State of the Nation 2015: Social Mobility and Child Poverty in Great Britain

Presented to Parliament pursuant to section 8B(6) of the Child Poverty Act 2010

December 2015

About the Commission

The Social Mobility and Child Poverty Commission is an advisory, non-departmental public body established under the Child Poverty Act 2010 (as amended by the Welfare Reform Act 2012) to assess progress towards improving social mobility and reducing child poverty in the United Kingdom. Its members are:

- The Rt. Hon. Alan Milburn (Chair).
- The Rt. Hon. Baroness Gillian Shephard (Deputy Chair).
- Paul Cleal, Partner at PwC.
- Paul Gregg, Professor of Economic and Social Policy, University of Bath.
- Douglas Hamilton, Director of the RS Macdonald Charitable Trust.
- David Johnston, Chief Executive of the Social Mobility Foundation.
- Catriona Williams OBE, Chief Executive of Children in Wales.

The Commission is supported by a Secretariat comprising: Paul Johnston, Kathryn Laing, Peter Brant, Jack Feintuck, Jodie Smith, Frank Soodeen, Claire Battersby, Gene Ward and Catherine Olsen-Saaler.

The functions of the Commission include:

- Publishing an annual report assessing improvement in social mobility in the United Kingdom, progress towards the 2020 child poverty targets and the implementation of the UK's child poverty strategy, and describing the Scottish and Welsh strategies;
- Providing advice to ministers on matters relating to social mobility and child poverty (which must be published);
- Undertaking social mobility advocacy.

This edition printed and published in the UK by The Stationery Office Limited

Printed on paper containing 75% recycled fibre content minimum.

Foreword

The Social Mobility and Child Poverty Commission is an independent statutory body which examines what is happening to child poverty and social mobility in the United Kingdom. This is the third State of the Nation report that the Commission presents to Parliament. In this report we assess: what the UK, Scottish and Welsh Governments are doing (our remit does not cover Northern Ireland); what progress is being made; and what we think will happen in the future. We also examine the contribution many others could make including employers and professions, schools and universities, parents and charities. We make a number of recommendations for action.

This is our first annual report since the 2015 UK General Election. On the morning after the election the Prime Minister set a One Nation agenda for this Parliament. Britain, he said, should be "a place where a good life is in reach for everyone who is willing to work and do the right thing". His would be a government for working people – it would ensure that those who made an effort were fairly rewarded. It would be a government that offered opportunity to all – no matter where they came from.

The Commission warmly welcomes this One Nation commitment and the Prime Minister's recognition that lower poverty and higher mobility are essential if Britain is to fulfil its potential, be at ease with itself and be confident about the future. In this report we take the Prime Minister's aspiration as our benchmark. A One Nation society is one where opportunities are shared equally and are not dependent on the family you were born into, the place where you live or the school you attend. It is a society where being born poor does not condemn someone to a lifetime of poverty. Instead it is a society where your progress in life – the job you do, the income you earn, the lifestyle you enjoy – depends on your aptitude and ability, not your background or your birth.

These are the hallmarks of a truly open, fair and meritocratic society. They are a long way from the Britain in which we live. In this report we explore in detail the gulf between where Britain is today and where the Prime Minister would like it to be. We do so not as a counsel of despair, but in order to set out the scale of the One Nation challenge facing the country and to provide the yardstick against which future progress can be judged.

Over many decades, successive governments have sought to boost social mobility and reduce child poverty. Contrary to today's prevailing climate of cynicism about politics, those efforts have produced real results. Child poverty has fallen by a third since 1997.[1] There are fewer children in workless households than at any time in two decades.[2] Employment

1 Institute for Fiscal Studies, *Incomes in the UK*, 2015
2 Office for National Statistics, *Working and Workless Households 2015*, 2015

is at record levels[3] and educational inequalities, though wide, have slowly narrowed.[4] More working class youngsters are benefiting from higher education than at any point in history.[5] Britain today has the fastest growing economy in the G7.[6]

It is also welcome that social mobility has become a new holy grail of public policy. It is a priority for government and in turn it has become a priority for many schools, colleges, universities and employers. Increasingly, many early years services, local authorities and voluntary organisations have also stepped up to the plate and made the social mobility agenda their own. These are solid foundations on which a One Nation agenda can be built.

There are many reasons to be optimistic about the future. Nonetheless, it is obvious that the progress to date has been too limited and too slow. In our report last year we warned that without a dramatic change in approach to how governments, employers and educators tackled child poverty and social mobility, Britain would become a permanently divided nation. Nothing we have seen in the last 12 months has made us change our view. In this year's report we expose some of the deep divides that characterise modern Britain.

There is a growing social divide by income and by class. Looking at earnings, the income share of the top 10 per cent has increased from 28 per cent to 39 per cent since 1979 and the income share of the top 1 per cent has more than doubled from 6 per cent to 13 per cent over the same time period. Looking at wealth, the wealth share of the top 10 per cent has increased from 59 per cent to 66 per cent since 1991 and the wealth share of the top 1 per cent has increased from 19 per cent to 23 per cent over the same time period.[7] At the very bottom of society there are more than one million children living a life of persistent poverty.[8] They are excluded from sharing in the many opportunities that life in modern Britain affords.

This form of social exclusion at the very bottom of British society finds an echo in the exclusive social make-up of those at the very top. Those who rise to the top in Britain today look remarkably similar to those who rose to the top half a century ago. In the professions, 71 per cent of senior judges, 62 per cent of senior armed forces and 55 per cent of Civil Service departmental heads attended independent schools – compared to just 7 per cent of the population who had a private education.[9] Of course, the best people need to be in the top jobs – and there are many good people who come from private schools and who go to top universities. But there can be few people who believe that the sum total of talent resides in just 7 per cent of pupils in the country's schools. The warning from the former Conservative Prime Minister Sir John Major applies to all parts of these islands – in every single sphere of British influence the upper echelons of power are held overwhelmingly by a small elite.

But, as we document in this report, social differences do not always follow common assumptions. Scotland, for example, has the smallest number of children living in poverty among the constituent nations of the UK[10], the lowest prevalence of low pay[11] and far more

3 Office for National Statistics, *Labour Market Statistics November 2015*, 2015. 73.7 per cent of 16 to 64-year-olds were in work in Q3 2015

4 For example, children eligible for free school meals were 55 per cent as likely as their peers to get five good GCSEs including English and maths in 2013–14 compared to only 39 per cent as likely in 2004–05. Department for Education, *GCSE and Equivalent Attainment by Pupil Characteristics 2014*, 2015; Department for Education and Skills, *National Curriculum Assessment, GCSE and Equivalent Attainment and Post-16 Attainment by Pupil Characteristics in England, 2005*, 2006

5 Higher Education Statistics Agency, *Widening Participation of Under-represented Groups*, 2015. An estimated 103,000 young people from working-class backgrounds (defined as NS-SEC 4-7) from the UK began a higher education course at university in 2013–14 compared to, for example, 77,000 a decade earlier in 2003–04

6 International Monetary Fund, *World Economic Outlook Database: October 2015*, 2015. The UK grew faster in 2014 than the USA, France, Germany, Italy, Japan and Canada

7 Data taken from Reed, H., 'Piketty, Chris Giles and Wealth Inequality: it's All About the Discontinuities', *The Guardian*, 29 May 2014, which is based on Piketty, T., *Capital in the 21st Century*, 2014

8 ONS, *Persistent Poverty in the UK and the EU, 2008-2013*, 2015

9 Social Mobility and Child Poverty Commission, *Elitist Britain*, 2015

10 Department for Work and Pensions, *Households Below Average Income*, 2015

11 Office for National Statistics, *Estimates of Employee Jobs Paid Less Than the Living Wage in London and Other Parts of the UK*, 2015

young people from deprived areas going on to higher education.[12] Wales has relatively high poverty rates and few poorer children leaving school with good qualifications, despite having more mothers with dependent children in work than most other parts of the UK.[13] [14] England has a higher proportion of poorer children leaving school with good qualifications than the other nations of the UK.[15]

These national differences are amplified at a more local level. A North:South divide has long been recognised. But that is only the tip of the iceberg when it comes to the fissures that have opened up in our country. It is only 100 miles from Norwich to St Albans, but they are like two different countries. On average, men live three years longer in St Albans than in Norwich, while women live nearly two years longer. The average salary in St Albans is £32,595 compared to £19,382 in Norwich. There are nearly twice as many professional jobs in the former compared to the latter. Unemployment in Norwich is almost double that of St Albans. While 75.9 per cent of children leave school with five A–C grade GCSEs in St Albans, only 43.8 per cent do so in Norwich. Not surprisingly, children in Norwich are over three times as likely to be in low-income families as children in St Albans.[16]

There are also big divides by gender and ethnicity. At school boys perform significantly worse than girls. In 2014, boys' GCSE results were 10 percentage points worse than girls' with 52 per cent of boys achieving five good GCSEs compared with 62 per cent of girls. The best results were achieved by Chinese girls (79 per cent) and the worst by black Caribbean boys (39 per cent). In the world of work, the educational attainment gap between boys and girls is reversed, with men getting paid more than women, especially after the age of 30.

So, social mobility is not just an issue about those at the very bottom of society or those at the very top. It affects the whole of our society and every part of our country. Middle England as much as Wales or Scotland. Rural communities as well as urban ones. At every level ours is a small country characterised by a large divide. We are a long way from being a One Nation Britain.

That is not to say that social mobility never happens. It does. There are countless stories of people succeeding against the odds. But that is the point – they have to swim against the tide in order to get on. Today's Britain does not provide a level playing field on which people can aspire to succeed. While educational attainment by children from disadvantaged families has improved over the last two decades, the gap between them and their more fortunate peers has improved only marginally.[17] The number of disadvantaged children going to university has increased but they have much less chance of going to the most sought-after universities than their privately educated peers.[18] Employment has grown considerably since 2010, yet despite recent improvements in real earnings, the number of workers who are low paid has also increased.[19] In recent times, more people are once again getting on to the housing ladder but home ownership rates among the under-25s have halved in just 20 years.[20]

The divisions in our nation run deep and, arguably, they are deepening. Unsurprisingly, the proportion of people believing that poverty and inequality are one of the most important

---

12 Higher Education Funding Council for England, *POLAR – Participation of Local Areas*, 2015

13 Office for National Statistics, *Families in the Labour Market 2013*, 2014

14 Welsh Government, *Achievement and Entitlement to Free School Meals*, 2014

15 Department for Education, *GCSE and Equivalent Attainment by Pupil Characteristics: 2014*, SFR 06/2015, Welsh Government, *Academic Achievement and Entitlement to Free School Meals*, 2014 and data for Scotland provided by the Scottish Government 2014; Adults Qualifications – Office for National Statistics, *Annual Population Survey*, 2014

16 HM Revenue and Customs, *Personal Tax Credits: Children in Low Income Families Measure: 2013*, 2015

17 Department for Education, *GCSE and Equivalent Attainment by Pupil Characteristics 2014*, 2015; Department for Education and Skills, *National Curriculum Assessment, GCSE and Equivalent Attainment and Post-16 Attainment by Pupil Characteristics in England, 2005*, 2006

18 Higher Education Statistics Agency, *UK Performance Indicators in Higher Education*, various years

19 Resolution Foundation, *Low Pay Britain 2015*, 2015

20 Institute for Fiscal Studies, *Living Standards, Poverty and Inequality in the UK: 2014*, 2014

issues facing the UK has increased threefold since 2007.[21] Those public concerns find echoes across the political spectrum. It is welcome that all the main political parties now advocate a Britain that is less elitist and more equal.

It seems that Britain may have reached an inflection point. If the trends of recent decades continue we will become a society that is ever more divided. If, on the other hand, the One Nation aspiration can be translated into real action, Britain could become the most open, fair and mobile society in the modern world. In this report we assess whether the desire for a different sort of society is being matched by policies capable of delivering it. Our conclusion is that, despite many welcome initiatives, the current policy response – by educators and employers as much as governments – falls well short of the political ambition. The gap between rhetoric and reality has to be closed if the Prime Minister's One Nation objective is to be realised.

In the chapters that follow we examine how, across the lifecycle of individuals, the policy and practice of governments, educators and employers has to move up a gear if we are to make progress towards Britain becoming a One Nation society.

Early years

A One Nation early years system would be one where every child whatever their background was school-ready by the age of five. But less than half of the poorest children in England are ready for school by then compared to almost two-thirds of other children, while a deep gender divide means girls from the poorest families do almost as well at age five as boys from better-off families. The North East and rural areas in the west of England do particularly badly in under-fives development. It is welcome that policies introduced by successive governments to create comprehensive early years services are continuing and, arguably, accelerating under this Government, but efforts to improve the school-readiness of the poorest children are uncoordinated, confused and patchy. Meanwhile, the complexity of the childcare funding system is hampering efforts to increase maternal employment.

It is welcome that the Government is increasing the childcare support it offers parents but a genuinely One Nation early years system needs a new scale of ambition. So we recommend that Government should end the strategic vacuum in the early years by introducing two clear, stretching, long-term objectives: to halve the development gap between the poorest children and the rest at age five; and to halve the gap in maternal employment between England and the best-performing nations, both by 2025. To help more parents to parent well the Government should establish an innovation fund designed to test new ways of improving parenting skills; to increase the take-up of free childcare it should radically simplify the multiple streams which finance it; and to improve pre-school development a national definition of school readiness should be established and the Government should unite all those involved in the early years behind delivering it.

Schools

A One Nation schools system would ensure that every child had the chances and choices to fulfil their potential, regardless of birth, background or geographical location. Schools are the cornerstone of efforts to improve social mobility and in some parts of the country – London especially – they are breaking the link between demography and destiny. But schools where poor children do well are the exception rather than the rule and there are some areas – Portsmouth and Bracknell Forest – where no pupils eligible for free school meals went on to a top university. Overall, children who receive free school meals are nearly half as likely to get five good GCSEs as their better-off peers and fewer than one in six get two or more A levels. Poorer children remain more likely to attend weaker schools, especially at secondary level.

21 Ipsos-Mori, *Issues Index*, 2015. This records the proportion of respondents who named poverty and/or inequality as one of the most important issues facing Britain today.

The Government is doing a lot to make schools engines of social mobility and there are welcome efforts to drive up standards by toughening exams and by focussing on a core curriculum. But we recommend that the Government should set its sights higher and aim for poor children elsewhere to do as well as they currently do in Inner London by 2030, which would reduce the educational attainment gap between the most disadvantaged children and everyone else by two-thirds. That would mean adopting a new zero tolerance approach to schools whose results remain below the floor standards for a five-year period by making wholesale changes in the leadership of such schools and requiring them to become part of an academy chain. A prestigious new fellowship of Change Leaders – Heads who have previous experience of successfully turning around schools – should be created to lead efforts to put failing schools on the path to success. Finally, we recommend that pay for new teachers should be improved and fees for Initial Teacher Training should be scrapped while the National Teaching Service should be turbo-charged with local trials of better incentives – including a new help-to-buy scheme exclusively for teachers – to get more of the best into the worst schools in disadvantaged areas.

Non-graduates

A One Nation vocational education system would be one which abolished the '16+' divide between youngsters who go on to university and those who do not. Today non-graduates tend to come from low income backgrounds and often end up in low pay, low-progression careers. There is a jungle of qualifications, courses and institutions which students find hard to penetrate. Quality is variable and there is little or no visibility about outcomes. Nor is the system working as well as it should for the economy with skills shortages in precisely those areas – construction, technical and scientific skills – that vocational education is supposed to supply. Unlike higher education, where the cap on student numbers has been lifted, there is more demand for apprenticeships than there are places and a dramatic under-supply of higher-level apprenticeships. Meanwhile, while it is welcome that youth unemployment is falling, there remains no solution to the phenomenon of young people not in education employment or training (NEET).

There is a welcome government focus on improving the life chances of non-graduates with major commitments to expand apprenticeships, embed a system for those who did not get good English and maths GCSEs to re-take them and develop new vocational routes from school to work. But the non-graduate track into employment remains too low a priority. We recommend that new apprenticeships should be targeted at higher-level courses and by 2020 there should be 30,000 young people a year starting a higher apprenticeship. A new UCAS-style website should be created for vocational education within two years so that young people can see what progression, employment and earnings opportunities they are likely to get. Failing further education colleges should become further education academies along the lines of the initial city academies with an external business sponsor. Finally, by 2020 the Government should reduce the NEET rates of 16–18-year-olds to around 55,000 young people (3 per cent or less) in line with the best performing Organisation for Economic Co-operation and Development (OECD) countries, underpinned by a new social investment fund worth around £50 million.

Higher education/professions

A One Nation higher education and professional employment system would be one where access to the top jobs and the best universities is fair and based on aptitude and ability, not background or birth. Substantial effort has been made by some universities and firms to increase the socio-economic diversity of their intakes but young people from poor families are still far less likely to go to university, attend a top institution or access certain elite professions. Law and professional service firms are doing most to improve social mobility; engineering and construction firms least. Privileged youngsters are disproportionately likely to attend selective universities and seven of 10 recruits in some elite accountancy firms still come from an independent or selective school.

It is welcome that the Government has set a challenging target of doubling the number of students from areas where participation is low. This will involve increasing by around 12,000 the number of students from such areas. There is little chance of success unless universities work together to focus more outreach activity on the schools and the places where HE access lags behind. A £40 million fund taken from universities' widening participation budgets should fund this vital effort. Professional employers similarly need to up their game. We propose that top professional firms should follow the lead of those making the greatest progress in opening up opportunities by changing recruitment processes and we urge the Government to make public sector internships transparent with a new interns.gov.uk website.

In-work poverty

A One Nation country would be one where work offered a guaranteed path out of poverty and where hard-working parents who worked the number of hours society expects would be able to deliver reasonable living standards for their families. But today 1.5 million children are in poverty because their working parents do not earn enough to secure a basic standard of living and the risk of absolute poverty for working families after housing costs has increased over the last decade. The percentage of UK full-time employees in low pay is 20.5 per cent and rising, compared to an OECD average of 17.1 per cent. We are also not as good as other countries in getting households to work as many hours as they reasonably might. Four out of 10 children in working poor households live in families where parents might be expected to enter work or work more hours.

The Government is aiming to tackle this issue by creating a higher pay, lower tax, lower welfare society, where the balance of responsibility for supporting living standards shifts away from the state towards employers and individuals themselves. There are some positive aspects to this approach, but also many risks. Many families will find it very difficult to increase their earnings enough to make good the cuts in state support even if they benefit from the welcome introduction of the National Living Wage. While its focus on tackling low pay and increasing parental employment is encouraging, recent changes to Universal Credit will make many working families significantly worse off.

So we recommend that the Government should, as the public finances improve, revitalise employment incentives in Universal Credit. Employers should take more responsibility for their employees' living standards with change led by a vanguard group of 'One Nation Employers' who act as a beacon for others. The Government should set a clear objective for the UK to become a Living Wage country by 2025 at the latest, and work with business to develop a comprehensive pay, progression and productivity plan that aligns Government programmes behind that goal. This will mean putting the UK on a par with the best performing countries in Europe by halving the proportion of people who earn less than two-thirds of median hourly pay to 10 per cent of employees.

Persistent poverty

In a One Nation country child poverty would be a transient experience and would not inflict lasting damage into adulthood. But today as many as one in six children spend large parts of their lives living in households which are persistently poor. The one million children in this situation are often those from families characterised by ill health and low skills rather than simply by parental addiction or broken relationships.

The Government's focus on getting these families into work is right, but to succeed it will need to focus harder on tackling the multi-causal nature of the persistent poverty problem.

The way the welfare-to-work system currently operates is incapable of meeting the needs of these families. So we recommend that Government should set a goal of making the UK one of the top five OECD countries for having the fewest children in workless households – so that by 2020, 500,000 fewer children live in households where no one works. This new national effort should be led by a refocused and rebranded Troubled Families programme with a remit to offer personalised help to get persistently poor families into secure employment. A new drive to improve the skills of the persistently poor should give personal learning accounts to long-term unemployed adults so they have more responsibility for raising their skill levels.

If we are serious about healing the social divisions that scar our nation then a new scale of ambition and action is required at every level. A wind of change needs to sweep through our country. As a nation, we should refuse to accept that child poverty – particularly when it is persistent – is inevitable. We should not be prepared to see people in work earning below the poverty line. We should not tolerate early years services that do not prepare children for school. We should take action when schools and colleges fail to raise attainment and training levels for the poorest. And we should be prepared to shine a spotlight on those universities and professions that refuse to throw open their doors to a far wider pool of talent.

In our view, poverty and mobility are two sides of the same coin. Without less of the former it is hard to imagine a society with more of the latter. Social justice cannot just be about establishing a new floor below which no one should be allowed to fall. It also has to be about unleashing people's aspiration to succeed. To have a good life, not just a better one. Not just to leave school with good results but to get into a good university. Not just to get a job but to progress in a career. Not just to have affordable housing but to own a home. Social justice means people having more of an equal opportunity to move up and get on.

This may be our last report on the current legal basis. Legislation before Parliament will change our terms of reference so that we lose our child poverty remit. This is part of the Government's wider intention to move its focus from the targets enshrined in the 2010 Child Poverty Act towards improving life chances. It has long been obvious that the existing child poverty targets are not going to be met. In fact they will be missed by a country mile. That is a matter of deep regret. A country that is the fifth richest in the world should not have 2.3 million children officially classified as poor. The Commission has long argued that a more rounded way of measuring poverty – taking greater account of causal risk factors – is sensible. The life chances of children, the poorest especially, depend on many things including good parenting, childcare, education and employment. For that reason we think the Government is right to want to measure worklessness and educational attainment as part of its new focus on improving life chances. But it is not credible to try to improve the life chances of the poor without acknowledging the most obvious symptom of poverty, lack of money. Without the specific inclusion of an assessment of income, these new measures are inadequate. And unless the Government sets a clear target for improving the life chances of the poorest families its agenda for healing social division in our country will lack both ambition and credibility. It will end up measuring life chances but not working towards a clear goal of improving them.

Abolishing the legal targets does not make the issue of child poverty go away. It remains a deep scar in the fabric of our nation. The issue is less how child poverty is measured and more how it is tackled. Far more needs to be done to make sure that the poorest families share in the proceeds of economic growth. That is why we look to decision-makers at every level to make Britain's welcome economic recovery the basis for a sustainable social recovery. Economically, there is a growing sense of confidence about our ability to grow and prosper as a nation. That confidence is borne not just of the UK's recovery from recession but from a belief that we possess the essential attributes needed for success in the future – an open economy, a flexible workforce, a spirit of innovation and enterprise.

It is hard to find the same level of confidence about our social prospects as a nation. Instead there is growing unease – even tension – about the lack of fairness in our society, a sense that our best days lie behind us not ahead. It feels like Britain faces an existential crisis about what sort of society we want to be.There is much talk of less elitism and more equality, of less poverty and more mobility. But willing the ends without the means is a recipe for more division, not less. It is the job of employers, educators and policymakers to reconcile the ends they aspire to see with the means they are willing to deploy. It is the Commission's job to assess whether they are doing so. Our conclusion in this report is that there are some signs of progress but they do not nearly go far enough or fast enough to address the gulf between the divided Britain of the present and the One Nation Britain we aspire to become.

Social mobility overview

Britain's social mobility problem

Britain has lower levels of social mobility than most other comparable countries. In Britain, income persistence between fathers and sons is the strongest of all Organisation for Economic Co-operation and Development (OECD) countries. In other words, ours is a country where the class and income of children when they grow up is more related to the class and income of their parents than elsewhere in the developed world.

In a society with high levels of mobility, origins would not determine destinations. Instead, how far a person progressed in terms of income, employment or social class would be based on ability and ambition alone – but today, despite most people moving up or down the class and income ladder at some point in their life, four times as many professionals in their 40s are from professional families than from working-class families (39 versus 10 per cent).[1] There is a class ceiling in British society and it inhibits the life chances of hundreds of thousands of children – those from the poorest households the most.

1 Goldthorpe, J.H., *Understanding – and Misunderstanding – Social Mobility in Britain*, 2012

How socially mobile is Britain – and are things getting better or worse?

Measuring mobility

Social mobility is measured in terms of **social class** or **income**.

Social class looks at whether individuals are in the same or different social classes to their parents. Social class is usually described using the National Socio-Economic Classification. In its simplified form there are eight classes ranging from higher managerial, administrative and professional occupations to long-term unemployed.

Income mobility considers the relationship between the income of parents and that of their children in adulthood.

Social mobility can be measured in **absolute** or **relative** terms.

Absolute mobility is the class or income position of an adult compared to their parents. For example, if the child of a shop assistant becomes a university professor, they have experienced absolute upward mobility.

Relative mobility is a measure of the class or income outcomes of different groups in society when compared to each other. It assesses the likelihood of achieving a particular adult class or income outcome, given where an individual starts out. For example, if children of working-class parents are, on average, much less likely to end up in professional employment than children of professional parents, relative social mobility is low.

Post-war Britain has seen high levels of absolute social mobility. Around 80 per cent of individuals born in the early 1980s (and who are in their 30s today) are in a different social class to that of their parents. This is the most recent point on a trend of rising absolute mobility, up from around 75 per cent for those born in the 1940s.[2] However, much of this social mobility is short-range, with relatively few from working-class backgrounds entering managerial or professional occupations and vice versa.

Many people also experience absolute income mobility. For example, of those born in 1970, 63 per cent of those with parents in the poorest 25 per cent escape low income as adults. However, most of this mobility is short-range and only one in seven reached the top 25 per cent as adults. Looking at those with parents in the richest 25 per cent, almost half – 45 per cent – remained there as adults.[3]

In the post-war period upward mobility in class terms exceeded downward mobility; but today, moves up and down are split equally.[4] This is largely due to changes in the structure of the economy – there are relatively more people in higher social groups, meaning the experience of downward mobility has become a more common one even though the chances of an individual in a given social class being downwardly mobile have hardly changed. British society is not rigid and many people do see improvements during their lives, albeit generally modest ones.

The situation in relation to relative social mobility is more complex and less positive. Relative class mobility rates for men have flatlined, whereas for women relative mobility appears to have improved. Comparing those born in the 1970s to those born in the 1940s, the odds

2 Bukodi, E., Goldthorpe, J.H., Waller, L. and Kuha, J., *The Mobility Problem in Britain: New Findings from the Analysis of Cohort Data*, 2015

3 Blanden, J., and Machin, S., *Recent Changes in Intergenerational Mobility in Britain*, 2007

4 Bukodi, E., Goldthorpe, J.H., Waller, L. and Kuha, J., op. cit.

ratio[5] of a man from a managerial or professional background remaining there as an adult compared to a man from a working-class background moving up so has stayed more or less the same, at around six. However, the same odds ratio for women has improved from nearly eight for women born in the 1940s to four for those born in the 1970s.[6] So while the relative mobility rates of working-class women have caught up and overtaken that of men, it remains the case that those born in working-class families face challenges in breaking through the class ceiling to professional work.

In terms of income, relative social mobility appears to have declined. Of those born in the lowest income quartile in 1958, 31 per cent were in the poorest 25 per cent as adults; whereas of those from the poorest families in 1970, 38 per cent remain there as adults. Conversely, of those born in the highest income quartile in 1958, 35 per cent remained there as adults compared to 45 per cent of those born in 1970.[7] Put simply, the link between parental and child income appears to be stronger for those born in 1970 compared to those born in 1958 (see Figure SM1).[8] For cohorts born after 1970, most experts believe that mobility did not deteriorate further, but neither did it improve.[9]

Figure SM1: Declines in income mobility: estimated income persistence between parents and offspring, comparing those born in 1958 to 1970

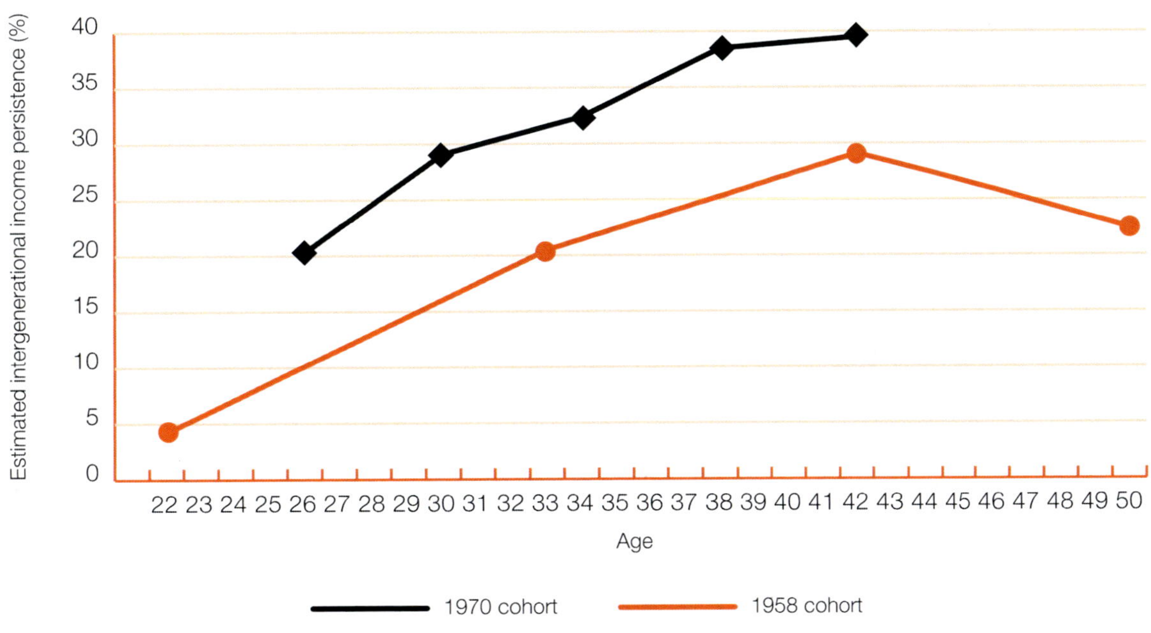

Source: P. Gregg, L. Macmillan and C. Vittori, *Moving Towards Estimating Lifetime Intergenerational Economic Mobility in the UK*, 2014

Note: The gap between the two lines reflects the decline in income mobility

The findings in relation to income mobility show that adults are more likely to be wealthy if their parents are wealthy, and that this connection has strengthened over time. The impact can be seen starkly when the employees of high-prestige occupations are examined. Recent entrants to law, medicine, accountancy and other professions are more likely to come from households with above-average income than previous cohorts entering these professions –

5 An odds ratio is the odds of one group achieving a given outcome divided by the odds of a different group. For example, if there were three men from middle-class backgrounds who remained there as adults for every one who was downwardly mobile – odds of 3:1 – and only one man from a working-class background who was upwardly mobile for every three who were not – odds of 1:3 – the odds ratio would be 9
6 Bukodi, E., Goldthorpe, J.H., Waller, L. and Kuha, J., op. cit. These figures are the central point from a range of probabilities
7 Blanden, J., Gregg, P. and Machin, S., *Intergenerational Mobility in Europe and North America*, 2005
8 Gregg, P., Macmillan, L. and Vittori, C., *Moving Towards Estimating Lifetime Intergenerational Economic Mobility in the UK*, 2014
9 Blanden, J., Gregg, P. and Machin, S., op. cit.

but they are also likely to have scored less well than their predecessors in IQ tests.[10] These findings are supported by Commission research which identified that less able but better-off children are 35 per cent more likely to become high earners than bright but poor children.[11] Money speaks more than ever in a way that is economically inefficient and socially unfair.

These mobility findings also show that, despite major changes to the education system and labour market, working-class men born in 1970 are just as unlikely to make it to the top as working-class men born at the close of the Second World War. Predictions that the decline of traditional working-class jobs and the rise of white-collar professional work would herald an era of continual social progress have proved premature.[12] [13] However, the evidence for increasing female mobility suggests that change is possible. The challenge is to achieve across-the-board improvement.

What explains these trends?

There is an apparent conflict between on the one hand the findings that class mobility is flatlining for men and improving for women, and on the other the economic evidence that concludes income mobility is in decline. However, they are not inconsistent.

Firstly, income inequality in the UK between different social class groups has increased significantly since 1979. A given pattern of social class mobility today will therefore give rise to a stronger connection between adult and child incomes than in the past.

Second, income inequality within individual social class groups has also increased. As those from better-off social backgrounds are more likely to be found in the highest earning jobs in each individual social class – and it is possible this polarisation by social background has increased over time – this will also explain some of the apparent disconnect between the economic and sociological evidence.

All of these findings are the product of three common social and economic drivers:

- Structural changes in the jobs market;
- The enduring and increasing impact of background on adult outcomes;
- Unequal access to higher education and professional jobs.

Changes in the jobs market

The increases in absolute class mobility – the finding that more people in Britain born in the post-War period end up in a different social class to their parents – was driven significantly by the changing face of the British jobs market. Over the last hundred years, an increase in professional jobs combined with declines in agricultural and traditional blue-collar work created openings for individuals of all backgrounds in higher social classes. Baby boomers benefited from the expansion of professional employment, and therefore their children were born in professional families. This in part could explain why young adults today may be less likely to experience upward social class moves, and more likely to experience downward moves.[14] Unlike those born in the 1940s, those born after the 1970s do not benefit from the same rate of expanding professional jobs as their parents.

10 Macmillan, L., *Social Mobility and the Professions*, 2009
11 Social Mobility and Child Poverty Commission, *Downward Mobility, Opportunity Hoarding and the Glass Floor*, 2015
12 Erikson, R., Goldthorpe, J.H., and Portocarero, L., *Intergenerational Class Mobility and the Convergence Thesis: England, France and Sweden*, 2010
13 Bukodi, E., Erikson, R., and Goldthorpe, J.H., *The Effects of Social Origins and Cognitive Ability on Educational Attainment: Evidence from Britain and Sweden*, 2013
14 Bukodi, E., Goldthorpe, J.H., Waller, L. and Kuha, J., op. cit.

The improvement in relative class mobility observed for women is not yet fully understood, neither is the exact reason why their relative mobility appears to be better than that of men. The change since the 1940s is likely to be due to several social changes that developed in parallel. These could include a general rise in women in work, an increase in middle-class women returning to work following childbirth, and perhaps more women achieving highly at university, unlocking jobs in the senior occupational classes.[15] If these are the main drivers of increased relative mobility for women, it is possible some further progress can be made; but the most dramatic changes in labour market participation are already likely to have happened.

The effect of background on outcomes

The second driver of changing social mobility is the enduring and increasing effect of social background on outcomes. The decline in income mobility observed for those born in 1970 compared to those born in 1958 is in part a result of how family resources can be increasingly deployed to affect a child's outcomes. When comparing young men assessed as most able, those from the most privileged backgrounds are found to be twice as likely to achieve upper secondary qualifications – a key driver of success in the labour market as an adult – compared to the least privileged. This effect was unchanged between cohorts born in 1946, 1958 and 1970. However, the connection between low cognitive ability and outcomes has weakened between those born in the 1950s and 1970s, suggesting that social background now has a greater effect on whether a child struggling in school will make progress. This is more pronounced in Britain than in other northern European countries (Figure SM2).[16]

Figure SM2: Strength of the link between individual and parental earnings across OECD countries

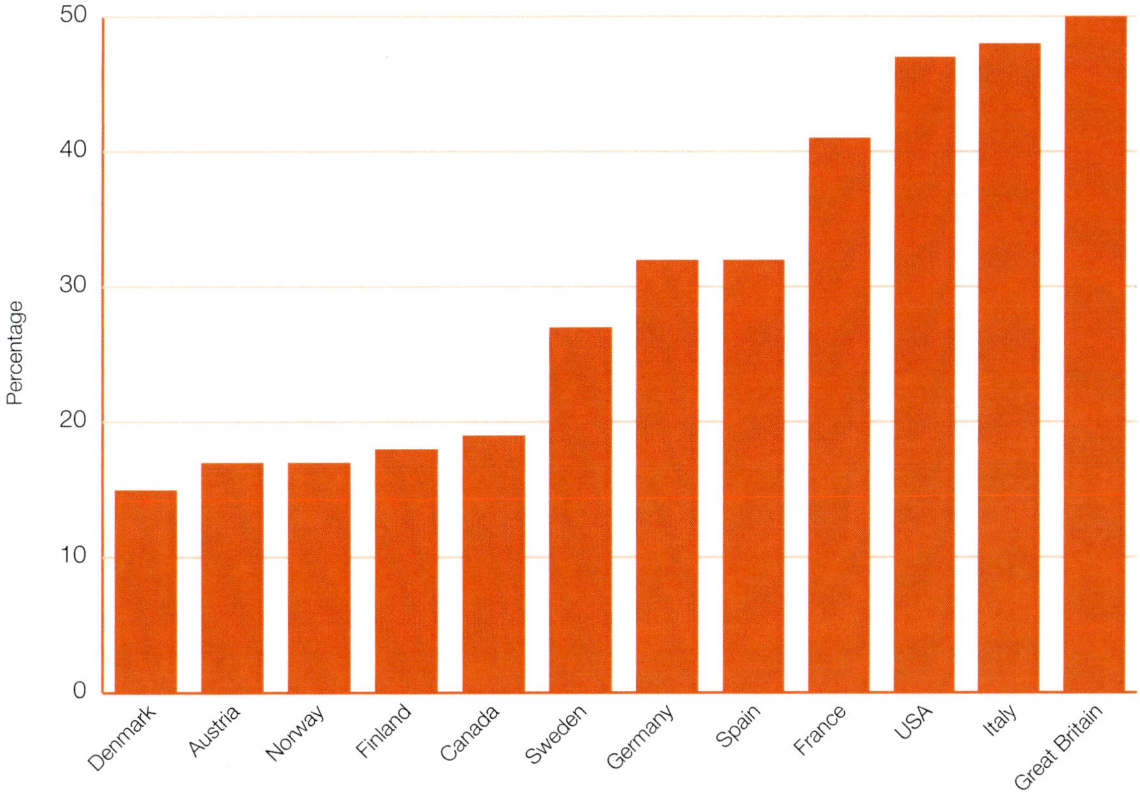

Source: OECD, *Economic Policy Reforms: Going for Growth 2010*, 2010

Note: The height of each bar measures the extent to which sons' earnings levels reflect those of their fathers

15 Erikson, R., and Goldthorpe, J.H., *Has Social Mobility in Britain Decreased? Reconciling Divergent Findings on Income and Class Mobility*, 2010

16 Erikson, R., and Goldthorpe, J.H., *Trends in Class Mobility: The Post-war European Experience*, 2006

Arguments have been made that genetics play a major role in the connection between background and origins. Genes may play a part in determining social success, but doing well at school, in exams and job interviews requires a wider suite of reasoning and interpersonal skills than those that may be passed down from parent to child. Perhaps as much as 80 per cent in the change in income persistence between the 1958 and 1970 cohorts can be explained by a combination of non-cognitive skills, cognitive traits, attainment and labour market attachment.[17] Non-cognitive skills have a big part to play in changes to mobility, accounting for as much as 10 per cent of persistence of top job status between parents and children.[18] The role of genetics in these important drivers of success is unlikely to be substantial, and certainly not the main factor.[19]

Unequal access to education and professional jobs

The third explanation for changing mobility patterns – specifically in relation to the growing correlation between the income of parents and their children – is unequal access to the best education and professional jobs. From the 1960s onwards, rising participation in higher education has not been equally shared. Between the 1980s and 1990s participation increased by 26 percentage points for the top fifth (20 to 46 per cent), 15 percentage points for the middle (8 to 23 per cent) and by only three percentage points for the least advantaged (6 to 9 per cent). Combined with increasing wage differentials between those in high-skilled and low-skilled jobs and the opening up of pay differences within occupations, differing rates of access to higher education could account for some of the declines in income mobility.[20] [21] [22] Increasing the total stock of education in a population in itself does not automatically lead to more social mobility; what matters is whether attainment between individuals from different class origins widens or narrows.[23]

It is possible that unequal access to the best professional positions also underpins the increasing connection between the income of parent and child. Of all adults in professional employment today, earnings are higher for those whose parents were also in professional employment. The finding that income persistence between parents and children has increased is not just a matter of those from privileged backgrounds getting a greater share of top jobs. Even when those from working-class backgrounds get professional jobs, they are likely to earn less than their colleagues who started off in professional families.[24] Causes could include those from better-off backgrounds having the knowledge to seek work in elite firms and the characteristics to fit in.[25] Conversely, research by the Commission suggests that some elite firms may be selecting candidates on the basis of middle-class characteristics, unintentionally or otherwise reinforcing wider trends.[26]

17 Blanden, J., Gregg, P., and Macmillan, L., *Accounting for Intergenerational Income Persistence: Noncognitive Skills, Ability and Education*, 2007

18 Social Mobility and Child Poverty Commission, *Social and Emotional Learning: Skills for Life and Work*, 2015

19 Jerrim, J., Vignoles, A., Lingam, R. and Friend, A., *The Socio-economic Gradient in Children's Reading Skills and the Role of Genetics*, 2014

20 http://www.oecd.org/unitedkingdom/OECD-Income-Inequality-UK.pdf

21 Schmidt, J., Shierholz., H. and Mishel, L., *Don't Blame The Robots: Assessing the Job Polarisation Explanation of Growing Wage Inequality*, 2013

22 Lindley, J. and Machin, S., *The Quest for More and More Education: Implications for Social Mobility*, 2012

23 Sturgis, P. and Buscha, F., *Increasing Inter-generational Social Mobility: Is Educational Expansion the Answer?,* 2015

24 Laurison, D. and Friedman, S., *Introducing the Class Ceiling: Social Mobility and Britain's Elite Occupations*, 2015

25 Scherger, S. and Savage, M., *Cultural Transmission, Educational Attainment and Social Mobility*, 2010

26 Social Mobility and Child Poverty Commission, *Non-educational Barriers to the Elite Professions Evaluation*, 2015

Conclusion

The social and political changes of the latter 20th century led to much progress. Increased participation in education and the opening up of elite universities and the professions all added to opportunity for some. Yet the 'dice-roll' of birth continues to have an overbearing effect on life chances. We live in a society where people can, and do, move up and down the class and income scale, but being born to a less privileged family is still far too likely to mean disadvantage as an adult.

There is hope of progress. As we chart in the main chapters of this report, the gaps between disadvantaged young people and others are wide but many are closing, albeit too slowly. The social mobility agenda will need to be pursued with consistency and clarity if improvements in schooling and access to higher education are to translate into better social outcomes.

It is not good enough to cross our fingers and hope. If we do, evidence suggests that those with family resources will outcompete everyone else for the places at the best universities and the jobs which bring greatest reward. Adopting and incubating practice that supports social mobility is the task of a wide range of institutions. Government, families, schools and businesses among others should recognise the fundamental inequality of opportunities that exist, and take steps to address them. Urgent action is required if a One Nation Britain is to be secured.

Housing and social mobility

Housing is a key engine of social mobility. Children need a reasonable home environment if they are to develop and learn well. Whatever sector they live in, their accommodation needs to be appropriate for the number of people in their household, in a reasonable condition and not constantly changing. However, housing is also important for other reasons. Home ownership is the main way that we hold and hand down wealth, so for most people, owning their own home is a key part of achieving a good life.

Nonetheless, in 21st-century Britain, home ownership is increasingly difficult to achieve. 25-year-olds born in the mid-1980s are now half as likely as those who were born in the mid-1960s to own their own home.[27] A combination of rising prices and higher rents is making it harder to assemble the large deposits required to get on the housing ladder. For couples with children, a decade of saving (and more than two decades in London) is not enough to buy even an average-priced family home unless they can get help from their parents.

The Government is committed to reversing the trend of declining home ownership (down from its 2001 peak of 69 per cent).[28] It has pledged to build a million new homes by 2020, including 200,000 new starter homes at 80 per cent of market rate for first-time buyers under 40, 135,000 new Help to Buy shared ownership homes and 10,000 Rent to Buy homes. It has introduced a new London Help to Buy scheme that will offer interest-free equity loans of up to 40 per cent of the value of the property. This is in addition to the Help to Buy ISA which tops up personal savings towards deposits. From next year, people renting from housing associations will also gain a discounted route to home ownership as the Right to Buy scheme is extended.

Despite these measures, the Government is unlikely to hit its million new homes target. In 2013/14 around 140,000 permanent dwellings were completed, an increase on the previous year but less than in any year in the 20 years from 1990–2010.[29] This figure also falls short of annual demand, estimated at between 230,000 and 300,000 new

27 Institute for Fiscal Studies, *Living Standards, Poverty and Inequality in the UK: 2014*, 2014
28 Office for National Statistics, *A Century of Home Ownership and Renting in England and Wales (Full Story)*, 2013
29 House of Commons Library, *Housebuilding: Social indicators*, 2015

units a year.[30] The mismatch between supply and demand means that for many – especially those on low incomes in areas where prices are high and supply is sluggish – costs to buy or to rent will continue to rise in the short to medium term.

The Government's liberalisation of the planning system does seem to be having an impact, with the number of planning permissions for new homes reaching 240,000 last year (up from 158,000 in 2011). But strong headwinds continue to hold back progress: business models that depend on restricting supply, the continuing unavailability of sufficient amounts of land and skilled workers, and lack of housebuilding materials all increase the challenge. These will need to be addressed more systematically if the Government is to deliver levels of home ownership at or above the 70 per cent mark.

30 House of Commons Library, *Housing Supply 2015–2020: Key Issues for the 2015 Parliament*, 2015

Chapter 1: Building the right foundations

- **Fewer than half of the poorest children in England are ready for school at age five, compared to almost two-thirds of other children. A deep gender divide means girls from the poorest families do almost as well at age five as boys from better-off families.**
- **The North East and rural areas in the west of England are blighted by particularly low pre-school development.**
- **Policies introduced by successive governments to provide comprehensive childcare services appear to be accelerating under this government.**
- **But the challenges to be overcome are significant – and three stand out in particular. First, opportunities are being missed to influence parenting, the biggest driver of the child development gap. Second, efforts to improve the school-readiness of the poorest children are uncoordinated, confused and patchy. And third, the complexity of the childcare funding system is hampering efforts to increase maternal employment.**
- **Government should end the strategic vacuum in the early years by introducing two clear, stretching, long-term objectives – to halve the development gap between the poorest children and the rest at age five and to halve the gap in maternal employment between England and the best performing nations, both by 2025.**
- **To help more parents to parent well, an innovation fund should be established to test new ways of improving parenting skills.**
- **The take-up of free childcare should be increased (and its costs decreased) by radically simplifying the multiple streams which finance it.**

1.1 Introduction

A child's development in the first five years of life is crucial to their future success. The scars of weak development in the earliest years are carried through school, adulthood and employment and affect a child's own behaviour as a parent. The weeks and months to age three, in particular, are vitally important as children go through significant developments in their cognitive, linguistic, social, emotional and motor development skills.

The period between 15 and 18 months is especially important for vocabulary growth, which is a key predictor of later attainment at school.[1] By age five, a large amount of the gap in educational attainment visible throughout the school years between disadvantaged children and their better-off peers has already opened up. Fewer than half of the poorest children in England reached a good level of development by age five in 2014, compared to almost two-thirds of other children.[2] And on average, that large gap between poorer children and their wealthier peers will increase over the school years as poorer children make less progress.[3]

Above all, it is parents who, in these earliest years and beyond, shape their child's future opportunities. What parents do has far greater effect than any intervention at primary or secondary school. It is for this reason that successive governments have built up an infrastructure of support to help parents. From antenatal care to maternity and paternity leave, to children's centres and funded childcare, there have been significant developments in universal publicly funded services designed to give children the best start in life.

The uncomfortable truth, however, is that family background remains highly consequential for children's futures. Parents' wealth and education not only go a long way towards explaining the gap observed at the start of school, but they also go on to determine future outcomes over and above their child's ability. Research for the Commission has shown that for many children, family background is a far greater determinant of future success than ability. Children from wealthier families who are assessed at age five as having low cognitive ability are significantly more likely to become high earners as adults than children from poor families assessed to be high ability at age five. In fact, low-ability children from wealthy families were 35 per cent more likely to be high earners as adults than high-ability children from poorer families.[4]

At their well-designed, evidence-based best, services to help parents and their children in the earliest years can help all families and give an extra boost to those who need them most. The key areas where services can make the biggest difference to social mobility is in getting mothers into work and in narrowing the child development gap at the start of school, so that children from all backgrounds commence their school life on an equal footing. This is why high-quality early education, available particularly to poorer children who would otherwise lose out on development, can pack a double punch by delivering both outcomes.

In this parliament, the Government has committed to an expensive and potentially ground-breaking addition to early years services with the doubling of the current free childcare provision for three- and four-year-olds. Increased devolution and new local structures, which bind local authorities and public health officials together, also provide welcome impetus to reform. But there is a concerning lack of clarity from the Government both about how it intends to capitalise on this – and importantly – what it wants to get from the £6 billion a year of funding it will be spending on childcare by the end of the parliament. This does raise concerns about the extent to which the pending reforms will fulfil their potential. They will

1 Parker, I., *Early Developments: Bridging the Gap Between Evidence and Policy in Early Years Education*, Institute for Public Policy Research, 2013
2 Department for Education, *EYFSP Attainment by Pupil Characteristics 2013 to 2014*, National and Local Authority tables
3 Department for Education, *GCSE and Equivalent Attainment by Pupil Characteristics: 2014*, 2014
4 Social Mobility and Child Poverty Commission, Press Release, 'New research exposes the "glass floor" in British society', 26 July 2015, https://www.gov.uk/government/news/new-research-exposes-the-glass-floor-in-british-society, 18 November 2015

only do so if the families who most need extra help are aware of, and are actually accessing, a coherent set of well-functioning services which help them to make the right choices about their own employment and about their child's education.

1.2 Does today's reality meet the One Nation vision?

The fundamental test for any early years system is the extent to which every five-year-old has a chance to fulfil their potential irrespective of family background. On this measure, England does badly: the variation in children's development across income groups is shockingly wide. Nationally, the child development gap between the poorest children and their better-off peers opens up very early and increases as children progress through school. The gaps at school entry by social class are significant. Longitudinal research shows that at the point of school entry in England, low-income children are almost one year behind middle-income children on vocabulary tests.[5] This creates a significant challenge for primary schools as they seek to ensure that all children, but particularly the poorest, make sufficient progress.

Government data on the Early Years Foundation Stage Profile (EYFSP) shows that in 2013/14, children eligible for free school meals were two-thirds as likely to achieve a 'good level of development' as other children at age five, with 45 per cent of poor children achieving this level of development compared to 64 per cent of other children.[6] This means that over half of children from poor families are failing to reach a basic development standard by the end of their reception year at school.

One of the most concerning social mobility problems in the early years is the disparities in outcomes for poor children between different areas of the country. There are particularly intense clusters of poor pre-school development in rural areas in the west of England (Herefordshire, Gloucestershire, Bath & North East Somerset) and in the North East. By contrast, London is doing much better – there the gap in development between the poorest and the rest is 13 percentage points, compared to 22 percentage points in the North East (see Figure 1.2).

Zooming in further, there were 39 top tier local authorities (over a quarter) in 2014 in which less than four in 10 poor children demonstrated a good level of development at age five. This is a significant improvement on the previous year, but still far from adequate. Most worrying were the five authorities – Blackburn with Darwen, Wigan, Halton, Stockton-on-Tees and Bath & North East Somerset – in which only one-third of poor children achieved a good level on this measure. These areas are storing up major problems for their primary schools. The progress of children who failed to meet key developmental benchmarks by five will need to be caught up before the levels of attainment expected for their age can be reached.

5 Waldfogel, J., and Washbrook, E., *Low Income and Early Cognitive Development in the UK*, Sutton Trust, 1 February 2010
6 Department for Education, *EYFSP Attainment by Pupil Characteristics 2013 to 2014*, National and Local Authority tables

Figure 1.1: Proportion of children eligible for free school meals reaching a good level of development at age five (2014) – highlighting the top 20 per cent and bottom 20 per cent

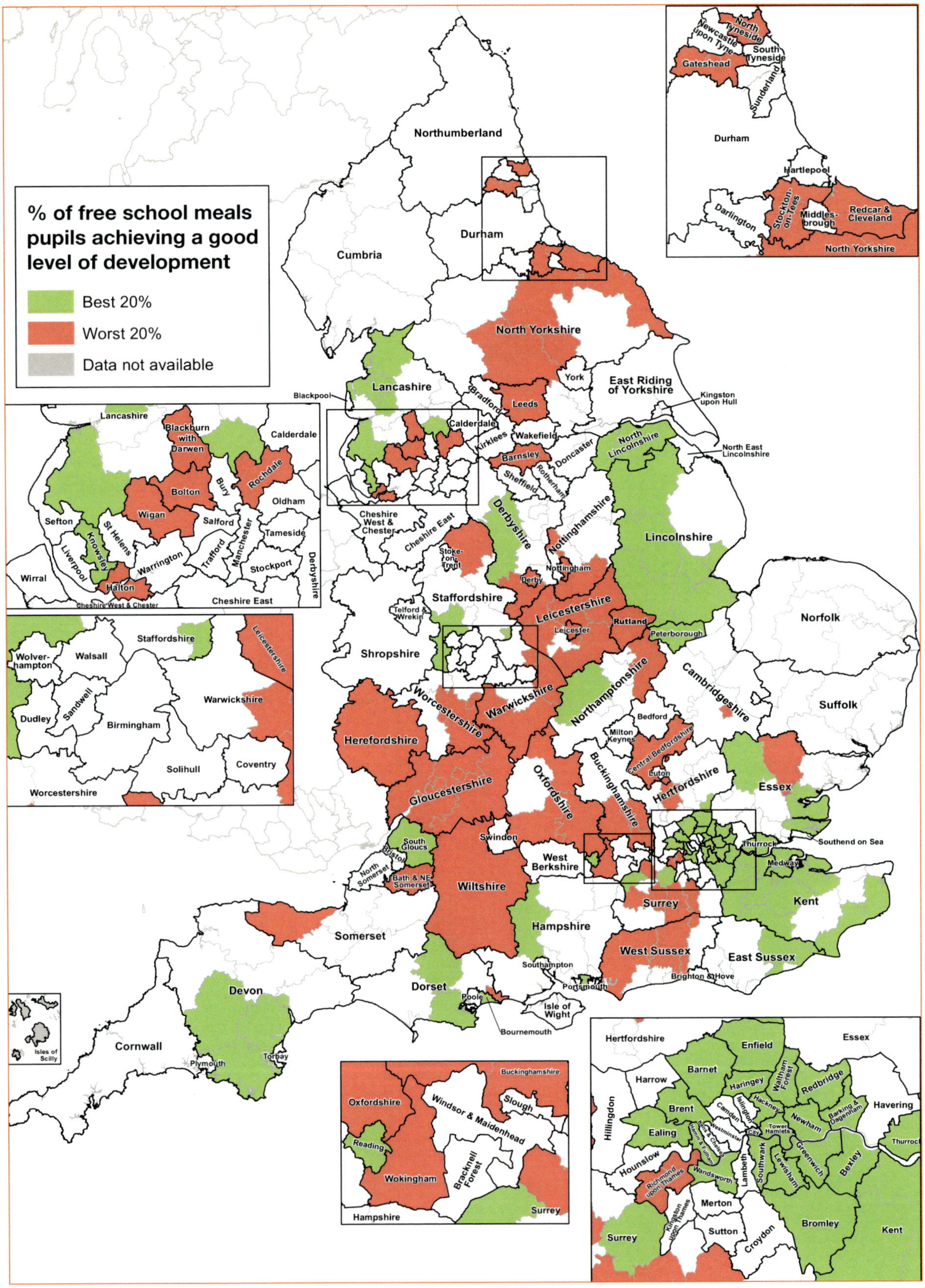

Source: Reproduced by permission of Ordnance Survey on behalf of HMSO, 2015

Figure 1.2: Percentage of children reaching a good level of development in the Early Years Foundation Stage 2014, according to pupil characteristics and location

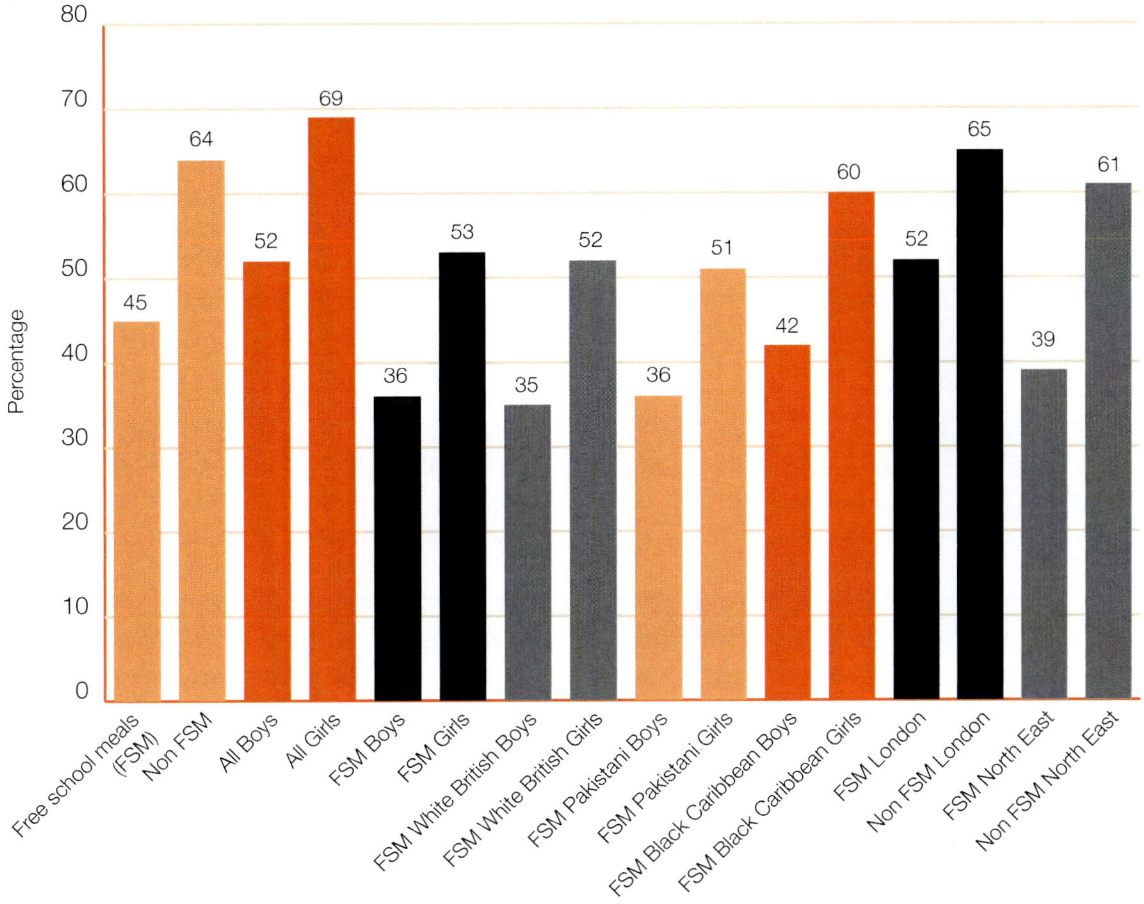

Source: Department for Education, *EYFSP Attainment by Pupil Characteristics 2013 to 2014*, National and Local Authority tables

There are also large child development gaps by gender. Most notably, girls far outperform boys in development checks at age five. Girls from the poorest families do almost as well at age five as boys from better-off families, with half reaching the expected standard. At 17 percentage points, the gender gap in child development between the poorest boys and girls is almost as large as the gap between the poorest and other children (see Figure 1.2).

There are some nuances within this overall picture. Boys do considerably worse in language tests than girls, while they do slightly better when it comes to numeracy.[7] Looking at ethnicity and gender, the data shows that white British and Pakistani boys from poor families do particularly badly. Just over one-third of both groups achieved a good level of development by age five.[8]

There are a number of possible explanations for this, including the different developmental patterns of boys and girls, and specific cultural influences which bear differently on girls and boys.[9] What is perhaps most notable is that it is the poverty rather than the gender gaps that have the greatest labour-market consequences. In fact, the gender pay gap turns the gender development gap on its head, with men earning significantly more than women.

7 Kirstine, H., and Jones, E.M., 'Ethnicity and gender gaps in early childhood', *British Educational Research Journal*, 37:6, pp973-91, 2011

8 Department for Education, *EYFSP Attainment by Pupil Characteristics 2013 to 2014*, National and Local Authority tables

9 Kirstine, H., and Jones, E.M., op. cit.

Beyond these specific geographical, gender and ethnicity inequalities in the early years, there are three more general problems which this chapter will now focus on.

Problem 1: Poor parenting is a significant contributor to the big child development gaps at age five, but public policy is failing to address it.

Parents from all backgrounds have high ambitions for their children and dedicate enormous time and resource to getting things right for them. Ninety-six per cent of mothers of seven-year-olds want their children to attend university, even where they have no qualifications themselves.[10] Parents' engagement with their children makes a big difference to their future prospects. Children's development is significantly better where their parents read to them frequently, where rules are enforced and bedtimes kept to, where there is a strong bond between parent and child, and where parents do not experience financial stress or mental health concerns.[11]

Evidence of young children's language skills provides perhaps the most specific insight into the impact that parenting can have. Language, that vital precondition to learning, is driven by conversation with and between adults, by reading and by other interactive activities that require comprehension and discussion.[12] Of course, not every parent from the same social background is the same. Parents at all points in the income scale can, for a whole variety of reasons, struggle to provide the routines, structures and opportunities for development which would benefit their children. But the evidence shows that the poorer parents are, the more likely they are to struggle with this. Under half of children (45 per cent) from the poorest fifth of families were read to daily when they were three years old, compared with eight in 10 (78 per cent) of children from the richest fifth.[13] The aggregate effect of this is marked gaps in children's cognitive development according to socio-economic group.[14]

One important contributor to varying effectiveness in parenting is the networks families are able to draw on for help and advice. New and worrying research for the Commission shows that while three in 10 parents from all backgrounds feel isolated after the arrival of their first child, this isolation appears to be much more intense for those who are poorer. The Commission's survey found that those with GCSE level or no qualifications were more than twice as likely as those with at least a degree-level qualification to report no contact at all with parents of similarly aged children (19 per cent versus 8 per cent). A comparable picture emerges from analysis of take-up of antenatal classes. Parents from the lowest socio-economic group are more than twice as likely as parents from the highest socio-economic group not to take part in any classes at all (35 per cent versus 15 per cent), with a worrying 28 per cent citing unavailability or inconvenience as a reason.[15] These classes can be very rewarding: they prepare individuals for birth and parenthood, but perhaps more importantly they foster new friendships with other parents-to-be. The socio-economic gap in participation is a problem.

Further evidence from the same survey suggests that there is not a clear difference by socio-economic group in attitude towards advice. A tiny proportion (5 per cent) of respondents indicated that they did not feel they required any advice, and the vast majority of the remainder cited the most valued source of support as their midwife or health visitor.

10 Hansen, K., et al., *Millennium Cohort Study: Fourth Survey, a User's Guide to Initial Findings*, 2nd Edition, Institute of Education: London, December 2010

11 Jones, E., Gutman, L., and Platt, L., *Family Stressor and Children's Outcomes*, Department for Education, 2013

12 Thompson, S., and Ben-Galim, D., *Childmind the Gap: Reforming Childcare to Support Mothers into Work*, Institute for Public Policy Research, February 2014

13 Waldfogel, J., and Washbrook, E., *Low Income and Early Cognitive Development in the UK*, Sutton Trust, 2010

14 Dearden, L., Sibieta, L., and Sylva, K., *The Socio Economic Gradient in Early Childhood Outcomes – Evidence from the Millennium Cohort Survey, Longitudinal and Life Course Studies*, vol. 2, issue 1, pp19-40, 2011

15 Silversides, K., and Gulc, B., *Experiences of Parenting in the Early Years by Social Background*, Social Mobility and Child Poverty Commission, forthcoming. Almost half (47 per cent) of those with either just GCSEs or no qualifications had not undertaken classes, compared to 17 per cent of those with a degree or postgraduate qualification

But middle-class parents reported seeking advice more regularly and from a wider range of sources than working-class parents.[16] However, these findings strongly suggest that it is time to drop the still prevalent received wisdom that parenting should be beyond the public policy pale. Parents of all income brackets do want advice on parenting. Policymakers must of course tread carefully: parents are understandably protective of their autonomy in this highly personal area of life. But it is time for a more activist approach.

Unfortunately, there are large gaps in the evidence on how to improve parenting on a grand scale. While high-quality (generally US-based) interventions have been shown to be effective in improving parenting and child development outcomes,[17] they are often intensive, hugely expensive, highly targeted and therefore difficult to replicate.[18] When it comes to universal programmes for wider groups of parents, the majority of those that are well evidenced are designed to address specific issues, such as behaviour or language development, rather than more general approaches to improve parenting.[19]

Over recent years, services for parents have shrunk in many areas of the country. Some areas have now stopped providing face-to-face antenatal classes, instead opting to put material online.[20] Budgets in children's centres have been squeezed.[21] Between 2010/11 and 2014/15, the removal of the ring-fence from the Early Intervention Grant to local authorities resulted in a 40.9 per cent real-terms fall in central funding for early intervention. The November 2015 Spending Review announced a 3.9 per cent annual real terms cut to the public health budget, which comes on top of a £200 million cut already announced in the Summer Budget 2015. Taken together, these cuts are highly likely to store up much more expensive problems for public services to deal with later down the line. They make sense only within a public finance model which cannot account for the savings accrued by early investment because savings benefit multiple departments, often not including the one which spent the original money. This is exacerbated by the political cycle, which disincentivises long-term investment, despite the considerable dividends it could reap for the public purse.[22]

By its very nature, early intervention only pays a dividend over time, rendering the question of how to finance it a difficult one for policymakers. In the last decade, more use has been made of social impact bonds and payment-by-results models; flagship government initiatives like the Work Programme and the Troubled Families initiative have been funded on this basis. The Government's devolution agenda could also herald a new dawn in this area by giving local authorities greater incentive to pool budgets and look long-term. If the devolution agenda could be twinned with an early-investment agenda, it could provide the foundation for real progress.

16 Ibid.

17 Barnes J., *The Family-Nurse Partnership Programme in England: Wave 1 Implementation in Toddlerhood and a Comparison between Waves 1 and 2a Implementation in Pregnancy and Infancy*, Department of Health, 2011

18 Like Perry Pre-School, which combined high-quality, low-ratio childcare with home visits to parents, and Nurse Family Partnership (Family Nurse Partnership in the UK), an intensive home-visiting programme starting during pregnancy until the child is age two

19 Education Endowment Foundation Early Years toolkit – https://educationendowmentfoundation.org.uk/toolkit/early-years/; and Early Intervention Foundation Guidebook – http://guidebook.eif.org.uk/programmes-library/search?outcomes%5B%5D=10&min-age=4.00&max-age=20.00&rating%5B%5D=3&rating%5B%5D=4&submit=search&s=

20 http://www.bbc.co.uk/news/uk-england-york-north-yorkshire-24265728; http://www.theargus.co.uk/news/11370236.Criticism_over_antenatal_cuts/; and http://www.bexhillobserver.net/news/local/local-antenatal-classes-are-cut-1-6212640

21 Pre-School Learning Alliance, *Pre-School Learning Alliance response to the Department for Education call for evidence on the cost of providing childcare*, 2015

22 Chowdry, H., and Oppenheim, C., *Spending on Late Intervention: How we can do Better for Less*, Early Intervention Foundation, February 2015; Heckman, J.J., *The Case for Investing in Disadvantaged Young People*, http://heckmanequation.org/content/resource/case-investing-disadvantaged-young-children, 18 November 2015

Problem 2: Efforts to ensure that children are school-ready are uncoordinated, confused and patchy.

School-readiness is an incredibly important milestone for young children. Dame Clare Tickell was right to describe the skills required as 'skills for life'.[23] So it is of great concern that children eligible for free school meals are two-thirds as likely as other children to have achieved a 'good level of development' at age five.[24]

The early years system, which in theory prepares children for school, is well provided for. There are now more health visitors than five years ago, and they work within a clear structure for engagement with families. All three-, four- and disadvantaged two-year-olds should now receive 15 fully funded hours of early education. The delegation of responsibility for commissioning public health to local authorities has made it easier to join up traditionally segregated health and education work by, for example, getting health visitors to work from children's centres.

However, there is a striking lack of consensus about what the term school-readiness actually means and poor coordination in preparing young children to achieve it. Ofsted pointed out in a report last year that there is no nationally agreed definition of school-readiness and no set age of child to which it should apply.[25] Effective measurement is also undermined by the fact that the current measurement regime for this age group, the EYFSP (which will become non-statutory in 2016) was designed to be conducted after children have been in school for a year. The Government's new baseline tests – which will at least take place at the start rather than at the end of the reception year and begin this year – do not resolve these problems and add a major additional one. Unlike the EYFSP, the baseline test will not allow for comparisons to be made of the relative development of children from different backgrounds and regions. Without this, policymakers will be reduced to guessing what is going on, rarely a recipe for successful reform.

Any parent who has read about age-specific developmental milestones and compared them to their own child will recognise the flaws in a specific, skills-based assessment, because all children develop so differently. Indeed, there is considerable debate about the so-called 'schoolification' of the early years as a precursor to school-readiness. However, it is reasonable to assume that as all children are required to commence compulsory schooling at age five, there are a set of understandings as well as cognitive, social and emotional skills that they will need to be able to cope – and thrive – in such an environment. The best early education providers and schools develop their own school-readiness definition, as well as determining an informal accountability system alongside parents and primary schools. But there are many that do not, a failure which is highly consequential for the child.[26]

The lack of a common-sense, clear, shared understanding of what constitutes school-readiness between parents, public health officials (health visitors), local authorities, schools and early education providers is a wasted opportunity. Similarly, the fact that development is not evaluated until months after the child has entered school dilutes accountability and reduces the use of such a measurement. The need for change here is particularly urgent given that the free childcare offer for children is set to be doubled to 30 hours for the school term, in effect shadowing the school day for three- and four-year-olds. A focus on school-readiness, combining a clear definition and a means of measurement which is reported nationally – whether by reforming and maintaining the EYFSP or by introducing a new approach – must be a priority for Government. In addition, the proposed gap in data for a start-of-school development measure is a concerning step backwards that would hinder efforts to focus parents, schools and early years providers on a highly important shared outcome.

23 Tickell, C., *The Early Years: Foundations for Life, Health and Learning, an Independent Report on the Early Years Foundation Stage to Her Majesty's Government*, 30 March 2011

24 Department for Education, *EYFSP Attainment by Pupil Characteristics 2013 to 2014*, National and Local Authority tables

25 Ofsted, *Are You Ready? Good Practice in School Readiness*, 3 April 2014

26 Ibid.

Problem 3: The complexity of the childcare funding system is suppressing take-up by parents and hampering efforts to increase maternal employment.

There are numerous benefits to increased maternal employment. These include improvements in the wellbeing of the mother, better child development, and reductions in the large maternal pay gap, which the Organisation for Economic Co-operation and Development (OECD) suggests is typically 21 per cent by the time a mother returns to full-time work (compared to 7 per cent between childless couples).[27] For Government, higher maternal employment means higher tax revenue and lower spend on benefits and tax credits. But the UK maternal employment rate of 66 per cent, while at about the OECD average, continues to languish some way behind the best-performing western nations like Denmark and Sweden, which enjoy a rate of over 80 per cent.[28]

A comparison of the childcare funding system in the UK and that in Denmark and Sweden is instructive. The system is simpler in much of Scandinavia – a progressive contributory model based on family income, rather than the English system combining free childcare, a voucher system and tax credits. It is also more affordable for parents. Denmark and Sweden prioritise public spending on services (like childcare) as opposed to cash benefits, with most recent OECD estimates suggesting that they spend two-and-a-half times more on services than they do on cash benefits, compared to the UK, where we spend just 50 per cent more on services than on cash benefits.[29] The result, as the Institute for Public Policy Research (IPPR) has found, is that on average 10 per cent of families' disposable income is spent on childcare in Denmark and Sweden, compared to one-third (and rising) for employed couples in the UK.[30] Although there is some research which suggests that lone parents in the UK face substantially lower childcare costs than the OECD average, the average full-time nursery bill for a child under two is now £11,000 a year in England and nearly £15,000 in London, according to the Family and Childcare Trust.[31] [32] Those costs simply price too many families out of the market altogether.

New research for the Commission underlines this as a major issue. When asked about their attitude to returning to work, parents of children under four years old in the lowest socio-economic group were more than twice as likely to say they would like to be able to do so but were put off by the cost of childcare, compared with people in the highest socio-economic group (67 per cent versus 32 per cent).[33] Worryingly, 20 per cent of working-class respondents said they had no idea that any financial help was available to them and a further 33 per cent of the same group said they were confused about what funding was available and where to get it. These figures were also significant for middle-class respondents at 17 per cent and 28 per cent, respectively.[34]

This is supported by other research which highlights the same issue. The IPPR found employment gains from a simpler, clearly communicated childcare system would not be significant for the middle classes, but that conversely there is huge potential to change employment outcomes for mothers at the bottom of the income scale.[35] They estimated that a childcare offer that is more in tune with the needs of working-class parents and which gets mothers currently out of work into work could create a £750 million net positive fiscal impact

27 http://www.theguardian.com/money/2015/oct/05/childcare-expensive-mothers-want-work-trapped-home
28 OECD, *OECD Family Database*, Table 1.2, http://www.oecd.org/els/family/database.htm
29 OECD, PF1.1: *Public spending on family benefits*, last updated 19/09/2014
30 Thompson, S., and Ben-Galim, D., *Childmind the Gap: Reforming childcare to support mothers into work*, Institute for Public Policy Research, February 2014
31 Richardson, L., *Can Parents Afford to Work? An Update*, European Population Conference 2012, Stockholm
32 Family and Childcare Trust, *Childcare Costs Survey 2015*, February 2015
33 Silversides, K., and Gulc, B., *Experiences of Parenting in the Early Years by Social Background*, Social Mobility and Child Poverty Commission, forthcoming
34 Ibid.
35 Thompson, S., and Ben-Galim, D., *op. cit.*

from increased tax revenue and decreased benefit expenditure. The IPPR estimates a further £700 million could result from encouraging mothers already in work to increase their hours.[36]

1.3 How are these problems being addressed?

Support for parents

The final evaluation of the previous government's parenting programme pilot, CANparent, was published in July 2014. Its findings identified some of the challenges in delivering voucher-based universal parenting programmes.[37] Providers including the Race Equality Foundation, City Lit, Parent Gym and Save the Children delivered programmes for parents in three pilot areas which sought to change the attitude of parents towards formal parenting advice. These initial pilots were succeeded by an amended programme, funded by the Department of Health, which ended in March 2015. The key change was a replacement of the voucher system by a joint funding structure combining contributions from public health, parents and the voluntary and community sector. The resulting evaluation should be published shortly.[38] Other than CANparent, there has been no explicit central-government-supported, universal programme which seeks to improve parenting.

But this does not mean that there is no support available to parents. A range of (generally targeted) programmes have been developed by health and local authority partners, and the Early Intervention Foundation has supported 20 Early Intervention Places, with many areas offering specific support to parents. In addition, a £215 million suite of interventions and evaluations designed to support parents to give their children the best start in life, funded by the Big Lottery Fund, is currently under way in five areas of England.[39]

The role of health in the early years has become more prominent since October 2015 when early years health services were integrated into public health structures and budgets and transferred to the responsibility of local authorities. This is illustrated in the NHS Five Year Plan (2014), which sets out proposals for local democratic leadership of public health, including the new statutory responsibility for local authorities to improve the health of their population.[40]

Health visiting services are the most prominent element of this new transfer to affect the parents of young children, with a continued expectation that as well as general access to health visitors, five universal health reviews would be conducted up to age two to two-and-a-half (the new integrated review), and there would be continued delivery of the Healthy Child Programme, which among other things coordinates immunisation and health and development reviews.[41] Other services, like the Family Nurse Partnership, an intensive health visiting service for vulnerable young mothers from 20 weeks of pregnancy to the child's second birthday, have also been transferred.[42]

This new approach is yet to bed in and, although there is great potential in a public health approach focused on getting things right from the start, how these services really deliver for families in the context of fiscal restraint, is yet to become clear.

---

36 Ibid.

37 Department for Education, *CANparent Trial Evaluation, Final Report*, July 2014

38 Warwick University, http://www2.warwick.ac.uk/fac/soc/cedar/canuniversalparentingevaluation/, 30 November 2015

39 Big Lottery Fund, https://www.biglotteryfund.org.uk/betterstart, 18 November 2015

40 NHS England, *Five Year Forward View*, October 2014

41 NHS England, *Health Visiting Programme*, https://www.england.nhs.uk/ourwork/qual-clin-lead/hlth-vistg-prog/, 18 November 2015

42 Family Nurse Partnership, *Family Nurse Partnership Core Service Specification for 2015/16*, 7 May 2015

School-readiness

This chapter has already discussed the limitations of the current approach to school-readiness. Because of these limitations, Government is failing to achieve what should be its prime objective for the early years, unifying parents, schools and providers around shared development goals.

There are changes in the pipeline which have the potential to address these issues, some are new and others have been in the pipeline for some time. The Commission strongly welcomes the bringing together of the education and health reviews for two- to two-and-a-half-year-olds into the appropriately named Integrated Education and Health Review. This review offers the potential for the high-quality developmental data resulting from health and education assessments to be shared between practitioners. The intention to reform the current Early Years Foundation Stage by making the profile assessment non-statutory and to introduce in its place a new reception baseline check (which started this year) is similarly a significant change for the system, with the Government having implemented a process by which schools can choose from a range of different providers of the new baseline tests. Government has been clear, though, that the reception baseline tests have been designed for school accountability purposes, rather than necessarily to resolve some of the problems set out above.

Childcare

There is a core early education offer of 15 hours per week of free childcare over 38 weeks of the year to all parents of three- and four-year-olds. This was extended during the last parliament to include around the 40 per cent most disadvantaged two-year-olds which includes children eligible for free school meals, children looked after by the local authority and two-year-olds from low income working families. Related to this, local authorities have a duty to secure sufficient childcare for working parents, and early education free of charge for eligible children.[43] The Government specified that, as far as possible, early learning for two-year-olds should be delivered by providers who have achieved an overall rating of 'outstanding' or 'good' in their most recent Ofsted inspection report and that all provision should be offered between 7am and 7pm in sessions no shorter than two and a half hours or longer than ten hours. As a minimum, parents should be able to take up their child's funded place across three or five days of the week.[44]

The end of the last parliament also saw the introduction of the Early Years Pupil Premium to help early years settings improve the education they provide for disadvantaged three- and four-year-olds. This was recommended by the Commission and others to recognise the importance of high-quality provision to address the child development gap. The funding provided is relatively modest, at 53p per hour or £302.10 for the full year if there is take-up of the full 15 hours, but the Commission welcomes the policy.[45]

In addition, the last parliament saw the introduction of a new Tax-Free Childcare scheme, which has now been delayed to 2017, but will mean that working parents with a joint income of up to £200,000 (amended from £300,000 in the November 2015 Spending Review) will in effect be able to claim back 20 per cent of their childcare costs up to a total of £2,000 per child.[46] This is an alternative to childcare vouchers, a tax-relief scheme that many parents make use of at present, but that excludes parents working for some smaller employers and those parents who are self-employed. Government also revised proposals for childcare relief under Universal Credit, so that from April 2016, recipients will be able to claim back 85 per cent of childcare costs.

43 Department for Education, *Early Education and Childcare, Statutory Guidance for Local Authorities*, September 2014
44 Ibid.
45 Department for Education, *Early Years Pupil Premium: Guide for Local Authorities*, https://www.gov.uk/guidance/early-years-pupil-premium-guide-for-local-authorities, 18 November 2015
46 HM Treasury, *Spending Review and Autumn Statement 2015*, 25 November 2015

In terms of new proposals, the Government has made one notable addition to the suite of funded childcare policies by pledging to double the current early education offer for three- and four-year-olds from working families to 30 hours, from the current 15 hours. The conditionality associated with this policy was clarified at the November 2015 Spending Review and means that eligible families must have one parent working at least 16 hours and that joint parental income can be no more than £200,000 (with the same conditions announced for tax-free childcare).[47] The Commission welcomes the provision of this additional funded childcare, in the main because there is a need for more, affordable childcare for working families in order for the UK to fulfil its potential on maternal employment.

Although the Government specifically chose to deliver this new commitment through its current, Department for Education-led, free early education provision funding stream, it seems to be based on a quite different rationale. From its inception the Department for Education-led early education policy has been explicitly aimed at child development, based on the good evidence that high-quality early education is beneficial for all children and especially the most disadvantaged.[48] However, the language now being used to describe this policy, as well as the now clarified conditions for eligibility, place the emphasis on childcare rather than early education, with a clear focus on reducing cost pressures for working families and improving maternal employment. This is a tension that needs to be resolved, as one objective should not lose out to another.

1.4 How can more progress be made?

The Commission believes that there are three key ways in which the Government and others can make faster progress in narrowing the gap in early outcomes.

Support for parents

Adopting an exclusively childcare-centred approach to the early years leaves huge holes for a Government that seeks to give every child a fair chance in life. Government must go further to acknowledge the importance of children's home lives in shaping their outcomes from the earliest age. Waiting until three, when they may or may not receive high-quality early education, risks wasting three vital years. Similarly, Government must ensure that it recognises the importance of parenting throughout childhood, including in the school years. Too often it seems that all attention is placed on schools as the mediator of the large attainment gap, when the vast majority of that gap is explained by home and individual factors.

School-readiness

There is an urgent need to end the strategic vacuum in the early years. A cross-cutting strategy which has an overall objective of achieving school- or life-readiness (as the Tickell review termed it), uniting the many departments, public bodies and providers active in this area is needed now more than ever.

Successive governments have talked the early years talk but failed on substance, including in the last parliament where numerous reviews by high-profile experts did not catalyse real action or long-term planning. The Government's proposal to double the fully funded childcare offer for three- and four-year-olds provides a potentially powerful tool to ensure the school-readiness of large numbers of children and to increase maternal employment. But the policy will fail to improve school-readiness if the Government does not get the quality of the offer right. These concerns will be heightened if the Government does not reverse its plans to

47 Ibid.
48 Education Endowment Foundation Early Years toolkit – https://educationendowmentfoundation.org.uk/toolkit/early-years/

remove the national measure of child development. With funding for local authorities and public health set to become ever tighter, and with devolution increasing the potential for complexity, there is an even greater need for clear objectives and strong accountability on school-readiness which ties in all actors in this area, including parents, providers of childcare and early education, and primary schools.

Childcare

Government's new proposal to double funded childcare provision for three- and four-year-olds is a high-stakes policy. It could, in fact, amount to a fully funded universal childcare offer for working parents. However, other than the new announcements about eligibility (minimum number of working hours and an income cap) and the hourly rate (for which an additional £300 million per year was found in the November 2015 Spending Review), there has been little clarity about the principles that will guide the delivery of this new policy. These proposals are hugely expensive (with £1 billion a year earmarked by 2019/20, bringing total Government funding for childcare to £6 billion a year)[49] but, if done right, could see significant gains reaped both in school-readiness and in maternal employment.[50] The Commission takes the view that the following framework represents a bare minimum:

- Protection of a 15-hour high-quality offer in a good or outstanding setting for the 40 per cent most disadvantaged two-, three- and four-year-olds, irrespective of their parents' employment status – using the Government's current definition of the most disadvantaged 40 per cent which applies to two-year-olds;
- The inclusion of incentives for providers, particularly to the 40 per cent most disadvantaged children, to offer provision beyond 9–5 Monday to Friday to support shift and flexible working patterns;
- Careful tracking of take-up of the offer among the 40 per cent most disadvantaged to better understand the reasons for low take-up – and to seek to address them;
- Genuine incentivisation of employment, by simplifying and joining up the offer of financial support to parents, including addressing the cliff edge between Universal Credit/tax credit funded childcare and tax-free childcare and the 30-hour offer.

There are a number of challenges the Government faces in delivering this framework, of which the most obvious is funding. Before the 2015 Spending Review, the IPPR estimated a funding gap of up to £1 billion by 2020/21,[51] a criticism which the Chancellor partially responded to. But without clarity on the Government's assumptions, it does still seem that a large shortfall remains, particularly if the key to this offer in terms of improving the attainment of the poorest children – high-quality early education, as opposed simply to childcare – is not to be watered down. It may be that Government is intending to rely on low take-up – an approach which would seem to run against its ambitions to boost maternal employment.[52]

One remaining concern of the Commission is the extent to which the current childcare provision market for three- and four-year-olds can absorb the increased requirements of a 30-hour offer without significant reform. There is a more specific problem in poorer areas, which have until now been characterised by a higher proportion of provision from the maintained sector, mainly schools and children's centres.[53] However, the schools sector faces particular capacity challenges and has warned that they are unlikely to be able to deliver the increased

49 HM Treasury, *Spending Review and Autumn Statement 2015*, 25 November 2015

50 Ibid.

51 Cory, G., *Extending the Early Years Entitlement: Costings, Concerns and Alternatives*, Institute for Public Policy Research, October 2015

52 *Nursery World*, http://www.nurseryworld.co.uk/nursery-world/news/1154964/lower-staff-child-ratios-to-bring-down-costs-says-dfe, 30 November 2015

53 Stewart, K., *Do Poorer Children Receive Lower Quality Childcare?*, http://www.lse.ac.uk/researchAndExpertise/researchHighlights/socialPolicy/Childcare.aspx, 18 November 2015

hours.[54] This is partly because many schools currently take two cohorts of children for 15 hours each. They often do not have the space to double their numbers, as the change will require. It is also because schools have tended to cross-subsidise the funding of their early years provision from elsewhere in their budgets to ensure quality. The Commission welcomes the Government's announcement in November 2015 of at least £50 million of new capital funding to support providers in the roll-out of the extended offer, which will be an important resource for providers who will struggle to deliver within current capital and funding constraints, but it is unclear that this will respond to providers' concerns.[55]

The role of the private sector in disadvantaged areas in delivering childcare is one that the Government must also consider carefully. Providers report that they sustain provision of funded childcare at a low rate by cross-subsidising from children whose parents pay for their care. There are fewer opportunities for this type of revenue in disadvantaged areas and the additional 15 hours funded at government rates will further reduce the potential for additional revenue.

Beyond the challenges of delivering a well-designed childcare system, it is also important to consider the extent to which such a system can increase maternal employment. In 2014, after the announcement of the Government's new tax-free childcare funding, but before the proposal to double the funded childcare hours, the Institute for Fiscal Studies (IFS) roundly criticised the complexity and effectiveness of current policy.[56] Their critique centred on the fact that the new tax-free childcare policy introduced a third way by which childcare is funded in the UK (joining tax credit childcare funding and fully funded hours for two- to four-year-olds). All three have different eligibility rules, different levels of support, and some perverse cliff edges. There is also a lack of clarity over the objectives of, and evidence for, the different schemes, particularly when it comes to maternal employment. These concerns combined add up to a real risk that precious financial resources may be being wasted in an inefficient and ill-targeted maze of schemes. The IFS called for a single funding scheme for Government to subsidise childcare, open to all parents where top-ups relate to parental income, age of children and work status of parents. It concluded:

> *Given all these uncertainties, the case for extending universal provision of nursery education for pre-school children is in fact not easy to make. There is a danger that the current policy bidding war – welcome as it will be to many parents looking for additional support – will result in ill-targeted and inefficient use of scarce public resource. We have already stumbled a long way in the dark in this policy area. It is time to stop stumbling, shine a light on the policy landscape, and plot an effective route forward.*[57]

Government plans to spend £6 billion a year on childcare by 2019/20, suggesting the need to put a rocket behind a review of the overall funding system for childcare. While early childhood education and care has huge potential to deliver on Government's One Nation aim, the risks of an ill-targeted, inefficient system are too important to ignore.

---

54 National Association of Head Teachers, *An Early Years Place for All, The NAHT Childcare Bill Report*, September 2015

55 HM Treasury, *Spending Review and Autumn Statement 2015*, 25 November 2015

56 Institute for Fiscal Studies, *Green Budget 2014: Chapter 8 – State Support for Early Childhood Education and Care in England*, 2014

57 Ibid.

1.5 Conclusion and Recommendations

It is conceivable that this parliament could prove a revolutionary juncture in the history of early years policy. The Government's commitment to large increases in fully-funded childcare, increased devolution and the new local structures which bind public health officials into early years care provide very significant opportunities to integrate efforts to narrow the gap in early child development and to boost the maternal employment rate. This would be an achievement of which a One Nation government could be proud.

But if that is the scale of the possible achievement, there are significant potential pitfalls along the way, many of which have been examined in this chapter. The recommendations which follow are aimed at avoiding the pitfalls and realising the potential – above all, ensuring that the £6 billion of public money spent by the state each year allocated to childcare and early education is spent wisely. This will require Government to end the damaging strategic vacuum in the early years. The cumulative effect of recent changes to policy here is to move ever closer to universal state-funded childcare for all three- and four-year-olds. But there is little sense of what ends the Government wishes this policy to achieve. This is particularly problematic given that it is managed by a range of government departments, and delivered in the main by local providers from a range of sectors. Childcare policy is split across the Department for Education, the Department for Work and Pensions and HM Revenue and Customs. Each works to differing objectives and with different target groups. There are similar concerns with wider early intervention policy, where good intention is not always translated into action. To correct these deficiencies, we make the following recommendations:

Recommendation 1: Set out a long-term early years strategy which binds all those involved in early years care together behind two clear, stretching objectives.

A universal state-funded childcare system could be a very significant policy tool with which to begin to deliver a genuinely One Nation Britain. However, if this is really Government's aim then it needs to raise its sights and set a truly ambitious objective behind which all those involved in this area can unite. The Government should set out its ambitions in a long-term strategy for the early years, which has a specific focus on its objectives for childcare policy and explicitly sets out how the different Government departments and childcare providers from all sectors will contribute to achieving it. This will help drive a more rigorous focus on evidence-based policy, as well as improve the focus on the specific design of policies and accountability of providers. In the Commission's view this ambition should be twofold:

- To halve the child development gap by 2025 (currently better-off children do 42 per cent better than poorer children);
- To halve the gap in maternal employment between England and the best-performing nations (most recent OECD data records the UK maternal employment rate as 66 per cent, compared to over 80 per cent in Denmark and Sweden – currently these nations perform 24 per cent better than the UK), by 2025.[58]

The pursuit of these long-term objectives should drive Government to be more evidence-based in its approach to policy, as well as more focused in its design of specific policies and the accountability of providers. A clear ambition which focuses on the outcomes of children and their mothers will go some considerable way to realising the Government's One Nation goal.

58 Thompson, S., and Ben-Galim, D., *Childmind the Gap: Reforming Childcare to Support Mothers into Work*, Institute for Public Policy Research, February 2014

Recommendation 2: End the received wisdom that parenting is beyond the reach of public policy by establishing an innovation fund designed to road-test and evaluate policies which aim to help improve parenting skills.

The lack of new, high-quality evaluation and innovative programmes to help a wide spectrum of parents to parent is striking. While previous parenting policies have not proved hugely successful, new evidence for this report shows that parents are hungry for advice at key points in their children's development and that they do trust health visitors and midwives to deliver that advice. This suggests that there is scope to do more to help parents to parent, so it is now time to think differently about what support for parents looks like and how it is delivered. We shouldn't give up just because it is difficult.

The Commission recommends that Government create an innovation fund of £10 million, similar to the £30 million fund set up by the Department for Work and Pensions for NEETs (young people not in education, employment or training), to support payment-by-results programmes that enable disadvantaged young people to participate and succeed in education and training. This innovation fund to support parents should seek to receive bids for programmes which are both universal – to enable social mixing – and targeted, for example, at the 40 per cent poorest parents. They should be designed so that they are accessible and of particular benefit to disadvantaged parents. The key outcomes sought should be related to attachment, child development and school/life readiness. Key to this proposal is evaluation. The Government should designate a specific evaluation budget, amounting to 20 per cent of the total fund. They should task the Early Intervention Foundation and the Education Endowment Foundation with overseeing providers' evaluation plans. No programme should be granted funding without clear, measurable outcomes and high-quality trial evidence should be collected from each.

Recommendation 3: Remove the damaging confusion that exists about the concept of school-readiness by introducing a single, national, easy-to-use definition, and unite all those involved in early years services behind it.

There are many unknowns about the Government's new 30 hours of funded childcare for three- and four-year-olds. The Government has clearly made assumptions about take-up, potential increases in maternal employment, provider mix and the delivery of the 30 hours that are not yet clear to the Commission. Whether, and the extent to which, the offer will reduce the large gaps in school-readiness that exist between the poorest children and the rest in England remains in doubt, particularly given the severe cost pressures. There is therefore a clear need to focus all those involved in delivering this policy on a specific objective to improve school-readiness. At a minimum, the Commission believes that the Government should:

- Develop a new definition of school-readiness to be achieved at the transition between early education and reception class, which seeks to engage parents, health professionals, early education providers and schools in this shared concept;
- The extent of school-readiness by social background should be reported by all local authorities in new league tables and action taken to address the gap in data left from making the EYFSP non-statutory. Either by reversing that decision, while focusing the EYFSP more explicitly on school-readiness and moving it to the start of the reception year, or by supplementing the new school-readiness definition proposed above with a simple new measurement tool;

- Introduce a new stipulation that the 15 hours of high-quality early education for the most disadvantaged 40 per cent can only be funded in good or outstanding settings. Where this is not possible, local authorities should report publicly on the numbers of disadvantaged children in lower-quality provision;
- Use area-based pilots to test the market's response to the 30-hour offer, in particular how it affects the inclination and ability of the highest-quality settings in the poorest areas to deliver it according to demand.

Recommendation 4: Increase take-up of free childcare, and decrease its cost by radically simplifying the multiple streams which finance it.

The Government's highly fragmented childcare offer is failing on efficiency for the taxpayer and on maternal employment. In order to deliver more effectively on both, it must be simpler. Government's inclination to tack on new additions to an already complex system further exacerbates the problem. We believe there is a long-term and short-term answer to this.

- **In the short term**: all parents entitled to Universal Credit and Child Benefit should receive a childcare entitlement statement, setting out the childcare support that they are (or are likely to be) entitled to from across the different schemes (tailored according to HM Revenue and Customs data about their income/tax). This document should stress the importance of the quality of early education and emphasise the choices that parents have.
- **In the long term**: the Government should look to streamline its highly complicated childcare offer across the wide range of current funding schemes. This is likely to realise savings through increased efficiency and improve incentives to employment by making the net cost of childcare clearer to all parents.

Chapter 2: Schools – the engine of social mobility

- **Schools are the cornerstone of efforts to improve social mobility and in some parts of the country – London especially – they are breaking the link between demography and destiny.**
- **But schools where poor children do well are the exception not the rule and in two areas – Portsmouth and Bracknell Forest – no pupils eligible for free school meals went on to a top university.**
- **Overall, poor children – even the brightest – do less well than their wealthier peers and the gap widens throughout school.**
- **Government is doing a lot to make schools engines of social mobility and there are welcome efforts towards tougher standards, a core curriculum and a greater focus on progress in accountability measures.**
- **But Government should set its sights higher and aim for poor children elsewhere to do as well as they currently do in Inner London by 2030, which would reduce the educational attainment gap between the most disadvantaged children and everyone else by two-thirds.**
- **It should adopt a new zero tolerance approach to schools which are in terminal failure. Those schools failing to perform for five consecutive years should face wholesale changes in their leadership and be required to become part of a high-performing academy chain.**
- **A prestigious new fellowship of Change Leaders – Heads who have previous experience of successfully turning around schools – should be created to lead efforts to put failing schools back on the path to success.**
- **Pay for new teachers should be improved and fees for Initial Teacher Training should be scrapped.**
- **The National Teaching Service's efforts to get more of the best teachers into the worst schools in disadvantaged areas should be turbo-charged with local trials of better incentives – including a new help-to-buy scheme exclusively for teachers.**

2.1 Introduction

Governments through the decades have recognised that schools are the cornerstone of efforts to improve social mobility. Indeed, for much of the past 30 years the English education system has found itself in the political cross-hairs. Schools have been subject to significant funding increases in the Blair years, combined with relative protection in the leaner Coalition years, as well as wide-ranging reforms to increase school autonomy and accountability, improve literacy, numeracy and standards for the most disadvantaged children, and most recently inject more rigour into the curriculum and qualifications.

There are now areas of the country as well as individual schools demonstrating the cumulative effect of these efforts, with some of this country's highest achieving schools now operating in some of our poorest areas. The successful turnaround of large numbers of previously written-off London schools has transformed the life chances of many of the capital's children. Beyond London too, some schools see their poor pupils do better at GCSE than the national average for all children. The simple inevitability of richer children doing better than poorer has been disproven.

But, there is still unfinished business. These turnaround schools and areas remain the exception. The English schools system is characterised by its patchiness and the continuing low attainment of many of the poorest children. While in 2014 there were nearly 60 non-selective schools in which at least three in four disadvantaged children left school with five good GCSEs[1] (above the national average for all children), there were nearly 600 schools where that figure was just one in four.[2] As research for the Commission shows, the tragic cumulative effect of this is that low ability children from wealthy families catch up with bright children from poor families at school.[3]

The attainment gap is not simply a matter of the poorest 10 or 20 per cent doing badly at school and the rest doing well. Attainment rises incrementally as deprivation reduces.[4] This is very important to social mobility, because it means that lost potential continues some way up the income scale – disadvantage affects the attainment of more than just the poorest children eligible for free school meals. It is also extremely important for later opportunities in life, as the labour market increasingly rejects those who were not successful at school, a trend that is particularly strong for the poorest children.[5] The lifetime returns of five or more good GCSEs, compared with no qualifications, is £283,000 for men and £232,000 for women. Even those who achieved five to seven low GCSE passes can expect increased lifetime earnings of £73,000 for men and £55,000 for women compared with those who achieved three to four low passes.[6]

These figures pose a particular problem for the Government's ambition to spread the recovery beyond the south-east. Schools in London enable 50 per cent more of their poorest children to obtain five good GCSEs compared with elsewhere.[7] This exacerbates the opportunity gap between London and the rest of the country, wasting both vast individual potential and significant sums in lost productivity and competitiveness in areas that need these the most.

1 Social Mobility and Child Poverty Commission, new analysis using the *National Pupil Database – 2013–14 GCSE results by pupil characteristics*, November 2015

2 Ibid.

3 Social Mobility and Child Poverty Commission, *New Research Exposes the 'Glass Floor' in British Society*, press release, 26 July 2015, https://www.gov.uk/government/news/new-research-exposes-the-glass-floor-in-british-society

4 Institute for Public Policy Research, *Excellence and Equity: Tackling Educational Disadvantage in England's Secondary Schools*, June 2013

5 Lindley, J., and Machin, S., *The Quest for More and More Education: Implications for Social Mobility*, in *Fiscal Studies*, Institute for Fiscal Studies, vol. 33, no. 2, 2012, pp265-86

6 Department for Education, *The Economic Value of Key Intermediate Qualifications: Estimating the Returns and Lifetime Productivity Gains to GCSEs, A levels and Apprenticeships*, December 2014

7 Department for Education, *GCSE and Equivalent Attainment by Pupil Characteristics: 2014*

There is growing consensus that the key ingredient in successful schools is a highly effective teaching workforce. And notably, Ofsted has judged teaching quality in the capital's secondary schools to be higher than in any other region.[8] Good teachers make a difference for all students, but make more difference for the most disadvantaged, because this group are least likely to fulfil their academic potential – a fact borne out by the experience in London, where the attainment gap is 10 percentage points smaller than in the rest of the country.[9] This is the direction in which we urge the Government to dedicate its education reforms in this parliament. The remainder of this chapter will develop this theme, first by assessing the country against the Government's One Nation ideal, second by examining current government policy, and third by identifying in more detail the further action that is needed. Finally, we draw some specific conclusions and recommendations.

2.2 Does today's reality meet the One Nation vision?

The One Nation vision is one in which every child has the chances and choices with which to fulfil their potential, regardless of birth, background or geographic location. There are some good signs of progress towards that goal. Since 2005, children eligible for free school meals have become considerably more likely to achieve the key threshold measures at the end of primary and secondary school (see Figure 2.1). The attainment gap between the poorest and other children at primary school is now 18 percentage points, an improvement of 7 percentage points since 2005.[10] The extent to which children not eligible for free school meals are more likely to achieve a good level at the end of primary school than their poorer peers (those eligible for free school meals) has also reduced since 2005. Children not eligible for free school meals' chances of achieving a Level 4 at Key Stage 2 reduced from 1.5 to 1.3 times more likely between 2005 and 2014 (Figure 2.1). At secondary school, these more affluent children are now 1.8 times more likely to gain five good GCSEs than their poorer peers, down from 2.5 times in 2005.

8 Ofsted Data View, quality of teaching as at 31/03/2015, http://dataview.ofsted.gov.uk
9 Department for Education, *GCSE and Equivalent Attainment by Pupil Characteristics: 2014*
10 Department for Education, *National Curriculum Assessments at Key Stage 2, 2014 (revised)*

Figure 2.1: Attainment at 11, 16 and 19 in 2014, compared to 2005, according to free school meal (FSM) status

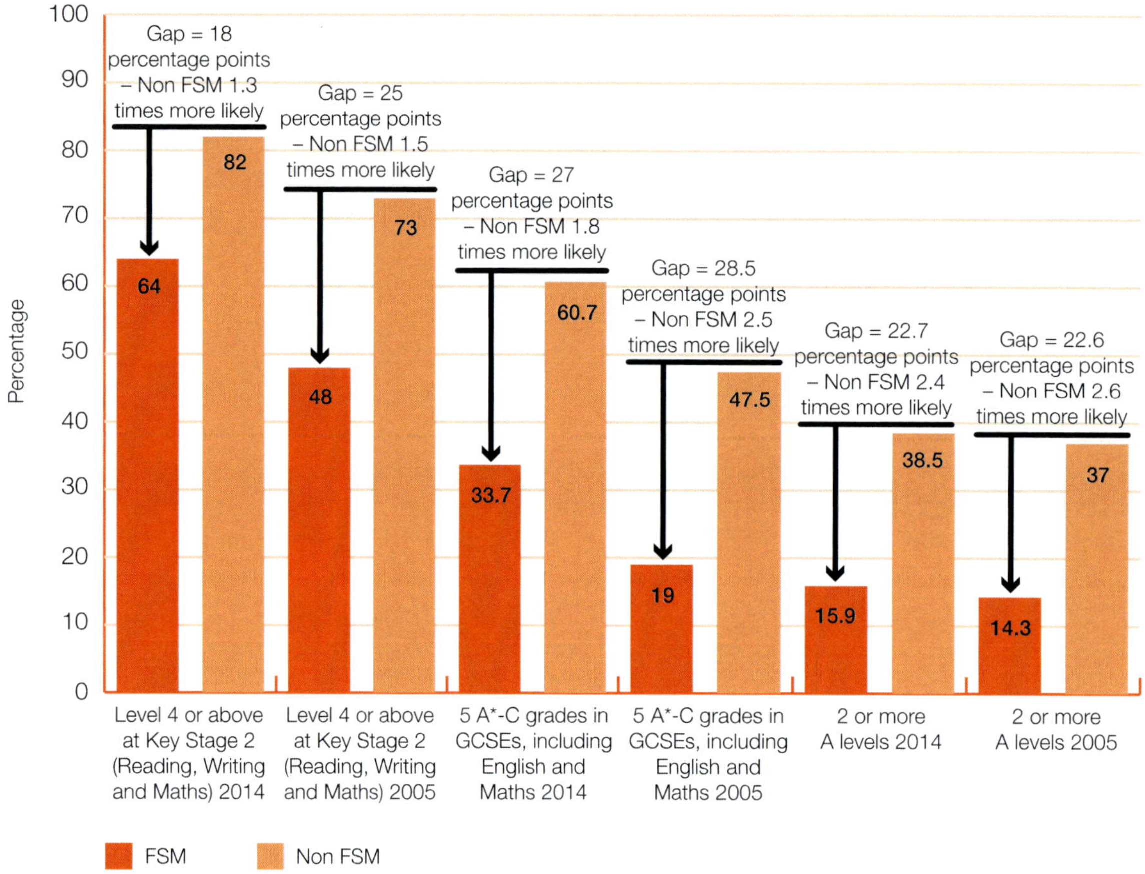

Source: Department for Education, *National Curriculum Assessments at Key Stage 2, 2014 (revised)*, Department for Education, *GCSE and Equivalent Attainment by Pupil Characteristics*, 2014, Department for Education, *Level 2 and 3 Attainment by Young People Aged 19 in 2014*, Table 15a , 31 March 2015

Family income

The attainment gap between children from families with the lowest incomes and their better-off peers remain large, both at Key Stage 2 and GCSE. The attainment gap also grows as children progress through school, with the gap at GCSE wider than the gap at Key Stage 2 (see Figure 2.1). The higher the initial level of attainment,[11] the wider this gap gets (see Figures 2.2, 2.3 and 2.4), demonstrating that beneath the headline indicators lies an even more worrying story. This is reinforced by another gap, in the abilities of children from different social backgrounds to achieve expected levels of progress during secondary school. This serves to highlight the absolute importance of detailed attainment tracking in order to fully understand where and how poorer children fall behind.

11 Level 4b rather than Level 4 at 11, EBacc (English Baccalaureate) rather than GCSE at 16, and A levels rather than Level 3 qualifications at 19

Figure 2.2: 11-year-olds achieving Level 4 and Level 4b in 2013–14

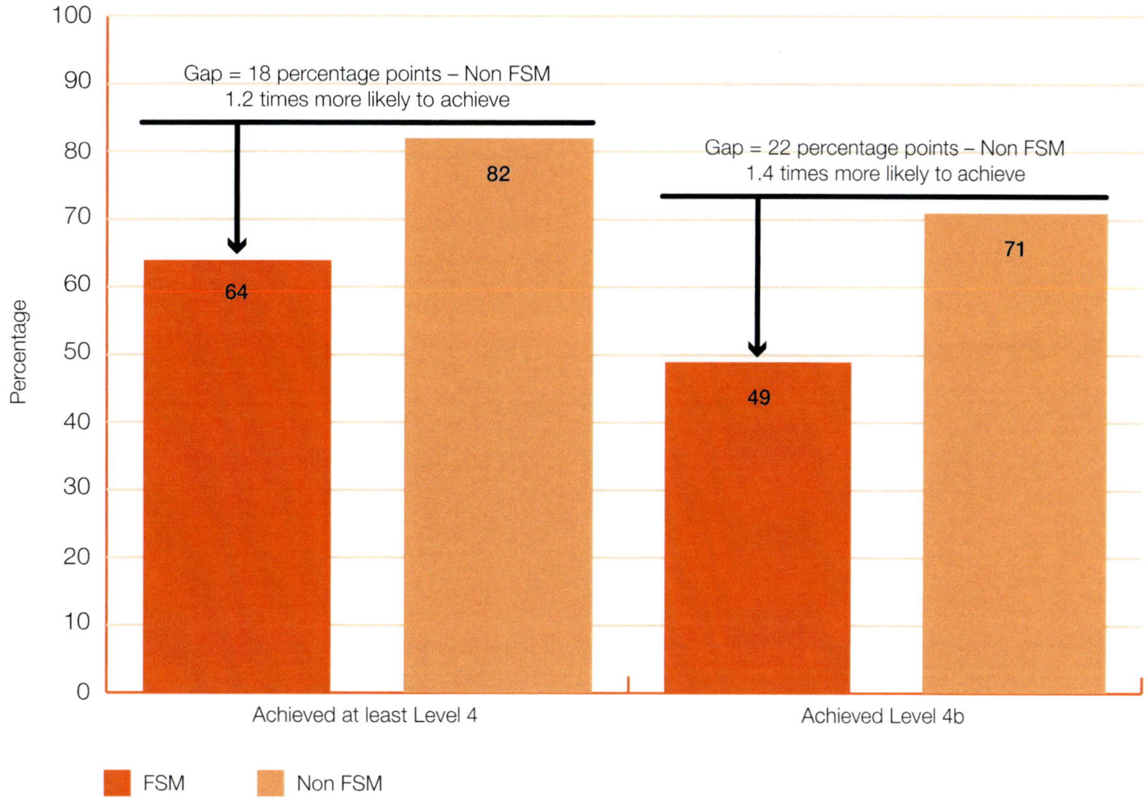

Source: Department for Education, *National Curriculum Assessments at Key Stage 2, 2014 (revised)*, 2014

Figure 2.3: 16-year-olds entered for and achieving the EBacc (English Baccalaureate) in 2013–14

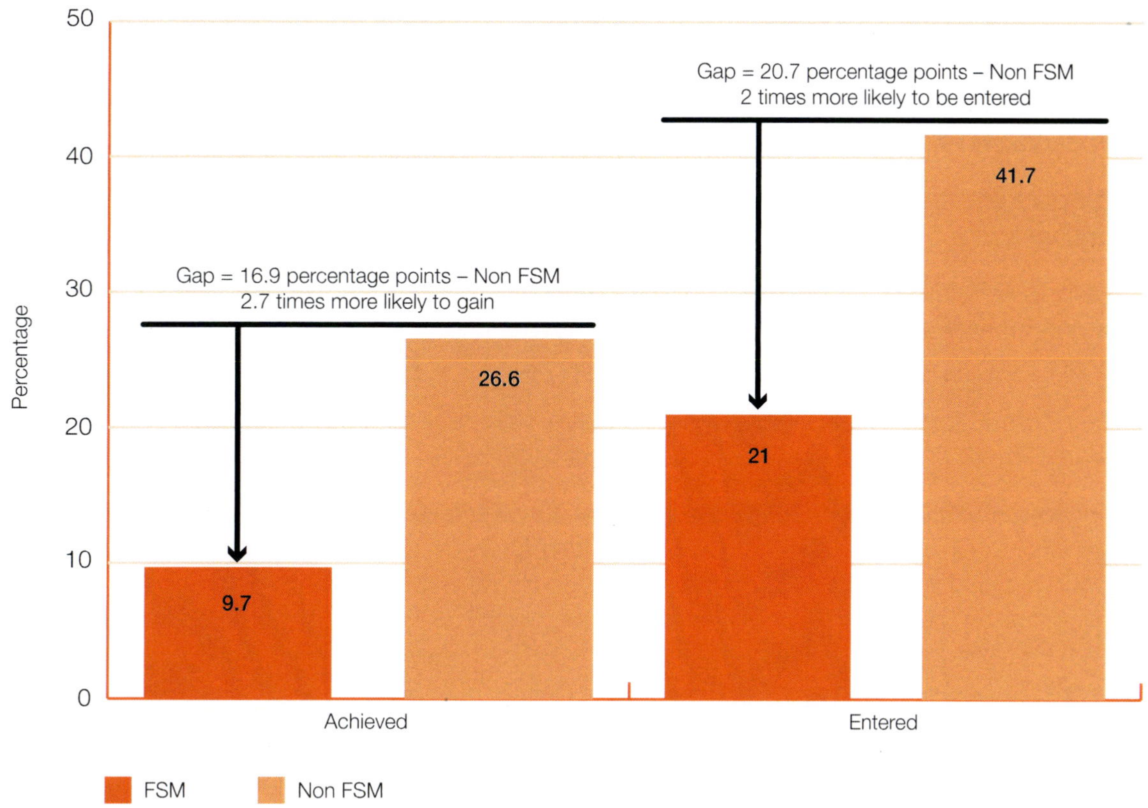

Source: Department for Education, *GCSE and Equivalent Attainment by Pupil Characteristics: 2014*, 2015

Figure 2.4: Qualifications gained by 19-year-olds in 2013–14

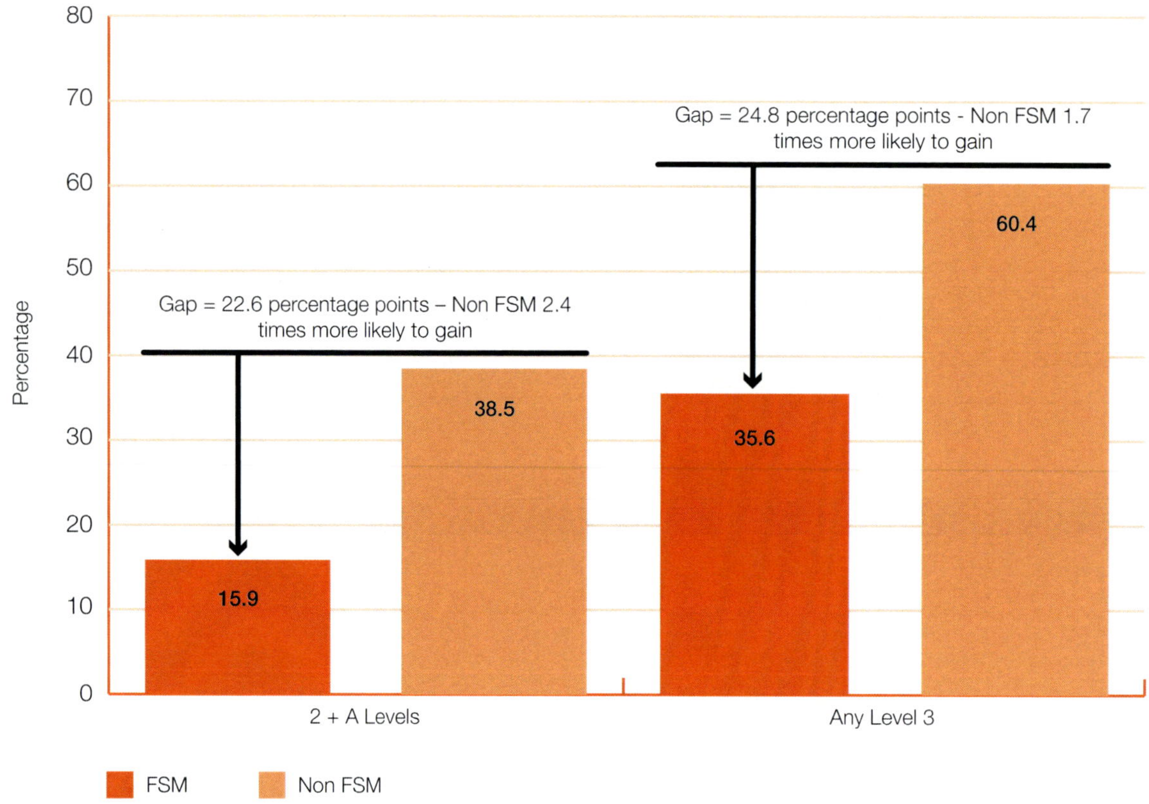

Source: *Department for Education, A level and other level 3 results: 2013 to 2014 (revised)*, 29 January 2015

Perhaps most worryingly, poor children do not only start school at a lower base, but they also make less progress while they are there. The attainment of wealthier children accelerates during their school years, while it stalls for the poorest. This means that wealthier children exceed their educational potential, but the poorest do not get near to fulfilling theirs. The most recent data available shows that:

- 57 per cent of the poorest pupils made the expected level of progress in English during secondary school, compared with 74 per cent of all other pupils;[12]
- 46 per cent of the poorest pupils made the expected level of progress in maths during secondary school, compared with 69 per cent of all other pupils;[13]
- Of the poorest children achieving the lowest levels in Key Stage 2 maths tests (at the end of primary school), 12 per cent went on to achieve a C or more in GCSE maths, compared to 20 per cent of wealthier children who got the same low level;[14]
- Of the poorest children reaching the highest level in Key Stage 2 maths, 29 per cent translated it into an A or A* in GCSE maths, compared to 49 per cent of other children.[15]

The progress gap increased in 2014, the last year for which data is available (Table 2.1). This coincides with the implementation of the Wolf reforms which, among other things, increased qualification requirements at GCSE. While this period saw a drop in the proportion of children of all backgrounds translating a good level of attainment[16] at the end of primary school into

12 Department for Education, *GCSE and Equivalent Attainment by Pupil Characteristics: 2014*

13 Ibid.

14 Defined as Level 3a and below. Ofsted and Department for Education, RaiseOnline, https://www.raiseonline.org/documentlibrary/ViewDocumentLibrary.aspx (under Transition Matrices heading), https://www.raiseonline.org/OpenDocument.aspx?document=381

15 Defined as Level 5. Ofsted and Department for Education, RaiseOnline, https://www.raiseonline.org/documentlibrary/ViewDocumentLibrary.aspx (under Transition Matrices heading), https://www.raiseonline.org/OpenDocument.aspx?document=381

16 Level 4b

five good GCSEs, the drop was more dramatic for poorer children. The resulting gaps in qualifications are marked: Six in 10 disadvantaged children who had gained a level 4b (so above the Government's current threshold at Key Stage 2) went on to achieve five good GCSEs in 2014, compared to eight in 10 other children (see Table 2.1).

The impact of these trends is demonstrated by research for the Commission which shows that high-ability children from disadvantaged families at age seven are overtaken by lower-ability wealthier children by the time they take their GCSEs, with the fastest drop-off occurring between Key Stages 2 and 4.[17] Secondary school marks a particularly risky time for disadvantaged children, with too many failing to fulfil the trajectory that their previous attainment would suggest.

Table 2.1: Students gaining at least Level 4b at the end of primary school who went on to gain five A*-C grades including English and maths at GCSE – 2011–14

	2011	2012	2013	2014
Disadvantaged	63.2%	63.4%	64.6%	58.5%
Non-disadvantaged	81.8%	81.1%	82.4%	78.4%
Percentage point gap	18.6	17.7	17.8	19.9
Non-disadvantaged more likely to achieve	29.5%	27.9%	27.5%	34.1%

Source: Ofsted and Department for Education, *Raise Online Transition Matrices for 2013/14*, 2015

Gender

Boys are doing worse than girls at every stage in education, from the Early Years Foundation Stage to A level. In 2014, boys' GCSE results were 16 per cent worse than girls', with 52 per cent of boys achieving five good GCSEs compared with 62 per cent of girls.[18] While this gap isn't replicated in the labour market (where the gender pay gap remains the other way around), there is evidence of an increasing gender gap in the labour market for lower socio-economic groups, with men more likely than women to have no qualifications at all.[19] There are signs that the gender gap at school has widened over time, with an increase of nearly two percentage points between boys' and girls' results from 2006 to 2014.[20] Commitment to homework is thought to be one explanation for the large gaps in attainment between boys and girls, but girls' success in English is also a key differentiator, with little difference in performance in maths between genders. The particularly low performance of boys is clearly concerning, but the attainment of poor girls is also unacceptably low.

Ethnicity

Of the group of children eligible for free school meals, white British boys are by far the lowest performers (of the major ethnic groups), with just 23.8 per cent gaining five good GCSEs (see Figure 2.5), compared with 30.8 per cent of black Caribbean boys. Of the 53,607 children eligible for free school meals who did not achieve five good GCSEs in 2014, over 20,000 (or 37 per cent) were white British boys (compared to the 32 per cent of white British boys eligible for free school meals overall). Disadvantaged white boys have been shown to have a particularly problematic time throughout secondary school, with research showing that, controlling for other characteristics, all ethnic minority groups make greater progress

17 Commission for Social Mobility and Child Poverty, *Progress made by High Attaining Children from Disadvantaged Backgrounds*, June 2014

18 Department for Education, *GCSE and Equivalent Attainment by Pupil Characteristics: 2014*, 2015

19 Lindley, J., and Machin, S., *The Quest for More and More Education*, op. cit.

20 2005/06 results taken from GCSE and equivalent attainment by pupil characteristics in England: 2009 to 2010 – attainment gap on five A*-C grades including English and maths between boys and girls 8.3 percentage points in 2005/06 and 10.1 in 2013/14

throughout secondary school than white students.[21] There has been considerable debate about the particular barriers to attainment faced by poorer white children. At a recent select committee meeting on the attainment of white working-class boys, Baroness Professor Alison Wolf concluded:

> *We do need to recognise that a lot of the low achievement that is concentrated among white working-class children is also related to where they live and, in many cases, to the fact that there are large parts of this country … where you have got an economy that is still bearing the scars of the end of manufacturing and industrial employment … A lot of the careers and jobs that were the bedrock of white working-class family life for many decades and generations have vanished and have not been well replaced.*[22]

When looking at the attainment of all children not just the poorest, black Caribbean children are the lowest-performing major group – 47.0 per cent gained five good GCSEs in 2014, compared with the national average of 56.6 per cent. The gender gap for black Caribbean children is also larger than for other ethnic groups, with girls doing comparably well. Notably, the rate of improvement in the attainment of black Caribbean boys from the poorest families has far exceeded the improvements for poor white British boys since 2006 (see the dotted lines in Figure 2.5).

21 Wilson, D., Burgess, S., and Briggs, A., *The Dynamics of School Attainment of England's Ethnic Minorities*, Centre for Analysis of Social Exclusion, January 2006

22 Education Select Committee, *Underachievement in Education by White Working Class Children*, 18 June 2014, http://www.publications.parliament.uk/pa/cm201415/cmselect/cmeduc/142/14206.htm

Figure 2.5: Percentage of students achieving five A*-C grades in GCSE examinations (including English and maths) by gender, free school meal (FSM) status and selected ethnicity, 2006–14

Source: Department for Education, *GCSE and Equivalent Attainment by Pupil Characteristics: 2014,* 2015 and Department for Children, Schools and Families, *Achievements at GCSE and equivalent for pupils at the end of Key Stage 4 by Pupil Characteristics, 2009/10 (with data back to 2005/06)*, 2010

Note: the reductions in performance in 2013–14 reflect the new methodology for calculating five A*-C recommended in the Wolf report, where there were limitations on the qualifications that count towards the five

Underlying these three gaps in attainment are three key structural problems that affect schools in England and prevent them from effectively tackling the attainment gap.

Problem 1: Despite progress in some English schools, the biggest weakness in the schools system is the large variation in standards.

The quality of schools in England is highly variable. Schools that are apparently similar in terms of relative deprivation of area or disadvantage of intake can perform very differently.[23] This map (Figure 2.6) highlights the patchiness of the system across England for children eligible for free school meals, with the large urban centres that were once the weakest performing now among the strongest.

23 Social Mobility and Child Poverty Commission, *Cracking the Code*, September 2014

Figure 2.6: Proportion of children across England eligible for free school meals gaining five A*-C grades at GCSE, including English and maths, 2014 – highlighting the top 20 per cent and bottom 20 per cent

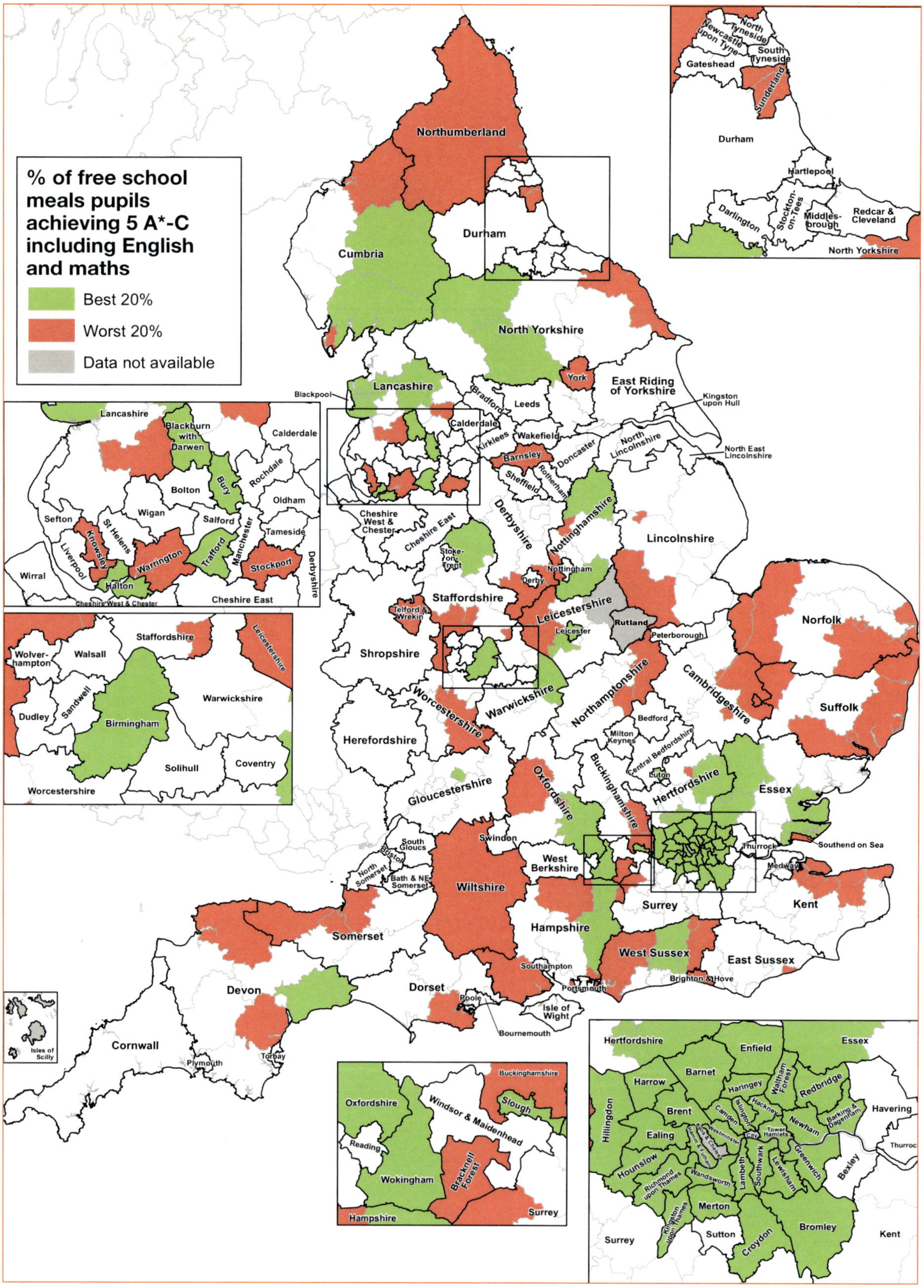

Source: Reproduced by permission of Ordnance Survey on behalf of HMSO, 2015

Attending a good school is important for all children, but particularly so for the poorest because they are more likely to have more ground to make up and have been shown to make less progress overall.[24] But in England, poorer children are more likely to attend weaker schools, which acts as a double disadvantage. A primary school age child living in one of the poorest areas of England is twice as likely as a child living in one of the wealthiest areas to go to a school which is less than good, according to Ofsted (22 per cent versus 10 per cent). At secondary level, the difference is larger still, with a child living in one of England's poorest areas three times more likely to go to a school which is less than good, compared to a child living in one of the wealthiest areas (34 per cent versus 11 per cent). While there has been a notable improvement in primary schools since 2010, the quality of secondary schools in the poorest areas of England remains far too low.[25]

Figure 2.7: Percentage of learners in good or outstanding schools, primary and secondary, by deprivation of area, change 2010–15

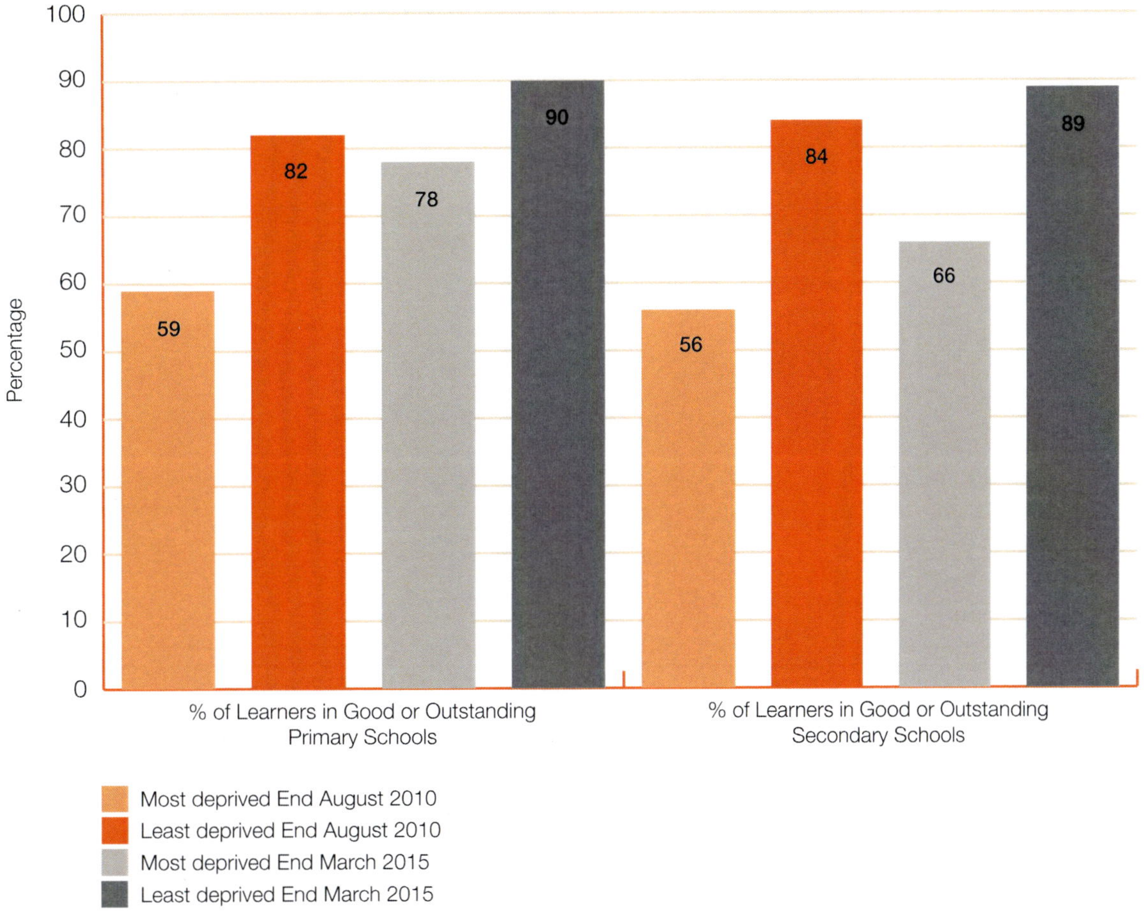

Source: Ofsted Data View, overall school effectiveness as at 31 March 2015

The fact that children in the poorest areas of England are far more likely to attend a weaker school is concerning, particularly because the relationship between disadvantage and attainment remains so strong in areas other than London. In London, some of the poorest areas are now home to England's most impressive schools. Poor children living in deprived London boroughs such as Southwark, Newham and Hackney[26] are likely to go to a school that is good or outstanding and to gain five good GCSEs at the end of secondary school. The old excuse of underperforming schools – that demography should dictate expectations – has been comprehensively undermined. This means that the Government's lens should be firmly focused on the areas in which poverty and low attainment remain unforgivably linked. Looking

24 Department for Education, *GCSE and Equivalent Attainment by Pupil Characteristics: 2014*
25 Ofsted Data View, overall school effectiveness as at 31/03/2015, http://dataview.ofsted.gov.uk
26 All among the 25 per cent most deprived areas of England

at the effectiveness of all schools in an area shows some stark differences across England. Figure 2.8 shows the areas of England with the highest and lowest proportion of schools that are at least good according to Ofsted – some of the same areas are highlighted in Figure 2.6. This illustrates the ongoing, stand-out success of schools in many areas in London.

Figure 2.8: Proportion of schools across England rated good or outstanding according to Ofsted as at end December 2014 – highlighting the top 20 per cent and bottom 20 per cent

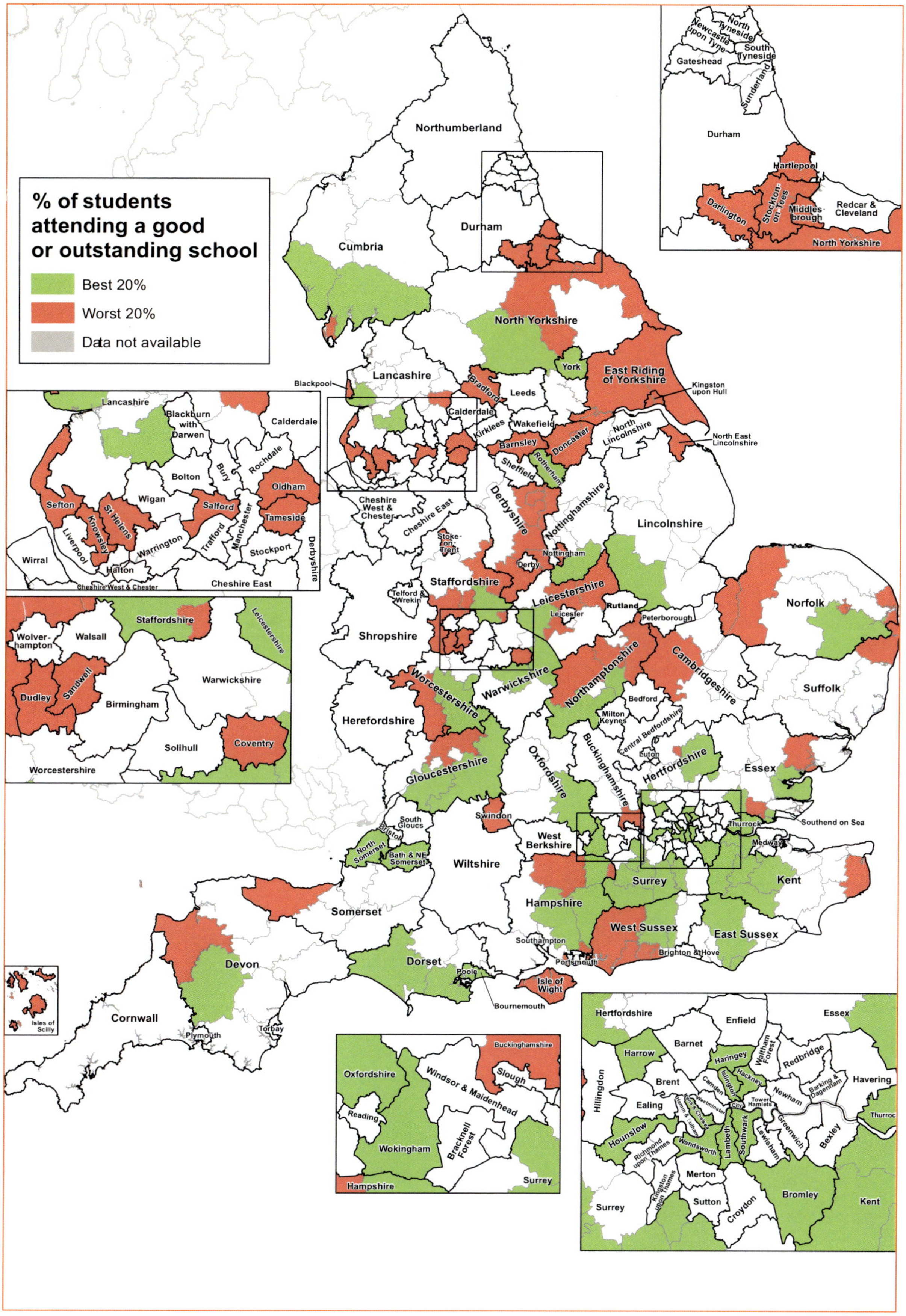

Source: Reproduced by permission of Ordnance Survey on behalf of HMSO, 2015

Bringing together the data set out in Figures 2.6 and 2.8, Figure 2.9 presents the results of a One Nation index of top-tier local authority areas by secondary school quality and the attainment of children eligible for free school meals at GCSE. The chart shows high-performing areas (better than average secondary schools and above average GCSE results for poorer children) in the top-right corner, and the inverse, the weakest areas, in the bottom-left corner. This bottom-left corner includes large industrial towns within the shadows of some of our major cities, such as Barnsley, Knowsley and Stockton-on-Tees. Here, nearly half of secondary schools require improvement or are in special measures and fewer than a quarter of poor children achieved five good GCSEs in 2014. It is in these areas, where parents have little or no choice of good schools and where the vast majority of poor children fail to achieve basic qualifications, that attention is most needed. Perhaps most strikingly, analysis in Table 2.2 shows that there is no clear deprivation trend, with deprived areas present equally in both the top 10 and bottom 10.

Figure 2.9: Secondary schools and social mobility – index based on performance by students eligible for free school meals and quality of schools by local authority area

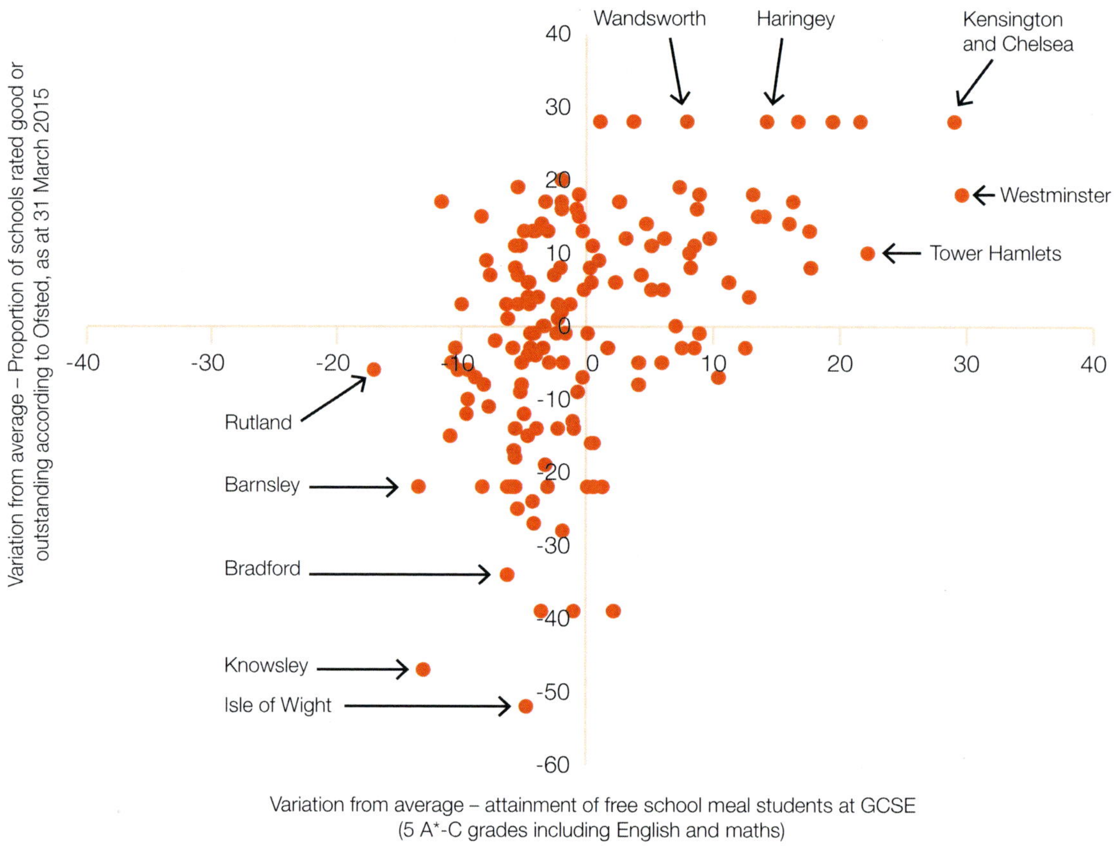

Source: Ofsted Data View, overall school effectiveness as at 31/03/2015, http://dataview.ofsted.gov.uk, and Department for Education, *GCSE and Equivalent Attainment by Pupil Characteristics: 2014*, 2015

Table 2.2: Underlying data in rank order (from Figure 2.8) – top 10 and bottom 10 areas with Indices of Multiple Deprivation (IMD) rankings

Index rank (based on FSM GCSE results and secondary school quality)	Area	% FSM students 5+ A*-C grades inc. English and maths at GCSE 2014	% Secondary schools good or outstanding (Ofsted – as at 31 March 2015)	Indices of Multiple Deprivation (IMD) – Rank of average score (1 = most deprived)
1/150	Kensington & Chelsea	62.0	100	75
2/150	Islington	54.6	100	22
3/150	Southwark	52.4	100	33
4/150	Hounslow	49.7	100	80
5/150	Haringey	47.2	100	24
6/150	Westminster	62.6	90	45
7/150	Redbridge	49.3	89	91
8/150	Hammersmith & Fulham	46.1	90	68
9/150	Wandsworth	40.9	100	103
10/150	Kingston upon Thames	41.9	90	144
	Average IMD rank of top 10 areas			**68.5**
141/150	East Riding of Yorkshire	27.1	50	118
142/150	Cambridgeshire	27.5	47	134
143/150	Kingston upon Hull	27.0	50	3
144/150	Northumberland	23.4	60	90
145/150	Stockton-on-Tees	26.7	50	65
146/150	Warrington	24.7	50	94
147/150	South Gloucestershire	22.1	57	143
148/150	Bradford	26.7	38	18
149/150	Barnsley	19.6	50	32
150/150	Knowsley	20.0	25	2
	Average IMD rank of bottom 10 areas			**69.9**

Source: Ofsted Data View, overall school effectiveness, op. cit.; Department for Education, *GCSE and Equivalent Attainment by Pupil Characteristics: 2014*; Office for National Statistics, *English Indices of Deprivation*, 30 September 2015

Below these areas which are underperforming for their poorest children are a small, but notable, number of schools in terminal failure. That is, at secondary level those schools which have failed to get to floor standards (40 per cent of students achieving five A*-C grades) for five consecutive years. The Commission's analysis suggests that between 2011 and 2015 there have been 30 such secondary schools across England. None of these schools are to be found in London, there are two in Nottingham, but Yorkshire and the Humber is home to nine, including four in Leeds. These schools represent less than 1 per cent of all secondary schools in England. They are consistently and tragically failing their pupils. The systemic response to this failure must be both swifter and bolder.

Overall, the large variations in attainment and school quality highlighted in this section, particularly among areas and schools with similarly disadvantaged populations, provide great grounds for optimism. There are tried and tested ways of tackling these issues, and there are huge gains to be made where this is done successfully. Analysis for the Commission's *Cracking the Code* report found that if schools closed half the gap in performance compared with the top 20 per cent of schools with similar concentrations of disadvantage, over 14,000 more disadvantaged students would get five good GCSEs each year.[27]

Problem 2: The incentives and structures that determine the recruitment, retention, development and deployment of teachers in England are failing to deliver enough high-quality teachers in the numbers required, especially in the most disadvantaged areas.

One of the key means at the Government's disposal to improve the social mobility problem in England is to address the issue of teacher quality and ensure that the poorest children have greater access to highly effective teaching. But there is increasing evidence that the teacher labour market is misfiring badly, accentuated by wider economic, population and policy factors.

Teacher training

Efforts to increase the number and quality of trainee teachers have had mixed success at best and it is clear that teacher-training places for many subjects are not being filled. The problem is most marked at secondary level, where just 82 per cent of the target number of places were filled in 2015/16.[28] We welcome the growth of school-based initial teacher training (ITT), which has the potential to improve the quality of training as well as the numbers recruited. However, the arrival of School Direct has only complicated the already highly fragmented offer for potential applicants. People interested in teaching as a career will find little information which compares the real costs, benefits and effectiveness of different teacher training routes or institutions, despite their wide variation.[29]

This is further complicated by the complexity of the financial packages available to help teachers finance their training. Two in 10 teacher-training places from 2015/16 were salaried, either through School Direct or Teach First,[30] and so required no upfront payments. The remaining eight in 10 (including seven in 10 of School Direct places) required applicants to pay tuition fees of up to around £9,000, just as for any undergraduate course in England. Students are entitled to full tuition-fee loans and other student finance, as well as various subsidies in the form of scholarships and bursaries, which vary according to subject specialism and degree classification. While financial assistance outside of the mainstream student finance system is extremely rare for primary school trainees (other than maths specialists), a secondary school physics trainee with a first-class degree or PhD might receive a bursary of £30,000[31] in addition to their student finance (see Table 2.3). Bursaries are extremely expensive and the evidence on their effectiveness in attracting individuals to teaching (who would not previously have considered it) is not clear.[32] Also, characteristics such as degree classification, which determine the amount of the bursary, have no bearing on the potential of the individual to be an effective teacher.[33] In addition, a recent evaluation by the Institute for Fiscal Studies (IFS) found that, under the new student finance system, the average teacher will never pay off the borrowing accrued for fees and living costs for their ITT year.[34] The IFS found that the combination of unpaid loans and subsidies mean that the cost

27 Social Mobility and Child Poverty Commission, *Cracking the Code*, September 2014
28 Department for Education, *Initial Teacher Training: Trainee Number Census – 2015 to 2016*, SFR 46, 19 November 2015
29 UCAS Teacher Training, *Postgraduate Routes into Teaching*, https://www.ucas.com/ucas/teacher-training/getting-started/postgraduate-routes-teaching, accessed 18 November 2015
30 Ibid.
31 Get Into Teaching website, https://getintoteaching.education.gov.uk/bursaries-and-funding, accessed 18 November 2015
32 See, HB., *Determinants of Teaching as a Career in the UK*. Evaluation & Research in Education, 2004 and National Foundation of Educational Research, *Who Would be a Teacher? A Review of Factors Motivating and Demotivating Prospective and Practising Teachers*, 2000
33 Allen, R., and Burgess, S., *Reforming Teacher Training to Find the Best Teachers*, Centre for Market and Public Organisation, http://www.bristol.ac.uk/media-library/sites/cmpo/migrated/documents/reformingteachertraining.pdf
34 Institute for Fiscal Studies, *The Costs and Benefits of Different Initial Teacher Training Routes*, IFS report R100, November 2014

to the state of fee-paying teacher training options (for shortage subjects) was as much as 50 per cent higher than for salaried ITT routes.[35]

Table 2.3: Bursaries for fee-paying Initial Teacher Training routes, 2016/17[36]

Specialism	Scholarships	Bursaries			
		Trainee with 1st/PhD	2:1/Master's	2:2	Other
Physics	£30,000	£30,000	£25,000	£25,000	£9,000
Maths	£25,000	£25,000	£25,000	£25,000	£9,000
Languages	N/A	£25,000	£25,000	£20,000	£0
Chemistry, computing	£25,000	£25,000	£20,000	£20,000	£0
Biology	N/A	£20,000	£15,000	£15,000	£0
Geography	N/A	£15,000	£15,000	£15,000	£0
Design and technology	N/A	£12,000	£9,000	£0	£0
English, history, music, religious education	N/A	£9,000	£4,000	£0	£0
Primary maths	N/A	£6,000	£6,000	£6,000	£3,000
Primary	N/A	£3,000	£3,000	£0	£0

Source: Get Into Teaching website, op. cit.

Teacher pay

Entry-level teacher pay is falling further and further behind other graduate jobs and teacher pay elsewhere in the OECD. Here we compare teacher salaries to the salaries offered by top graduate employers to understand the extent to which teaching presents an attractive financial package for top graduates. In 2015, the median salary for top graduate vacancies was £30,000, compared with a starting salary for teachers of £22,244 in most of the country and £27,819 in London.[37] Starting salaries for qualified teachers outside of London have increased by 16 per cent (just over £3,000) in 10 years (2005/6 to 2015/16), held down by public sector pay constraint, compared with a 30 per cent increase (£6,900) in the median graduate starting salary which reflects recent improvements in the economy.[38] While the majority of new teachers in England are young (55 per cent were under 25 in 2015/16), teachers' starting salaries also need to attract career changers, with, for example, 57 per cent of the flagship School Direct cohort in 2015/16 being made up of over 24s.[39] Starting salaries for teachers in England are also in effect deferred until after the initial teacher training year (which students may have to pay for), so do not become a reality as immediately as for other graduate jobs. A recent OECD report commented on the fact that while teacher pay in England is notably low compared to the OECD average at the start of teachers' careers, when additional allowances (for leadership responsibilities, which can be acquired once teachers are more experienced) are included teachers in England become – overall – better remunerated than teachers elsewhere.[40] While it does not make up for the low starting salary, this evidence from the OECD raises an important point. There is clearly an opportunity to do more to sell the potential for career progression and accompanying salary uplifts, as well as addressing the pay shortfall at the start.

35 Institute for Fiscal Studies, *The Costs and Benefits of Different Initial Teacher Training Routes*, IFS report R100, November 2014

36 Get Into Teaching website, op. cit.

37 Association of Teaching Leaders; https://www.atl.org.uk/Images/School%20Teachers'%20Pay%202015-16%20Pay%20Scale%20Points%20-%20National%20Joint%20Advice.pdf

38 Comparing median graduate salary from http://www.highfliers.co.uk/download/2015/graduate_market/GMReport15.pdf to teacher pay rates on M1 (the first point on the teacher pay scale) – outside of London – £19,161 in 2005 and £22,224 in 2015

39 Department for Education, *Initial Teacher Training: Trainee Number Census – 2015 to 2016*, SFR 46, 19 November 2015

40 OECD, *Education at a Glance: Country Notes – United Kingdom*, November 2015

Teacher numbers

There is a teacher numbers problem, which risks creating a quality problem. Put simply, if school leaders do not have sufficient high-quality candidates to choose from, they will be left with the option of appointing someone below par or with a vacancy that requires them to use temporary teachers and non-specialists. At the end of 2014, teacher numbers were 5,000 up on the previous year, bringing the total to 455,000 full-time equivalent teachers in England.[41] This increase not only responds to increases in pupil numbers, but it is also accounted for by 6,000 new nursery and primary school teachers. Over the same period there were 800 fewer secondary school teachers. The result is that secondary schools in particular are finding it harder to fill posts. At the end of 2014, there were over 1,000 more vacancies and temporarily filled posts compared with the same point in 2013.[42] Surveys of school leaders show this to be a significant problem, with eight in 10 saying that recruitment is a problem, with the most stark issues at secondary schools in English, maths and science. Just over half attributed their recruitment struggles to overall shortages and just under half to the suitability of the candidates applying. Almost two-thirds of those in London said that the high housing and living costs were a specific barrier to recruitment in their area.[43] This highly unsatisfactory situation is likely to get worse, not better, as we approach a period in which the pool of potential graduates is declining at the same time as the number of school-age children is increasing considerably. In 2012, there were 10 school-age children per 21-year-old, which will increase to 12 for each 21-year-old in 2020.[44]

Teacher quality and incentives

What is perhaps most worrying about this numbers squeeze is the potential knock-on effect it has on teacher quality. In 2014, 20 per cent of maths lessons in secondary schools were being taught by teachers without a relevant qualification, an increase from 17 per cent in 2013.[45]

In addition, there are few incentives available to encourage teachers to work in the most challenging schools. A survey for the Commission in 2014 found that just 15 per cent of teachers would actively seek out a school that was more challenging than their current school and over half said that the pressure of working in a weaker school was a significant deterrent.[46] There are marked contrasts between the lack of incentives to teach in challenging schools and areas, and the incentives to encourage subject specialists – even in subjects where there is not strong evidence of shortages. This is exacerbated by the fact that, below senior leadership level, teachers are not a mobile workforce, with most working in the region where they grew up. Travel-to-work time is of primary concern as they seek new roles.[47]

Problem 3: Schools are not sufficiently focused on preparing the poorest children for life after school.

At the sharp end of schools' success – or otherwise – in breaking the cycle of disadvantage lies the destinations of their pupils after school. The picture is not good, with big geographic variations in the extent to which young people from poor households access the best universities. At the worst end of the scale, in two local authorities, no pupils eligible for free school meals progressed to the top third of higher education institutions in 2013/14, the last year for which data is available. In 13 of the worst 20 performing local authorities, 2 per cent or less of the poorest children doing A levels progressed to the best universities. In the same local authorities, pupils not on free school meals who attained A level or equivalent

41 Department for Education, *Statistical First Release, School Workforce in England, November 2014*, July 2015
42 Ibid
43 National Association of Headteachers, *The NAHT School Recruitment Survey 2015*, 9 December 2015
44 Office for National Statistics, *Principal projection – England Population, Single Year of Age, 2012-based, Table A3–4*, 2013
45 Department for Education, *Statistical First Release, School Workforce in England, November 2014*, July 2015
46 Social Mobility and Child Poverty Commission, *Cracking the Code*, September 2014
47 LKMCo, *Why Teach?*, October 2015

qualifications at schools and colleges within the area were five times more likely to progress to top universities.[48]

Yet Figure 2.10 also highlights some authorities that buck the trend in the cluster to the top left. Examples include Bournemouth and Wigan. There is a further worrying trend at a local level. In the majority of places where overall progression to top universities is above average, the gap in progression between youngsters eligible for free school meals and others is wide. If opportunities were fairly shared, we might expect local authorities with high overall proportions of students progressing to top universities to do better for all. This is not the current position. As illustrated below, in too many places the balance goes against those from poor families (as indicated by free school meal eligibility).

Figure 2.10: Comparison of young people progressing to top third of higher education institutions by English local authority area

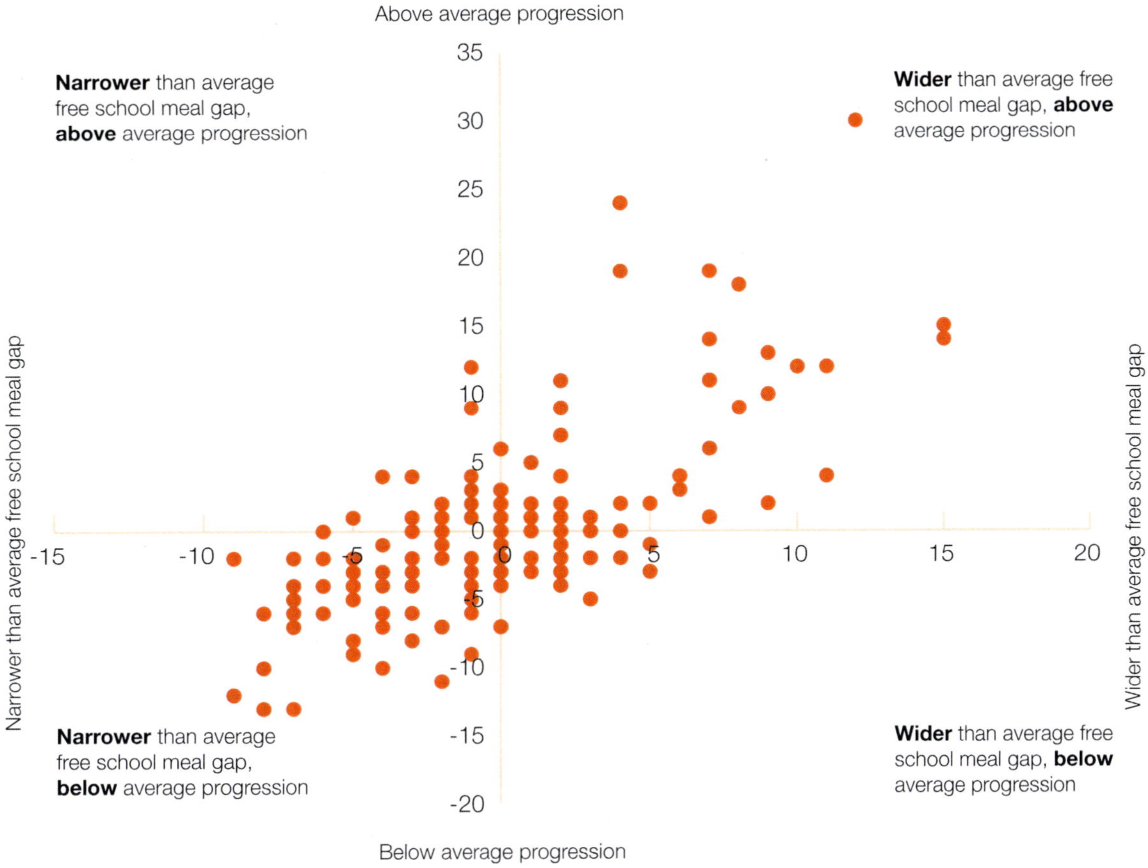

Source: Department for Education, *Destinations of Key Stage 4 and Key Stage 5 Pupils 2013 to 2014,* 23 October 2015

Note: Both axes are in percentage points from average. The X-axis represents the free school meal progression gap; the Y-axis the overall progression to top universities in that local authority

More areas serving large proportions of poor pupils clearly need to replicate the performance of the areas with high progression – and that needs to start at school. This means going above and beyond the traditional narrow focus on the academic curriculum. The Commission's *Cracking the Code* report, published in 2014, highlighted many of the practices undertaken by some of the schools that do particularly well for poor children. We found that the best schools proactively set out to broaden the experiences of their poorest students to prepare them to compete in the world beyond school. Approaches taken included looking beyond academic results, social and cultural capital building, early engagement with

48 Department for Education, *Destinations of Key Stage 4 and Key Stage 5 pupils: 2013 to 2014,* 23 October 2015. The data excludes local authorities where the number of free school meal-eligible pupils progressing to top HE is small (one or two pupils). These have been reconstructed in the data by assuming the maximum – two free school meal pupils progressing to top HE. The City of London, Isles of Scilly and Rutland are excluded entirely due to small numbers

universities, a knowledge-based curriculum tailored to individuals and early engagement with employers. One secondary school head teacher told the Commission:

> *It's just the right thing to do ... It's us being socially responsible – if we do not do it, we're setting them up to fail. We're measured in the same way as other schools – mainly on attainment – but we have to make sure that kids who leave here are ready to walk into great careers ... and they absolutely won't if we do not look at the wider set of things stopping our students from succeeding.*[49]

As this head teacher points out, schools' direct incentives to look beyond exams are relatively weak. The accountability system remains strongly focused on academic performance, and the much-lauded destinations data relates only to institutions where students undertook their post-16 studies, not the ones where they spent their secondary school career (which is different for many students). It also does not tell us enough about the destinations of students who do not progress to higher education.

49 Commission for Social Mobility and Child Poverty, *Cracking the Code*, September 2014

A levels: the stepping stone to university

A levels are and will remain the stepping stone to university, and are therefore the biggest rung on the social mobility ladder. So it is a major problem that poor, bright children are far less likely than their wealthier peers to gain good A levels.

Only 2,000 (or 2.2 per cent) of the most deprived children gain the good grades in their A levels that top universities demand (3 grades A*-B). The figure is 10 times higher (20.6 per cent) for the least deprived children (see Figure 2.11). This yawning chasm represents a real risk to the Government's ambitious widening university participation target, particularly if top universities are to participate fully. As one study shows, extremely high attaining poor children[50] at 11 are four times less likely to go on to an elite university than their high-attaining, wealthier peers.

Figure 2.11: High attainment at A level

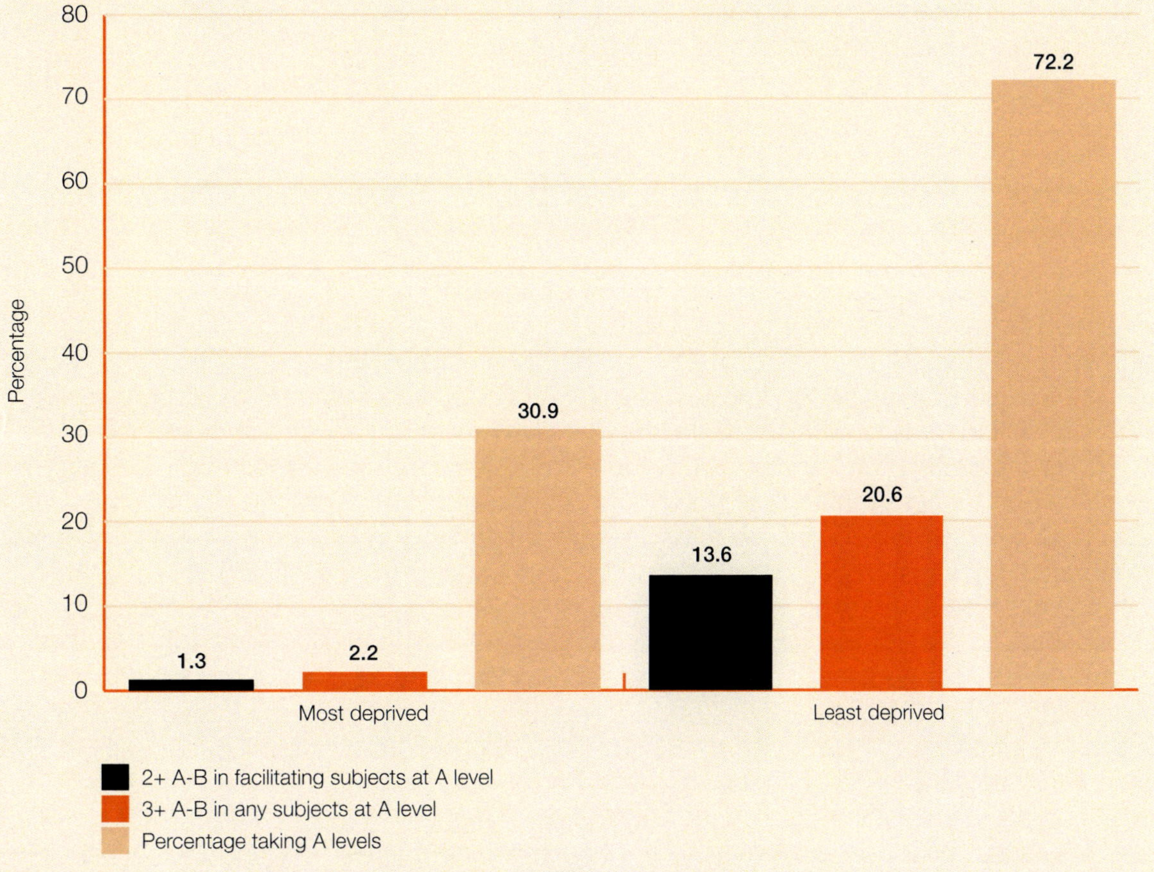

Source: Crawford, C., Macmillan, L., and Vignoles, A., *Progress made by High Attaining Children from Disadvantaged Backgrounds*, Commission for Social Mobility and Child Poverty, June 2014

Successive governments have sought to increase the proportion of students gaining A level equivalent qualifications, and have had considerable success in doing this. Ninety per cent more 19-year-olds from the most deprived areas hold Level 3 qualifications than 10 years ago.[51] However, this increase is driven, almost entirely, by students holding non-A level qualifications which often do not offer the same access to top universities.

These figures are a wake-up call to both state schools and top universities. Both need to do more to ensure that the brightest but poorest children are able to access the top universities.

50 Those who achieved Level 5

51 Department for Education, *A Level and Other Level 3 Results: 2013 to 2014 (revised)*, 29 January 2015

In schools there needs to be a renewed focus on ensuring that those children who are identified as high attainers early in their academic career are aiming for A levels and university beyond. This means preparing the path from the start of secondary school, including access to the best teachers who can ensure they choose core GCSE subjects and do well in them. This is exacerbated by the fact that one-third of secondary schools have no responsibility for their pupils' education after GCSE because they lack a sixth form. That is why we call in this report for a new destinations measure which links an individuals' progress back to their secondary school, regardless of where they undertook further education.

Universities have a stake in this too – they should be assessing how they can use widening participation funds in a much more focused manner to increase the likelihood that those children identified as capable of going to university at an early age, take and then excel in A levels. Universities – especially those elite institutions that are currently the most socially exclusive – also need to ensure their admissions processes are looking at potential by, for example, taking fuller account of the type of school and the family background from which applicants come.

2.3 How are these problems being addressed?

While there have been some new policy approaches for schools announced in this parliament, there are a number of significant changes that were developed during the last parliament that are still to come to fruition. All of this is happening in the context of schools with financial challenges on the horizon. Despite Government's recent commitment to real terms protection for schools and the welcome commitment to protect the Pupil Premium on a per pupil (cash) basis, analysis from the IFS suggests that the figures imply a real terms cut of 7.5 per cent in spending per pupil in this parliament.[52] Schools are facing a number of new pressures over the coming years as a result of the rise in pupil numbers, and the cost pressures of increases in pension contributions and National Insurance. The IFS suggest that the next five years will be considerably more challenging for schools than during the last parliament, and the first time schools have seen a real-terms cut in per pupil funding since the mid-1990s.[53] In addition, there are wide-ranging implications of the announcement in the recent Autumn Statement of the introduction of the national funding formula for schools. Government has announced plans to consult in 2016 and commence roll out in 2017.[54] This move to address the historical unfairness in school funding is welcome, but Government has some complex choices to make about how to implement the formula. There will be significant implications for some schools (particularly those considered to be overfunded); so it is important that Government gets the formula and the transition arrangements right.

The Government's reforms fall in two broad areas: improving standards across the system, which includes failure regimes for schools, and raising standards within schools and across the workforce.

Improving standards across the system

The Government has focused heavily on failure regimes in recent years, with the introduction of regional schools commissioners to identify struggling schools and promote academies and free schools, and proposals for a coasting schools accountability measure from 2016.

52 Institute for Fiscal Studies, *School Funding Reform*, http://www.ifs.org.uk/uploads/publications/budgets/Budgets%202015/Autumn/Sibieta_Schools.pdf, 2 December 2015

53 Institute for Fiscal Studies, *Observations: English Schools Will Feel the Pinch Over the Next 5 Years*, 21 October 2015 http://www.ifs.org.uk/publications/8027, 18 November 2015

54 HM Treasury, *Spending Review and Autumn Statement 2015*, 25 November 2015

This new measure focuses on overall attainment as well as progress over a three year period – and will commence when 2016 test data has been analysed. Until 2018, when there will be three years of new data, plans are to use an interim measure for previous years in combination with the new data. For primary schools, the 2016 measure will be where fewer than 85 per cent of children achieve the new higher expected standard at the end of primary and pupils do not make good enough progress. In the interim for 2014 and 2015, the measure will be where fewer than 85 per cent of pupils achieved Level 4 in reading, writing and mathematics and below the median percentage of pupils made expected progress in reading, writing and maths. For secondary schools, the 2016 measure will be where schools are performing below a level set against the new progress 8 measure. The interim measure for 2014 and 2015 for secondary schools will be where fewer than 60 per cent of pupils achieved 5 A*-C grades including English and maths and the school has a below median percentage of pupils making expected progress in English and maths.

The Government has also recently announced that five academy sponsors have been awarded grants of £5 million in total and tasked with driving up standards in particular areas of the north of England where performance has been low.[55] Detailed plans for this arrangement have not yet been published.

In addition to these wider structural reforms, the accountability and exam reforms begun under the previous government have started to bed in. This includes the new Progress 8 and Attainment 8 measures at GCSE. These measures aim to capture both attainment and progress in eight subjects (including a set of core subjects) through secondary school, and will compare the attainment of pupils that started school at the same level. In addition, levels have been scrapped at primary school, new progress-focused accountability for primary schools have been introduced, and the bar for tests at Key Stage 2 and GCSE have been raised. These measures will support the Government's plans for coasting schools described above, which will increasingly reflect the new progress-based measures year-on-year as there is more data.

Secondary schools in particular face a wide set of reforms affecting Key Stage 4. The new GCSE scoring system, replacing letters with numbers, commences for the cohort starting English and maths GCSEs this year and other subjects from next year. The raised bar means that the new threshold measure will be equivalent to the top third of a current C grade and adds more scope for differentiation between performance at the top of the ability range. Alongside this, wider exam reforms will make GCSEs more stretching. The Government also announced this year that from 2018, secondary schools will be required to ensure that 90 per cent of students study English, maths, science, either history or geography and a language at GCSE (the compulsory English Baccalaureate, or EBacc). Schools that do not conform will not be eligible for an outstanding Ofsted rating.

There have also been important reforms at A level. The decoupling of A and AS levels has commenced and all students failing to achieve a C grade in GCSE English and maths must now continue their studies in these subjects into the sixth form or college.

In primary schools, the Government has recently announced proposals for new Key Stage 1 tests at age seven as well as plans for children who do not reach the required level in Key Stage 2 tests at the end of primary school to be retested at secondary school. In addition, primary schools are now required to undertake a baseline assessment for children in reception class.

As well as this, the Government has committed to 500 new free schools in this parliament, in addition to just over 400 already open or planned to open in 2016 and beyond.[56] While these individual schools will of course affect the students that attend them, the numbers of schools

55 Department for Education, press release for speech by the Secretary of State for Education, 3 November 2015, https://www.gov.uk/government/news/nicky-morgan-no-tolerance-of-areas-where-majority-of-pupils-fail

56 Department for Education, *Free Schools: Open Schools and Successful Applications*, last updated 2 September 2015

and attendees remain proportionately small, making up less than half a per cent of all schools in England.

There are encouraging signs of progress. Increasing numbers of schools are turning previously accepted wisdom about the inevitability of poor children's outcomes on their head. The schools which perform best for their disadvantaged students are taking on board the Government's school reform programme, using the Pupil Premium strategically, and maintaining a strong focus on standards. Government reforms have clearly led many schools in the right direction, but there are limits to its control. The best performers push their responsibility for their poorest children above and beyond the areas where Government has explicit levers, taking responsibility for the attainment and long-term outcomes of their poorest students, driven by the highest expectations of their students and their teachers.[57] These schools have shown that ensuring that their poorest children fulfil their potential requires ambition and innovation, as well as an explicit commitment to ensuring that poor children have the chances and choices that reflect their potential, rather than their background.

Teacher numbers, deployment and quality

The Government has continued to back a more market-based approach to teacher training, with increasing numbers of places being offered by individual schools through School Direct, the school-based ITT programme, with the stated aim of improving quality. For the recruitment year 2015/16, there is also one significant reform to the teacher training landscape. The Government has in effect deregulated the teacher training market, maintaining an overall target figure, but removing the specific allocations that were previously in place for each training institution (which now includes individual schools). What this means for training providers is that they can recruit entirely freely until the Government's national totals are reached for each subject, phase (primary or secondary), or route in (i.e. School Direct or Higher Education Institution).

Bursaries and scholarships continue to be offered to trainee teachers on fee-paying (student rather than salaried) routes, with rates depending on subject specialism, school phase and degree classification. Table 2.3 sets out the bursaries recently announced for the 2016/17 school year.

The Government has also set out to address the underperformance of schools in areas that struggle to recruit, through its new National Teaching Service programme. The intention is to deploy high potential teachers and leaders to some of England's most challenging schools for up to three years, with plans for 1,500 participants by 2020 and a pilot in the North West starting in September 2016.[58]

In addition, the Government has sought to recognise the large workloads of teachers in England, which include substantial amounts of activities that do not necessarily add value to students. It has undertaken a Workload Challenge review, which sets out a new protocol, including longer lead-in times to major reforms and a commitment that Ofsted will not make substantive changes to the assessment handbook mid-year. This has been accompanied by a myth-busting drive by Ofsted to clarify what activities are and are not expected.

2.4 Assessment: what further action is needed?

The key priorities for schools introduced over the last parliament and into this one have in the main been the right ones. Under the Coalition, various actions were taken to address flaws that had proved to further the disadvantage of the poorest children. Notably, this includes the move away from the five A*-C threshold at GCSE, the recognition of the importance of the

57 Social Mobility and Child Poverty Commission, *Cracking the Code*, September 2014
58 Department for Education, press release regarding speech by the Secretary of State for Education, op. cit.

study of core subjects for all students in preference to low- or no-value vocational courses, the drive to address failing schools and the championing of the Pupil Premium and the work of the Education Endowment Foundation. The Government elected in May 2015 has committed to support all of these policy strands and has continued to support Teach First, which places excellent teachers in some of the most disadvantaged areas of England.

But it is the Commission's judgement that without efforts to build capacity in schools and in the teaching workforce, and in the absence of careful monitoring, some of the Government's policy approaches could further disadvantage some of the poorest children – those who have the most to gain from many of these new reforms. There are particular risks with regard to:

- Implementing the new national curriculum at primary schools;
- Raising the bar for tests at Key Stage 2 and GCSE;
- Teaching the EBacc subjects to all secondary school pupils;
- The requirement for retakes of GCSE maths and English during Key Stage 5 study.

For these policies to have the desired impact, they require schools to be firing on all cylinders. They need a highly effective teaching workforce; schools with the leadership and capacity to deliver to a (rightly) demanding set of new reforms; efficient and effective use of the pupil premium to channel money directly to the most disadvantaged children; and a well-designed accountability system to back it up. Below we look in more detail at the risks associated with these four elements of the system.

Improving standards across the system

The Government's new accountability regime, combined with the introduction of the coasting schools measure, have the potential to classify many more schools as ineffective. This means that those schools that are not already academies are likely to become sponsored academies if they do not demonstrate their potential to improve, and quickly. The Commission supports this broad approach.

The implications for primary schools are particularly significant here. First because the new accountability demands on primary schools are so far above current standards, and second because the proportion of primary schools that have converted to become academies is still relatively low and the market is not well developed. The think-tank Policy Exchange estimates that the new accountability standards could mean that 20 per cent of primary schools – 3,300 schools – could fall into the failing category.[59]

But there does not seem to be a clear plan to address the gaps in capacity in the schools themselves which might lead to self-improvement. Neither does there appear to be a plan to ensure that where schools are required to convert to academy status under a sponsor, there are a sufficient number of well-equipped, high-quality sponsors available to take on the job, particularly outside of London and the South.

The Government has broadly gone in the right direction on its accountability regime, which is an important piece in the jigsaw of any effective strategy to drive out underperformance and incentivise high expectations. The Commission has strongly welcomed the shift from the five A*-C measure at GCSE to the Progress and Attainment 8 approach. It is absolutely right that all children have access to an academic curriculum to age 16, and Progress and Attainment 8 is a well-designed approach. The focus on progress across the eight subjects also addresses some of the problems of the previous threshold-based accountability regime – there is recognition of progress between any given grades, rather than focusing closely on the C/D borderline as at present.

---

59 Policy Exchange, *Primary Focus: The Next Stage of Improvement for Primary Schools in England*, Policy Exchange, 2014

However, the recent addition of the compulsory EBacc to the core accountability measures seems out of sync with the intention behind Attainment and Progress 8. The policy objective behind the EBacc was addressed effectively and flexibly by Attainment and Progress 8. In addition to the capacity and availability of the teachers required to teach the EBacc, which is discussed above, there is a risk that an inflexible EBacc will disengage some children. There is some evidence from Germany that a more academic curriculum resulted in an increase in disengagement with school and an attendance drop-off.[60] Avoiding this kind of outcome requires a careful balancing act and the Government should be aware of the implications of its recently announced requirement for 90 per cent of children in each school to undertake the EBacc from 2018. A move to determine a proportion of students in a school likely to be capable or not of achieving the EBacc seems inconsistent with a system of autonomy and, indeed, a system where we know that each school inherits students of widely differing ability and engagement. In one school, it may be that 100 per cent of students should be studying for a core set of subjects, whereas in others that figure may well be far lower. Attainment and Progress 8 offered schools the flexibility to determine this, which it seems was an approach more fitting with the autonomy granted to them.

The elements of government policy described in this chapter should certainly go some way towards driving up standards. However, it remains vital that specific additional focus remains on the troubling attainment gap. While the Commission welcomes the Government's commitment to continue to fund the Pupil Premium, we are deeply concerned at suggestions of a move away from a focus on narrowing the attainment gap, replacing this with an objective of raising standards for all. We recognise that when applied to individual schools, an exclusive focus on narrowing the attainment gap could only be as stretching as the non-pupil premium students are wealthy. We understand the risk that this could lead to an unambitious lowest common denominator approach for individual schools.[61] However, disregarding the objective at a national level would be a major mistake. Raising standards for everyone is a reasonable and ambitious aim, but the lesson has been learnt by previous governments that without specific focus on the poorest children within schools, progress across the board stalls. The evidence is absolutely clear that the particular disadvantages faced by the poorest children drag their actual attainment way below their potential, which is evident from the bottom to the top of the attainment distribution, not just in the proportion of children achieving the basics:

- Poorer children start school almost a year behind their wealthier peers;[62]
- Children in the poorest areas of England are less likely to attend the best schools and therefore have less access to the best teaching (see Figure 2.7);
- Once they are at school, poorer children make less progress than their wealthier peers, in effect widening the gap throughout school;[63]
- Children from wealthy families tend to significantly exceed their potential based on ability, whereas children from poorer families too often fail to fulfil their potential, even where they demonstrate high ability at a young age. Research for the Commission showed that low-ability children from wealthy families are 35 per cent more likely to be high earners as adults than high-ability children from poorer families;[64]
- Even where poorer children can compete on grades, their wealthier peers are likely to benefit from other factors that boost their attainment further and unlock wider opportunities, including private tutoring and access to extracurricular activities.[65]

60 Gorlitz, K., and Gravert, C., *The effects of Increasing the Standards of the High School Curriculum on School Dropout*, IZA DP No 8766, January 2015

61 Speech by the Secretary of State for Education, 18 June 2015, https://www.gov.uk/government/speeches/nicky-morgan-discusses-the-future-of-education-in-england

62 Waldfogel, J., and Washbrook, E., *Low Income and Early Cognitive Development in the UK*, Sutton Trust, 1 February 2010

63 Department for Education, *GCSE and Equivalent Attainment by Pupil Characteristics: 2014*

64 Social Mobility and Child Poverty Commission, *New research exposes the 'glass floor' in British society*, op. cit.

65 Francis, B., Hutchings, M, *Parent Power*, Sutton Trust, 18 December 2013

For these reasons, the Government's attention must remain unwaveringly on both raising standards across the board, and on the gap between the richest and the poorest. A move away from this approach would adversely affect both practices and outcomes, and the system itself would fail to fulfil its potential.

Teacher numbers, deployment and quality

Wider reforms, including those set out above, will not have the desired impact if they are not accompanied by a major drive to increase the number of good teachers in the system. There are two broad issues that the Government must review and should address as a matter of urgency.

System management: While the Commission welcomes the contribution of School Direct, the move to more school-based ITT has led to a system of teacher supply that is not social-mobility friendly. The laissez-faire system of teacher recruitment and retention undoubtedly favours the best performers in the most desirable areas, so accentuating the gap between the best and the weakest schools. Other than through Teach First, the system in effect encourages new and existing teachers seeking employment to go to better-performing institutions in better-off areas. This problem could be accentuated by the new deregulated approach to ITT, which would appear to incentivise providers to take the earliest rather than the best applicants – to avoid their allocations being closed down once the national quota is exceeded. While schools as recruiters (through School Direct) in theory have more at stake than universities if they select weaker applicants, in a market where there are shortages, they may feel that they have little choice – and prioritise quantity of early candidates over quality.[66] How far this plays out, only time will tell. In the Commission's view, it would be perfectly reasonable to create a diverse market for teacher recruitment if the incentives in the system were well aligned to the problem. But they are not.

Creating a 21st-century teaching profession: Teaching is struggling to keep up with other graduate career paths in terms of pay, training and career development, with profound implications for recruitment and retention. There is evidence that concerns about debt and increases in student fees, may shift career patterns away from lower-paid roles, including teaching.[67] The IFS suggests that, at current ratios, population increases mean there will be a need for 480,000 teachers by 2020, 25,000 more than at present.[68] Delivering this requires schools to keep their best teachers, recruit high-potential new ones and possibly attract former teachers back into the fold, while retaining the bandwidth to remove underperformers.

In its teacher recruitment strategy, the Government needs to move away from its current use of large bursaries, which, as described earlier, are an unproven and expensive approach. A long-term strategy is required that should aim to remove the current barriers to entry to the profession, identify what is required to improve retention, and further identify and trial incentives to get the best teachers into challenging schools. Three key ingredients are:

- **Pay reform**: while public sector pay restraint has been an important part of the drive to balance the books it has had a significant impact at the bottom of the teacher career ladder, with a large and increasing gap between teacher starting salary and the median graduate salary offered by top recruiters. Government encouragement for schools to pay better teachers more is welcome but, in reality, schools have little flexibility to do anything meaningful in this regard.
- **Workload**: the Government clearly recognises the fact that many teachers are being driven, for a variety of reasons, to undertake a wide range of administrative and

66 Husbands, C., *'Tragedy of the commons': How the government abandoned the pursuit of teacher quality,* blog post, Institute of Education, 16 November 2015, https://ioelondonblog.wordpress.com/2015/11/16/the-tragedy-of-the-commons-how-the-government-abandoned-the-pursuit-of-teacher-quality/

67 Policy Exchange, *Education Manifesto*, 2014

68 Institute for Fiscal Studies, http://www.ifs.org.uk/publications/8027

preparatory tasks outside of the classroom which may not be adding value to their teaching. It clearly does not make for a desirable career if only half of a teacher's working week of 46 hours is spent in the classroom.[69] Neither is this good for students. Government and Ofsted must continue to clarify what practices are and are not required so that the Workload Challenge is not a tokenistic gesture but instead genuinely drives teachers and leaders to focus on what is important.

- **Training and development**: Teachers' probation periods are relatively short – in effect just made up of the one newly qualified teacher year which follows the initial teacher training year. And evidence suggests that after the first three years, teachers develop very little.[70] Both of these are perhaps a symptom of systematic under-investment by schools in their workforce. Schools are spending just £15 per pupil on the continuing professional development of their workforce, over half of which goes on costs to cover teachers while they are training. Fewer than one in 10 schools evaluate the impact of their training spend on student attainment.[71] The Teacher Development Trust reports that most schools use training and development to react to changes in government policy and to understand how to deal with Ofsted, rather than to develop their workforce.[72]

The Government's recent proposal for a National Teaching Service (NTS) is welcome, and in line with proposals made earlier this year by the Commission for a fast stream for teaching. There is significant potential for the NTS to help to shape teaching into a more desirable career – able to compete with other graduate careers on factors other than pay – and to carve out a clearer career structure for ambitious potential recruits and current teachers. However, in the context of the entire system, the scale of the NTS is relatively small, with proposals for a cumulative total of 1,500 participants by 2020, and it is likely that this kind of route will be suitable only for a relatively small proportion of teachers. The problems set out earlier in this chapter – of teacher shortages, concerns about quality and the necessity for high-quality teachers to deliver on Government's reforms demand much greater breadth and more scale in the Government's response.

2.5 Conclusion and Recommendations

If the Government is to realise its One Nation ambition, it must raise its sights. A step change in ambition is required. Its education objective should be to reduce the attainment gap between the most disadvantaged children and everyone else by two-thirds by 2030. This would involve poor children elsewhere doing as well as they currently do in Inner London. Achieving that challenging objective requires significant further reforms.

Recommendation 1: Government should adopt a new zero tolerance approach to schools in terminal failure, which fail their pupils and their communities for more than five years in a row.

There are too many schools which have consistently failed their communities, churning out some of the poorest results in England year after year – even after various efforts to turn things around. These schools are failing all their pupils, but it is the poorest who suffer the most.

69 OECD, *New Insights from TALIS 2013: Teaching and Learning in Primary and Upper Secondary Education*, 2014

70 Written evidence to the Education Select Committee from Rebecca Allen (Institute of Education) and Simon Burgess (CMPO, Bristol University), http://www.publications.parliament.uk/pa/cm201012/cmselect/cmeduc/1515/1515vw40.htm

71 Teacher Development Trust, *CPD in England: The Good, the Bad and the Ugly*, https://docs.google.com/presentation/d/1wUrlfDFaTGGUdFe8rCGmo6ZRGgTUMGbxs1EJEhXiw7A/edit?pli=1#slide=id.g24793c2e_0_51, accessed 18 November 2015

72 Teacher Development Trust, *CPD in England: The Good, the Bad and the Ugly*, op. cit.

The failure framework for schools is complex, inconsistent, drawn out and treats academies and maintained schools differently. Understanding it is a test in itself. It serves no-one well. It should be replaced as a matter of urgency. The Commission recommends:

- A new national framework for terminal failure should apply to all schools equally. Terminal failure should be classified as falling below the floor standard for five years in a row, and where there have not been substantial changes in a school's leadership and governance in that period.
- The leadership and governance of a terminally failed school should be replaced – with an expectation that a (new) multi-academy sponsor will be sought.
- Given the intensified problems associated with primary school failure, an early warning point should be established for primaries, which will encourage schools to voluntarily combine with a successful academy group prior to the point of final sanction.
- In addition a prestigious new cadre of Change Leaders – head teachers with previous experience of successfully turning around schools – should be created to channel and support the best leaders into schools with the greatest turnaround challenges. This programme should be modelled on the current Talented Leaders Programme, and include a centrally administered salary boost to reflect the challenge of the role, as well as a relocation budget and a leadership fund, to be used to bring talented senior leaders into the support team and for wider staff development.

Recommendation 2: The Government should make clear its absolute commitment to narrowing the educational attainment gap at a national level and confirm it by launching a new set of social mobility measures at a national, local authority and school level.

The Commission is extremely concerned by suggestions that the Government might reduce its focus on narrowing the attainment gap. Raising standards for everyone is a reasonable and ambitious objective but the lesson has been learnt by previous governments that without specific focus on the poorest children within schools progress across the board stalls. As long as poorer children make far less progress, are less likely to attend good schools, and are overtaken academically by wealthier children of lesser ability, the attainment and the progress gap remain important indicators of our nation's success.

The Commission recommends that alongside a relaunch of the pupil premium, a new set of One Nation social mobility measures should be introduced to take a more nuanced look at attainment in schools and the extent to which poorer children are falling behind. The new data should include:

- Performance at primary school, secondary school and A level and equivalent study to age 19;
- A specific focus on the socio-economic gap at the top and the bottom of the attainment distribution as well as on achievement at a standard performance threshold and on gaps in progress;
- Rankings of schools based on similar-schools analysis according to the performance of the most disadvantaged students;
- A new destinations measure, which relates all students' outcomes post-18 to their secondary school, regardless of whether or not they conducted their post-16 study at the same institution. Government should seek to use new data-linking models to build in data on the destinations of students who are not in higher education post-19.

The Government should then enshrine a new objective for all schools to narrow the gap with the best similar schools, supplemented by the Education Endowment Foundation's Families of Schools database. This data should be published annually by the Secretary of State for Education in the form of a schools social mobility index.

Recommendation 3: Pay and reward for new teachers should be overhauled.

There are gaps emerging between teacher pay and that of other top graduate professions which have grown significantly over the past decade and which are exacerbating problems with recruitment. The majority of recruits commence their teaching career with a year as a student (with the additional debt that this entails), rather than with a salary, which doesn't commence until after their teacher training year. In response, the Government is pursuing an expensive bursaries policy based on subject specialism and degree grade. There is very limited evidence that such a system will work. Despite the bursaries policy, the fee-paying (so bursary-eligible) School Direct training route filled only six in 10 of its target places in 2014/15. If the Government is to attract the additional 25,000 teachers that the system requires by 2020 (as well as replacing those that leave the profession each year), it needs to take more drastic action. It should do this by:

First, getting more new teachers into the system. Government should do this by taking seriously the gaps emerging between teacher pay and that of other professions, particularly at the bottom of the pay scale. While pay restraint has played an important role in the Government's fiscal plans, this risks creating a long-term problem for the profession if the gap between teacher pay and other top graduate professions continues to increase. An important gesture that could be made here would be to scrap fees for Initial Teacher Training, paid in 2014/15 by almost 30,000 trainees. The Institute for Fiscal Studies has highlighted that these fees will never be paid off by the average teacher, so the costs of our proposal would be minimal. Beyond this, the Government should review entry- level pay to ensure that the teaching profession competes with its competitors, including top graduate employers. There is also more that could and should be done to clarify and explain the potential career paths of teachers, including the many opportunities to take on additional responsibilities and leadership positions that can come relatively early in a teachers' career.

Second, the *quid pro quo* for increased entry-level wages should be an increase in the probation period for teachers from the current one year to three. This should be joined by a raising of the bar on the criteria required to be certified as a fully-fledged teacher – an approach first proposed by experts in 2012.[73] This approach should be developed in line with recent proposals for a curriculum for the teacher training period – and would lead to the development of a higher-quality training offer with a clear end point at which those who fail their training period would not be eligible for continued employment. In addition, the door to teaching should be opened to high potential people from a wider range of backgrounds, by stopping the current approach which places such heavy emphasis upon degree classification.

Third, to help finance changes in pay, the Government should change track on the large bursaries it offers to enter the profession. The evidence for such large financial incentives is weak and there is no evidence that candidates with better degrees make better teachers. In fact, it is very hard to determine who will be a good teacher before they are practised in teaching.

73 Allen, R., Burgess, S., *Reforming Teacher Training to Find the Best Teachers*, CMPO, http://www.bristol.ac.uk/media-library/sites/cmpo/migrated/documents/reformingteachertraining.pdf, 2012

Recommendation 4: New incentives should be introduced to get more good teachers into the most challenging schools.

Until the senior leadership grades are reached, teaching is not a mobile profession, with many teachers working in the area in which they trained. There are few incentives for new and current teachers to move to schools that are weaker or in less desirable areas. The Government's National Teaching Service is very welcome, but does not go far enough in addressing the wider lack of incentives in the system to get teachers to the places where they are most needed. The move towards more school-led teacher training with no central management exacerbates this problem from the start of teachers' careers. More needs to be done to get promising teachers who have proven themselves to the schools and areas that most need them.

The Commission recommends that there should be area-based trials of a number of different approaches designed to incentivise teachers to move to schools that are more challenging, including:

- Committing to write off a proportion of teachers' student loans for each year that they teach at a particularly challenging school. This would form part of a robust performance management system, so weaker performers would not get the benefit. For example, a teacher has £45,000 of outstanding student loans, accrued over their three-year degree and one year of teacher training. If they move to a qualifying school (from a non-qualifying school), they could have 10 per cent of their student loan paid off each year (£4,500 in year one), subject to meeting agreed performance management standards. The real cost of this policy would be low over the long term, particularly since the teacher will also be repaying their loan. The real cost would be further reduced because of the likelihood that a proportion of the average teachers' student debt will never be paid off in any case (according to the IFS).
- Committing to implement a new help-to-buy scheme exclusively for teachers, targeted at first-time buyers moving to eligible areas (where they must also teach) from a non-eligible one. Rather than the current general Help to Buy scheme, where recipients can purchase new or old properties with a 5% deposit and a government-backed loan, this scheme would be more generous – and require the Government to match the teacher's 5% deposit for properties worth up to £250,000. This would be on the condition of a commitment to the area of at least five years. The cost to the Government would be relatively low compared to incentives such as bursaries. Even at full property value (which few would be eligible to borrow against), the Government's contribution would be £12,500, or £2,500 per year for each of the five years. This compares with, for example, a bursary of £30,000 for someone with a first-class degree training to be a physics teacher, who can teach in any school with no long-term commitment.
- Taking on board a suggestion made by Policy Exchange, the Government should work with areas with new devolved powers, such as Manchester, to support the creation of area-wide relocation packages, which might include incentives on housing, training, childcare and transport.[74] In practice, this could promote collaboration between academy chains, individual schools and local government. This approach would also provide an excellent opportunity to test and thoroughly evaluate a range of different incentives and promote the ownership of teacher recruitment among the areas involved.

74 Simons, J., Porter, N., and Briggs, A., *Education Manifesto*, Policy Exchange, 2014

Chapter 3: Improving life chances for non-graduates

- **There is a '16+' divide between youngsters who go on to university and those who do not with non-graduates, who tend to come from low income backgrounds, ending up in low-pay, low-progression careers.**
- **Youth unemployment is falling, but there remains no solution to the phenomenon of young people not in education, employment or training (NEET).**
- **There is a welcome government focus on improving the life chances of non-graduates, with major commitments to expand apprenticeships, design new routes to technical jobs and establish a retake system for those who did not achieve good English and maths GCSEs.**
- **But more than two in five apprenticeships go to adults over 25 and the non-graduate route into employment is complex and fractured.**
- **The Government should make the non-graduate track into employment a priority for reform.**
- **New apprenticeships should be targeted at higher-level courses and there should be at least 30,000 young people starting a higher apprenticeship a year by 2020.**
- **A new UCAS-style website should be created for vocational education within two years so that young people can see what progression, employment and earnings opportunities they are likely to achieve.**
- **Failing further education (FE) colleges should become FE academies along the lines of the initial city academies, with an external business sponsor.**
- **By 2020, the Government should reduce the NEET rates of 16–18-year-olds to 3 per cent or less (or around 55,000),[1] in line with the best performing Organisation for Economic Co-operation and Development (OECD) countries.**

1 This is 3 per cent of the projected 16–18 population in 2020. Office for National Statistics, *Young Age Structure Variant – England Population Single Year of Age, 2012-based*, 2013

3.1 Introduction

The old 11-plus created a social divide at the end of primary school. It was rightly criticised for the advantages it conferred on some children over others.[2] Although the old exam is mostly gone, its spirit remains. The divide between grammar and secondary modern has been replaced by the split between sixth form and further education (FE). The 11-plus has become a 16-plus. Young people who end up on the wrong side of the educational divide at this point in their lives find it much harder to get on track to good careers.

The public's views on 16-plus choices tell their own story. Nearly three-quarters of parents think vocational education is not worthwhile.[3] Of mothers of children born at the turn of the century, 96 per cent aspired to university for their children, regardless of their own education.[4] In part, this reflects real difficulties in the FE sector. Despite improvements in many areas, last year nearly 390,000 young people were in provision rated inadequate or requires improvement by Ofsted, and 16 colleges were unable to improve from the lowest Ofsted ratings.[5][6] Overall, the non-graduate track continues to be seen, in the words of Baroness Wolf, as a "great idea for other people's children"[7] – yet it remains the mainstream option for young adults: the last Census showed that two-thirds of young people in their early 20s did not have a degree.[8]

For too many, non-graduate routes lead to outcomes that are simply not good enough. **At the top**, non-graduate routes that deliver high-level technical skills and professional jobs are very much an exception. **In the middle**, for the majority on vocational courses, the system is complex and confusing, and progression to a good career is far from guaranteed. **At the bottom** of the ladder, hundreds of thousands of young people are neither learning nor earning, with no clear policy for re-engaging them. By the age of 19, few that leave school with low attainment have secured the basic qualifications employers seek. The contract between government and those on the non-graduate route is stretched to breaking point. There is no guarantee that if you carry on in vocational study you will have decent outcomes.

There are strong economic reasons for tackling this situation. Persistent levels of job vacancies and growing requirements in high-skill industries show that the current skills system is not delivering.[9] UKCES report that around 22 per cent of all vacancies are due to skills shortages.[10] At current levels of job vacancies the skill gap might be the cause of over 150,000 unfilled roles. Year-on-year vacancies are up 5 per cent in construction and scientific work to almost 90,000. The demand for more proficient workers cannot be delivered by the university sector alone.

There are social justice arguments too. Those from working class backgrounds (NS-SEC 5-7) are much more likely to go to FE colleges and vocational education. So it is vital that the mainstream non-graduate route offers real chances to do well.[11] A One Nation society would be one where non-graduates had much better opportunities to progress up the social ladder.

2 Hart, A. Moro, M. and Roberts, E.J., *Date of Birth, Family Background, and the 11 Plus Exam: Short- and Long-term Consequences of the 1944 Secondary Education Reforms in England and Wales*, 2012
3 Edge Foundation, *Children Labelled 'Too Clever' for Vocational Education*, 2014
4 Centre for Longitudinal Studies, *Millennium Cohort Study Fourth Survey: A User's Guide to Initial Findings*, 2010
5 Ofsted, View Data View, 2015, http://dataview.ofsted.gov.uk/
6 Ofsted, *Education and Skills*, 2015
7 Wolf, A., *Does Education Matter?*, 2002
8 Office for National Statistics, *Qualifications and Labour Market Participation in England and Wales*, 2014
9 Office for National Statistics, *Labour Market Statistics*, 2015
10 UKCES, *UK Commission's Employer Skills Survey 2013: UK Results*, 2014
11 Social Mobility and Child Poverty Commission, *Downward Mobility, Opportunity Hoarding and the 'Glass Floor'*, 2015

3.2 Does today's reality meet the One Nation vision?

Of those enrolled in full-time education at age 17, youngsters whose parents were in routine occupations are two-and-a-half times as likely to be in an FE college as those whose parents were in higher managerial and professional roles.[12] Half of young people eligible for free school meals who stay in education post-16 progress to FE colleges compared to just over one-third (36 per cent) of their peers.[13]

However, it would be wrong to assume that the non-graduate route is only for the less able. Of those in the top one-fifth of GCSE scores in education at 17, more than 10 per cent go to FE colleges.[14] In the early 2000s, just over one-quarter of those taking vocational A levels at Level 3 had more than 10 GCSE passes.[15]

Depending on the route of study, graduate or non-graduate, there is a divide in whether young people continue or complete their courses. Those taking courses at FE colleges, excluding A levels and A/S levels in 2013 were twice as likely to withdraw as those on A level courses (a 10.8 per cent drop out versus 4.8 per cent). Furthermore, those on FE courses were 12 times more likely to finish without a qualification than those studying A levels (15.7 per cent failure rate versus 1.3 per cent A levels without a grade). Although there has been improvement in retention over recent years, the cost of this is still substantial: £814 million.[16] Young people and the taxpayer are being let down.

Those who study towards A level or equivalent qualifications at FE colleges are around one-third less likely to progress to higher education (HE) than those studying in state schools (39 per cent versus 58 per cent) and less than half as likely to attend one of the most selective third of universities (10 per cent versus 26 per cent).[17] This reflects both the courses followed and type of qualifications achieved.

In general, those that leave FE colleges with A level or equivalent qualifications have positive outcomes. In 2013/14, nearly seven in 10 of those leaving FE sector institutions continued into further study, training or work.[18] However, as currently constituted, FE all too often leads to a lower occupational status and lower-paying jobs. Those who follow a non-graduate route are more likely to end up in lower socio-economic groupings. They are more likely to work in lower-paying industries, with fewer opportunities for progression. Fewer than one in 10 adults (6.7 per cent) aged 25–49 whose highest qualification is Level 3 (A level equivalent) find themselves in higher managerial and professional roles. This compares to three in 10 (28.1 per cent) of those qualified to Level 4 (the lowest level of HE) and above.[19] Non-graduates are twice as likely as graduates to work in distribution or hotels: jobs associated with lower pay and fewer opportunities to increase salaries.[20] Conversely, non-graduates are one-quarter less likely to work in banking and finance, and half as likely to work in public administration or education – jobs which traditionally have strong chances for progression and high pay.[21]

Finally, social background and choices at 16-plus have an impact on whether people are in work at all. In 2014, those qualified above degree level were 18.2 per cent – nearly one-fifth – more likely to be in work than those without (85 versus 72 per cent). Looking across the UK, the biggest gap in the employment rate between those with degrees and those without is in

---

12 Meschi, E., Crawford, C. and Vignoles, A., *Post-16 Educational Choices and Institutional Value Added at Key Stage 5*, 2010
13 Department for Education, *Destinations of KS4 and KS5 pupils, 2013 to 2014*, 2015
14 Meschi, E., Crawford, C. and Vignoles, A., *Post-16 Educational Choices and Institutional Value Added at Key Stage 5*, 2010. Attending an FE college is not itself proof that an individual will follow a non-graduate route, but they are more likely to
15 Vickers, P. and Bekhradnia, B., *Vocational A Levels and University Entry: Is There Parity of Esteem?*, 2007
16 Centre for Economic and Social Inclusion, *Achievement and Retention in Post-16 Education*, 2015
17 Department for Education, *Statistics: Destinations of Key Stage 4 and Key Stage 5 Pupils*, 2015
18 Department for Education, Statistics: *Destinations of Key Stage 4 and Key Stage 5 Pupils*, 2015
19 Office for National Statistics, *Census 2011 Tables: NS-SEC by Highest Level of Qualification, by Age*, 2011
20 Social Mobility and Child Poverty Commission, *Escape Plan: Understanding Who Progresses from Low Pay and Who Gets Stuck*, 2014
21 Office for National Statistics, *Graduates in the Labour Market*, 2013

inner London at 39 per cent – the lowest is in the East Midlands, but it is still more than 10 per cent (see Figure 3.1).[22]

Figure 3.1: Percentage difference in employment rates between non-graduates and graduates in Britain in 2014

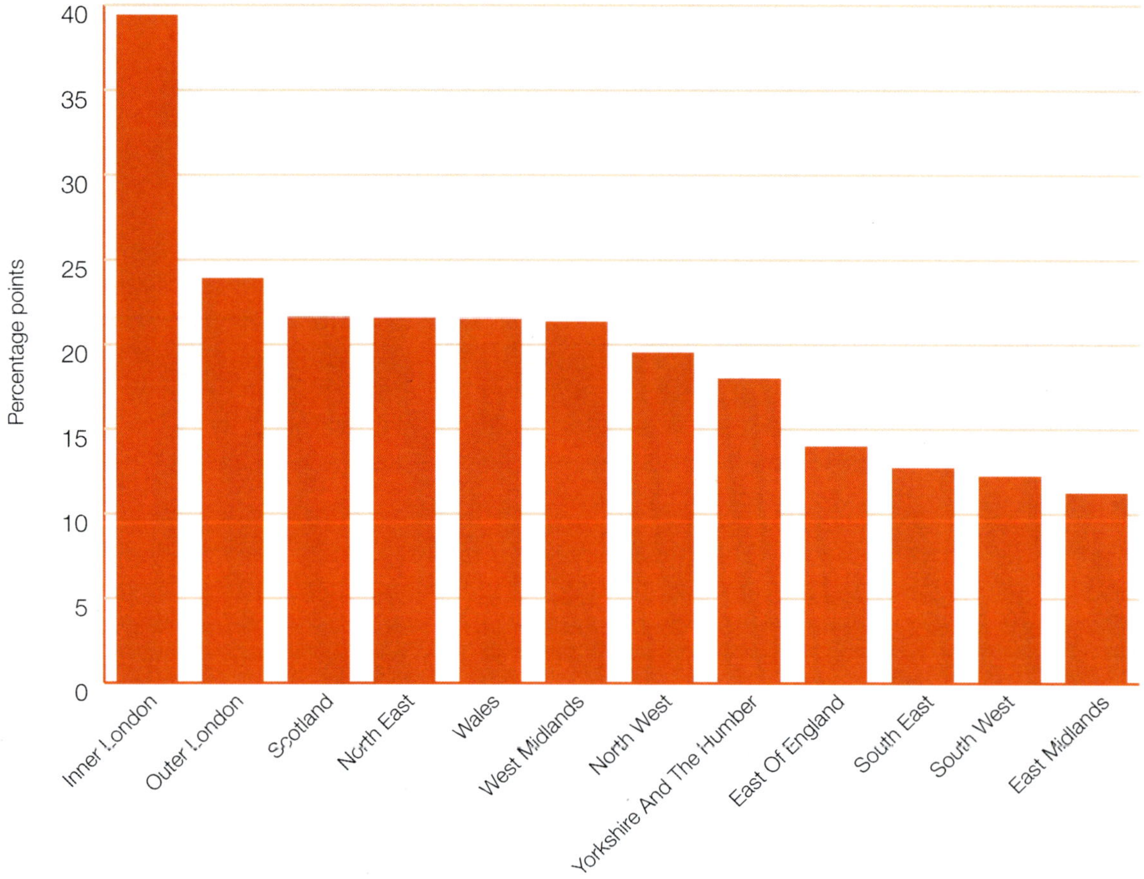

Source: Data provided by Office for National Statistics, Commission analysis

The effect of the 16-plus reverberates across lives. These sharply different outcomes pose fundamental questions about the state of Britain's vocational education system. Currently, for youngsters with options to take either an HE or FE route, the non-graduate track is generally less attractive than a university degree.[23] For those currently on the vocational track, there is a need to improve the quality of vocational education. In the following sections, the three challenges to One Nation laid out at the start of this chapter are examined in detail.

First, we assess the lack of non-graduate options with the greatest potential for social mobility: apprenticeships. Second, we examine the extent to which the majority of 'quality' non-graduate routes offer chances for progression to decent jobs and pay. Third, we consider the absence of a national solution to youth disengagement and low attainment. If we are to achieve a high-functioning, British non-graduate system, these are the barriers that must be overcome.

22 Commission analysis of Labour Force Survey data, provided by the Office for National Statistics
23 Sutton Trust, *Levels of Success: The Potential of UK Apprenticeships*, 2015

Problem 1: Too few non-graduate routes deliver good life chances.

The One Nation challenge of expanding high-quality, non-graduate routes is not new. It has been recognised for half a century that those who fall between the disengaged not in education, employment or training (NEET), and the university track elite categories, are losing out. A 1959 government report on the education of 15–18-year-olds concluded:

> *In the middle... the deficiencies [of the educational offer], relatively to the need, are greatest of all, for it is in this "second quartile" that the richest vein of untapped human resources lies, which will have to be exploited if this country is to keep a place among the nations that are in the van of spiritual and material progress.*[24]

The conclusion is as valid in this century as it was in the last. The majority of those on the non-graduate track are neither disengaged nor in remedial study, but neither are they offered vocational options that provide a path to top employment opportunities. There is huge potential for the sector to do more. Consider two simple facts. Demand from youngsters for apprenticeships far outstrips supply. In 2014/15, just over 190,000 apprenticeship vacancies were posted, compared to well over 1.5 million applications: a ratio of more than 8:1.[25] Businesses also report major skill gaps: around three in 10 vacancies are reported to be hard to fill because of skill gaps, most likely in skilled trades – the area where many apprenticeships focus.[26]

Unlike in HE, where government took the bold step to remove any cap on university places, currently the best vocational options are limited. In 2014 only 6.5 per cent of 16–18-year-olds were on an apprenticeship.[27] For Higher Apprenticeships, which at Level 5 offer better lifetime earnings than undergraduate degrees from all universities (bar the most selective), the opportunities are similarly limited.[28] In 2013/14, only 2,900 people aged 19–24 started Higher Apprenticeships, compared to nearly 170,000 first-year undergraduate degree starts in the same age range. This is a ratio of nearly 60:1.[29] [30] There is no way that the non-graduate route can become attractive for young people when it offers so few top opportunities.

Of course, it is welcome that apprenticeship numbers are set to rise, but the apprenticeships that young people take are mostly below the skill level that one would expect or want. If 16–19-year-olds progress in line with the English curriculum, they should have achieved Level 2 (five GCSEs at A*–C) by 16, and ideally be studying at Level 3 (A level equivalent) aged 16–18. Students aged 19–24 should be aiming for Level 4 or above. However, in 2014, seven out of 10 under-19s (the age definition used in apprenticeship statistics) who started apprenticeships were working towards a GCSE equivalent (Level 2) qualification, which offer only slightly better earnings than secondary school qualifications alone.[31] Nearly all 19–24 apprenticeship starts were at Level 3 or below (97 per cent). In comparison, 19–24-year-olds who start an honours degree are progressing towards Level 6. Apprenticeships ask less of young people than those on the academic track. This reinforces the attitude that if you can, you do A levels and if you can't, you take the other route. The 16-plus has driven down ambitions and opportunity for the majority of young people.

Widespread concerns about the quality of apprenticeships compound the general lack of stretch that apprenticeships provide. Recent inspections by Ofsted paint a worrying picture. It finds apprentices completing their course by making coffee, serving sandwiches or cleaning floors, adding little value and underlining the disconnect between the current national skill

24 Ministry of Education, *15 to 18*, 1959
25 Department for Business, Innovation and Skills, *FE Data Library: Apprenticeship Vacancies*, 2015
26 UK Commission for Employment and Skills, *UK Commission's Employer Skills Survey 2013: UK Results*, 2014
27 Department for Education, *Participation in Education, Training and Employment: Age 16 to 18*, 2015
28 Sutton Trust, *Levels of Success: The Potential of UK Apprenticeships*, 2015
29 Department for Business, Innovation and Skills, *Further Education and Skills: Statistical First Release – Learner Participation, Outcomes and Level of Highest Qualification Held*, 2015
30 UCAS, *End of Cycle Report 2014*, 2015
31 Sutton Trust, *Levels of Success: The Potential of UK Apprenticeships*, 2015

gaps and training provided. Even worse, Ofsted found that some learners were not even aware that they were on an apprenticeship. Successful apprenticeships were identified in sectors more traditionally associated with the model: engineering and construction. It is beyond bizarre when people who, as far as they are concerned are doing their day job, are counted as apprenticeship successes.[32] The challenges identified need urgent remedy, or a headline policy risks becoming tainted by its failing parts.

What is more, too few young people start apprenticeships, and the number has declined over recent years. The total number of apprenticeship starts by people under 19 in 2015 is up on the previous year – but over 5,000 fewer than in 2010/11 or 2011/12. For the 19–24 group, total starts are less than any year since 2011. Much of the growth in apprenticeships over the last Parliament was due to apprenticeship starts by over-25s. These increased by one-quarter (or almost 50,000) between 2011 and 2012, when previous adult training schemes were reclassified as apprenticeships. After a dip in 2014, apprenticeships for over-25s are on the rise again, making up more than two in five of all starts in 2015.[33] There is a social mobility problem when fewer young people are on the best non-graduate routes. There is also a problem with the brand 'apprenticeship' when so many of those on it are adults over the age of 25 already in work rather than young people being introduced to a trade.

Apprenticeships: fewer opportunities for the young?

Since 2010 the age profile of people starting apprenticeships has altered dramatically. In 2010 the majority of starts were young people, with fewer than one in five over-25s starting an apprenticeship. Since then, the age profile has been turned on its head. The proportion of apprenticeship starts by over-25s has more than doubled, and under-19s are now the fewest (Figure 3.2).

Figure 3.2: Apprenticeship starts by age, 2009/10 to 2014/15

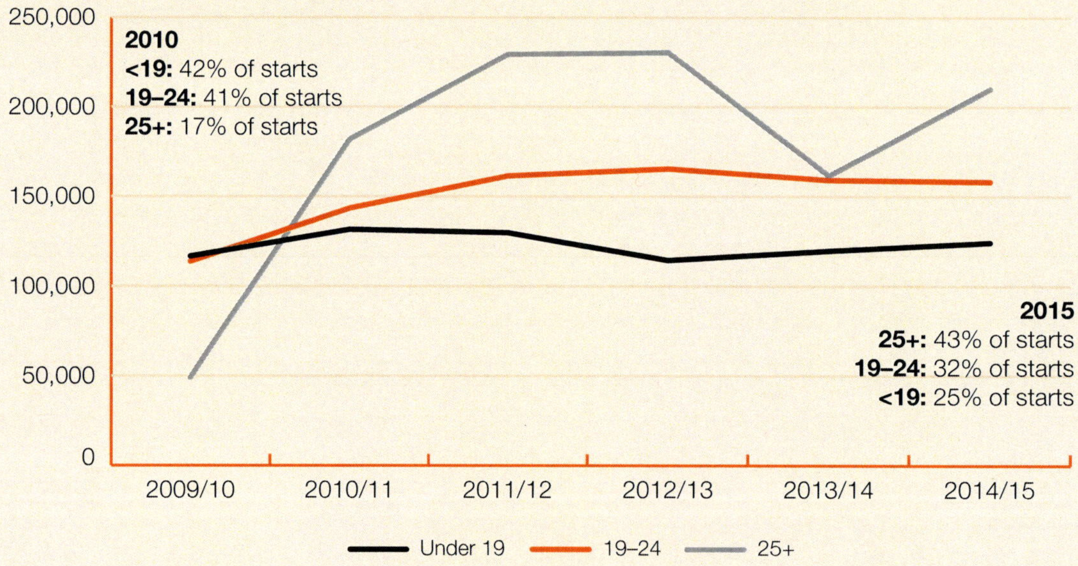

Source: Department for Business, Innovation and Skills, *Further Education and Skills: Statistical First Release*, 2015

32 Ofsted, *Apprenticeships: Developing Skills for Future Prosperity: How Well Do Apprenticeships Meet the Needs of Young People, Their Employers and the Economy?*, 2015

33 The dip in 25+ apprenticeship starts was possibly due to a requirement for adults to take out loans for some 24+ apprenticeships, a policy later reversed

Despite the high return to apprenticeships on average, there are big differences depending on gender and the sector in which an apprenticeship is taken. The earnings premium for a Level 3 apprenticeship compared to those who remain at Level 2 is more than 50 per cent greater for men than women.[34] This is likely driven by the sector in which people choose to take apprenticeships. Apprenticeships at Level 2 and 3 lead to the greatest increase in earnings in construction and planning, and the lowest increase in health, public services and care.[35] The former are more likely to be chosen by men and the latter by women. Of engineering apprenticeships, 96 per cent are male.[36] Young people are not making the best choices, which suggests the advice being given to them is poor.

As access to better apprenticeships is imbalanced by gender, neither is access to the best apprenticeship frameworks balanced across the country. Last year there were twice the number of Higher Apprenticeship starts in the North West, compared to the East Midlands or the North East.[37] More generally, there is a national skew away from apprenticeships in science, technology, engineering and maths (STEM), which can carry higher rewards, to other subject areas.[38] In London there are more than five non-STEM starts for every STEM apprenticeship. In the South East, South West and West Midlands the ratio is 3:1 – better, but still poor.[39]

In short, there are too few top apprenticeship opportunities, and they are not shared fairly. The lack of top-end, non-graduate options reduces the attractiveness of the route, despite some leading to better earnings than university degrees. So most of the brightest young people simply opt out of this route altogether. Young people who do well in exams at the point of the 16-plus choose the A level option because they believe it is better. This is reinforced by teachers, parents and careers advisers. It has led to the current situation where the non-graduate track is perceived as a route for those who are less capable.

Similarly, the lack of top non-graduate options leads employers, especially in many professional occupations, to prefer graduates. In most circumstances, non-graduate certificates are not competitive with degrees. Many professional occupations have extremely limited or no non-graduate entry routes. It is hardly surprising that parents with higher levels of qualification take a dimmer view of vocational education than higher education, and advise their children accordingly.[40] The consequence is to reinforce the class divide in post-16 education where children from better-off backgrounds tend to go to HE, while those from poorer backgrounds tend to be in vocational education.

Problem 2: The mainstream non-graduate track lacks coherence and does not prioritise career progression.

The characteristics of the graduate route which make it easy to understand and navigate are lacking in the non-graduate track.

First, university has a national admissions process. The UCAS system provides a straightforward gateway by which a young person can apply to a number of institutions for their subject of choice. The non-graduate route has no single admissions process, and certainly no national arrangements. Young people not heading to university will not be

34 Department for Education and Skills, *Research Report 834: A Cost–Benefit Analysis of Apprenticeships and Other Vocational Qualifications*, 2007

35 Department for Business, Innovation and Skills, *Research Paper 105: Review of the Economic Benefits of Training and Qualifications, as Shown by Research Based on Cross-Sectional and Administrative Data*, 2013

36 Sutton Trust, *Levels of Success: The Potential of UK Apprenticeships*, 2015

37 Department for Business, Innovation and Skills, *Apprenticeships by Geography, Age and Level 2005/6 to 2014/15*, 2015

38 STEM apprenticeship sectors are science and mathematics, ICT, engineering and construction and planning

39 Department for Business, Innovation and Skills, *Apprenticeships by Geography and Sector Subject Area: Starts 2005/6 to 2014/15*, 2015

40 City and Guilds Centre for Skills Development, *New Directions: Young Peoples' and Parents' Views of Vocational Education and Careers Guidance*, 2011

automatically able to access the best options nationally, and will end up constrained by what local providers offer and what the local labour market needs.

Second, universities have a place in the public consciousness. Providers of non-graduate options do not. There are numerous kinds of FE college, 14–18 institution, schools and private providers where non-graduate training can take place. Some areas have a range of choices, and others few. It is not straightforward for a young person to understand which institution is good and which should be avoided. Defaulting to the nearest option may not be the best, but it may not be at all easy to work out where a better option lies. The university degree is an unambiguous qualification. If a student achieves a degree such as law, it signals certain skills and is common currency in the jobs market. However, there is no equivalent for the non-graduate route. There are four documents totalling 75 pages that list all of the current technical and vocational qualifications for young people at Levels 2 and 3, and these documents only relate to courses recognised in performance tables: there are still nearly 16,000 qualifications available for 16–19-year-olds.[41] The performance table simplification is significant but still a maze, especially in relation to courses outside the science and technology subjects which may have multiple and similar options.[42]

Third, the vocational courses that young people (16–18) take offer less attractive routes into the world of work or chances to transfer from the non-graduate to the university track. Of most popular vocational Level 3 courses taken up in 2014, sports studies and business studies made up more than one-fifth of the total.[43] These qualifications provide ways into work and HE, but will be less likely to unlock places at top universities or in top professional firms. A student gaining CDD at A level is still more likely to go to university than a student gaining three distinctions in Level 3 BTEC courses.[44] The best results in vocational courses, especially if outside areas where skills are in demand such as engineering and construction, do not match up in terms of progression.

For those over 19, health and social care is the largest category of courses taken – one-third of the total.[45] Around half of the top category is in social care: a sector which has been in focus for poor pay and limited progression opportunities, driven by expanding demand and tight local government finances.[46] Sectors with greater earning potential, engineering and construction, make up less than 5 per cent of the top 100 Level 3 vocational qualifications by certificates awarded (see Figure 3.3).[47] [48] Yet presently there are around 25,000 vacancies in construction.[49]

41 Department for Education, *Section 96 – Qualifications* lists just short of 16,000 qualifications: http://www.education.gov.uk/section96/download.shtml

42 Department for Education, *Technical and Vocational Qualifications for 14- to 19-year-olds*, 2015. For example, in the performance tables there are two Level 3 qualifications for mechanical engineering, one for medical services and three for heavy vehicle repair. On the other hand, there are eight for horse management, 13 for hairdressing and 16 for beauty

43 Department for Education, *A level and Other Level 3 Results: 2013 to 2014 (Revised)*, 2015

44 Higher Education Funding Council for England (HEFCE), *Young Participation in Higher Education: A Levels and Similar Qualifications*, 2015

45 First Aid qualifications make up around half of the total. If these are discounted, on the basis of often being a mandatory part of a job, the category would be roughly joint first

46 Resolution Foundation, *As If We Cared: The Costs and Benefits of a Living Wage for Social Care Workers*, 2015

47 Ofqual, *Vocational Qualifications Dataset: Dataset 2009 to Present – England, Wales and Northern Ireland*, 2015

48 National Foundation for Educational Research, *A Literature Review of the Value of Vocational Qualifications*, 2015

49 Office for National Statistics, *Labour Market Statistics, Table VACS02 – Vacancies by Industry*, 2015

Figure 3.3: Top 100 Level 3 vocational courses (by certificates awarded in 2014–15) by subject area

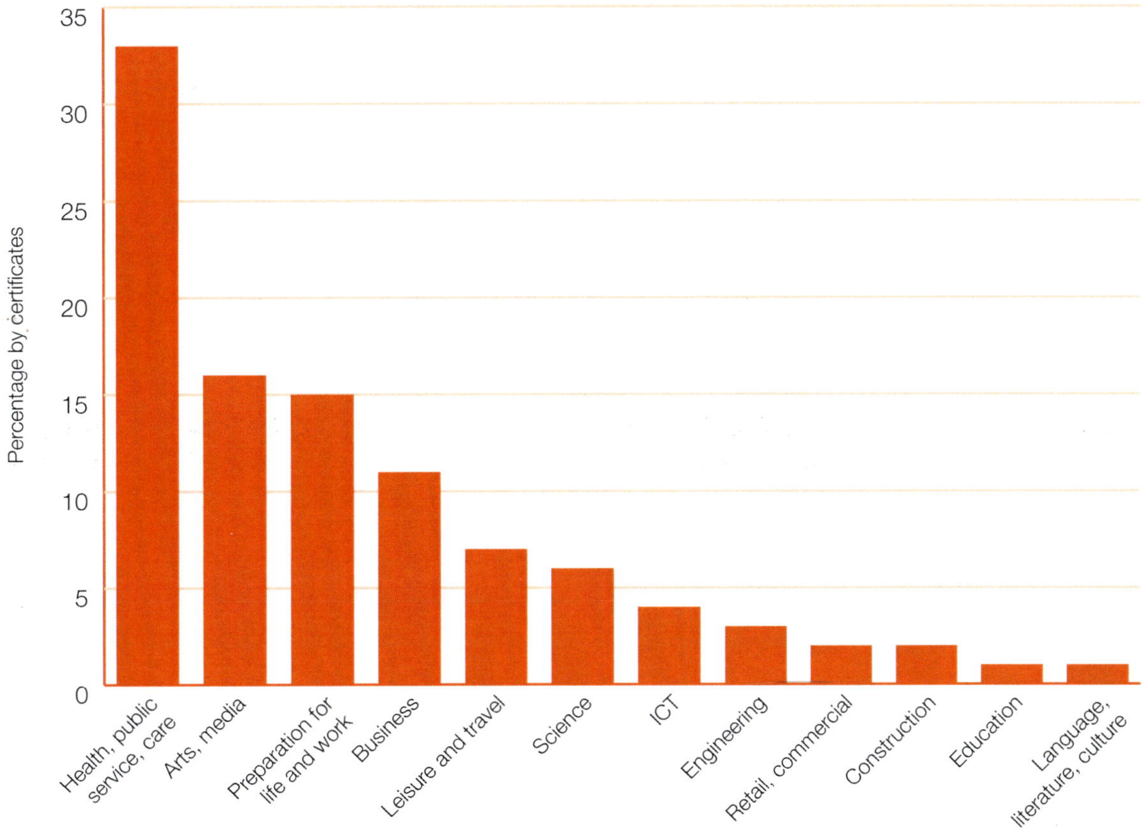

Source: Department for Business, Innovation and Skills, *Adult Further Education Learners: Destination Rates for National Qualifications – Experimental Data*, 2014

The future of young people who do not go to university is as important as those who do. However, vocational education is not currently structured in a way that maximises its social mobility potential. Compared to the relatively coherent university system, the FE system offers a fragmented application process, a proliferation of institutions with no clear signal of quality, and a range of qualifications with different value to different employers. This leads to some areas where young people are much less likely to attain benchmark Level 3 qualifications by 19 (see Figure 3.4).This poses a fundamental challenge to closing the opportunity gap between the university and the non-graduate track.

Figure 3.4: Social mobility cold spots: English local authority districts with the fewest poor (free school meal-eligible) 19-year-olds qualified to Level 3

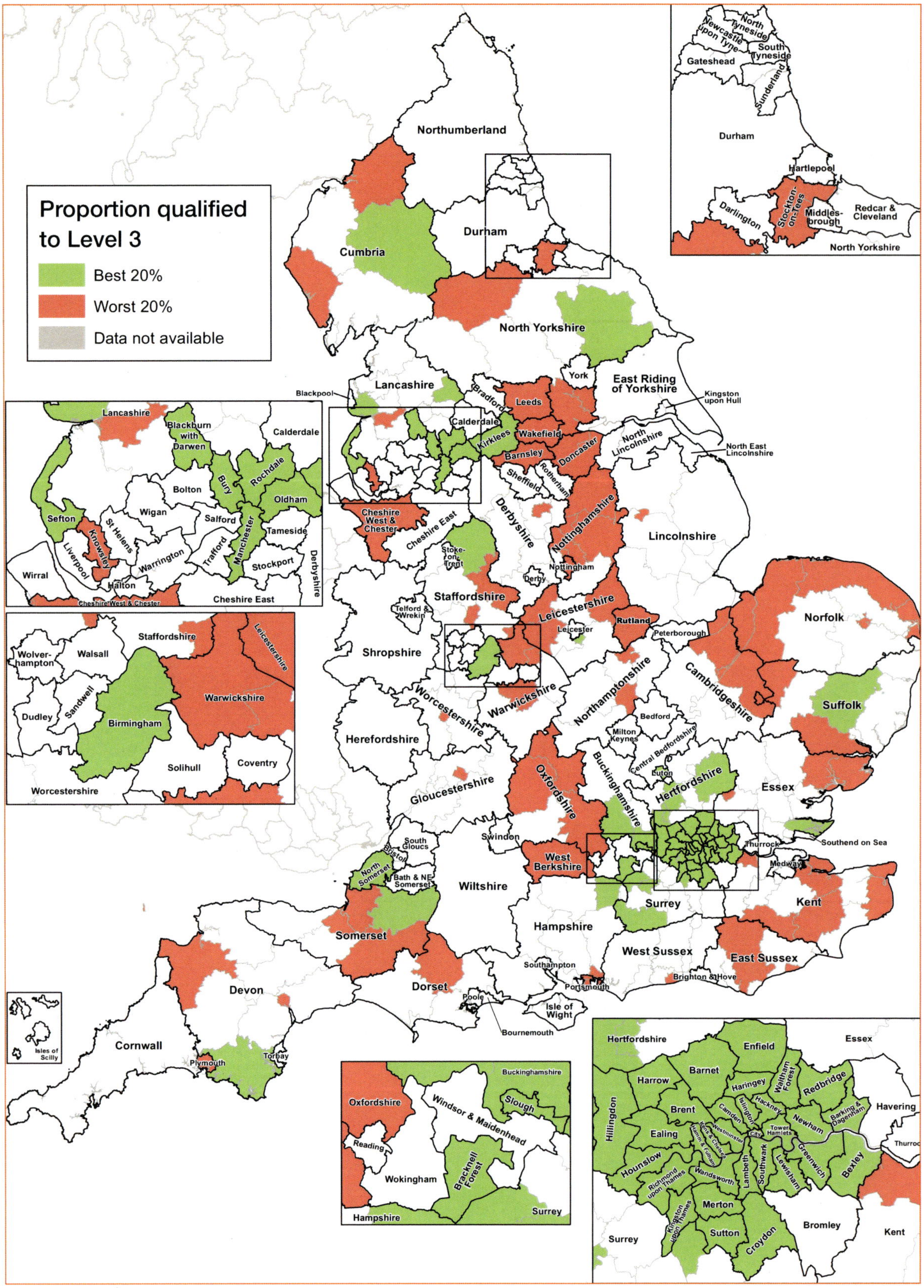

Source: Department for Education, *Level 2 and 3 Attainment by young people aged 19 in 2014*, 2015

Problem 3: There is no solution to chronic levels of youth unemployment and the NEET phenomenon.

In 2014 around 10,000 school-leavers achieved no GCSEs at all: more than double the figure in 2012/13 and the highest number since 2008.[50] [51] The size of the group with no GCSEs is the equivalent of more than 60 schools' year 11 cohort.[52] In the 10 lowest performing local authorities, on average more than 3 per cent of their pupils achieve no passes at GCSE (see Table 3.1). Part of the reason for the increase in those with no passes has been the removal of qualifications perceived as lower value from the GCSE league tables. This reform, while understandable, has not been accompanied by the right support to give all young people the chance to succeed.

Table 3.1: Local authorities with the highest proportion of pupils achieving no passes at GCSE

Local authority	% of pupils achieving no GCSE passes
Knowsley	6.7
Leicester	3.9
Wandsworth	3.8
Wolverhampton	3.7
Middlesbrough	3.5
Manchester	3.2
Stoke-on-Trent	3.1
Haringey	3.0
Newcastle upon Tyne	2.9
Redcar and Cleveland	2.9

Source: Department for Education, *GCSE and Equivalent Results in England 2013/14: Subject and Local Authority Tables*, 2015. Data relates to state-funded schools only

Being qualified to less than Level 2 (achieving less than five GCSEs at grade A*–C) has a damaging effect on employment. On average, only half of 21–24-year-olds with one to four GCSEs or no qualifications were employed at the time of the last census, compared to an employment rate of more than 70 per cent for those with Level 2.[53] Yet those who did not get good GCSEs at 16 and try for their Level 2 qualifications in their later teens tend not to make good progress. Of those who have not achieved Level 2 qualifications including English and maths by 16, only 20 per cent achieve this by 19. In other words, around eight out of 10 young people who did not get a C in GCSE English and maths by 16 still had not got this mark of employability by the end of their time in compulsory education.[54] Increasing the proportion of young people that reach this level will increase their employability, boost their potential to progress to higher levels of study and fill skill gaps in the economy.

The outlook for those who become unemployed or NEET after leaving school remains poor. Despite the proportion of 16–24 NEETs with no qualifications almost halving since 2005 (28 versus 16 per cent), the overall number of 16–24 NEETs is only 10,000 less (780,000 versus 770,000), suggesting a major structural challenge.[55] Although young NEET numbers are the

50 Department for Education, *GCSE and Equivalent Results in England 2013/14*, 2015. Data for all state-funded schools
51 Department for Education, *Review of Vocational Education: The Wolf Report*, 2011.The number of pupils obtaining no GCSEs has been driven up by changes to GCSE rules which removed courses deemed to be of lower quality from the statistics. This change is referred to as the 'Wolf Rules', as it arises from the 2011 Wolf Report of Vocational Education
52 Department for Education, *Schools, Pupils and Their Characteristics*, 2015. In 2015 there were 3,381 state-funded secondary schools, 543,526 pupils in year 11. An average year 11 had 161 pupils
53 Office for National Statistics, *Qualifications and Labour Market Participation in England and Wales*, 2014
54 Department for Business, Innovation and Skills, *Level 2 and 3 Attainment by Young People Aged 19 in 2014, Table 14b*, 2015
55 Office for National Statistics, *Highest Attained Qualification for Those Who are NEET (Not in Employment, Education or Training) in England as a Percentage of all NEETs*, 2015

lowest ever recorded, 140,000 16–18-year-olds are still currently disengaged from learning or earning.[56] This is progress from a high of more than 200,000 in 2008, but a long way from success. In fact, when compared to other countries the UK comes close to the bottom of the table. The five OECD members with lowest levels of 15–19-year-old NEETs have rates around 3 per cent – the UK had a rate of 8.4 per cent at the point of comparison. Only seven countries do worse, including Greece, Spain and Turkey, which have faced far longer and deeper youth employment crises than Britain.[57] On one estimate, the lifetime costs of a young person being NEET is around £56,000[58] – around £7.8 billion for the total group. Successful schemes to tackle the NEET problem are needed, and they pay for themselves.

For the young adult group, around 430,000 18–24-year-olds who are not in full-time education are unemployed, above the pre-recession levels of early 2008 (see Figure 3.5).[59] The progress in reducing youth unemployment from the highs of more than 1 million during the recession has been substantial. Yet for a large number of young people, the economic recovery has still not produced a social recovery.

Figure 3.5: Employment rates of 18–24-year-olds and 16–17-year-olds not in full-time education and in full-time education (FTE)

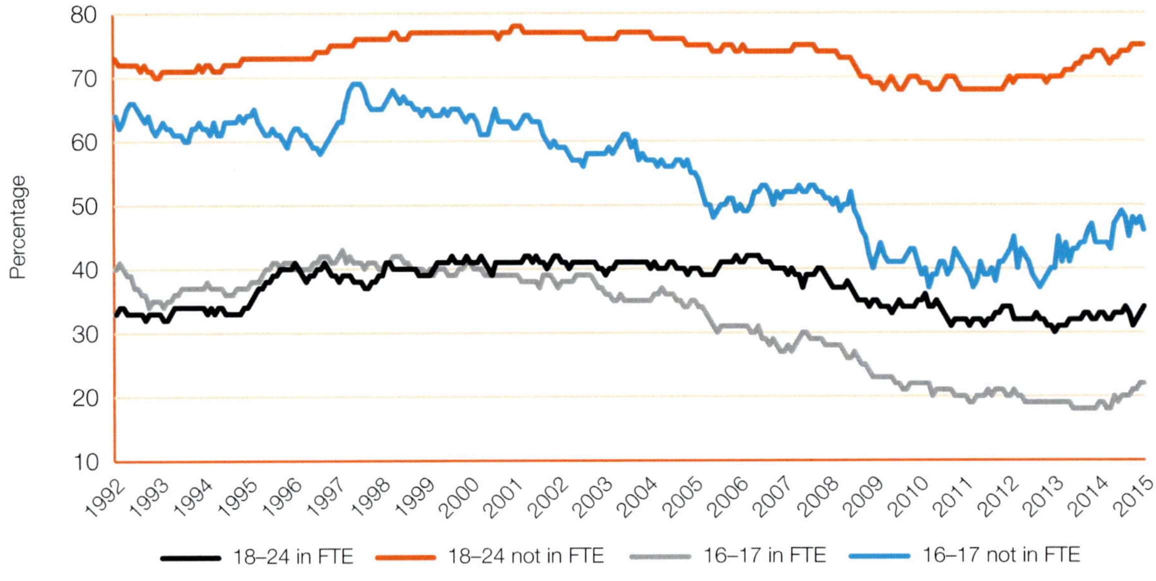

Source: Office for National Statistics, *Labour Market Statistics*, 2015

Note: 18–24-year-olds not in study are in employment at pre-recession rates. The 16–17-year-old group is still more likely to be out of work than in 2008

The unemployment challenge applies to older non-graduates as well as those under the age of 25. Non-graduates aged 21–30 felt the sharpest rise in unemployment following the recession. In 2012 the unemployment rate of young non-graduates was 80 per cent higher than that of recent graduates (15 per cent versus 8 per cent).[60] The wages of people born in 1983 are now the same as the wages that those born 15 years earlier experienced at the same age, despite significant economic growth (see Figure 3.6). The growth in earnings of the 1983 cohort came to a halt as GDP shrunk in 2008/09.[61] The recession had a profound impact on young people's life chances – and more so for those without a degree.

56 Department for Education, *Participation in Education, Training and Employment: Age 16 to 18*, 2015
57 OECD, *Education at a Glance: Percentage of 15–29-year-olds in Education/Not in Education, by Work Status, Age Group and Gender*, 2015
58 University of York, *Estimating the Lifetime Cost of NEET: 16–18 Year Olds Not in Education, Employment or Training*, 2010
59 Office for National Statistics, *Unemployment by Age and Duration (Seasonally Adjusted)*, 2015
60 Office for National Statistics, *Graduates in the Labour Market*, 2013
61 Gregg, P., *Making Steady Progress: Policies to Help Long-term Earnings Growth*, 2015

Figure 3.6: Comparison of the weekly earnings of cohorts of young people born between the 1960s and 1980s

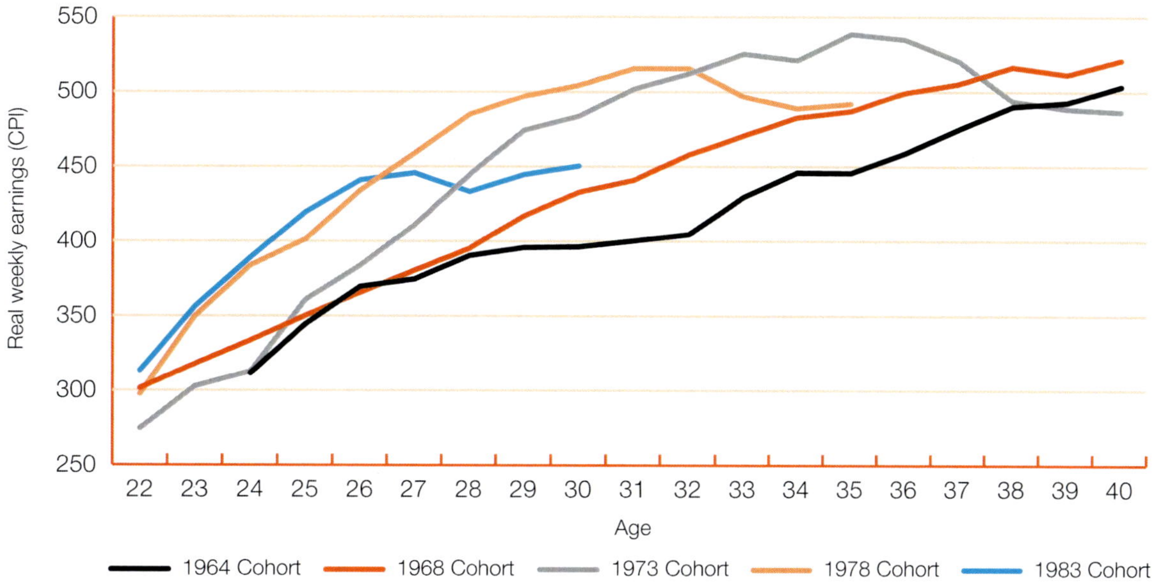

Source: P. Gregg, *Making Steady Progress: Policies to Help Long-term Earnings Growth*, 2015

The introduction of the National Living Wage may also have unforeseen consequences for young people. With the higher National Living Wage rate starting for those aged 25 and over, there will be an incentive for employers to create roles for young people, but not necessarily with skill and progression opportunities: once a person reaches the age of 25 some may seek to replace these workers with younger, cheaper, staff. As the policy is phased in there will be a need for government to monitor the jobs market effect, to ensure that a drive to increase opportunity for some does not increase disadvantage for others.

Although youth unemployment continues to decline in the UK as a whole, in some areas it remains high and is rising. In the North East and Wales more than two in 10 16–24-year-olds are unemployed. Over the last year (comparing May–July 2014 with May–July 2015), the proportion of unemployed young people has increased in three regions: by 14 per cent in Wales, 9 per cent in the West Midlands and 8 per cent in London (see Figure 3.7).[62] The regional NEET challenge mirrors the unemployment problem. In the North East, where youth unemployment is worst, on average 7 per cent of 16–18-year-olds are NEET. In Stockton-on-Tees almost one in 10 (9 per cent) young people are NEET: the highest level in the country.[63] This continuing level of disengagement is unacceptable.

62 Office for National Statistics, *Regional Labour Market Statistics: Regional Unemployment by Age (Experimental Statistics)*, 2015

63 Department for Education, *2014 Local Authority NEET Figures*, 2015

Figure 3.7: Change in rate of 16-24 unemployment by region: May–July 2014 versus May–July 2015

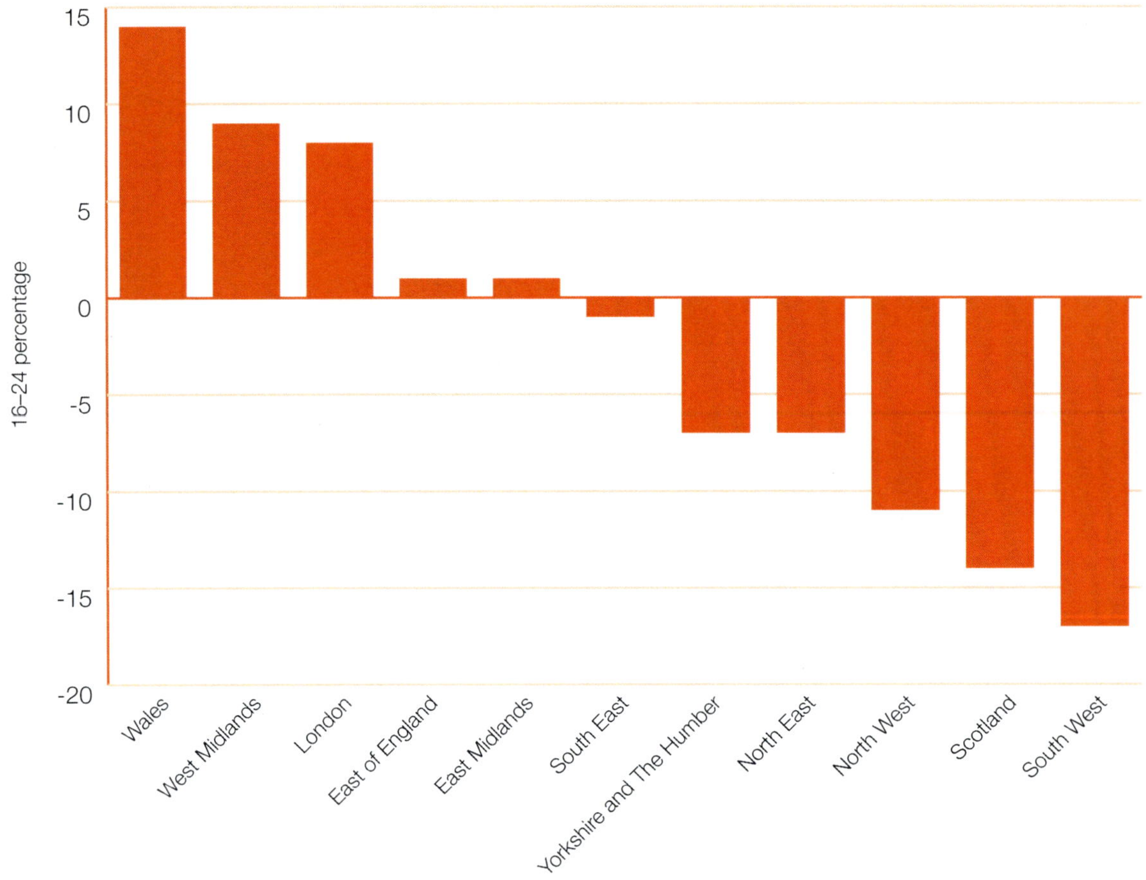

Source: Office for National Statistics, *Regional Labour Market Statistics: Regional Unemployment by Age (Experimental Statistics)*, 2015

3.3 How are these problems being addressed?

In relation to apprenticeships, the target for 3 million starts by 2020 is core to the Government's agenda. Apprenticeship growth is welcome: the contribution of vocational skills to productivity is greater where it is embedded in an apprenticeship system – as in Denmark, Germany and the Netherlands, for example.[64] Of all vocational routes, apprenticeships consistently bring higher returns for individuals and the wider economy than other qualifications.[65] Nonetheless, as assessed below, growth in apprenticeship numbers does not automatically translate into more social opportunity. In addition, by 2017 the Government plans for all new apprenticeships to be on revised frameworks that have been designed by the employers that will use them. In theory, this employer buy-in should put the scheme on a more sustainable and long-term footing, and is based on trailblazer schemes that have been rolled out over the past five years. On top of the plans to grow numbers, Degree Apprenticeships were introduced in September 2015, many in ICT subjects, as part of a drive to expand higher-skill routes.[66] To fund this expansion the Government has announced a levy of 0.5 per cent of firms' paybill if it is greater than £3 million, which will raise £3 billion a year by 2020.[67] Finally, legislation is being developed to restrict use of the term 'apprenticeship' in law to government-approved schemes.

64 European Centre for the Development of Vocational Training, *Macroeconomic Benefits of Vocational Education and Training*, 2014

65 Department for Business, Innovation and Skills, *Measuring the Net Present Value of Further Education in England*, 2015

66 The Tech Partnership, *Degree Apprenticeships*, https://www.thetechpartnership.com/recruit-and-train/degree-apprenticeships/

67 Department for Business, Innovation and Skills, *Apprenticeships Levy: Employer Owned Apprenticeship Training – Government Response*, 2015

In relation to vocational education and training in general, there is substantial policy activity. For 16–19-year-olds in FE, per-pupil funding has been protected in cash terms to 2020 which equates to a real terms cut, depending on inflation. Sixth-form colleges have been given the green light to become academies, thereby allowing them to avoid VAT charges they currently face.[68] Responding to the need to improve training in higher technical skills (at Levels 4 and 5), the Government has put in place plans for a new generation of national colleges – such as the College for High Speed 2, which will operate from Birmingham and Doncaster. Other new institutions are focused on technical training, such as university technical colleges; while others provide 14–18 routes that span academic and vocational courses such as careers colleges; and yet others provide a mix of work experience and classroom study, such as studio schools. Further, reforms to technical and professional education have been announced to create around 20 new routes to employment through study and apprenticeship, designed by employers and overseen by an expert panel.[69] To fund some of these courses, 19–23-year-olds will be able to take out loans to fund study at Level 3 or 4, and anyone over 19 can take out loans for FE study at Level 5 or 6.[70]

In relation to reducing NEET numbers, the Government has a package of measures planned to ensure that young people are in work. Jobcentre Plus is working with schools to provide advice to 16- and 17-year-olds. Plans are in development to add conditions to youth benefits, referred to by some as 'earn or learn', making participation in an apprenticeship or community activity mandatory. Traineeships have been introduced as programmes to prepare for work or an apprenticeship. In 2014/15 only 58 per cent of traineeships were completed – but of those that were finished, on average just over half progressed to a job, apprenticeship or other training.[71] These decent early results suggest that the model has potential, but needs further refinement to reach more young people and ensure good outcomes. There are also broad commitments for a new social impact bond (a payment-by-results scheme) to target youth unemployment.

Spanning the challenges of youth unemployment and the vocational route is the fledgling policy to drive up retakes of GCSEs. The Government has identified the premium that employers put on these qualifications, especially in English and maths, and requires those who fail to secure a C in these subjects by 16 to work towards achieving these qualifications as part of their study programme. Institutions that do not put such students on approved English and maths courses will have their funding reduced.[72] Recent data suggests some impact of the 2014 requirements. The most significant increases are in English retakes and successes, up by half and three-quarters respectively, although this may have been partly caused by a rise in those with grade D English entering for these exams. Despite this initial sign of progress, there remains a way to go. Three out of four of those who did not get a GCSE C in English, and four out of five of those without GCSE maths, were not retaking in 2014. Building a proper retake system is necessary, but it appears some way off.[73]

68 HM Treasury, *Spending Review and Autumn Statement 2015*, 2015
69 Department for Education, *Technical and Professional Education Revolution Continues*, 2015
70 HM Treasury, *Spending Review and Autumn Statement 2015*, 2015
71 Department for Business, Innovation and Skills, *Further Education and Skills Statistical First Release*, 2015
72 Education Funding Agency, *16 to 19 funding: Maths and English Condition of Funding*, 2015
73 Department for Education, *Level 1 and 2 Attainment in English and Maths by Students Aged 16–18: Academic Year 2013/14*, 2015

3.4 How can more progress be made?

On the trajectory of current policy and wider trends there are a number of areas of continued concern.

First, the Government's main target for vocational education – the creation of 3 million apprenticeships by 2020 – could be met without substantially increasing opportunities for young people. Increasing the number of over-25 apprenticeships would be the easy option. They already make up a large proportion of apprenticeship starts – as much as 45 per cent in recent years – and are a low-risk choice for firms, as often the candidates have been in their current role for many months. One government report suggests that seven out of 10 adult apprenticeships have already been working with a company for at least a year before they start their apprentice programme.[74] It would be the path of least resistance for firms if they want to reinvest their apprenticeship levy contribution on training existing staff. If apprenticeships are to become a byword for opportunity and social mobility, the real challenge is to make sure that the target and the incentives presented by the levy are used to increase the number of young people on high-quality apprenticeships at Level 3 and above.

There is a further risk that the 3 million target puts too much focus on the creation of apprenticeships, and not enough on their completion. The target is based on apprenticeship starts, yet between 2011/12 and 2013/14 apprenticeship success dropped by nearly 7 per cent in just two years (from 74 per cent to 69 per cent).[75] On a broad calculation, should successes continue to fall, 3 million apprenticeship starts would amount to just fewer than 2 million apprenticeship successes. The risk is that a sensible objective – more opportunity through the vocational route – loses out to a numerical target. More clarity is needed on how the Government will work with firms and training providers to ensure that more of those that start apprenticeships actually finish them.

Working futures? Scenarios for apprenticeship growth

The Government faces a range of challenges in relation to growing apprenticeship numbers:

- Meeting its target of 3 million apprenticeship starts by 2020;
- Tackling the decline in youth apprenticeship starts;
- Reversing the decline in the apprenticeship success rate.

The Government's 3 million apprenticeship starts target appears to be stretching. Figure 3.8 shows three scenarios of growth for apprenticeship starts based on recent trends. A 3 per cent growth rate (the average between 2011/12 and 2014/15) misses the target by 300,000. An ambitious 6 per cent growth scenario still undershoots by around 50,000. A lower rate of 1.5 per cent misses the target by 400,000.

74 Department for Business, Innovation and Skills, *Prior Qualifications of Adult Apprentices 2012/13*, 2014

75 Department for Business, Innovation and Skills, *Further Education and Skills Statistical First Release*, 2015.

Figure 3.8: Three scenarios of apprenticeship growth 2015–20

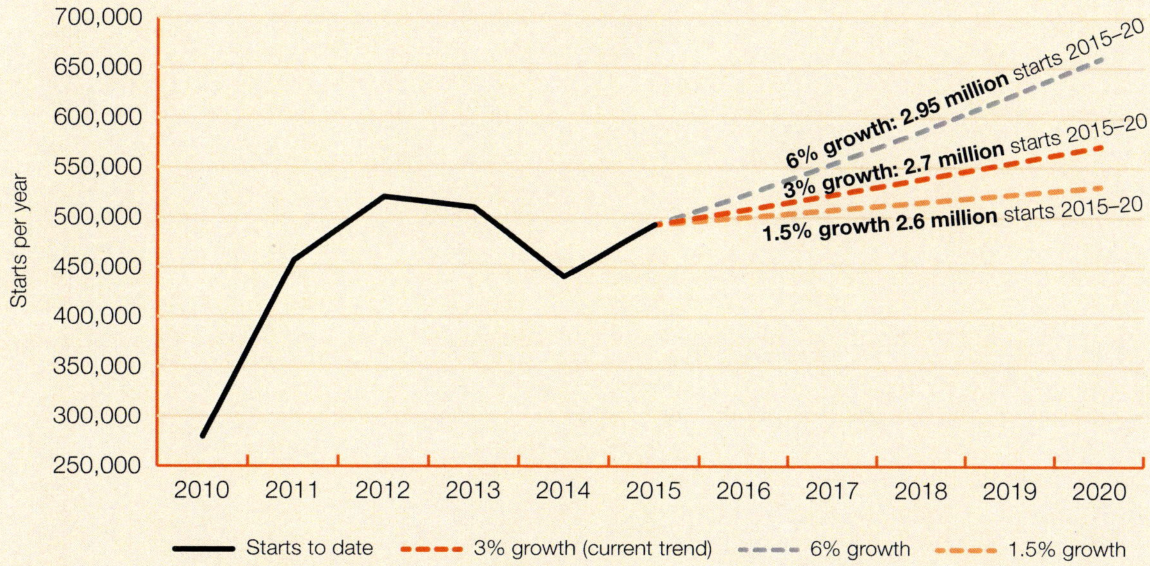

Source: Department for Business, Innovation and Skills, *Further Education and Skills: Statistical First Release*, 2015 (Commission projections)

Yet even if the target is met, urgent action is required to prevent young people missing out (see Figure 3.9). Since 2011/12 the growth in numbers of apprenticeship starts has differed significantly between age groups. Starts by the 25+ group have grown on average by 7 per cent a year, the 19–24 group by 3 per cent and the under-19s by -1 per cent. Taking these trends and projecting them forwards implies the gap in starts between age groups may widen.

Figure 3.9: Trends of apprenticeship starts per year by age group

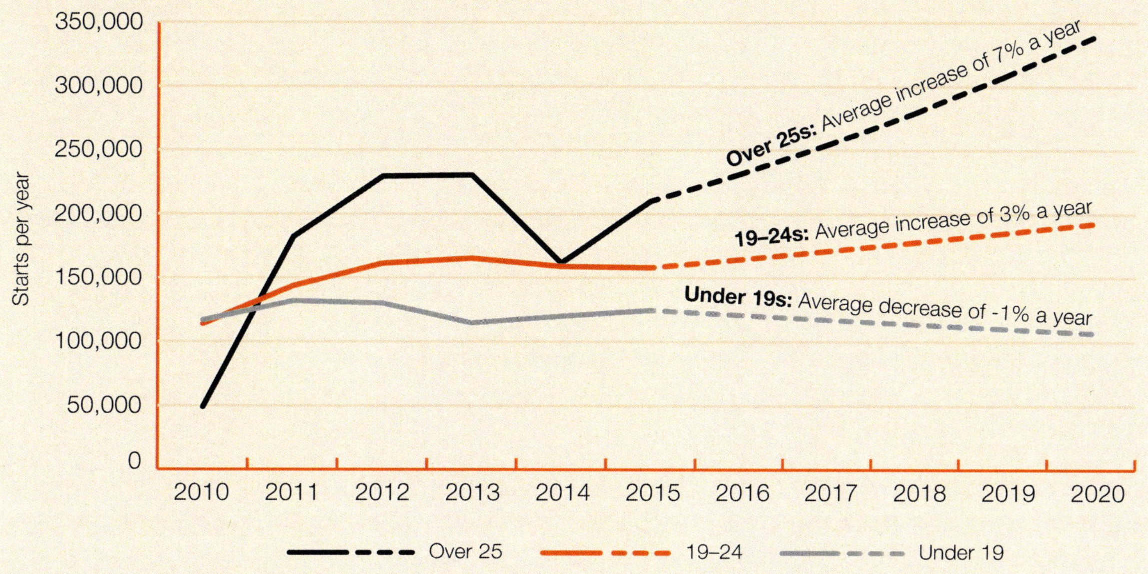

Source: Department for Business, Innovation and Skills, *Further Education and Skills: Statistical First Release*, 2015 (Commission projections)

Perhaps as few as three in five of all apprenticeships started between 2015 and 2020 will result in successful completion (see Figure 3.10). Today, fewer than seven in 10 of starters have completed their apprenticeships by the target date. This rate declined by 3.4 per cent a year between 2011/12 and 2013/14. Should this trend continue, even if numbers of starts increase by 3 per cent a year (the current trend), growth will be offset by higher proportions of people starting but not finishing their apprenticeship.

Figure 3.10: Trends in apprenticeship success rates, 2015–20

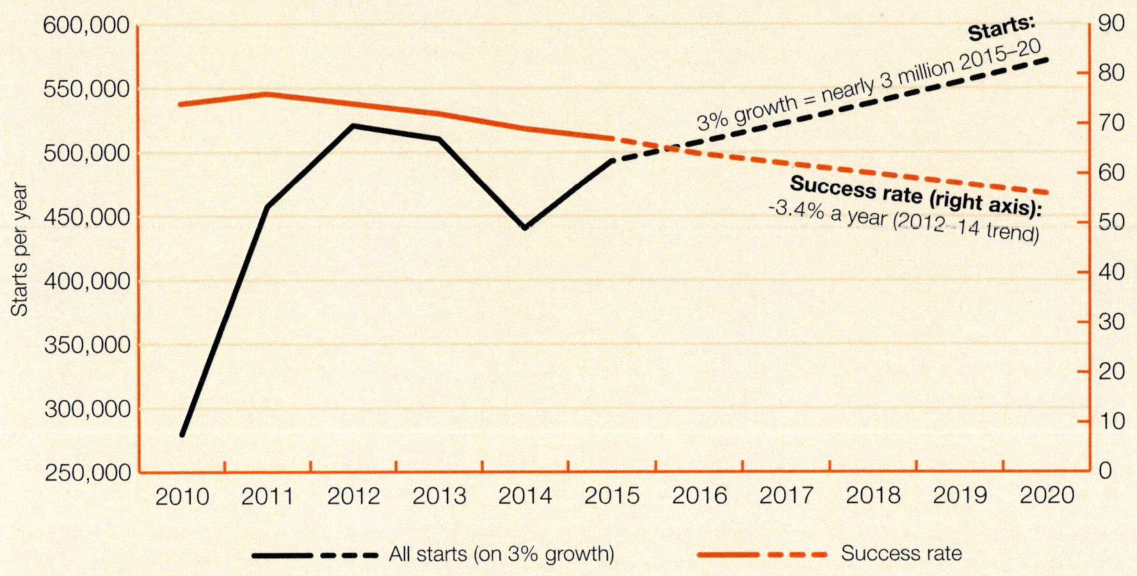

Source: Department for Business, Innovation and Skills, *Further Education and Skills: Statistical First Release*, 2015 (Commission projections)

An additional challenge to ensuring apprenticeship growth and opportunity is bringing firms on board. The burden of responsibility and funding for training will be further shifted to firms through the new levy and longer-term declines in funding for classroom vocational education. How this will change firms' approach and attitude is unclear. Early responses to the levy suggest that there is a distance to go before employers are bought in.[76] Also, over recent years, while the number of firms offering apprenticeships has increased, this rate of expansion is slowing. Between 2010/11 and 2012/13 the number of workplaces employing apprentices increased by 13 per cent a year on average. However, for the last two years the number of employers with apprenticeships has increased by less than 5 per cent a year.[77] Current firms cannot offer unlimited additional apprenticeships; new firms must buy in. This urgently needs to be escalated to the top of the Department for Business, Innovation and Skills' 'worry list'. If business does not embrace the opportunity to take the lead, there is a risk of a void left where chances for progression once were.

Second, skill gaps at a higher technical level may persist if the right structures do not exist to deliver them.[78] State-driven solutions to the FE system – such as colleges for High Speed 2 – are not an adequate response to the current employer demand for skills at Levels 4 and 5. There is no reason why, in 2015, an FE system should look so much like a flashback to the 1970s. The implication of the current situation continuing is twofold: potential productivity will be lost to the economy, and individuals will miss out on opportunities that provide chances for social mobility. Getting the higher vocational solution right will unlock opportunity for those not

76 Chartered Institute of Personnel and Development (CIPD), *Employers Split over Plans to Introduce Apprenticeships Levy According to CIPD Survey*, 2015

77 Department for Business, Innovation and Skills, *Workplaces Employing Apprentices by Region (2009/10 to 2014/15 In-year Estimates)*, 2015

78 Higher Education Policy Institute, *Raising Productivity by Improving Higher Technical Education: Tackling the Level 4 and Level 5 Conundrum*, 2015

following traditional graduate routes. The greatest productivity returns to a well-functioning higher vocational system are in the production sector. Of all the parts of the economy that employ non-graduates, manufacturing has the most potential for pay and skill progression.[79] There is a potential virtuous circle if more young people enter higher vocational training in the right areas – but at present it is unclear whether FE reforms are underpinned by a strategy to deliver this.

More broadly in relation to classroom-based vocational training, it is unclear whether innovations will fill the gaps that exist. Creating a range of different institutions does not respond to the fundamental problems, not least a system that is difficult for young people to navigate. The fact that some university technical colleges have had to close due to low demand, with public sunk costs in excess of £15 million, suggests that the Government should exercise caution in expanding untested models.[80] The implication of longer-term funding arrangements for the sector is potentially severe. More than one-third of sixth-form colleges believe that, under current 16–19 funding arrangements, it is likely that they will cease to be a going concern by 2020.[81] Planned funding reductions are made even more challenging by additional costs imposed by the expansion of apprenticeships. Even with the proposed levy on firms, the cost to the Government may need to be met from elsewhere.

Third, at present, evidence suggests that the vocational route only partly delivers for those who move across to the university track. The positive story is that former apprentices do well when they progress to HE. One in five of a cohort of apprentices progressed to HE in the seven years since 2006/07. Nearly seven in 10 former advanced apprentices (Level 3) who went on to study a first degree achieved a 2:1 or first – a rate above the UK average. Further, annual salary for former apprentices with degrees was higher than HE leavers in general.[82]

However, for young people on general vocational tracks, despite the increasing popularity of BTEC, this route to university does not match up to A levels in its outcomes. Those with BTEC qualifications at Level 3 are found to be less than half as likely to progress to HE compared to those with A levels (29 versus 64 per cent). Those who do progress to HE with BTEC qualifications are nearly seven times less likely to enter highly selective Russell Group institutions (17.9 versus 2.6 per cent). Further, those who do progress are likely to be less successful. BTEC students taking first degrees are one-fifth (19 per cent) less likely to achieve a degree, and nearly 30 per cent less likely to achieve a first or 2:1 than those who studied A levels.[83] Young people progressing to HE who started on the vocational track are seeking opportunity, but not all are finding it. To provide genuine choice, more high-quality, non-academic routes are needed.

Fourth, the changing shape of the jobs market means that in some areas the vocational track, especially in relation to qualifications that carry less purchase with employers, will be more likely to lead to low-paying work. The trend of growth in both high-paying and low-paying jobs at the expense of certain intermediate roles is exaggerated in some cities. Between 2001 and 2011 the share of employment in low-paid jobs increased by 5 percentage points in Coventry, Luton and Stoke – more than double the average increase.[84] If young people are to make the most out of vocational options, there needs to be more clarity than at present about the job and progression opportunities to which courses or apprenticeships might lead. The local option may be far from the best, but the evidence to help young people decide is absent from the debate.

79 New Economics Foundation, *Good Jobs for Non-graduates*, 2012
80 Times Educational Supplement, *Government Spent £15m on UTCs that Closed or Did Not Open*, 2015
81 Sixth Form Colleges Association, *SFCA Funding Impact Survey Report 2015*, 2015
82 Department for Business, Innovation and Skills, *Progression of Apprentices to Higher Education: Second Cohort*, 2015
83 Department for Business, Innovation and Skills, *Progression of Further Education Students to Higher Education*, 2015
84 Centre for Cities, *Unequal Opportunity: How Jobs are Changing in Cities*, 2014

Fifth, current low rates of success in English and maths retakes for those who have not achieved Level 2 by 16 suggest a deep problem. These young people are more likely to be unemployed, and without core qualifications will be unable to access training. Requirements for apprenticeships vary, but many employers ask for five GCSEs at grades A*–C, including English and maths.[85] Moreover, ensuring educational re-engagement is not just important for progression; it is the crucial link to prevent low attainment at school converting into unemployment and NEET status. With large numbers of young people unaccounted for in local authority data, there have been suggestions that there could be as many as 50,000 16–18 NEETs missing from official statistics.[86] This situation is difficult in the best of economic times; in the event of another downturn, this group risks falling even further behind. There is an urgent need for a local solution to this ongoing issue.

3.5 Conclusion and Recommendations

Over recent years, proposed solutions to the faultlines in the post-16 education landscape have fallen broadly into two categories. One approach suggests that the system as represented by the current institutions does not need changing. Instead, the options within the system, courses, qualifications and routes through the system need to be improved.[87] The other approaches favour a reformed system, perhaps localised and with new institutions, that brings those on the graduate and non-graduate route closer together.[88] If the objective is to increase social mobility, elements of both approaches are required.

Improving vocational education requires overturning decades of inaction and contradictory policies. Recently there has been a welcome push from the Government to improve vocational options, expand apprenticeships and bring employers into the fold. However, this alone will not fix the damaging effect of the 16-plus; neither will it overcome the entrenched negative attitudes held by many parents and students. To deliver a One Nation society a new contract is required between government, young people on the non-graduate track and their parents.

This new contract needs to focus on outcomes, not numbers. It should have four parts:

1. A commitment to rapidly increase participation of youngsters on high-quality courses;
2. Far better information on the employment prospects of vocational choices;
3. A new focus on improving the quality of failing colleges;
4. A commitment to reduce the dropout rate of 16–18-year-olds in line with the best international comparisons.

A non-graduate track that is firing on all cylinders can create both a virtuous supply of high-skilled workers and engaged firms who will employ them. Opportunity and social mobility will be enabled. If it is not, a sizeable proportion of the population will continue to fall behind, to the loss of us all.

85 UCAS Progress, *Apprenticeships*, https://www.ucas.com/ucas/16-18-choices/search-and-apply/apprenticeships
86 Fabian Society, *Out of Sight*, 2014
87 Examples being: HM Government, *Dearing Review of Qualifications for 16–19-year-olds*, 1996 and Department for Education, *Review of Vocational Education: The Wolf Report*, 2011
88 Examples being: Department for Education and Skills, *14–19 Curriculum and Qualifications Reform Final Report of the Working Group on 14–19 Reform*, 2004 (the *Tomlinson Review*); Nuffield Foundation, *Education for All: The Future of Education and Training for 14–19-year-olds*, 2009; Kenneth Baker, *14–18: A New Vision for Secondary Education*, 2013

Recommendation 1: New apprenticeships should be targeted at higher-level courses and young people: there should be 30,000 young people starting a higher-level apprenticeship a year by 2020.

If the Government and firms are serious about securing talent from all walks of life, expanding top non-graduate routes is essential. This means that the current dominance of apprenticeships by older people must come to an end. The Commission recommends the following:

- By 2020, increase by tenfold the number of 19–24-year-olds starting Higher Apprenticeships. This would change the ratio of degree starts to Higher Apprenticeship starts from 60:1 to around 6:1 on current levels. It would mean around 30,000 starts a year by this age group. There are more than 19,000 Higher Apprenticeship starts a year at the moment, although around three-quarters of these go to over-25s;

- Apprenticeship starts by older people who have been employed for over a year should be reclassified as in-work training. This could result in as much as a 70 per cent drop in the number of adult apprenticeship starts.[89] The effect, at current levels, would be a reduction of the proportion of adult apprenticeships to 20 per cent of the total, rather than 45 per cent as at present. This is vital to restore credibility to the apprenticeship brand.

Recommendation 2: A new UCAS-style website should be created for vocational education within two years so that young people can see what progression, employment and earnings opportunities they are likely to achieve.

To ensure that young people can make the most of changes to vocational study, there needs to be clear routes through – as there are clear routes through A levels to higher academic study. Clarity is all the more important since the announcement at the 2015 Spending Review that FE students (over 19) will be able to take out loans to fund their courses. To achieve this, better outcomes data is required at the point when young people apply to courses at colleges or for apprenticeships. The purpose is to ensure that young people know what a choice at 14 or 16 will lead to at 18 or 19 – or later – regardless of whether someone wants to enter employment, continue to higher levels of study or attend university. To achieve this, the Commission recommends:

- The Department for Business, Innovation and Skills accelerates the process of publishing outcome data for vocational courses, and expands this in collaboration with the Department for Education to cover those under 19. In specific terms, it is important to capture whether a qualification or apprenticeship will enable progression to the next level of study;

- Outcomes data to be published regularly that link FE and tax data, to show the earnings progression for those who follow vocational courses. This should be further broken down, where possible, to level and type of qualification, region and background of the individual, both social and ethnic;

- This data should be brought together in a UCAS-style website that allows pupils to apply for courses at 14 or 16, as appropriate. Further, it should have national coverage, so that young people at 18 or 19 can apply for courses in different parts of the country, if relevant.

89 Department for Business, Innovation and Skills, *Prior Qualifications of Adult Apprentices 2012/13*, 2014

Recommendation 3: Failing FE colleges should become FE academies along the lines of the initial city academies, with an external business sponsor.

The Government is taking action in relation to schools perceived as coasting. The same enthusiasm for high-quality provision should be applied to FE colleges. The purpose is to improve attainment, build links with the local jobs market and ensure that young people are equipped with the skills for work or progression to higher levels of study.

The Commission recommends that:

- Where colleges are failing – in terms of quality or finances – the Skills Funding Agency, Further Education Commissioner's Office and Department for Business, Innovation and Skills put in place a process by which they can become an academy;
- Any college that is rated requires improvement or inadequate one year and does not move out of this category the next should be urgently converted to an academy to protect pupils. The 16 colleges that Ofsted identified as failing to improve should be the primary targets of this academy programme;
- Where area reviews take place and mergers or closures are proposed, the academy model should be preferred to reinvigorate skills provision and progression on the vocational track in an area.

Recommendation 4: By 2020 the Government should reduce the NEET rates of 16–18-year-olds to 3 per cent or less (or around 55,000),[90] in line with the best performing OECD countries.[91] This should be underpinned by a new social investment fund worth around £50 million to pay for the successful outcomes of NEET prevention schemes.

There is an urgent need to establish a solution to prevent those at risk of dropping out from becoming NEET. The lesson from recent programmes is that that nationally imposed schemes can meet resistance, but a lack of central direction will result in local schemes of varying quality.[92] The key challenge to end the NEET phenomenon for the 16–18 group is to prevent young people from dropping out in the first place, then ensure they remain engaged. The Commission recommends:

- The Government expand existing commitments to social impact bonds for reducing unemployment, and establish a social impact bond with the core objectives of identifying those at risk of NEET when they are at school, preventing dropout and ensuring continued engagement in earning or learning. A social impact bond works by investors providing funding for an intervention, and the Government making success payments to investors when an intervention achieves specific outcomes. The payments are on the basis of current and future savings to government and the taxpayer: for example, from reduced benefits, prison places and remedial education costs. The Government's three-year, £30 million innovation fund has recently finished, leaving the future of this approach uncertain. A new extended fund would ensure a continued focus on delivering vital outcomes, scope to further build the market and establish this model;

90 This is 3 per cent of the projected 16–18 population in 2020. Office for National Statistics, *Young Age Structure Variant: England Population Single Year of Age, 2012-based*, 2013

91 In 2014, the youth (15–19) NEET rate in Britain was 8.4 per cent. The rate was 2.4 per cent in Luxembourg, 2.9 per cent in Germany, 3.2 per cent in the Czech Republic, and 3.5 per cent in Norway. OECD, *Education at a Glance 2015*, 2015

92 Department for Education, *The Youth Contract for 16–17 Year Olds Not in Education, Employment or Training Evaluation*, 2014

- An initial scheme should be targeted at the North East. Of the top five local authorities with the highest proportion of 16–18 NEETs and the greatest increase in proportion of NEETs between age 16 and 18, three are in this region (Gateshead, Redcar and Middlesbrough). A recent scheme to reduce NEETs in the North East as part of the Coalition Government's Youth Contract showed significant re-engagement and attainment of qualifications. Schemes under the Department for Work and Pensions Innovation fund have shown promising results;

- The Government should identify investors and run a competition in collaboration with local authorities in the area to select service providers. As the benefits of NEET reduction span a number of departments' outcome, payments should be managed centrally from the Cabinet Office or Treasury.[93] On the basis of initial evaluation, this scheme should be rolled out rapidly to other parts of the country, starting with the areas with the greatest problems.

93 The Department for Education will save through reduced requirement for Pupil Referral Units; the Department for Work and Pensions through reduced benefit payment; and the Department for Business, Innovation and Skills through a reduced remedial adult education bill. The Ministry of Justice and its agencies will benefit from reduced requirement for court time and prison places. Local government will save funds otherwise spent on NEET reduction

Chapter 4: Fair access to university and the professions

- **Substantial effort has been made by some universities and firms to increase the socio-economic diversity of their intakes, but young people from poor families are still far less likely to go to university, attend a top institution or access certain elite professions.**
- **Law and professional service firms are doing most to improve social mobility; engineering and construction firms least.**
- **Privileged youngsters are disproportionately likely to attend selective universities with independently schooled pupils making up nearly 40 per cent of the intake of the five most selective Russell Group universities.**
- **The Government has set a welcome target to double the proportion of students from low participation areas, but achieving it will be challenging.**
- **If the Government's target is to be met, by 2020 universities might need to increase by 12,000 per year the number of students from low participation areas. There is little chance of success unless universities work together to focus more outreach activity on the schools and the places where HE access lags behind. A £40 million fund taken from universities' widening participation budgets should underpin this vital effort.**
- **The Government should make public sector internships transparent with a new interns.gov.uk website.**
- **Top professional firms must follow the lead of those making the greatest progress in opening opportunities by changing recruitment processes.**

4.1 Introduction

For society to be socially mobile, access to higher education and to jobs that bring the greatest reward must be open to all with the ability to benefit from them. The members' club mindset that once dominated admission to university and the professions is no longer acceptable. Real equality, as the Prime Minister put it, is now the shared goal.[1] Over recent years good progress has been made. There has been a dawning realisation in both higher

1 David Cameron MP, *The Prime Minister's Party Conference Speech*, 2015

education and among our country's top professional employers that they have been missing out on talent by recruiting from too narrow a social stratum. Bigger efforts have been made to diversify their intakes. Yet the long shadow of the members' club remains. It can be seen in university interview questions that some are coached to answer but are a mystery to the rest. It is present in job assessments that rely on notions of talent or polish rather than purely on potential. And it hangs over internships reserved for those in the know rather than all who seek to establish their career. It leads to a situation where the holders of top jobs today too often represent a small selection of backgrounds and experience.[2] When aspiration and potential are held back – whether by lack of careers guidance, connections or finances – individuals and society lose out. It is vital that our universities and professions redouble their efforts to turn growing calls for equality of opportunity into meaningful, lasting change.

The benefits of universities to the economy and to individuals are significant. As a country, the skills that university education can provide are vital to our future economic growth. With the expansion of university provision over the final quarter of the last century, participation in higher education (HE) increased from around 15 per cent in 1988 to 47 per cent by 2013/14.[3 4] This has led to substantial gains in productivity and output in the economy. Graduate skill accumulation accounted for a fifth of UK Gross Domestic Product (GDP) growth between 1982 and 2005; productivity is estimated to rise between 0.2 and 0.5 per cent for each 1 per cent increase in the share of the workforce with a degree.[5] In 2011/12 universities contributed £40 billion to GDP or around 2.8 per cent of UK national income.[6 7] And for individuals today, the average premium for a degree across a lifetime is more than £200,000 and is higher for women (£277,000) than for men (£199,000).[8] Since the late 1990s further progress has been made, especially in recognising and responding to the challenge of widening participation and opening access to the most selective institutions. More people than ever from a greater diversity of social backgrounds are seeing the benefits of higher education. But there is still a long way to go.

A good degree unlocks the door to the professions and to positions in elite organisations. Firms are beginning to recognise the value of a diverse workforce and their own role in broadening the range of backgrounds of their employees. Initiatives in accountancy, professional services and other sectors are a good start but they remain the exception and need to become the norm across the economy.

A prosperous One Nation Britain is one that recognises and incubates talent from all walks of life. Clear pathways must be provided to jobs that the best and brightest can flourish in to drive growth and international competitiveness. We face not only a social crisis when access to some prestigious universities and jobs is limited to those from privileged families. As a nation we also face a crisis of growth and productivity. Over the current parliament, it is predicted that increases in jobs will be in higher skilled, white-collar services. The number of jobs in managerial, professional and assistant professional occupations is expected to increase by 2.3 million –17 per cent – over the next decade.[9] This growth provides an opportunity to open up the professions to a wider range of talent. Failing to do so would widen divisions that already exist and limit the productivity boost that the economic recovery is yet to deliver. It is time to turbo-charge efforts to make Britain a country that is more equal and less elitist.

---

2 Social Mobility and Child Poverty Commission, *Elitist Britain?*, 2014; Social Mobility and Child Poverty Commission, *Elitist Scotland?*, 2015

3 Participation of 17- to 30-year-old English domiciled first-time entrants to HE. Institute for Fiscal Studies, *Widening Participation in Higher Education: Analysis Using Linked Administrative Data*, 2010

4 House of Commons Library, *Participation in Higher Education: Social Indicators Page*, 2015

5 Department for Business, Innovation and Skills, *The Relationship Between Graduates and Economic Growth Across Countries*, 2013

6 Universities UK, *The Economic Role of UK Universities*, 2014

7 David Willetts MP, *Contribution of UK Universities to National and Local Economic Growth (speech)*, 2014

8 Walker, I., and Zhu, Y., *The Impact of University Degrees on the Lifecycle of Earnings*, BIS research paper 112, 2013. The figures presented here are for the net present value of obtaining a degree

9 UK Commission for Employment and Skills, *Working Futures 2012-2022*, 2014

4.2 To what extent does today's reality match up to the One Nation vision?

The gap in university access between those from poor households and others is wide, but narrowing. In this context the Government has committed by 2020 to double the proportion of young people entering higher education who live in areas with the lowest HE participation, compared with 2009 levels.[10] This is a hugely welcome commitment. It is also a daunting one. Currently, on average, young people from the areas with the lowest higher education participation are over two and half times less likely to attend HE compared with those from the areas with the highest higher education participation (18 versus 46 per cent).[11] The participation rate of young people from low participation areas in 2009 was 14 per cent, and has been rising by around a percentage point a year. At this rate the commitment will not be met until the mid-2020s. But even with this progress, the gap between poorer young people and others will remain. If recent trends continue, the gap in access will not close until the 2060s.[12]

Figure 4.1: Government commitment to increase HE participation by young people from low participation areas

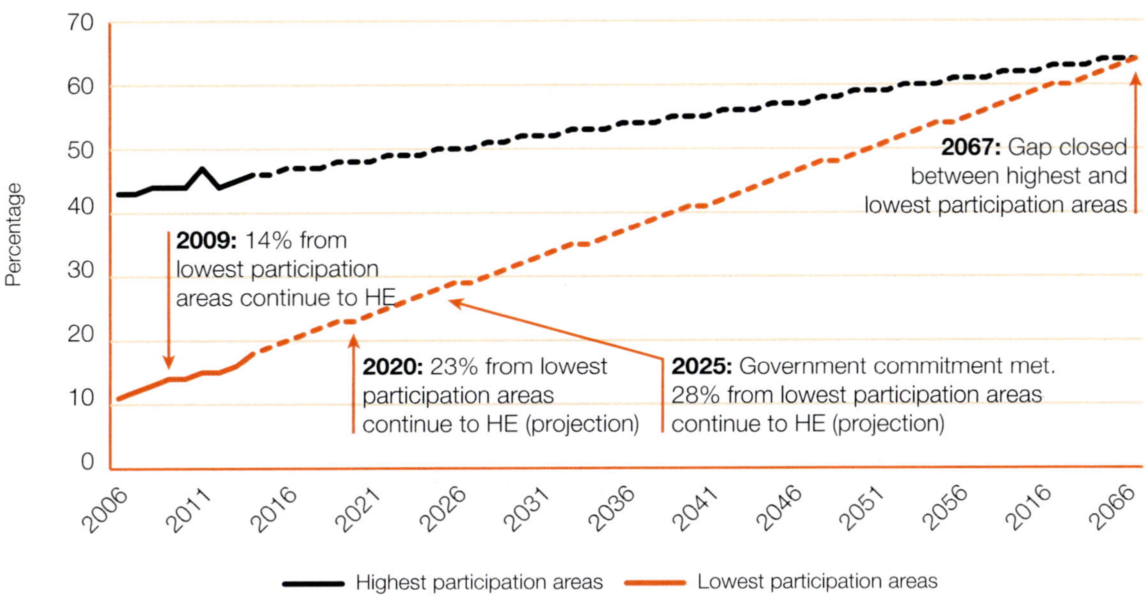

Source: UCAS, *End of Cycle Report 2014*, 2015 (Commission projections)

Just as the mix of students in universities fails to reflect wider society, so too does the social make-up of top firms. Research for the Commission shows that those who went to private or grammar schools make up 40 per cent of trainees in law firms and as many as 70 per cent in some elite accountancy firms.[13] Furthermore, young people from disadvantaged backgrounds who make it to top jobs are likely to be paid less than their counterparts who grew up in professional families. Those who are long-range socially mobile (who started off in families working routine or manual jobs and ended up in professional jobs themselves) earn on average £150 a week less than those whose parents worked in professional and managerial roles.[14]

10 Department for Business, Innovation and Skills, *Fulfilling our Potential: Teaching Excellence, Social Mobility and Student Choice*, 2015
11 UCAS, *End of Cycle Report 2014*
12 Department for Business, Innovation and Skills, *Widening Participation in Higher Education 2015*, 2015
13 Social Mobility and Child Poverty Commission, *A Qualitative Evaluation of Non-educational Barriers to the Elite Professions*, 2015
14 In this instance, an individual is considered long-distance socially mobile if, broadly, they grew up in families where the main occupation was routine or manual and gained a professional job as an adult. London School of Economics, *Introducing the Class Ceiling: Social Mobility and Britain's Elite Occupations*, 2015

The low proportions of less advantaged young people in top firms can partly be accounted for by the fact that few go to the most selective universities. This is because elite firms often recruit candidates from a narrow selection of HE institutions. But this only partly explains the dominance of privileged social backgrounds in some firms. In fact, in many cases, firms' own behaviour exaggerates the trend. Research for the Commission suggests that employers' preconceived ideas of talent cause them to headhunt new recruits in their own image, to the exclusion of others.[15] [16] While background still plays a central role in access to universities and the professions, even when attainment is accounted for, there will remain a distinct social mobility problem at the top of society.

In the remainder of this section, closely connected challenges to fair access to higher education and the professions are examined in detail. First, we assess the wide gap in HE participation between those from disadvantaged backgrounds and others. Second, we explore the acute problem of the gap in access to the most selective universities. Third, we examine the enduring effect of background in access to professional jobs, even after graduation.

Problem 1: The university participation gap is too wide.

Over the past decade there have been positive and welcome trends in university participation: from 2003/04 to 2013/14 the proportion of working-class students at all universities increased by almost a fifth (from 20.9 to 24.7 per cent).[17] Since last year alone there has been an increase of over 9 per cent in young people from areas with the lowest rates of participation accessing HE (from 27,500 to 30,000).[18] These achievements are driven by several factors: improved school results, increased efforts by universities to widen participation (including by those who have studied vocational BTECs rather than academic A levels), and individuals responding to the rising importance of university degrees in the jobs market.

But the participation gap remains wide. Young people eligible for free school meals are a little over half as likely to enter HE by the age of 19 than those not eligible. Because of the gap between the most and least advantaged, the university population fails to reflect the make-up of wider society. In the UK, 41.6 per cent of adults work in professional jobs, but 54.9 per cent of those at university have parents in professional jobs. At the other end of the scale, 30.4 per cent of adults work in routine and manual jobs yet only 24.4 per cent of those in universities have parents in routine and manual jobs.[19] Much of this gap can be explained by differing levels of attainment by social background. But, while universities continue to serve certain groups in society over others, social mobility will suffer.

15 Social Mobility and Child Poverty Commission, op. cit

16 CIPD, *A Head for Hiring: The Behavioural Science of Recruitment and Selection*, 2015

17 Higher Education Statistics Agency (HESA), SMCPC analysis. Working class is here defined as students who reported their parents working in lower supervisory and technical, routine and manual occupations, National Statistics Socio-economic Classification (NS-SEC) 5-7. This differs from the definition used in HESA analysis, which also includes young people whose parents worked in NS-SEC 4 occupations (small employers and the self-employed)

18 UCAS, *End of Cycle Report 2014*, 2014. This has been driven by steep rises in acceptances on the basis of BTEC rather than A level qualifications. As set out in Chapter 3, those accessing HE via this specific vocational route are less likely to access the most selective universities and less likely to achieve top degree results compared with the A level cohort

19 Commission analysis of data provided by HESA. Professional relates to NS-SEC groups 1 and 2; routine relates to NS-SEC 5–7; Office for National Statistics, *Table EMP11: Employment by Socio-Economic Classification*, 2015

Figure 4.2: People from professional backgrounds are far more likely to be in HE

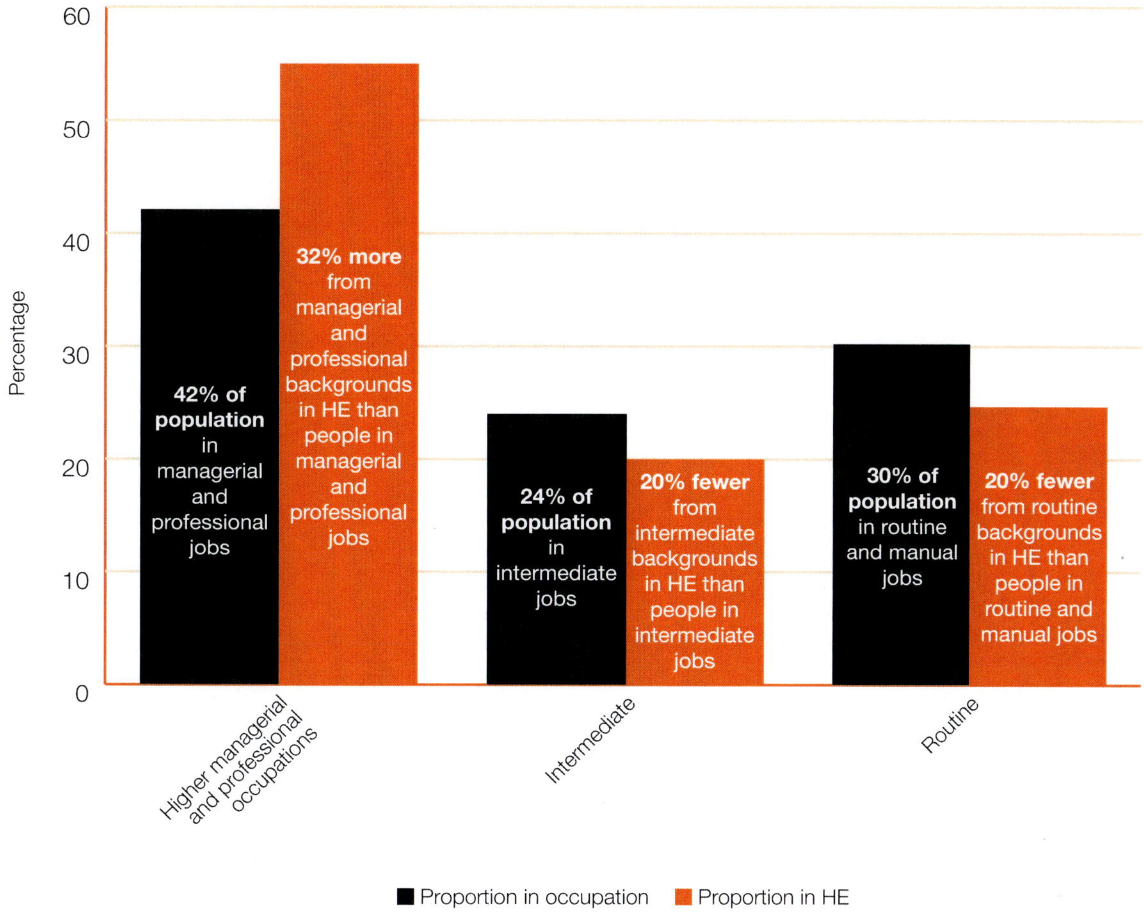

Source: Data supplied by Higher Education Statistics Agency (Commission analysis)

Universities have put their shoulder to the wheel in recent years to widen participation and ensure fairer access. But they are not helping their own efforts by focusing their activity in the wrong place. Despite substantial and rising expenditure on widening participation, the Commission is concerned that the balance is still tilted too far away from universities doing outreach activity in schools – especially those in less-advantaged areas – and too much towards financial support for individual students. The evidence for bursaries as tools to increase numbers of less advantaged pupils in HE is insufficient to justify their being the largest part of participation expenditure.[20 21 22] Last year the Commission called for 25 per cent of widening participation funding to be used to support strategic engagement with schools by 2020. In 2013/14 (the latest year for which there is data), £803 million was spent in total on widening participation driven by access agreements between universities and the Office for Fair Access (OFFA) and additional funding from the Higher Education Funding Council for England (HEFCE).[23] Of this, £122 million was used towards outreach work with schools and young people – around 15 per cent.[24] This is the same proportion as in the previous year.[25] Universities are a vital player in enabling social mobility. But to demonstrate their credentials as real agents of opportunity, more institutions will need to prioritise active outreach with schools, since the evidence suggests it is this activity that returns the greatest social mobility dividend.

20 OFFA, *What do we Know About the Impact of Financial Support on Access and Student Success?*, 2015
21 OFFA, *Do bursaries have an effect on retention rates?*, 2014
22 Widening Participation and Lifelong Learning, *Special Issue on Student Financial Support*, vol. 17, number 3, 2015
23 OFFA, *Outcomes of Access Agreement Monitoring for 2013-14*, 2015
24 Ibid.
25 OFFA, *Outcomes of Access Agreement, Widening Participation Strategic Statement and National Scholarship Programme Monitoring 2012-13*, 2014

There are big gaps between the English regions in the proportion of university widening participation spend that is dedicated to improving access. Universities in Greater London spend on average a quarter of their access agreement expenditure (25 per cent) on access activity (i.e. outreach), more than double the proportion universities spend in the East Midlands (11 per cent).[26] London is fortunate in having a large number of universities and a school system that outperforms many other places. It is therefore disappointing that areas outside of the capital where there is a clear case for more outreach to raise attainment, aspirations and admission continue to lag behind.

Figure 4.3: Average proportion of access agreement expenditure spent on access activity, 2013/14

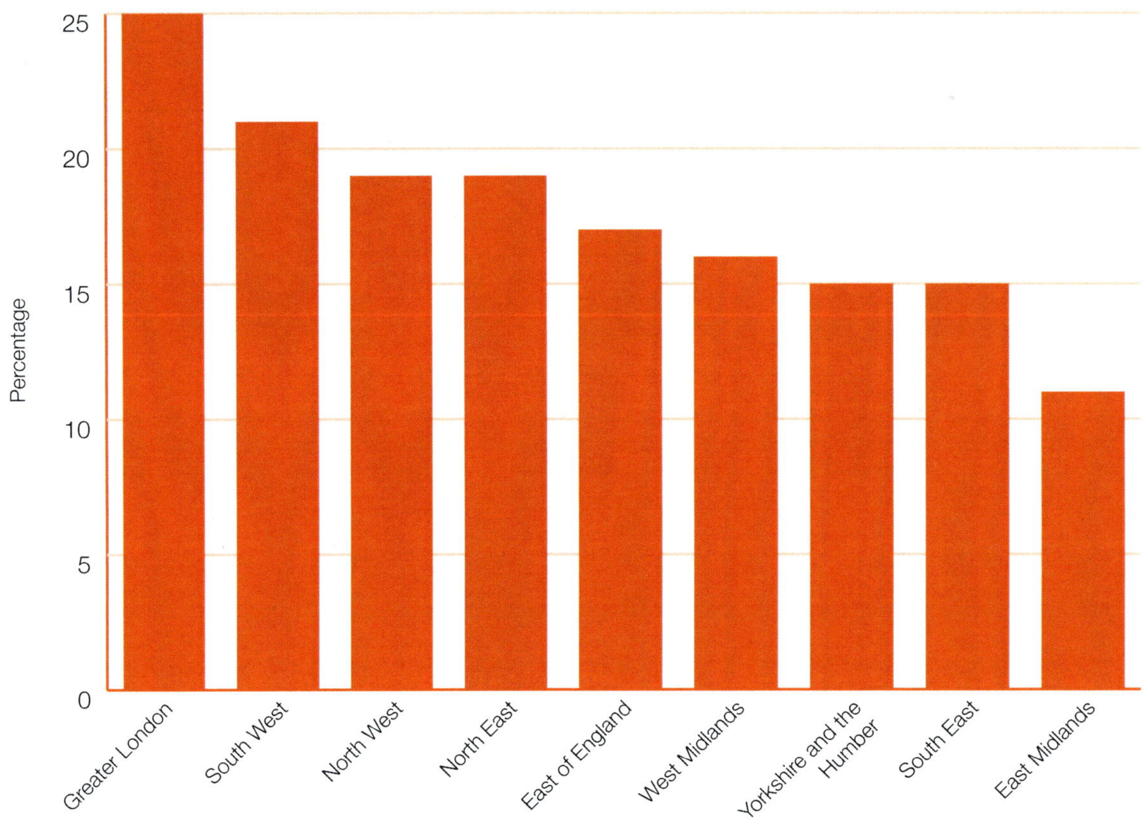

Source: OFFA, *Outcomes of Access Agreement Monitoring for 2013-14*, 2015

Greater focus is needed too to address worrying trends concerning mature and part-time HE students. The decline in numbers reported last year has continued: comparing 2012/13 with 2013/14, first-year undergraduate part-time students are down by around 12 per cent and first-year undergraduate mature students studying for their first degree or other undergraduate degrees are down by over 5 per cent year on year.[27] Overall, part-time student numbers dropped by nearly 50 per cent from 2010/11 to 2013/14.[28] This is an astonishing and deeply worrying trend. The Independent Commission on Fees concluded that there is a strong suggestion that the introduction of higher fees has had an impact on the numbers of part-time and mature students.[29] Despite student loans being made available for part-time students, a range of exemptions means that only one-third of this group were eligible

26 OFFA, *Outcomes of Access Agreement Monitoring for 2013-14*, 2015. The remainder goes towards schemes to improve student success, student progression and institutional financial support. London access spend is boosted by a number of arts and music institutions that allocate large proportions of access agreement expenditure to access activity

27 Numbers calculated from: HESA, *Table 2 – First year HE student enrolments by mode of study, sex, level of study and domicile 2009/10 to 2013/14*, 2015, and HESA, *Table H – Percentage of first year UK domiciled undergraduate students by age, level of study and mode of study*, 2015

28 Universities UK, *Trends in Undergraduate Recruitment*, 2014

29 Independent Commission on Fees, *Independent Commission on Fees 2015 Final Report*, 2015

for loans, and a smaller proportion took them out.[30] Higher education should provide routes to social mobility for people of all ages – not just the youngest. It must be a priority for universities and government to better understand, check and then reverse these trends.

Mature and part-time students are hit by the combined effect of lower participation and persistently high drop-out rates. In 2012/13 more than one in 10 full-time mature students (11.9 per cent) and over one in three part-time students (34.1 per cent) were not in HE a year after entry (two years after entry for part-time students). In comparison, around one in 20 young full-time entrants drop out of HE (5.7 per cent). There has been some improvement for mature students, the non-continuation rate falling by around a fifth from 2002/03 to 2012/13 (15.4 per cent to 11.9 per cent). However, the improvement for part-time students is much less marked. In the five years between 2006/07 and 2011/12 (the biggest gap for which data is available), the drop-out rate fell by only 3.4 per cent (1.2 percentage points).[31] Given that part-time and mature routes have been vehicles for social mobility and second chances in the past, this also merits further government attention.

Finally, the high university drop-out rates for young people from low-participation areas remains of concern. There has been some improvement over the longer term, the overall drop-out rate falling from 10 per cent in 2005/06 to 8 per cent in 2012/13. But in some institutions there is a wide gap between the rate for those from areas with the lowest participation and other areas. Of the 10 institutions with the highest ratio of low participation to high participation area drop-out rates, seven are selective Russell Group institutions.[32] It remains the case that even when the participation gap is closed, the retention gap is damaging the prospects of disadvantaged young people.

Table 4.1: The 10 universities with the greatest ratio of drop-outs among young people from low-participation neighbourhoods compared with those from other neighbourhoods

Institution	Drop-out rate: young entrants from low-participation neighbourhoods (%)	Drop-out rate: young entrants from other neighbourhoods (%)	Ratio of drop-outs: low participation vs others
Durham University	5.4	1.4	3.9
University of Sussex	8.2	2.8	2.9
University of Southampton	6.2	2.2	2.8
University of Oxford	3.6	1.3	2.8
University of Bristol	4.4	1.7	2.6
University of Cambridge	3.3	1.3	2.5
University of Exeter	4.3	1.7	2.5
Leeds College of Art	11.6	4.9	2.4
Newcastle University	4.8	2.2	2.2
Keele University	5.0	2.4	2.1

Source: HESA, *Non-continuation rates*, 2015

30 Higher Education Policy Institute, *It's the Finance, Stupid! The Decline of Part-time Higher Education and What to do About it*, 2015

31 HESA, *Non-continuation Rates*, 2015

32 Ibid.

Problem 2: There is a yawning gap in access to selective universities.

Attending a top university leads on average to better jobs and higher pay. Within four years of graduation, those who attend the most selective institutions earn over £4,300 per year more than those who attend universities created after 1992.[33] Comparing this to vocational options, only higher apprenticeships can compete with degrees in terms of lifetime earnings, but even they cannot match the earnings premium of the most prestigious UK universities.[34]

It is therefore welcome that there has been slight progress since our 2014 annual report in participation gaps at the 24 highly selective Russell Group universities. Over the past year the proportion of state school pupils increased by 1.7 per cent (75.9 to 77.2 per cent) and pupils from less advantaged social groups (NS-SEC 4-7) by 1 per cent (20.4 to 20.6 per cent).[35] These are small but welcome steps forward, but the job is far from complete.

These general improvements do not fix the fundamental issue: access to selective universities remains more likely for those from privileged backgrounds, even taking account of differences in A level grades.[36] In 2013/14 half of the Russell Group universities admitted significantly less state school pupils than their HESA benchmark figure (see Figure 4.4).[37] The HESA benchmarks are estimates of what the social mix of entrants to each university would be if the university's intake was representative of the general intake of those with the required grades entering a UK higher education institution in that year. In relation to access by students from NS-SEC classes 4 to 7,[38] over half of the Russell Group universities fall significantly short of their benchmark. There are an estimated 2,800 missing students at Russell Group universities from state schools and 1,900 missing students from class 4 to 7 backgrounds if the social mix of entrants is compared with the social mix of those with the right grades to enter.[39]

The scale of the fair access challenge becomes clear when individual selective universities are compared to one another (Figure 4.4). At one end of the scale, the five universities furthest from the benchmark set by HESA for admitting pupils from state schools would need to increase their state intake by a fifth or more on average – 28 per cent in the case of Bristol – if they were to achieve 'fair access' on this measure. At the other end, almost all of the students at Queen's Belfast come from the state sector – well above its benchmark of around 85 per cent. There are challenges to overcome, but high performance is certainly possible.

A similar trend (Figure 4.5) is seen in relation to access to the Russell Group by students from less advantaged social backgrounds (NS-SEC 4-7). Disappointingly, but perhaps unsurprisingly, many of the universities that are a way from meeting their HESA state school benchmark are also some distance from achieving the HESA measure of fair access for less advantaged students. Indeed, the bottom seven performers in both Figures 4.4 and 4.5 are the same institutions. However, Queen's Belfast, Queen Mary London and the London School of Economics all perform well against both the social class benchmark and the state school benchmark described above. These three examples confirm once and for all that world class reputation and a student population reflective of wider society are entirely compatible.

33 Sutton Trust, *Earning by Degrees*, 2014. The figures account for student characteristics, A levels attained, degree class and subject. The most universities referred to in the text are the 13 most selective as defined by the Sutton Trust

34 Sutton Trust, *Levels of Success*, 2015

35 HESA, *Widening Participation of Under-represented Groups*, multiple years' data

36 Boliver, V., 'How fair is access to more prestigious UK universities?', *British Journal of Sociology*, vol. 64, issue 2, 2013

37 Data supplied by the Higher Education Statistics Agency. This uses the working-class definition used by HESA social groups 4–7 as described in footnote 17 above

38 This is broader than 'working class' as NS-SEC class 4 includes small employers and the self employed

39 SMCP Commission, *Higher Education: the Fair Access Challenge*, 2013

Figure 4.4: Proportion of entrants from state schools and HESA benchmark by Russell Group institution, 2013–14

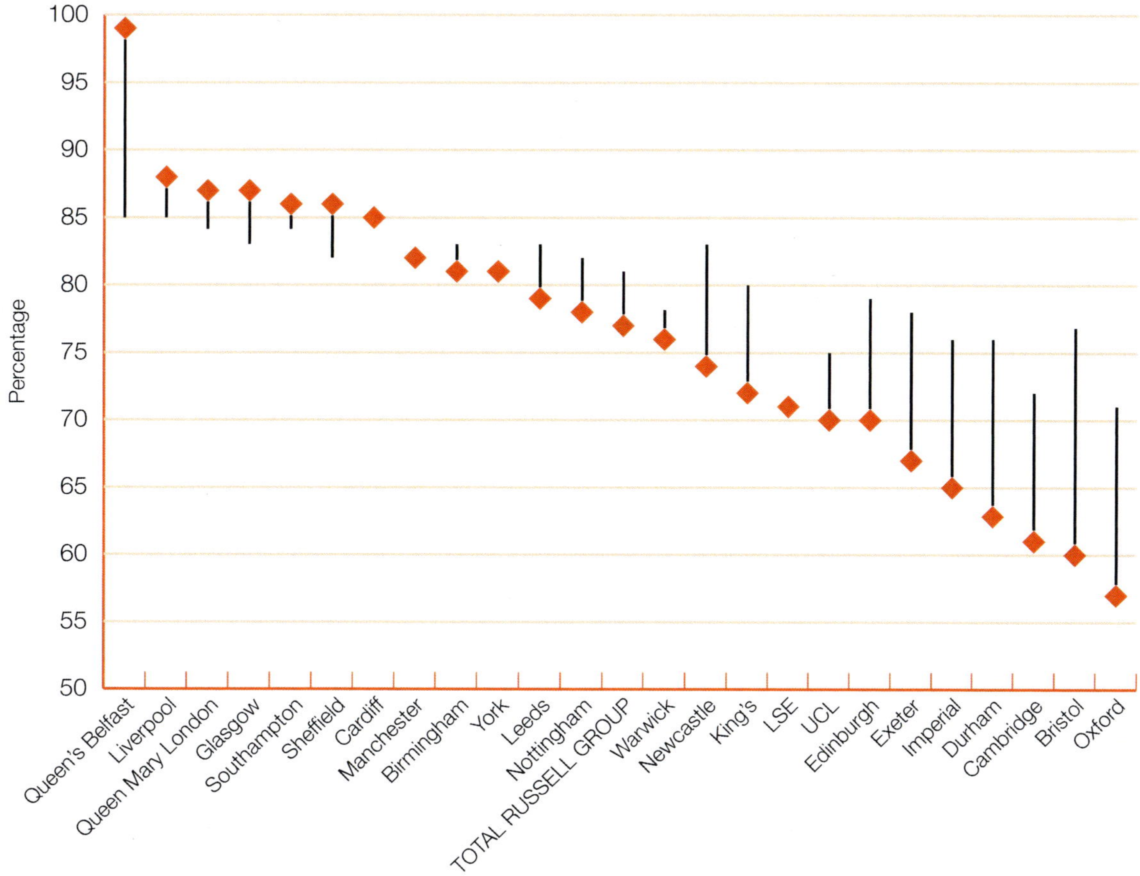

Source: Higher Education Statistics Agency, *Widening participation of under-represented groups*, 2015

Note: In this chart the diamond shows current proportion of state school entrants, the tail is the distance from the HESA benchmark. A diamond with a line beneath it is a university doing better than its benchmark; a diamond with a line above it is a university not meeting its benchmark.

Figure 4.5: Proportion of entrants from less advantaged social backgrounds (NS-SEC 4-7) and HESA benchmark by Russell Group institution, 2013–14

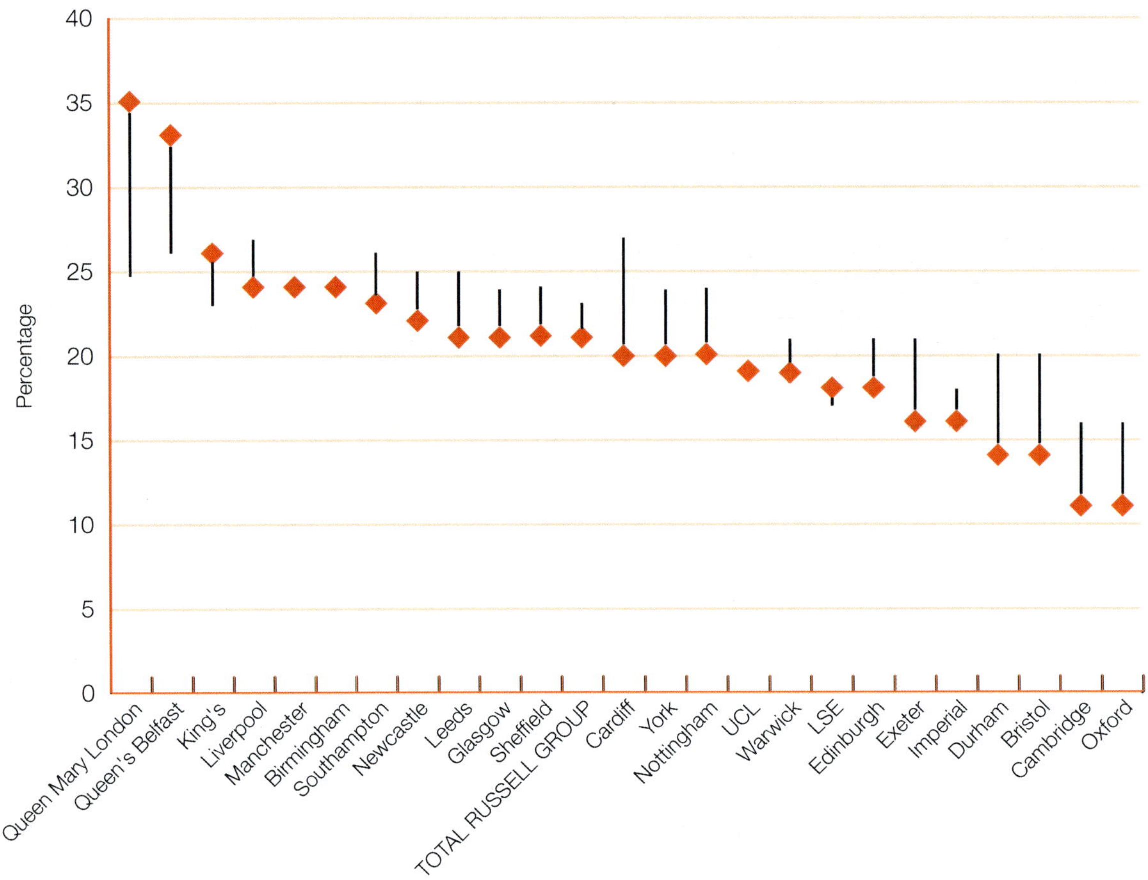

Source: Higher Education Statistics Agency, *Widening participation of under-represented groups*, 2015

Note: In this chart the diamond shows current proportion of pupils from less advantaged social backgrounds, the tail is the distance from the HESA benchmark. A diamond with a line beneath it is a university doing better than its benchmark; a diamond with a line above it is a university not meeting its benchmark.

The gap that remains between admissions and fair access in many universities should not overshadow examples of significant progress (Figure 4.6). Nottingham, University College London (UCL) and Kings' are notable for improving significantly over the last decade, in terms of admitting both state school students and students from less advantaged backgrounds. On the other hand, some universities which currently are behind their benchmarks have gone backwards, notably Bristol and Exeter in terms of admitting state school pupils. Some universities that are shown to have made little or negative progress are actually above their benchmarks (such as Queen Mary or Queen's Belfast) and their apparent lack of progress should be seen in this context. The takeaway message is that some universities have made improvements from a low base. There is no reason why others should not follow suit.

Figure 4.6: Russell Group universities ranked by combined progress in admitting state school pupils and pupils from NS-SEC 4-7 backgrounds, 2003/4 to 2013/14

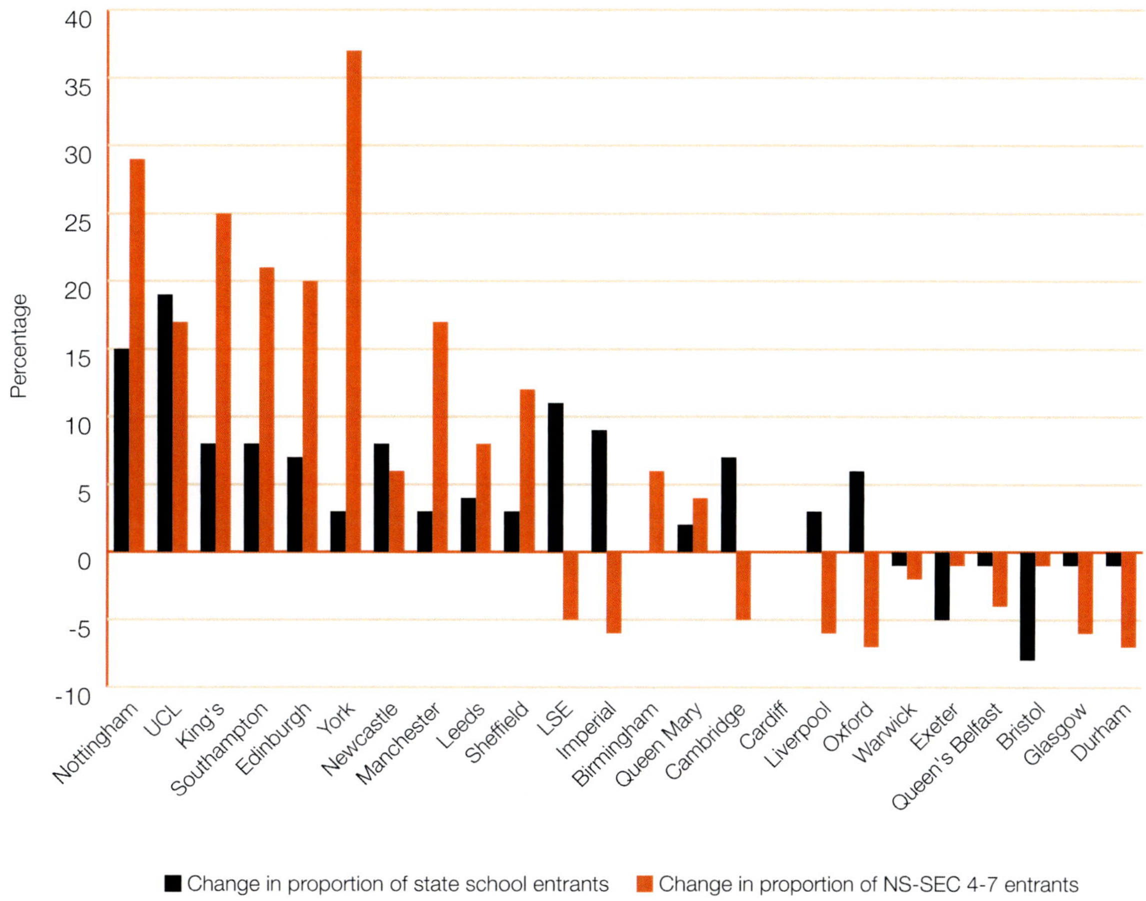

Source: Higher Education Statistics Agency, *Widening Participation of Under-represented Groups*, multiple years' data

Widening participation for ethnic minority students

There has been some, but not enough, progress in widening participation of young people from ethnic minority backgrounds. Over the decade from 2003/04 to 2013/14, the proportion of ethnic minority first-year students rose from 17.1 to 22.5 per cent, an increase of nearly one-third (32 per cent). The greatest proportion of ethnic minority students is found on courses in law, medicine and dentistry, and business studies.[40]

Recent research on ethnic inequalities in accessing selective universities has highlighted that ethnic minority students are less likely to receive offers from Russell Group universities than white applicants with comparable qualifications. This is the case even after the numerical competitiveness of a course is taken into account.[41]

Subsequent UCAS analysis has suggested that most of these inequalities can be explained by the fact that universities make entrance decisions based on predicted rather than actual grades. A limitation of the UCAS analysis is that it excludes the 36,000 students who either apply to Oxford and Cambridge, apply to Medicine or Veterinary sciences or are predicted to get three A*s at A level – a sizeable proportion of those who apply to the Russell Group universities.

40 HESA, *Students by Ethnicity*, 2015

41 Boliver, V., *Exploring Ethnic Inequalities in Admission to Russell Group Universities*, 2015

However, even if the UCAS analysis is right and the differential application success rates can be explained by predicted grades, it would still be extremely worrying – grade prediction is less accurate for disadvantaged young people and the end of modular A levels will increase this uncertainty.

These findings highlight a problem but further research is required to explain what is driving these outcomes. It is not yet clear whether the cause is intentional behaviour of universities, the application process or a combination of the two. To resolve this, UCAS should make the necessary fine-grained data available to researchers, ensuring individual information is anonymised to usual academic standards.

The most selective universities, Oxford and Cambridge, still recruit a disproportionate number of students from private schools. Despite an increase in the proportion of state-educated pupils of 6 per cent between 2003/04 and 2013/14, independently schooled pupils still make up around two-fifths of the intake at both Oxford and Cambridge. To meet their benchmarks, Oxford would need to increase the percentage of state school pupils by a quarter (24 per cent) and Cambridge by a fifth (18 per cent). Only Bristol, where the proportion of the intake from state schools is declining, fares worse on this measure. Part of the reason why the most selective universities admit such a large percentage of privately educated students is that top A level grades flow disproportionately from this group. In 2010 one-third of all pupils in England who achieved A*AA at A level, Cambridge's standard offer at the time, were educated independently.[42] As described in Chapter 2, there is much more work to do to raise the attainment of all pupils, especially those from disadvantaged backgrounds. And our analysis shows that even after taking into account differences in A level performance, unexplained gaps in access between advantaged and disadvantaged groups remain. The challenge faced by young people from poorer households or low-performing schools in achieving good grades, and the quality of advice and guidance from parents, teachers and universities all play a part in this continuing unwelcome trend.

The difficulties encountered by less advantaged young people in accessing Oxbridge is amplified when considered in terms of the colleges that make up the universities.[43] There are large discrepancies between colleges in the number of offers made to applicants from the state sector. Some make less than half of their offers to state-educated pupils, and even the highest performers in this regard still give a quarter or more of their places to the privately educated. Yet even given Cambridge's own estimate of a reasonable target for admissions from state schools on the basis of the social backgrounds of those achieving very high A level grades – somewhere between 60 and 63 per cent – it is clear that some parts of Oxbridge are falling far behind.

42 University of Cambridge, *UK State-Sector Undergraduate Admissions to Cambridge: What is an Achievable Target?*, 2011

43 The universities of Oxford and Cambridge are made up of a number of colleges. There are 38 at Oxford and 31 at Cambridge

Table 4.2: Colleges from Oxford (2013) and Cambridge (2014) with the highest and lowest percentage of offers made to applicants from the state sector [44] [45]

College	Proportion of acceptances by state sector applicants (%)
Colleges with greatest proportion of acceptances by state sector	
Churchill (Cambridge)	73.7
Mansfield (Oxford)	72.7
Girton (Cambridge)	70.2
Wadham (Oxford)	69.4
Homerton (Cambridge)	69.2
Colleges with lowest proportion of acceptances by state sector	
Christ Church (Oxford)	42.2
Trinity (Oxford)	44.3
St Peter's (Oxford)	47.1
Robinson (Cambridge)	47.4
University College (Oxford)	48.3

Source: University of Oxford, *Undergraduate Admissions Statistics: 2013 entry*, 2014; University of Cambridge, *Undergraduate Admissions Statistics: 2014 cycle*, 2015

Nonetheless, it is welcome that contextual measures are increasingly being used by elite universities, including Oxbridge, as a means of addressing the under-representation of lower-income and state-educated students.[46] [47] Too often in the past, university applicants have missed out because of a lack of opportunity to demonstrate their potential. So it is right that where a young person has attended a poor-performing secondary school, is a care leaver or comes from an area with stubbornly low HE participation, their predicted and actual grades should be considered in that light. This practice should be encouraged and continued.

Problem 3: Social background continues to drive graduate outcomes and access to the top professional jobs.

The sea of gowns at graduation ceremonies creates the false impression of a uniform student body headed for equally grand destinations. But differences become clear soon after graduation. Accessing top jobs is tightly connected to the university and the course a young person takes. But even accounting for institution and subject choice, there remains a gap. Young people from the most disadvantaged areas are almost a tenth less likely to be in professional employment three and a half years after graduation. Black African qualifiers are around 14 per cent less likely to be in professional jobs six months after qualification compared with white graduates, a problem that gets worse 40 months after graduation. Three and a half years after leaving university, black African pupils are 16 per cent less likely than white graduates to be in professional roles.[48] Hurdles to social mobility remain for those who have succeeded, perhaps against the odds, in getting into university once they leave.

44 University of Oxford, *Undergraduate Admissions Statistics: 2013 entry*, 2014
45 University of Cambridge, *Undergraduate Admissions Statistics: 2014 cycle*, 2015
46 University of Oxford, *Contextual data* (web page)
47 University of Cambridge, *Contextual data* (web page)
48 Higher Education Funding Council for England, *Differences in Employment Outcomes: Equality and Diversity Characteristics*, 2015

Non-educational barriers to the elite professions

The Commission carried out research into law and accountancy firms in England (primarily London) and financial services firms in Scotland. We found:

- Firms look for 'talent' in a small number of highly selective universities, which have very high proportions of middle-class and privately educated students. They then coach potential applicants through their recruitment processes. As a result, in some law firms around 40 per cent of staff were educated at fee-paying schools – compared with just 7 per cent in the wider population.
- Notions of talent can often be skewed towards middle-class characteristics. One recruiter interviewed for the research commented, "I'm very interested in people who've gone travelling"; another talked of the importance of "holidays that you've been on, places you've visited"; another revealed that "accents make a difference, [the] things people talk about".
- Disadvantaged graduates are less likely to be promoted, even if recruited. The report finds that "...while these patterns [of low social mobility] may be the result of conscious discrimination, they can also result from the tendency of more senior professionals to promote in their own image and thus 'misrecognise' merit".

The challenge for graduates from less advantaged backgrounds in accessing elite professions starts before they finish their course. One important factor in an individual gaining a position in a top firm is whether the university they attend is targeted by firms' outreach activity. Elite employers are more likely to focus their attention on a narrow group of universities, which less privileged young people are least likely to attend. On average, only one in 10 of the students in the universities most targeted by graduate employers are from working class backgrounds (NS-SEC 5-7). There is a self-fulfilling prophecy when firms seeking a certain kind of polish in their young recruits go only to a narrow selection of universities. Firms are missing real talent, and young people are missing out on the opportunities that they have been led to believe university will open.

Table 4.3: Proportion of students from working class backgrounds (NS-SEC 5-7) in universities most targeted by graduate employers.[49 50] Thirty per cent of those in employment are in NS-SEC 5–7, a far greater level than in the universities listed above.[51]

University	% students NS-SEC 5-7 in 2013/14
University of Oxford	7.2
University of Cambridge	7.2
University of Bristol	8.9
Durham University	9.5
Imperial College London	11.6
University of Warwick	13.1
University College London	13.6
University of Nottingham	14.1
University of Leeds	14.9
University of Manchester	17.0

Source: Office for National Statistics, *All in Employment by Socio-economic Classification*, 2015

49 Social Mobility and Child Poverty Commission, op. cit.
50 NS-SEC data supplied by Higher Education Statistics Agency
51 Office for National Statistics, *All in Employment by Socio-economic Classification*, 2015

In addition to the activity of graduate recruiters, young people's ability to access unpaid internships or other forms of work experience depends on background. In 2014 one-third of graduates working as interns were found to be doing so unpaid – and the Sutton Trust estimates that the cost of an unpaid internship is over £900 a month in London and nearly £800 a month in Manchester.[52] The implication is that young people from better-off backgrounds are far better placed to exploit these opportunities. On average, around one-third of placements are converted into graduate positions, which for some will make the expense more than worthwhile.[53] The Commission and others have previously called for this practice to be ended – and at the least for work to recognised as such and paid for. Until these changes take place, some routes into top jobs will be reserved for children who are fortunate enough to be able to draw funds from the bank of Mum and Dad.

Parental education and the school a young person attended also continue to have an effect on graduates' pay. There is some good news: students whose parents did not have degrees appear to earn more as new graduates if they graduate from the most selective universities. This amounts to just under £1,000 per year for Oxbridge graduates. On the other hand, a private school education also has a positive effect on earnings – even when university, subject and degree classification are accounted for – with starting salaries £1,350 higher than for state-school counterparts.[54] Three and a half years after graduation, privately schooled young people earn £4,500 more than their state-school educated peers. Half of this difference cannot be explained by the type of higher education institution attended or prior attainment – suggesting this gap could be driven by soft skills including character and a network of contacts.[55] Gaps that have opened early in life are once more seen to have enduring effects.

As well as the effects of individual and family education on adult income, there is a social mobility penalty imposed on graduates who make it to professional jobs from working-class backgrounds. The London School of Economics has identified a 'class ceiling' where two people in similar jobs are likely to earn very different salaries depending on whether their parents worked in the same area or whether they themselves achieved long-distance social mobility. The long-range socially mobile – those who work in top professional socio-economic groupings as adults but grew up in families where the main work was routine or manual – earn on average £7,700 less than those who grew up in families with jobs in the highest socio-economic bracket. This effect will in part be due to the kinds of schools and universities young people from different backgrounds attend. An additional explanatory factor is that different firms within 'top job' categories will have different pay and may seek to recruit, intentionally or otherwise, from a more or less privileged pool of candidates. But the fact remains that even when a child from a poor family accesses top jobs, it is probable their pay will be less than their privileged peers.[56] This is not a level playing field: those who grow up in disadvantaged families are playing uphill and towards narrow goals.

4.3 How are these problems being addressed?

Access to higher education

The November 2015 Green Paper *Fulfilling our Potential* lays out the Government's plans for higher education.[57] It makes a number of welcome commitments with the aim of driving improvements in social mobility. Primarily these are:

52 Sutton Trust, *Internship or Indenture?*, 2014
53 Association of Graduate Recruiters, *Summer Survey*, 2013
54 Sutton Trust, *Earning by Degrees*, 2014
55 Sutton Trust, *Private Pay Progression*, 2015
56 London School of Economics, *Introducing the Class Ceiling: Social Mobility and Britain's Elite Occupations*, 2015
57 Department for Business, Innovation and Skills, *Fulfilling our Potential: Teaching Excellence, Social Mobility and Student Choice*, 2015

- A commitment to improve access to HE by pupils from areas where participation is low;
- Streamlining of existing widening participation arrangements under a new umbrella body, the Office for Students. This will incorporate the role of OFFA – the fair access regulator – and the main functions of HEFCE, which also undertakes research and provides funding to open access to university;
- Use of linked data to hold universities to account for the employment outcomes of their students as part of a new Teaching Excellence Framework;
- New powers for the Office for Students to require data to be made available to tackle access issues.

The Green Paper confirms the Government's commitment to double the proportion of young people from low participation areas accessing HE by 2020, compared with 2009 levels. This is a substantial ambition. HEFCE finds the rate of increase in HE participation for the target group might need to as much as triple to achieve this.[58] Achieving the same target in relation to children on free school meals would require a doubling in the current rate of increase. It is important that a focus on low participation areas is not at the expense of disadvantaged youngsters, but however the target is measured, the objective provides welcome encouragement to focus more on increasing participation for all. Plans to reduce the £380m Student Opportunity Fund by up to half have also been announced.[59] This fund is focused on retention and progression of disadvantaged students. While cutting this fund may not have a direct impact on entry from disadvantaged areas there needs to be more clarity over how current levels of drop-out will be addressed. A comprehensive plan is needed that sets out how the Government's objectives in this area will be met while funding is being reduced.

Thankfully the Government has restated its commitment to an independent fair access regulator. OFFA, which will in due course become part of the new Office for Students, plans to target participation work further on retention and progression of disadvantaged groups. The Commission believes these are necessary areas for focus, not least because of the spending reductions above. The Commission looks forward to seeing how the new Office for Students takes this mission to heart – for mature and part-time students as well as young entrants – and how universities respond in their access agreements to this continued push for action.[60] Further, in the Spending Review the Government set out an intention to work with the Director of Fair Access to ensure universities take more responsibility for widening access, including collaborating on outreach to reduce inequality in admissions. This seems a sensible approach, but it will be important to target this at the right areas and ensure all universities – whether more or less selective – are involved.

Beyond the recent Green Paper, the Government has announced that from 2016-17 living-cost grants for less well-off students will become loans. For a three-year course, this means average debt will rise from £40,500 to around £53,000 for the poorest 40 per cent of students.[61] For those who go on to successful professional careers this will not be problematic. High earnings will more than make up for additional debt. But for those who do not convert their degree into a top job it will increase their debt burden and ultimately lead to a cost the Government will pick up if the debt goes unpaid.

The implications of this policy for widening participation are not clear. It is good news that previous increases in fees did not by and large reduce HE participation for young full-time students. But it also was the case that when higher fees were introduced in 2012, grants for

58 HEFCE, *Delivering Opportunities for Students and Maximising their Success: Evidence for Policy and Practice 2015-2020*, 2015

59 Department for Business Innovation and Skills and HM Treasury, *Department for Business, Innovation and Skills' Settlement at the Spending Review 2015*, 2015

60 Office for Fair Access, *Strategic Plan 2015-2020*, 2015

61 Institute for Fiscal Studies, *Analysis of the Higher Education Funding Reforms Announced in Summer Budget 2015*, 2015

the poorest students increased by 10 per cent.[62] Students are currently willing to shoulder substantial debts but it is less clear whether a point will be reached where the quantity of debt will seem too big and deter young people from applying to university. Trust in the student finance system may be further weakened following the decision to retrospectively change repayment conditions, freezing repayment thresholds in cash terms rather than increasing them in line with earnings. There is a need to proceed with greater caution, given the direct impact of the switch from grants to loans on the group whose participation in HE the Government seeks to increase. The confirmed freeze of the threshold at which student loans are repaid may also be significant, as students leaving university on lower incomes will see a proportional increase in repayments. Given that disadvantaged students are less likely to get into professional jobs, this could also have a deterrent effect.[63] Should early evidence come to light that this policy will reduce participation by disadvantaged students, the Government will need to intervene or risk missing its public commitment.

Conversely, the welcome uncapping of student numbers could have a broadly beneficial effect on increased participation. More students attending university will lead to a growth in opportunities. The Government estimates 60,000 additional students a year will be starting HE from 2016.[64] The immediate impact is clear: acceptances in 2015 are up by more than 12,000 (3 per cent) on the previous year.[65] Further, a commitment to allow part-time students to take maintenance loans and an extension of loans to postgraduates up to the age of 60 may help reverse recent declines. Should these trends in participation continue, the longer-term effect will be significant. Specifically it will present more chances for young people from less privileged backgrounds to access HE. This is positive news but it also comes with challenges, not least in ensuring that the rapid increase in numbers is met by support so that all entrants can succeed and that provision can expand in quantity without dilution in quality. For £9,000 a year, or more in the future, students and their families expect no less.

Access to the professions

The Social Mobility Business Compact, which began during the last parliament, continues under this Government. The compact is a voluntary commitment employers make to improve social mobility. In addition there is a 'champion tier' of firms that have agreed to stretching targets in relation to collection and publication of data about their own workforces and to examine how they can increase the number of people they recruit from less advantaged or minority backgrounds. The Department for Business provides a forum for the Champions' Tier of firms to discuss and share best practice and has done a good job in holding firms to account for the criteria they have committed to. A report will be published in 2016 detailing the progress the champion firms have made. This is clear evidence of how government can provide real leadership in an important area. Over the next five years there is a need to continue working with those already signed up but also to expand the number of firms working towards becoming national – and global – leaders in opportunity.

The past year has seen continued activity by professional employers to improve access and make the case for social mobility. A number of firms have taken action to build the evidence base for reform. This includes publishing diversity statistics, and demonstrating commitment to transparency in relation to the socio-economic background of those they employ.[66] The Civil Service has commissioned research into why those from lower socio-economic groups are less likely to apply to its Fast Stream graduate programme, and less likely to succeed if they do apply. Alongside an improved understanding of the barriers disadvantaged young people face in their careers, the Commission hopes the final report will provide the evidence and impetus to adjust the recruitment process itself. In financial services, J.P. Morgan has

62 Ibid.
63 Sutton Trust, *Unfair Deal*, 2015
64 HM Treasury, *Autumn Statement*, 2013
65 UCAS, *Interim Assessment of UCAS Acceptances by Intended Entry Year, Country of Provider and Qualifications Held*, 2015
66 For example, see Ernst & Young, *UK and Ireland Diversity and Inclusiveness Statistics*, 2015

started a residential scheme in partnership with the Social Mobility Foundation; early evidence suggests good outcomes for the young people who have taken part.[67] While it is critical that employers do not delay improving access, the specific barriers within the recruitment process – and what works in overcoming them – must be understood if real change is to take place.

Professional firms are also actively changing their hiring process. And firms have responded to the challenge of under-representation among new employees – either graduates or school leavers – of less advantaged socio-economic groups. Since our last annual report, firms in accountancy, law and professional services have ended A level and other academic criteria for graduate jobs, which disadvantage those who attended poorer schools,[68] [69] [70] and created new apprenticeship routes to top professional occupations.[71] A number of firms now subscribe to services that put young people's grades in the context of their social background when making hiring decisions.[72] [73] These are most welcome changes and a necessary first step in making professional jobs accessible to a greater proportion of the population.

Finally there has been a range of actions taken to advocate for social mobility, provide guidance and raise the profile of these issues. In the legal and accountancy professions, the Prime[74] and Access Accountancy[75] schemes have similar objectives to the Business Compact. As with the compact, good progress was made initially, with many firms signing up. There is a need to ensure that the profile of these schemes remains high – the recent best-practice event led by Access Accountancy is the kind of activity required. Other sectors have produced guidance to drive change. In medicine, Health Education England has published a widening participation strategy, aiming to tackle lack of social diversity in the profession,[76] including actions around widening access to medicine courses at university and reviewing admissions procedures at medical schools through the Medical Schools Council Selecting for Excellence review.[77] In engineering, the Institution of Mechanical Engineers has set out proposals for government and the industry to improve participation.[78]

All of this shows that an increasing number of sectors and employers have recognised the scale of the task and are beginning the tough process of working out how change can be achieved. There is no doubt the issue of fair access to professional employment is now on the agenda. The question is how to convert the welcome recognition of the need for change into real action to ensure it takes place.

67 Institute for Fiscal Studies, *An Evaluation of the impact of the Social Mobility Foundation Programmes on Education Outcomes*, 2015
68 PWC, *UCAS Tariff Changes*, 2015 (www.pwc.com)
69 Ernst & Young, *Joining EY*, 2015 (www.ey.com)
70 Grant Thornton, *Applications and Minimum Requirements*, 2015 (www.grantthornton.co.uk)
71 KPMG, *KPMG Announces Plans for a New Apprenticeship Programme*, 2015 (www.kpmg.com)
72 Deloitte, *Social mobility: it's Not Where You're From, it's Where You're Going*, 2015 (www.deloitte.com)
73 Linklaters, *We'll Look at Substance Rather Than Polish*, 2015 (www.linklaters.com)
74 www.primecommitment.org
75 www.accessaccountancy.org
76 NHS Health Education England, *Widening Participation: it Matters! Our Strategy and Initial Action Plan*, 2014
77 Medical Schools Council, *Selecting for Excellence Final Report*, 2014
78 Institution of Mechanical Engineers, *Social Mobility and the Engineering Profession*, 2015

4.4 How can we go further?

Higher education participation

The Government's commitments in the Green Paper to widening participation are the right starting point. Now there is a need to ensure that the opportunity presented by the creation of the Office for Students – not least putting all access activity under one roof – pays off. The most pressing challenge is the new commitment to double the proportion of young people from low participation areas entering HE. It is likely to be missed if recent trends continue. And even if the target is met, though more disadvantaged young people will be entering universities, the gap between poor students and others will barely have narrowed. Further, if widening participation activity over coming years serves the target exclusively there is a risk that disadvantaged pupils in high-participation areas (for example, many London boroughs) will lose out. By the end of the decade the Commission projects that those from low participation areas will still be less than half as likely to go to HE compared with those from areas with the highest participation. And youngsters eligible for free school meals will still be one-third less likely to go to HE by age 19 when compared with others.[79] Of course, a substantial responsibility falls on parents, schools and communities to ensure young people are able to succeed at school. But universities and experts in this area, namely OFFA and HEFCE, retain a vital role in directing access funding to ensure this continued progress.

The current access agreement system has put widening participation front and centre in universities' thinking but it does not yet present a solution to the problem of raising participation across the country. In response to this challenge, HEFCE has established 38 National Networks for Collaborative Outreach – schemes to bring institutions together to improve HE participation in their areas. These schemes are time limited, with funding available only until the end of the 2015/16 financial year. An evaluation is planned by HEFCE but will not be available until the end of 2016.[80] This gap in information is a challenge, especially as networks will need to become financially self-sustaining after current funding ends. But it would make it harder to widen participation – and for the Government to meet its target of doubling the proportion of young people from low participation areas entering HE – if the collaborative response to the participation problem was lost. It is right that the Spending Review has underlined the importance of collaborative action and that the government and OFFA will look into this. The university sector as a whole must spearhead the solution and the structures need to be in place to enable this.

The Government's endorsement of the role of OFFA provides welcome support for widening participation activity in England. But whether the model of individual access agreements can deliver the shift in pace needed to achieve the Government's ambitions is less certain. While on average progress is being made, some areas lag substantially behind. In the five local authorities with the lowest progression rates to HE for pupils from poor families, fewer than one in 10 disadvantaged young people are likely to progress to university. In the five authorities with the highest progression rates, nearly half of all young people eligible for free school meals progress to HE.[81] Unless the lowest-achieving areas make more progress in the next few years, the Government will most likely miss its target of doubling the proportion of young people from areas with low participation in HE by 2020. Even if it is hit, unless those poorly performing areas see focused action, some parts of the country might barely reach 2009 levels of progression by the end of the decade.

79 Projected from Department for Business, Innovation and Skills, *Widening Participation in Higher Education*, 2015
80 London Metropolitan University, *Evaluation of the National Networks for Collaborative Outreach (NNCOs)*, 2015
81 Department for Business, Innovation and Skills, *Widening Participation in Higher Education 2015*, 2015

Figure 4.7: English local authority districts with the highest and lowest progression of young people eligible for free school meals to selective universities

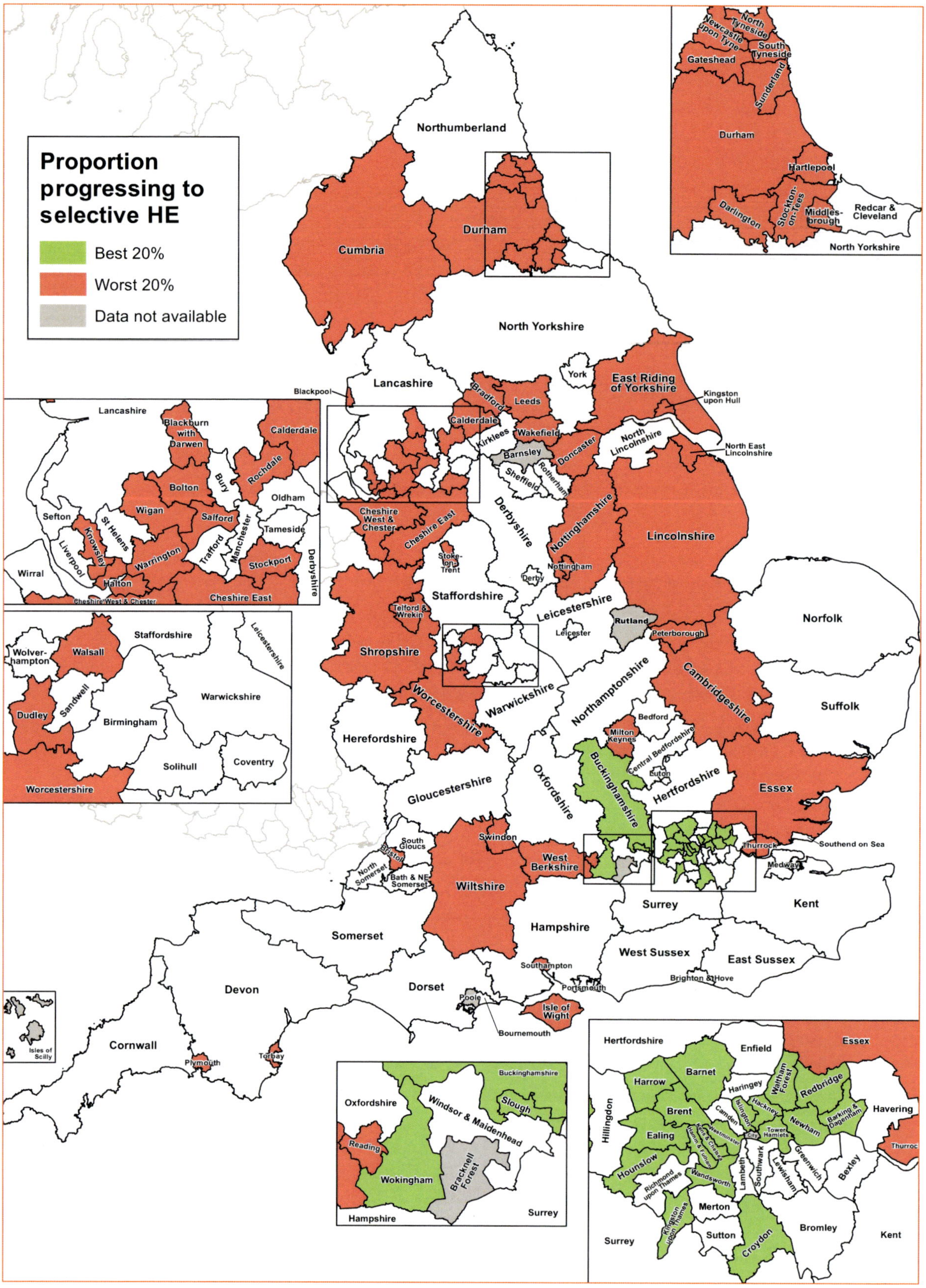

Source: Department for Business, Innovation and Skills. Reproduced by permission of Ordnance Survey on behalf of HMSO, 2015

The risk of current policy for widening access is that many universities, especially more selective institutions, will continue to focus narrowly on target groups of students, for instance exceptional candidates from under-represented backgrounds, and dismiss general activity to drive up participation among disadvantaged students as too difficult or not their responsibility.[82] On the other hand, universities that already attract large proportions of less advantaged pupils will spend their access funding, logically, on retention and success. These possible trends, combined with the preference for spending widening participation funds on bursaries and grants, seem likely to further squeeze out broad-based and shared programmes to increase participation of less advantaged young people. It is not acceptable for universities individually or collectively to in effect write off schools that send few or no pupils to good universities. Teachers and families alone cannot shift attitudes and ambitions to the extent required if lasting change is to be achieved.[83] Universities need to find new ways of collaborating so that they can use their collective muscle to crack the hardest nuts – those schools in those parts of the country that currently send the fewest disadvantaged children to HE. The opportunity to use the HE reforms in the pipeline to solve this problem should not be allowed to pass by.

Action is also needed to improve access to data on widening participation, as the HE Green Paper rightly acknowledges. The lack of availability of detailed UCAS data to identify specific outcomes and trends has been noted previously by the Commission as a block to progress.[84] UCAS is rightly concerned about broad access to information that may be used to identify individuals. But the Commission believes there are ways that data can be securely shared to allow vital questions to be answered, for instance via secure academic data portals. Without this, some issues in relation to participation will remain hidden, specifically the detailed selection decisions of universities, and trends in participation by background and location of residence. We hope that the Office for Students will work with UCAS to ensure future and historical data is made accessible, with stringent safeguards.

Uncapping of student numbers will lead to more HE entrants who have not followed the traditional academic A level route. There was an 8 per cent increase in HE applicants with BTECs between 2014 and 2015, while over the same period the proportion with A levels remained steady.[85] Lessons from Australia, which has a similar HE system and removed the numbers cap in 2012, suggest that universities will need to provide support for those who have gained entry via non-traditional qualifications or those less familiar with independent study.[86] Failure to do so risks lower degree outcomes and a greater chance of disadvantaged students dropping out.[87] There will need to be real clarity over how this will be pursued since the HEFCE budget used to support retention and progression of students, the Student Opportunity Fund, is being reduced. An increase in the stock of university places needs to be met by clear policy to ensure drop-out rates – particularly among disadvantaged students – come down.

Planned changes to A levels present further challenges to widening participation, to which the HE sector will need to respond. As detailed in Chapter 2, A levels are becoming two-year courses with exams at the end. A/S levels can still be taken but will no longer count towards final A level grades. Some schools, perhaps those with funding to spare, are likely to continue to enter students for A/S levels. Even though this will not count towards final A levels it will provide an invigilated grade that can be used on UCAS forms. Pupils in schools who choose not to or cannot afford to prepare pupils for A/S levels as well as A levels will lose out as they will lack objective scores to present to universities.

82 University of the West of England, *AIMS Project: Towards a New Understanding of Widening Participation*, 2015
83 Department for Business Innovation and Skills, *Understanding Progression into Higher Education for Disadvantaged and Under-represented Groups*, 2015
84 Social Mobility and Child Poverty Commission, *Data and Public Policy: Trying to Make Social Progress Blindfolded*, 2015
85 UCAS, *Interim Assessment of UCAS Acceptances by Intended Entry Year, Country of Provider and Qualifications Held*, 2015
86 Higher Education Policy Institute, *A Guide to the Removal of Student Number Controls*, 2014
87 Times Higher Education, *Clearing the Way to Higher Dropout Rates? Lessons from Uncapped Australia*, 2015

This fundamental change to the HE application process reopens the debate about whether to move the timing of the university application process so that students know their A level grades, rather than universities having to rely on predicted grades. There is a strong case to consider a shift to a post-qualification university admission process, despite the logistical challenges involved. First, with A/S levels being phased out, universities will be decreasingly able to predict reliably what applicants will actually get. And non-academic aspects of application may begin to take on a greater role, benefiting those from privileged backgrounds. Second, predictions based on GCSE scores will be more inaccurate than predications made on a track record of A/S level modules, and will be most inaccurate for the least advantaged.[88] Third, the reputation of a school may become disproportionately important in university selection decisions: admission tutors may use historical success of a school as a proxy for accuracy of grade predictions. This would assist those who can access the best schools. Taken together these risks pose substantial challenges to the achievement of the Prime Minister's widening participation objective. The Commission believes that the new Office for Students should take responsibility for reviewing the evidence and proposing a solution before the admissions process becomes a block to opportunity.

Student outcomes and access to top jobs

The Teaching Excellence Framework announced in the Higher Education Green Paper will create new and necessary accountability to ensure that universities are delivering value to their pupils. Quality of teaching is important to social mobility, and the framework may help some less advantaged pupils make informed choices about study. As the Green Paper acknowledges, the ultimate metric for social mobility is outcomes data. For young people, a clear picture of the kinds of employment and income a given course or institution provides is increasingly vital. Tuition fees make that data important for parents and families too. It is good news that the Government has put the legislation in place to enable data from different sources to be linked, and plans to act on this. The early studies using these approaches show their value and potential.[89] As part of its commitment to data transparency and widening participation, the Government should accelerate this process of linking and publishing data over this parliament so that students can make decisions informed by the outcomes that matter.

The growth in new schemes and strategies that professional employers have announced to broaden their intakes is welcome. But there remains a patchwork quilt of action. Some firms and professions have risen to the challenge and begun the painful process of change. Others are barely acknowledging the problem. If access to the top jobs in the economy is to be genuinely open and fair, the changes that some are making need to become the preserve of all. The fair access agenda needs to move from the margins to the mainstream of employment practice across the professions. The key recommendations of the Commission's research in this space,[90] and the champion tier of the Government's Social Mobility Business Compact (which the Commission helped design), are a good starting point and should be taken to heart by many more employers.[91]

Real change also requires collection and analysis of data to assess the scale of the problem. This means better understanding the social make-up of current staff as well as new recruits. The Civil Service's approach to this is an example of a thorough and serious attempt to start a programme of work.[92] The ideal would be for all major professional employers to routinely collect background data from their new recruits and current employees so they can track progress and act on problems.

88 Department for Business, Innovation and Skills, *Investigating the Accuracy of Predicted A level Grades as Part of the UCAS Admissions Process*, 2011

89 Institute for Fiscal Studies, *Comparing Sample Survey Measures of English Earnings of Graduates with Administrative Data During the Great Recession*, 2015

90 Social Mobility and Child Poverty Commission, *A Qualitative Evaluation of Non-educational Barriers to the Elite Professions*, 2015

91 Department for Business, Innovation and Skills, *Social Mobility Business Champion Criteria*, 2014

92 Civil Service, forthcoming

The public sector has made some progress in ensuring internships are available to those from disadvantaged backgrounds. The Whitehall Internship Scheme and the Summer Diversity Internship Programme currently provide around 400 places, around a quarter of the total paid work-experience places on offer in the state sector. In total, the public sector now offers the second-highest number of paid work-experience places, behind only investment banking.[93] Other organisations will need to follow suit to show that their intent translates into opportunities on the ground. We are a long way from access to internships being based on what, not who, you now. Many more professions and employers need to take action to set that right.

93 High Fliers, *The Graduate Market in 2015*, 2015 (www.highfliers.co.uk)

The distance to go in increasing access to the professions

Accountancy and law are farthest ahead in their efforts to improve social mobility for their graduate intake. In accountancy, nearly nine out of 10 recruiters report targeted strategies to address socio-economic differences; in law, the proportion is seven in 10. Fewer than half of all other sectors have similarly targeted approaches.

Monitoring the background of staff is an essential tool to understand the social mobility challenge faced by employers. Accountancy, law and the public sector all perform well in this regard, with over half of all recruiters reporting monitoring activity. In most other sectors, monitoring is a minority activity: on average only just over one in 10 firms monitors the social background of recruits or employees (12 per cent).

Figure 4.8: Proportion of graduate recruiters with target strategies or data monitoring programmes to address socio-economic diversity

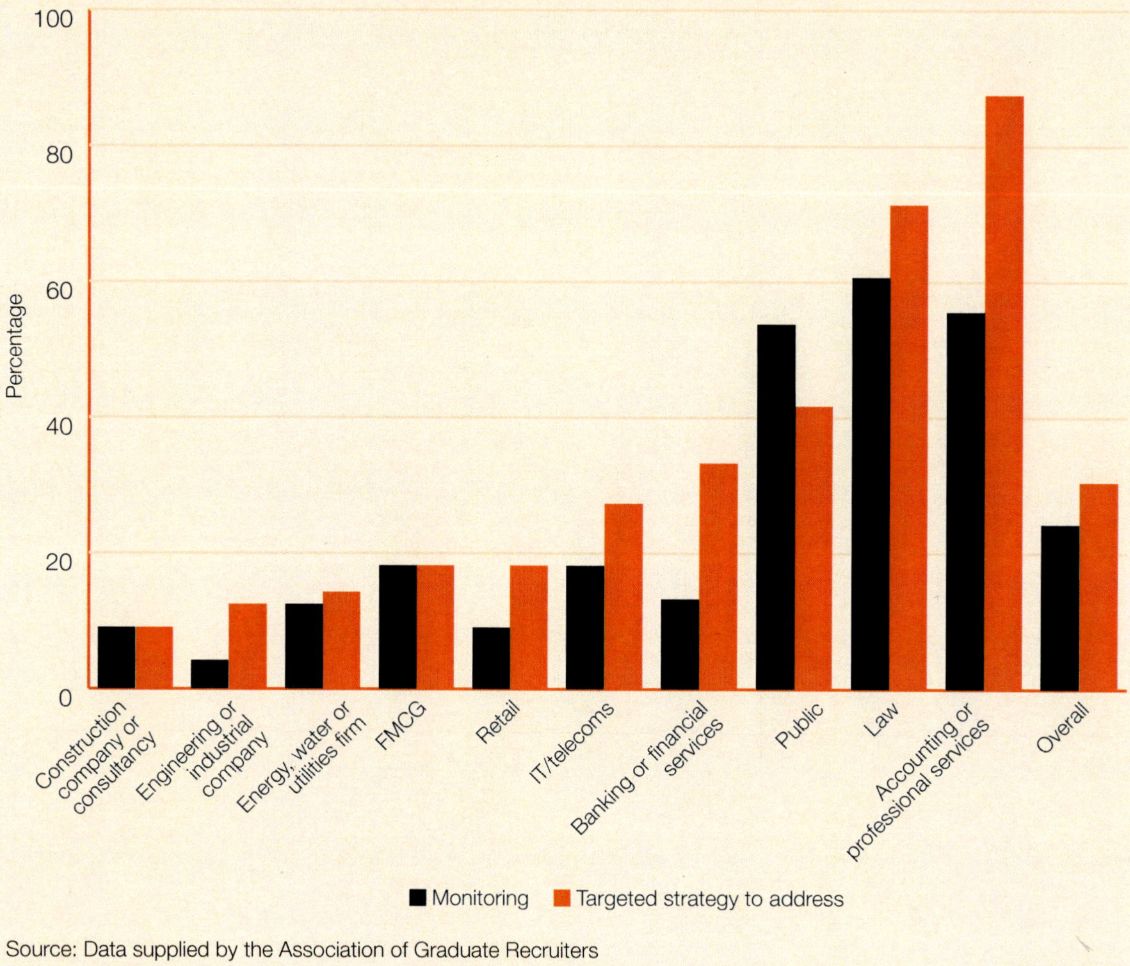

Source: Data supplied by the Association of Graduate Recruiters

Those sectors where progress lags need to look to those that have implemented their own schemes. Specifically, firms that are doing little need to consider what more they can do beyond targeting race and gender as priorities for action on inequality.

4.5 Conclusion and Recommendations

Despite much focus and more action over the past few years, the gaps in access to leading universities and to top jobs are a high-profile reminder of where our nation fails the fairness test. Schools, as described in Chapter 2, need to improve young people's outcomes but universities must match this by ensuring outreach activity gets where it is needed. The Government's target to increase the number of students from low participation areas in HE sharpens this challenge. Universities need to take greater ownership for the outcomes of their students, and professional firms must do more to ensure their approach to finding and choosing new staff members is genuinely open and fair. There is no lever in Whitehall that can be pulled to solve this, but the Government can provide leadership. As a nation we are rightly proud of our world-class universities and professional companies. At this point, those with responsibility must pull together to make sure opportunities for access are fairly shared and talent is not missed.

Recommendation 1: The Government's widening participation commitment requires around 12,000 more students from low participation areas to enter HE in 2020 compared to today. To ensure outreach activity accelerates to meet this vision, 5 per cent of universities' widening participation funding – around £40 million – should be ring-fenced for collaborative action and coordinated by OFFA and the new Office for Students.[94]

The current system of access agreements creates accountability for widening participation at the level of an individual university and ensures genuine consideration is given to this important issue. But universities as a body of organisations have no shared responsibility to increase participation in general and in all parts of the country. What this means is there can remain a large number of local authorities and schools that have significant problems in progressing disadvantaged students to higher education, yet participation activity is not targeted at these areas.

The Government has set its ambitions for widening participation. The university sector needs to rally around this, but a collaborative effort is required. Universities will need to significantly outdo recent progress. On a basic estimate this will require 12,000 more students from low participation areas entering HE by 2020 compared to 2014.

For these reasons we recommend that a portion of widening participation funding should be set aside to embed collaborative outreach at the heart of widening participation, to target areas where participation is low and to close the substantial gaps between poor students and others. This should be coordinated by OFFA and the new Office for Students to ensure collective effort across the HE sector in driving improvements. This will entail universities pooling their resources and skills to focus outreach activity on those schools and areas identified as the worst performers.

Recommendation 2: The Government should create a single online portal for young people to access public sector internships by 2017.

Despite increasing recognition that internships should be advertised openly and fairly paid, many are still secured through informal connections and remain unpaid. The public sector performs better than the private sector but the sheer range of internships it makes available – from defence

94 At current rates (18.2 per cent in 2014), based on HEFCE's POLAR measure, around 25,000 young people from low participation areas enter HE; at target rates (28.2 per cent in 2020) around 37,000 young people from low participation areas would enter HE via a UCAS application. HEFCE, *Polar – Participation of Local Areas*, 2015; UCAS, *End of Cycle Report*, 2015

to health, local to national government – makes access complex. Different organisations tend to have their own website or no website at all. There is a need to create a simple front-end so that students and young people can see what is available and then apply. The UK Government should make it a priority to bring order out of this chaos by creating a single interns.gov.uk website. In so doing, the public sector has the opportunity to blaze a trail for others to follow.

Recommendation 3: Professional employers should follow the lead of those making the most progress in opening up more opportunities to people from disadvantaged backgrounds.

The Commission recommends professional firms, especially major recruiters of graduates and school leavers, hold themselves to account on the basis of the following measures. These are based on the Commission's Business and Social Mobility manifesto,[95] the criteria for the Social Mobility Business Champions[96] and recent activity by firms:[97]

Table 4.4: Opening up opportunities to people from disadvantaged backgrounds

Objective	Why is it important?
Understand challenges. Collect data to understand the social background of applicants, recruits and current staff at different levels in the organisation. Review recruitment and selection procedures to identify where barriers exist and what can be done to overcome them – for both entry- and graduate-level positions.	In order to make progress, firms need to understand the social make-up of their organisations. Depending on the process a firm uses, disadvantaged candidates may fall behind at different stages in recruitment. Identifying where this happens is vital.
Remove roadblocks. Ensure initial thresholds for application are not exclusionary. Broaden the range of universities from which a firm recruits, reduce minimum academic/UCAS requirements and incorporate contextual admissions tools into the selection process.	Targeting only top universities and setting high UCAS-point thresholds will mean that some young people will not be able to apply at all. Changing such policies is important. Consideration of context is essential to understand the differences in opportunity candidates face.
Expand entry routes. Open up non-graduate entry routes with good progression prospects. Ensure entry requirements do not exclude disadvantaged young people.	The majority of young people do not follow the university route. Building work-based routes that recognise real-life experience is vital to social mobility.
Engage strategically. Forge connections with schools and young people. Encourage staff to become school governors.	Enduring relationships with schools will lead to changes in young people's attitudes and prospects. Businesses can help explain and support paths to professions for those lacking experience in the family.
Open opportunities. Pay and advertise for internships, targeting at least 25 per cent at disadvantaged groups.	Many internships convert into permanent jobs. Ensuring these are accessible to people from different backgrounds is an important part of opening up the professions.
Embed leadership. Appoint a board-level business leader to champion this agenda.	To achieve real change, social mobility needs to be a 'business as usual' aim – akin to tackling inequality based on gender, race and disability – not a separate corporate social responsibility.

95 Social Mobility and Child Poverty Commission, *Business and Social Mobility: A Manifesto for Change*, 2013
96 Department for Business, Innovation and Skills, *The Champion Criteria and 12 Month Timeline*, 2014
97 For example, the civil service research cited above

Changing employer practices to overcome the barriers young people from disadvantaged families face in accessing the best jobs must become a top objective for professional firms. As the arguments for reducing gender and ethnic inequalities were won in the 20th century, the arguments for reducing those that stem from family origins are gaining ground in the 21st. Firms that have committed to improving social mobility are making major changes to reduce the disadvantages some young people face. But if a One Nation vision is to be achieved, best practice must spread beyond the vanguard. The Commission will assess top employers throughout 2016 to see what progress has been made.

Child poverty overview

Britain's child poverty problem

Child poverty in Britain is about average for the EU, although it is significantly higher than in the Netherlands, Denmark or France.[1] Fortunately, child poverty in the UK has been on a downward trend since the early 1990s. At its highest level in 1992, nearly three in 10 children were in relative poverty (see Figure CP1). On the same measure, fewer than two in 10 children are in poverty today. Yet there are still 2.3 million children living below the current statutory child poverty line. These numbers hide the day-to-day tragedy of child poverty, from the effects of low-quality and insecure housing, through a lack of new, quality clothes that other children take for granted, to unhappy and anxious early years.[2 3 4] Child poverty imposes a lasting burden. When doors to opportunity are closed off early in life, the chance to do well as an adult is much reduced.

Progress in reducing child poverty has been welcome, but it must not be allowed to grind to a halt – or worse, reverse and undo years of improvements. If we are to achieve a One Nation Britain, first, today's level of child poverty must be reduced – and then eradicated for good.

1 Office for National Statistics, *Persistent Poverty in the UK and the EU: 2008-2013*, 2015
2 HM Government, *An Evidence Review of the Drivers of Child Poverty for Families in Poverty Now and for Poor Children Growing Up to be Poor Adults*, 2014
3 Joseph Rowntree Foundation, *A Minimum Income Standard for the UK in 2015*, 2015
4 Social Mobility and Child Poverty Commission, *Social and Emotional Learning: Skills for Life and Work*, 2015

How much child poverty is there in Britain – and are things getting better or worse?

Measuring child poverty

Under the Child Poverty Act 2010 there are four main ways in which poverty is measured – and against which targets have been set for 2020/21. Although the Welfare Reform and Work Bill will repeal the targets, data against the measures will continue to be published. The main measures (which all relate to income before housing costs) are as follows:

Relative low income: the proportion of children who live in households with income below 60 per cent of the current median (adjusted for household size). This currently equates to an annual income of £21,691 a year for a couple with two children – or just short of £17,000 for a single parent with two children. The target is to reduce this measure to 10 per cent or less.

Combined low income and material deprivation: the proportion of children who live in households with income below 70 per cent of the current median who experience material deprivation. Material deprivation refers to individuals' or households' inability to afford particular goods typically bought in wider society. The target is to reduce this to 5 per cent or less.

Absolute low income: the proportion of children who live in households with income below 60 per cent of the 2010/11 median. The target is to reduce this to 5 per cent or less.

Persistent poverty: the proportion of children who live in households with income below the current median in at least three of the previous four years. The target is to reduce this to 7 per cent or less. (Data is not currently reported against this target.)

In 2013/14, 2.3 million children (17 per cent) were in relative poverty, and 2.6 million (19 per cent) lived in absolute poverty. Relative poverty and absolute poverty have decreased by less than half a percentage point each since 2012/13. These decreases are not statistically significant, so the measures can be said to have remained flat.

On the sharpest measures of child poverty, there are 1.7 million children in combined low income and material deprivation (13 per cent), and half a million in severe low income and material deprivation (4 per cent). These have not changed since 2010. At the height of the recession, the fact that 1 million young people were unemployed was rightly described as a crisis – and more than double that number of children are in poverty. Yet unlike youth unemployment, poverty is not fading away with the economic recovery. Britain's child poverty crisis is a stubborn one that a return to economic growth alone cannot fix.

Figure CP1: Relative and absolute poverty trends over the long term, 1979–2013

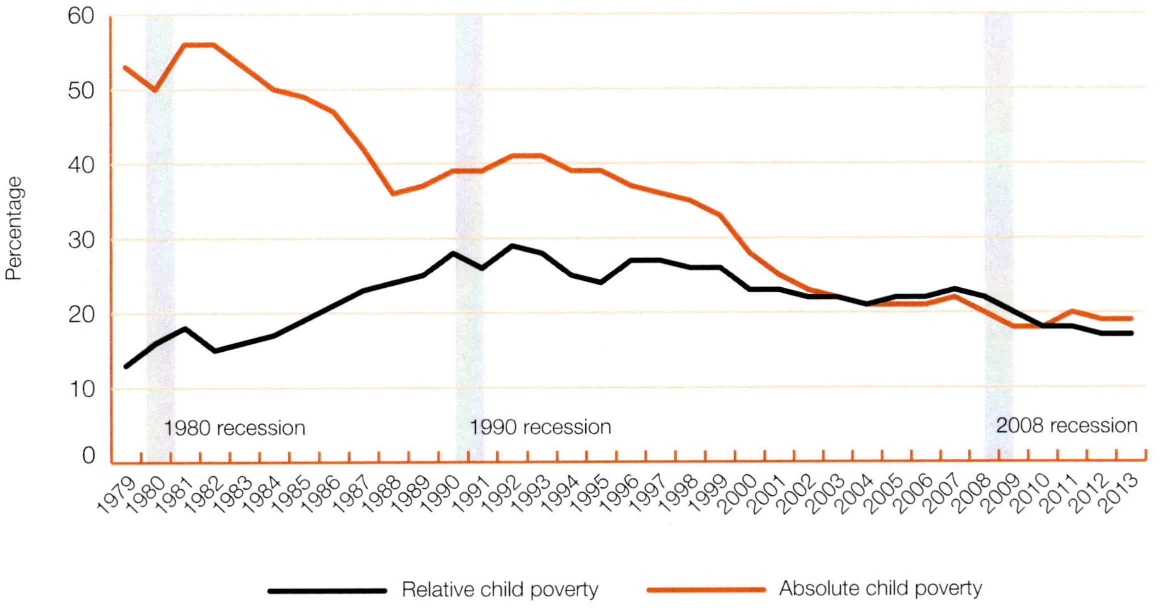

Source: Institute for Fiscal Studies, *Living Standards, Poverty and Inequality in the UK (supplementary data)*, 2014

Behind the shocking headline numbers, child poverty in Britain has changed. Once it was a problem of workless households – in 1996, 43 per cent of children in relative poverty were in working households, but now almost two-thirds (63 per cent) are.[5] To be clear, having parents out of work still makes it more likely that a child will be in poverty; however, the majority of poor children are poor not because their parents cannot find work, but because their parents are in work with income that is too low. Despite working hard, sometimes at more than one job, mums and dads across the country struggle to provide adequately for their kids. The underlying reasons for this are complex, spanning the jobs market and welfare system. As described in Chapter 5 (page 141) there is much scope for government and employers to make a real difference for the lives of the largest group of poor children.

There is also a powerful geographic dimension to child poverty in Britain. At the broadest regional level, children in the south east are 70 per cent less likely to be in poverty than those in Wales and Northern Ireland (13 versus 22 per cent). Once housing costs are taken into account, relative poverty ranges from one in five children in Scotland (21 per cent) to nearly twice this (37 per cent) in London.

Virtually every local area of the UK – even the most affluent local authorities – have significant pockets of disadvantage, but it is not evenly distributed across the country.[6] The proportion of children in low-income households varies from 5.5 per cent in Hart in Hampshire to 39 per cent in Tower Hamlets in London. Differences at a ward level are even more extreme.[7] One-third of children in poverty in the UK live in the most deprived 1,000 wards, whereas only one in 100 children in poverty live in the least deprived 1,000 wards. This illustrates the scale of the geographic divide in opportunity in the UK. There are 33 wards where more than half of children are in poverty (including 24 out of the 582 wards in Northern Ireland (see Figure CP2).

5 Institute for Fiscal Studies, *Nearly Two-thirds of Children in Poverty Live in Working Families*, 2015
6 This is based on HM Revenue & Customs' estimates of children in households that claim Income Support, income-based Jobseeker's Allowance or Child Tax Credit, where household income is less than 60 per cent of median. Therefore, it is not strictly comparable to headline poverty estimates
7 A ward is the smallest electoral division in the UK. There are just under 9,500 each with a population in the thousands

Figure CP2: The fifth of local authority districts with the highest concentrations of child poverty

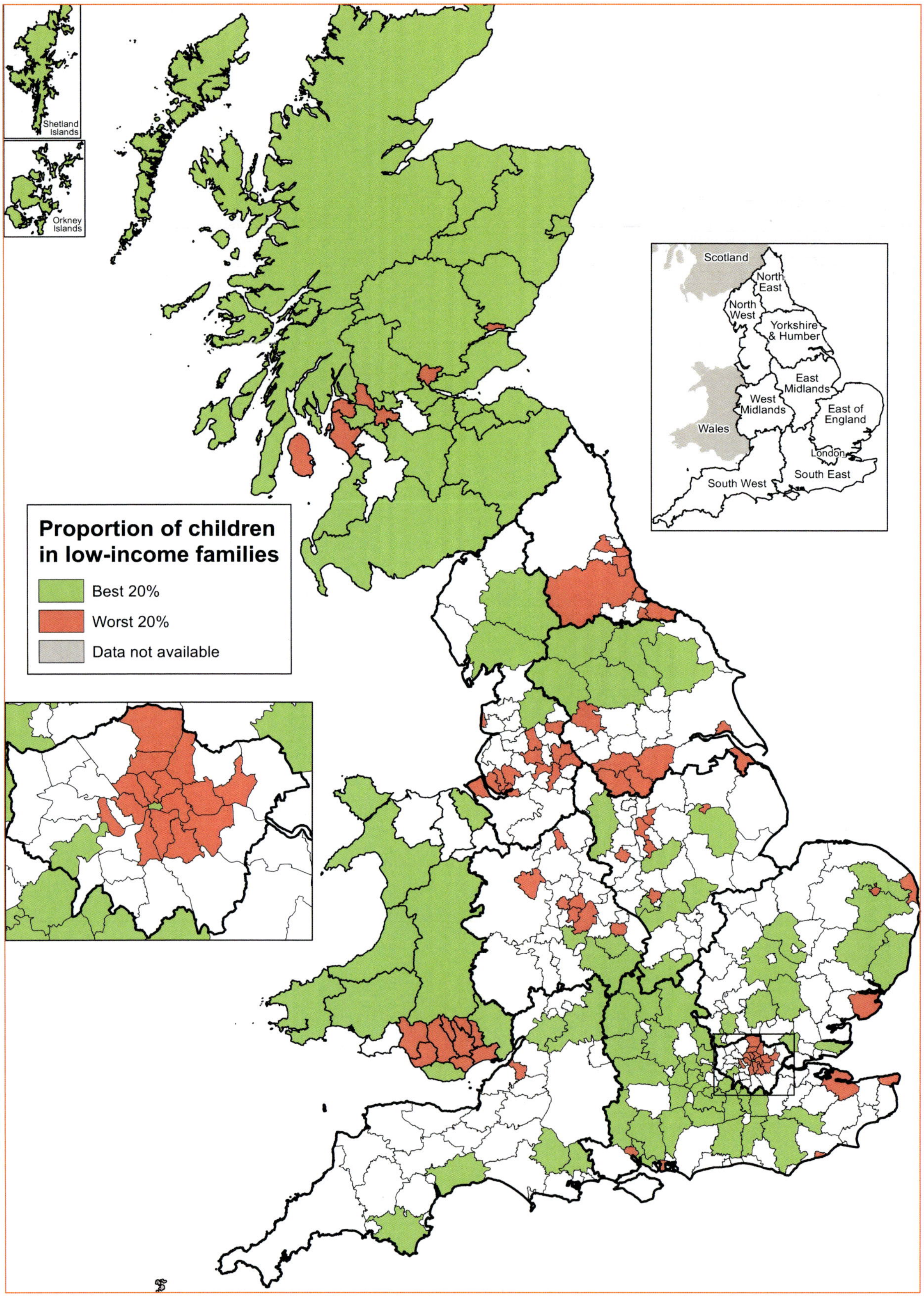

Source: HMRC, *Personal tax credits: children in low income families local measure: 2013*, 2015. Reproduced by permission of Ordnance Survey on behalf of HMSO, 2015

What explains these trends?

Progress has been made in reducing child poverty since the 1990s, demonstrating that improvement is possible in the right circumstances. As Figure CP1 illustrates, between 2000 and today, relative poverty has decreased by 9 percentage points. This is a drop of one-third. These most recent trends reflect decreasing worklessness in the period before the recession and increased support from the state for those with children.[8]

More recently child poverty against the headline relative measure has flat lined, contrary to forecasts that it would rise (though absolute poverty is higher than in 2010, especially once housing costs are taken into account). Predictions were based on the effects of the recession, reduced welfare entitlements and employment and earnings outlooks from the Office for Budget Responsibility.[9] Compared to the assumptions that underpinned the predictions of rising poverty, employment growth since 2010 has been faster than expected and earnings growth has been lower than expected. Faster employment growth, especially the 11 per cent rise in lone parent employment from 2010–14, has reduced the number of children in workless households and protected them from poverty. Slower earnings growth has resulted in falls in real earnings across the income distribution. However, low earners have been relatively protected as they tend to rely on the state for a greater proportion of their income. Additionally, low earners may have benefited from lower than expected council tax rises and increases in the personal allowance targeted at this group. A final consideration to bear in mind is that data on child poverty is produced with significant time lags – the latest data tells us what happened in 2013–14.

Even when trends over time are understood, it begs the question why Britain has such high levels of child poverty at all. After all, Britain is the fifth wealthiest country in the world, and today our economy is growing above the trend of many similar nations. There is no simple explanation, but a combination of increases in low-paid work and job insecurity, a decline in well-paid jobs for those with few skills, and the challenges of combining work and caring responsibilities across the generations all play their role. At a family level, lone parenthood and large families are also significant. These problems are not unique to the UK, but similar countries to ours have lower rates of child poverty (see Figure CP3). It seems they may have found better ways of reducing the incidence of child poverty.

8 Hills, J., *The Coalition's Record on Cash Transfers, Poverty and Inequality 2010–2015*, 2015

9 For detail of some of these benefit changes, see Institute for Fiscal Studies, *Living Standards, Poverty and Inequality in the UK: 2015*, 2015

Figure CP3: Absolute child poverty (60 per cent of 2008 median income) across the OECD

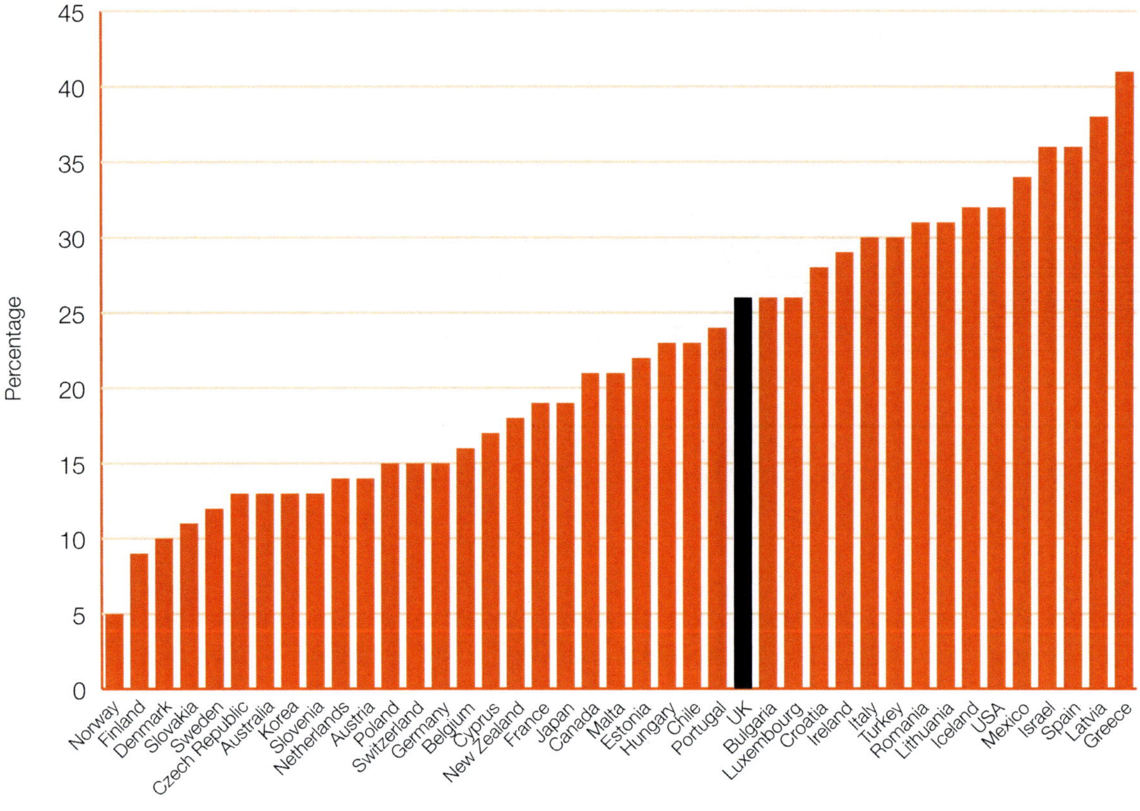

Source: UNICEF, *Children of the Recession: The Impact of the Economic Crisis on Child Well-being in Rich Countries*, 2014[10]

Note: This chart is based on an absolute measure anchored to 2008

Conclusion

After a decade and a half in which child poverty fell significantly, progress appears to have stalled. The Commission – along with the vast majority of independent experts – believes that the targets in the Child Poverty Act 2010 are certain to be missed. For example, to achieve the relative poverty target, progress over the next five years would need to be nearly as much as over the last 15 years. Worse still, it seems highly likely that child poverty will increase in the period to 2020: the Institute for Fiscal Studies forecasts that it is likely to rise to above 20 per cent on the headline relative poverty measure.[11] This is without taking into account the additional £12 billion of cuts to welfare entitlements announced by the Government since May 2015, which will increase poverty even further. In part, this reflects adverse economic circumstances. But in the Commission's view, it also reflects a clear reduction in the priority being given to this issue.

The Commission recognises that there are complex arguments about how best to measure poverty, and accepts that the target of abolishing child poverty by 2020 has ceased to be a realistic prospect. We welcome the Government's continued commitment to tackling the root causes of poverty, but remain convinced that assessment of progress must include an income measure. It would be counter-intuitive for any government to claim it was successfully reducing poverty if this was not reflected in smaller numbers of people living on low incomes. As this report demonstrates, if poverty is not tackled, real opportunity will be the preserve of those born to better-off parents. That is hardly the mark of a One Nation Britain.

10 To enable cross-country comparison, UNICEF uses a different method to official UK statistics. The UK child poverty level appears higher here than elsewhere in this section.

11 Institute for Fiscal Studies, *Child and Working-age Poverty in Northern Ireland over the Next Decade: An Update*, 2014

Housing and poverty

The targets in the Child Poverty Act relate to poverty before housing costs; the situation looks worse when housing costs are taken into account. In 2013/14 relative child poverty after housing costs was 28 per cent (compared to 17 per cent before housing costs), and absolute poverty after housing costs was 31 per cent (compared to 19 per cent before housing costs).[12] These differences reflect the high levels of housing costs in this country and the fact that housing benefit counts as a form of income, and so makes some households appear better-off compared to others than they actually are.

We welcome the Government's commitment to dramatically increase the number of houses built and its efforts to increase home ownership. However, it is regrettable that it is not taking more positive action to tackle the housing issues faced by those for whom home ownership is not a realistic option.

The Government is cracking down on private sector rogue landlords by creating a new database of offenders and introducing more stringent tests for those letting houses in multiple occupation.[13] Its decision – announced in the 2015 Summer Budget – to cut social housing rents by 1 per cent will benefit tenants who pay their own rents (while also reducing the housing benefit bill).

However, from April 2016 tenancies let at social rents will be capped to the amounts covered by relevant local housing allowances, which already have been frozen for the next three years. As a result housing benefit will no longer fully cover the costs that families pay to live in social housing.[14]

Traditionally, social housing was seen as the long-term option for low-income households, but successive governments have pushed up rents and moved away from providing subsidies that would support a large increase in supply. Right to Buy policies have led to a further diminution in the available stock. The result has been that the proportion of households living in the social housing sector fell to 17 per cent in 2013/14, its lowest point since the mid-1960s.

Most of the unmet need has been absorbed by the private rented sector. The proportion of households with dependent children living in the private rented sector trebled in the decade 2003–04 to 2013–14 from 8 per cent to 24 per cent. This includes almost one in three lone parent families.[15] Families living in this sector have much less stability and security than those who own their own homes or live in social tenancies. Just one-fifth (20 per cent) of renters have lived in their current homes for five years or more, despite 82 per cent saying that when choosing a home the option to live there for five years or more was important to them.[16]

In 2014–15, 9,590 social rented homes were delivered, less than half the number delivered in 2004/05.[17] Cuts to social housing rents (plus the uncertainty that this reversal of policy creates in relation to future rental streams) is likely to keep this figure low.

Against this background, it seems clear that many low-income families are likely to spend much or all of their lives in the private rented sector, where rents are likely to continue to rise dramatically. Forecasts made prior to the 2015 Autumn Statement suggest that private rents in England will rise by around 90 per cent in real terms between 2008 and 2040 – more than twice as fast as incomes. All other things being equal, this in turn will boost poverty rates among private renters to as high as 53 per cent by 2040 (compared to 43 per cent in 2008).[18]

12 Department for Work and Pensions, *Households Below Average Income, An Analysis of the Income Distribution 1994/95–2013/14*, 2015
13 Department for Communities and Local Government, *Tackling Rogue Landlords and Improving the Private Rental Sector*, 2015
14 HM Treasury, *Spending Review and Autumn Statement 2015*, 2015
15 Department for Communities and Local Government, *English Housing Survey: Table FT1241*, 2015
16 Shelter, *Making Renting Fit for Families: the Impact of Different Forms of Rent Regulation*, 2015
17 Department for Communities and Local Government, *Affordable Housing Supply: April 2014 to March 2015 England*, 2015
18 Stephens, M., *et al.*, *What Will the Housing Market Look Like in 2040?*, 2014

Chapter 5: Tackling low pay and in-work poverty

- **1.5 million children are in poverty because their working parents do not earn enough to secure a basic standard of living.**
- **The risk of absolute poverty for working families after housing costs has increased over the last decade.**
- **20.5 per cent of UK full-time employees are in low paid jobs, compared to an OECD average of 17.1 per cent.**
- **Four out of 10 children in working poor households live in families where parents might reasonably be expected to enter work or work more hours.**
- **The Government aims to tackle these problems by moving the UK from a "low wage, high tax, high welfare society to a higher wage, lower tax, lower welfare society" and has a number of policies – including the National Living Wage – to do so.**
- **The Government's plans will have a positive impact on some of the drivers of working poverty and the increased focus on tackling low pay and increasing parental employment is welcome. However, recently announced changes to Universal Credit will make many low-income working families significantly worse off.**
- **The Government should, as the public finances improve, revitalise employment incentives in Universal Credit.**
- **Employers should take more responsibility for their employees' living standards with change led by a vanguard group of 'One Nation Employers' acting as a beacon for others.**
- **The Government should set a clear objective for the UK to become a Living Wage country by 2025 at the latest and work with business to develop a comprehensive pay, progression and productivity plan that aligns Government programmes behind that goal.**
- **This will mean halving the proportion of people who earn less than two-thirds of median hourly pay to 10 per cent of employees, so putting the UK on a par with the best performing countries in Europe.**

5.1 Introduction

It is widely accepted that work is the best route out of poverty: children in workless families are almost three times as likely to be poor as those whose parents are in work.[1] However, finding a job is, on its own, not a guarantee of escaping poverty: for example, 1.5 million children in working families – more than one in eight – are in poverty. Working poverty on this scale is a sign that something is seriously wrong in our society.

The problem of in-work poverty has a significant impact on the welfare system. Forty-four per cent of children in working households – almost five million children – are in families in receipt of tax credits, and around 12 per cent of working families with children are in receipt of housing benefit. The combined cost of financial support for working families with children through tax credits and support with housing costs was an estimated £22.6 billion a year in 2013–14 – 1.6 per cent higher in real terms than in 2009–10, despite significant cuts in entitlements to these benefits over the last few years.[2]

The Prime Minister has said that he wants the country to move from "a low wage, high tax, high welfare society to a higher wage, lower tax, lower welfare society",[3] with responsibility for securing decent living standards for those in work shifting from the state towards employers and individuals.

The 2015 Summer Budget set out the Government's blueprint for achieving this goal. Key measures include:

- A £12 billion reduction in welfare entitlements between 2015 and 2020;
- A renewed commitment to full roll-out of Universal Credit;
- Increased work expectations on parents of pre-school children in receipt of tax credits;
- A higher minimum wage for over-25s through the National Living Wage;
- Increases in the income tax personal allowance to £12,500 by 2020;
- A series of changes to business taxation and regulation intended to support businesses in creating higher wage jobs.

The Government's hope is that the combined effect of these measures will help parents to increase their net earnings from employment (through, for example, entering employment, working longer hours, increasing their hourly earnings and paying less income tax), and reduce their living costs (for example, by moving to cheaper housing or choosing to have smaller families).

The risk of this approach is that while cuts in welfare entitlements are certain and affect family incomes immediately, the compensatory changes are less certain and will take longer to materialise. Unless the hoped-for impacts of the Government's reforms on employment, earnings and living costs are successful in fully offsetting reductions in benefits, it will become more difficult for low-income families to achieve decent living standards, and there will be increases in child poverty and income inequality.

This chapter explores the key drivers of the UK's working poverty problem, describes the UK Government's approach towards tackling working poverty, and identifies a number of areas where further action could help achieve the Prime Minister's vision.

---

1 All the data in this chapter about child poverty come from Department for Work and Pensions, *Households Below Average Income*, June 2015, unless otherwise stated

2 Commission analysis using data from the Department for Work and Pensions housing benefit extract from February 2015: https://stat-xplore.dwp.gov.uk/; Department for Work and Pensions, *Housing Benefit Caseload Statistics*, 2015; and HM Revenue and Customs, *Personal Tax Credits Statistics*, using gross domestic product (GDP) deflators to adjust for inflation

3 David Cameron, *Speech on Opportunity*, 22 June 2015: https://www.gov.uk/government/speeches/pm-speech-on-opportunity

5.2 Does today's reality meet the One Nation vision?

A One Nation Britain would be one where every child whose parents are fulfilling society's expectations about how many hours they should work, given their health and caring responsibilities, has a decent standard of living.

We are long way from achieving that vision. Too many hard-working families in Britain are unable to enjoy basic living standards. Two-thirds of children in poverty live in working households, and the best available evidence suggests that most of them – an estimated six out of 10 – have parents who are working sufficient hours to meet their responsibilities within Universal Credit.[4]

The relative importance of working poverty has been growing for the last 20 years. For example, in 1996–97 more children in poverty lived in workless families than in working ones. This is in many ways the flipside of success in tackling workless poverty: the number of children in workless households has fallen by 36 per cent since 1997,[5] and children in workless families are less likely to be in poverty than in the past.

The proportion of children in working families who are in relative poverty before housing costs – 13 per cent in 2013–14 – has changed little over time. However, after taking account of housing costs, recent trends are more concerning. Over the last decade, the risk of absolute poverty for working families after housing costs has increased from 17 per cent in 2003–04 to 23 per cent in 2013–14, suggesting that economic growth over the last decade has not translated into higher living standards for low-income working families (see Figures 5.1 and 5.2).

Figure 5.1: Proportion of children in the UK who live in working poor families

Sources: Institute for Fiscal Studies, *Incomes in the UK*, 2014; Department for Work and Pensions, *Households Below Average Income*, June 2015

4 Bradshaw, J. and Main, G., *How Many Working Poor Parents Might Be Able to Work More?*, March 2014. Available from http://spruyork.blogspot.co.uk/2014/03/how-many-working-poor-parents-might-be.html. This analysis is based on self-reported working patterns from the Family Resources Survey. It has been assumed that the hours of work of those who say they are working full-time/part-time correspond to the expectations that will be set within Universal Credit

5 Office for National Statistics, *Working and Workless Households*, 2015

Figure 5.2: Proportion of children in absolute poverty after housing costs by family type and work intensity

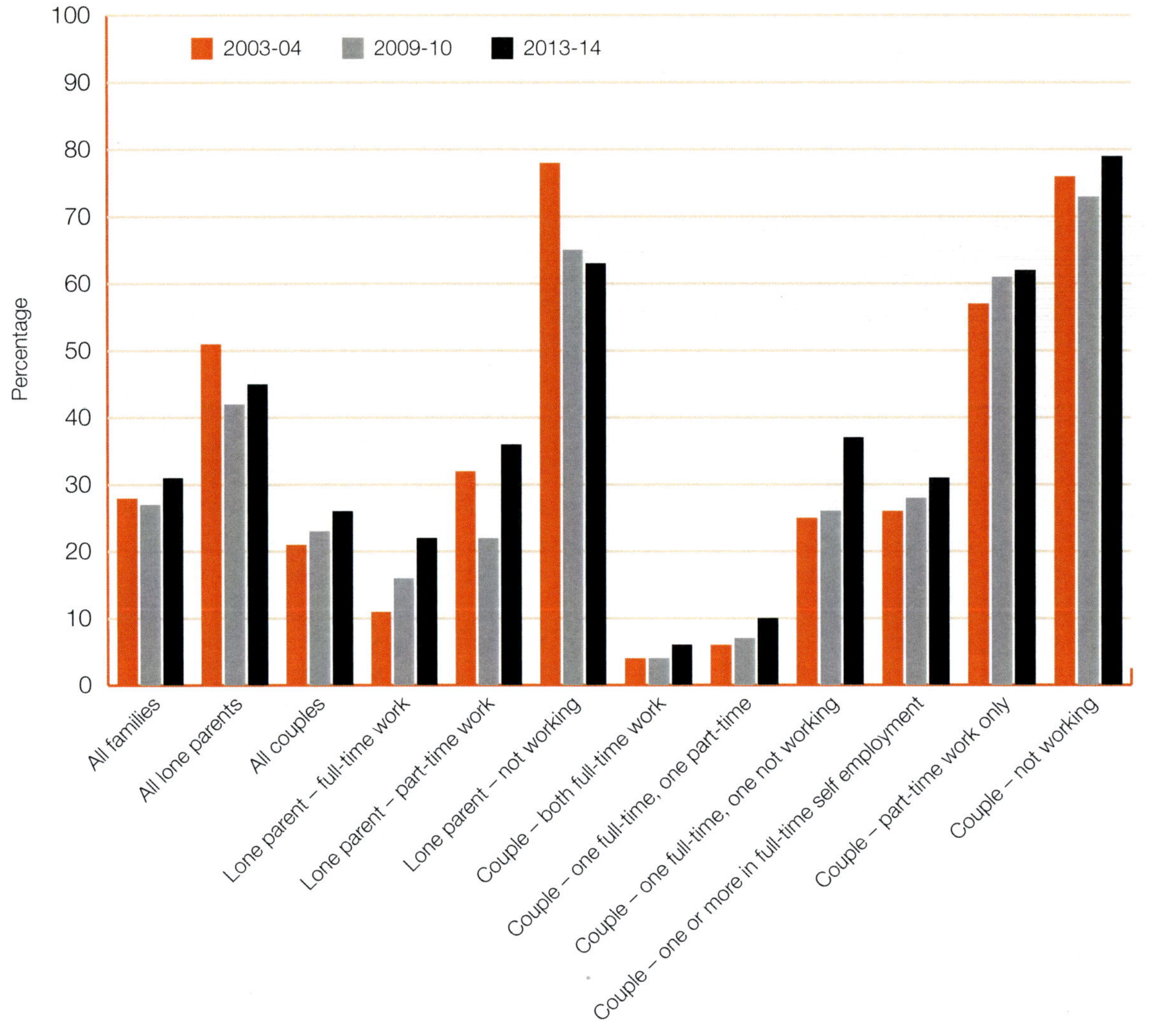

Source: Department for Work and Pensions, *Households Below Average Income*, June 2015

There are three aspects to the working poverty problem in the UK that we will focus on in the rest of this section. First, the extent of low pay and its impact on different groups. Second, the importance of second earner employment and part-time working patterns in affecting the chances that a family will be in working poverty. Finally, the difficulties many families face in escaping from working poverty.

Problem 1: The UK has more low-paid workers than most other developed countries.

The introduction of the National Minimum Wage in 1999 has virtually eradicated extreme low pay – defined as hourly pay below half of median hourly earnings – for those aged 21 and over in the UK. For example, the National Minimum Wage rate in April 2015 for this group was, at £6.50 per hour, 55 per cent of median hourly earnings of £11.75.[6]

However, low pay more broadly – defined as hourly pay below two-thirds of the median – has been broadly static since the mid-1990s, with around 22–23 per cent of employees paid at

6 Median hourly pay excluding overtime. Office for National Statistics, *Annual Survey of Hours and Earnings, Table 1.6b*, November 2015. We have used the April 2015 National Minimum Wage rate rather than the current rate (£6.70) to align with the latest reliable data on median hourly earnings

this level (see Figure 5.3).[7] The UK has the eighth highest rate of low pay in the Organisation for Economic Co-operation and Development (OECD) countries: 20.5 per cent of full-time employees are in low pay, compared to an OECD average of 17.1 per cent.[8] And the UK is a long way behind the best performing countries in Europe: Sweden, Finland, France, Belgium, Norway and Denmark all have fewer than 10 per cent of workers paid less than two-thirds of hourly median pay – less than half the levels of low pay seen in the UK.[9]

Over the last few years, the proportion of workers who are not paid enough to achieve a basic minimum standard of living – defined as being paid less than the voluntary Living Wage rates set by the Living Wage Foundation – has increased significantly due to a combination of falling real earnings, high inflation faced by lower income households, and decreases in the generosity of in-work benefits since 2010. These trends are expected to continue over the next few years despite the upward pressure on pay at the bottom of the earning distribution associated with the introduction of the National Living Wage in April 2016.[10]

The introduction of the National Living Wage will mean there will be three main types of wage floor in the UK:

1. The National Minimum Wage – the statutory minimum rates for apprentices and people aged 24 and under;
2. The National Living Wage – the statutory minimum rate for people aged 25 and over, excluding apprentices;
3. The voluntary Living Wage – a scheme operated by the Living Wage Foundation: employers can become accredited living wage employers by paying all their staff and on-site contractors at least this wage.

The only true living wage – by which we mean a wage based on an assessment of the income that different families need to secure a basic minimum standard of living – among these three is the one that is set by the Living Wage Foundation.

7 Resolution Foundation, *Low Pay Britain 2015*, October 2015
8 OECD, OECD Employment Outlook 2015, *Statistical Annex, Table O – Earnings Dispersion and Incidence of High and Low Pay*, 2015
9 *Eurostat, Statistics Explained: Earnings Statistics*, January 2013: http://ec.europa.eu/eurostat/statistics-explained/index.php/Earnings_statistics#Earnings_and_low-wage_earners_by_sex
10 Resolution Foundation, *Low Pay Britain 2015*, October 2015

Figure 5.3: Trends in low pay in the UK over the last 45 years

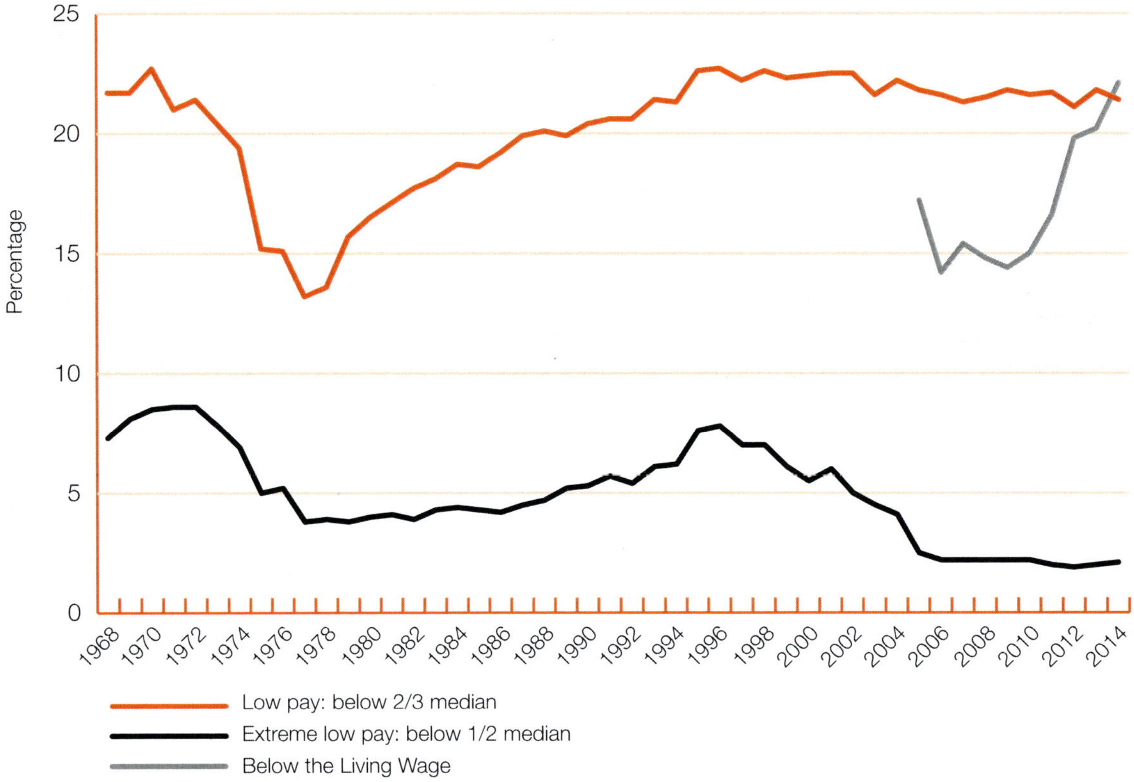

Source: Resolution Foundation, *Low Pay Britain 2015*, 2015

There are big differences in the prevalence of low pay between different groups of the population. For example, analysis by the Resolution Foundation[11] shows that:

- **By gender**: six out of 10 of those paid less than the Living Wage are women, and 27 per cent of women are paid less than the Living Wage compared to 17 per cent of men;
- **By age**: almost half (46 per cent) of those paid less than the Living Wage are aged between 16 and 30. Young people are two-and-a-half times more likely to be paid less than the Living Wage (39 per cent of those aged 16 to 30 versus 16 per cent of those aged 31 and above);
- **By working pattern**: almost six out of 10 (55 per cent) of those paid less than the Living Wage work part-time. Those who work part-time are more than three times as likely to be paid less than the Living Wage than those who work full-time (43 per cent versus 14 per cent);
- **By occupation**: almost three-quarters (71 per cent) of those paid less than the Living Wage work in personal services, sales and customer services or elementary occupations;
- **By industry**: more than half (55 per cent) of those paid less than the Living Wage work in the hospitality, wholesale and retail, and administrative and support services industries;
- **By sector**: 91 per cent of those paid less than the Living Wage work in the private and third sectors. Those in the private sector are three-and-a-half times more likely to be paid less than the Living Wage than those in the public sector (28 per cent versus 8 per cent).

There is wide variation across the country in people's ability to earn enough to support their families (see Figure 5.4). For example, at a regional level, the estimated proportion of workers paid less than the Living Wage rates set by the Living Wage Foundation varies from 19 per cent of employees who work in London, the South East of England and Scotland to 29 per cent in Northern Ireland. At a local level, it varies from 5 per cent of employees who work in the City of London to 42 per cent of employees who work in West Somerset.[12]

11 Resolution Foundation, *Low Pay Britain 2015*, 2015

12 Office for National Statistics, *Estimates of Employee Jobs Paid Less than the Living Wage in London and Other Parts of the UK*, October 2015

Figure 5.4: Proportion of employee jobs paid less than the Living Wage

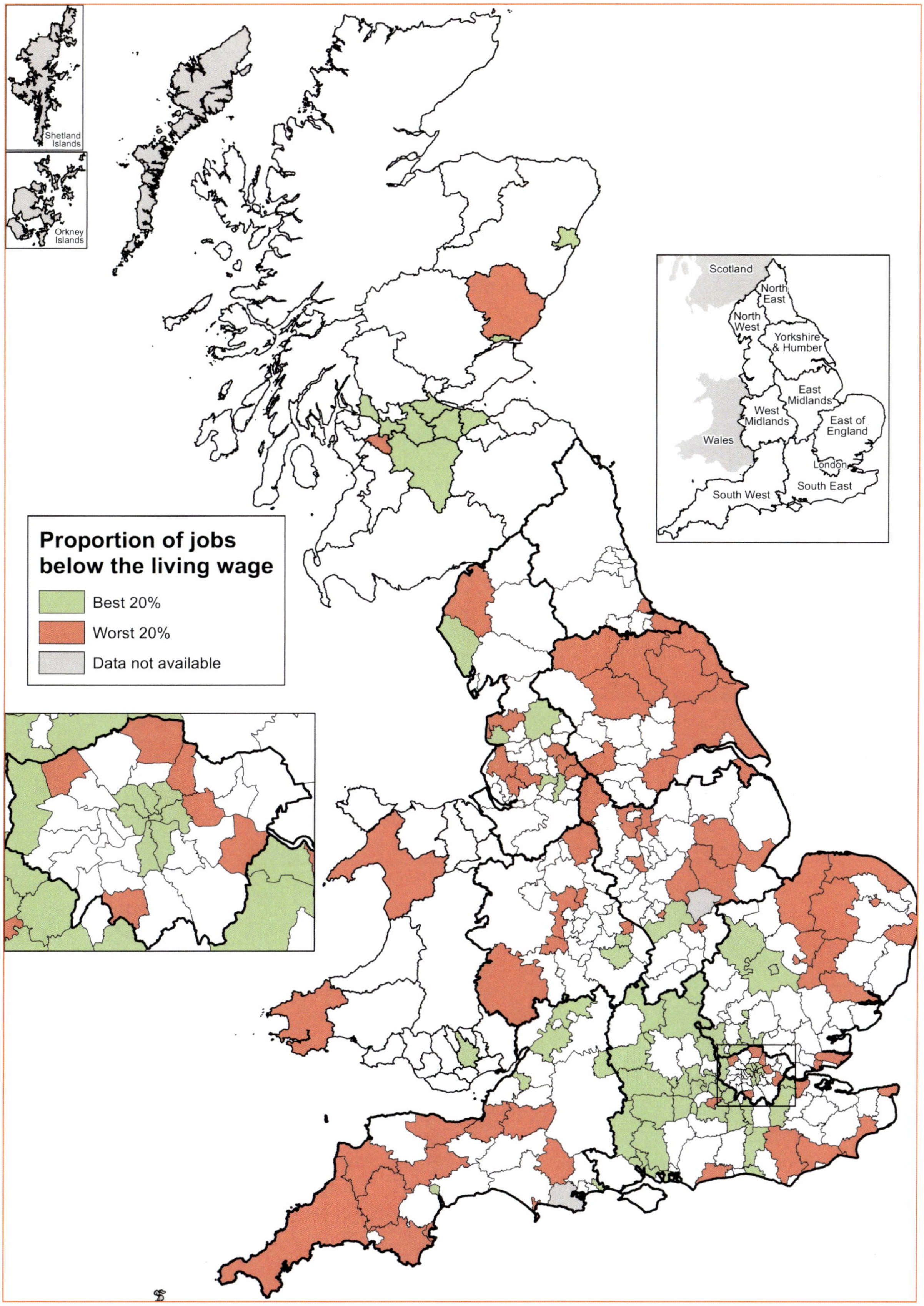

Source: Office for National Statistics, *Estimates of Employee Jobs Paid Less than the Living Wage in London and Other Parts of the UK*, October 2015

Problem 2: Many working poor families are not fulfilling society's expectations around how much they work.

The evidence is clear that for families in low-paid work to reliably escape poverty, at least one parent must work full-time and, for couples, both parents need to be in work:

- **Poverty risks are relatively low where a lone parent or both parents in a couple are in full-time employment:** 3 per cent of children with two parents in full-time work and 9 per cent of children with a lone parent in full-time work are in relative poverty before housing costs (although 20 per cent of children with a lone parent in full-time work are in poverty after taking housing costs into account);
- **Poverty risks are far higher in single-earner couple families:** 20 per cent of children in families where one parent works full-time and the other does not work are in relative poverty before housing costs;
- **Children in households where no one works full-time – especially those in couple families – are also at high risk of poverty:** 41 per cent of children in working couple families where no one works full-time are in relative poverty before housing costs, as are 16 per cent of children with a single parent in part-time work.

However, more than half (56 per cent) of children in working poor families either have no parent in full-time work, or live in couple families where only one parent is working:

- Almost one in three children (30 per cent) in working poor families live in single earner (full-time) couple families;
- 16 per cent of children in working poor families live in couple families where no one works full-time;
- 11 per cent of children in working poverty live in lone parent families with a parent who is working part-time.

Of course, society does not expect every lone parent to work full-time and both parents in every couple to be in work. For example, there is widespread acceptance that lone parents and one parent in a couple should not be expected to work at all when their children are very young, and should only be expected to work part-time at family-friendly hours when their children are toddlers and in primary school. For example, research by the Child Poverty Action Group[13] found that:

- Few people thought it was reasonable to expect lone parents and second earners in couples to work more than 20–25 hours a week until their youngest child was 13 years old;
- Only one-third of people said it was reasonable to expect lone parents and second earners to work outside of 9–5 Monday to Friday (although fewer than half said it was unreasonable, with the balance not expressing a view one way or the other);
- Only a fifth of people said it was reasonable to expect lone parents and second earners to work unpredictable hours, with 57 per cent of respondents saying that this was an unreasonable expectation.

The Government's work expectations for parents that will be embedded in the welfare system through Universal Credit are similarly tailored to family circumstances:[14]

- The main earner in couple families will be expected to work full-time, regardless of how old their children are (with some exemptions for those with limited capability for work or regular caring responsibilities for a disabled person);

13 Child Poverty Action Group, *Round the Clock: In-work Poverty and the "Hours Question"*, April 2015

14 Department for Work and Pensions, *Universal Credit and Your Family*, 2013 as amended by HM Treasury, *Summer Budget 2015*, 2015 (which reduced the age at which lone parents and main carers in couple families will be expected to find work, from when their youngest child is five years old to when they are three years old)

- Lone parents and the main carer in couple families will not be compelled to find work until their youngest child is three years old (currently, five years old), and allowance will be made for caring responsibilities (for example, only expecting them to work during their child's school hours);
- Lone parents and the main carer in couple families will not be compelled to find full-time work until their youngest child is 13 years old.

As noted earlier in this chapter, the best available evidence suggests that an estimated six out of 10 children in working poor households live in families where parents are working the hours that will be expected of them under Universal Credit.[15] This leaves almost four out of 10 children in working poverty living with parents who might be expected to enter work or work more hours. More than three-quarters of these children are in single-earner couple households where the youngest child is of school age, or couple households where no one is in full-time work. In other words, the key working poverty challenges in terms of parental employment are getting more second earners in couples into work and helping more parents in couple families to enter full-time work (see Figure 5.5).

The good news is that there has been a lot of progress over the past 20 years in increasing parental employment, which is at historically high levels: 92 per cent of fathers in couples, 73 per cent of mothers in couples and 64 per cent of lone parents were in employment in April–June 2015. As a result, the proportion of children in workless households is the lowest since records began in 1996: at 11.8 per cent of children, including 4.6 per cent of children in couple households and 38.5 per cent of children in lone parent households.[16]

Figure 5.5 Proportion of children in working families in poverty by whether their parents are working enough to meet current Universal Credit requirements

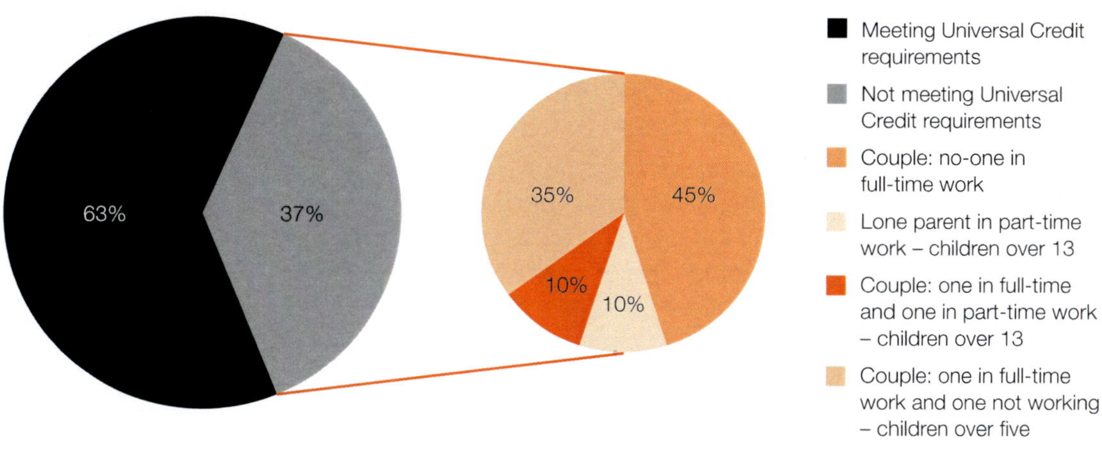

Source: J. Bradshaw and G. Main. *How Many Working Poor Parents Might Be Able to Work More?*, March 2014: http://spruyork.blogspot.co.uk/2014/03/how-many-working-poor-parents-might-be.html

However, the UK still has lower parental employment rates than many OECD countries: for example, the lone parent employment rate in the UK remains below the OECD average.[17] The UK also has a far higher prevalence of part-time working among lone parents and second earners: for example, only around a quarter of lone parents work full-time (compared to the OECD average of 49 per cent), and only around a quarter of couples with children are both in full-time work (compared to the OECD average of 38 per cent).[18] This latter issue has a double effect on working poverty, given that part-time work tends to be lower paid and associated with fewer prospects for progression.

15 Bradshaw, J. and Main, G., *How Many Working Poor Parents Might Be Able to Work More?*, op. cit.
16 Office for National Statistics, *Working and Workless Households 2015*, October 2015
17 OECD, *Families Database, Table LMF1.3*, 2015
18 OECD, *Families Database, Tables LMF2.2 and LMF2.3*, 2015

Problem 3: Working poor families often find it difficult to escape from poverty.

In a One Nation country, families would be able to escape working poverty by increasing their earnings through working more hours or developing and progressing up the career ladder over the course of their working lives, rather than finding themselves trapped in a dead-end job for years on end, or cycling between entry-level roles and unemployment.

However, many working poor families cannot earn enough to escape poverty even if they work long hours since they face high effective marginal tax rates which mean that if they increase their earnings their net income hardly changes. As noted above, the best available evidence suggests that 900,000 children are in poverty despite their parents working enough hours to meet the expectations that will be placed on them under Universal Credit.[19] Their parents find it extremely difficult to escape poverty as, in the current tax credits system, if they pay income tax they will only keep £27 out of every additional £100 they earn, with the £73 of lost earnings split between income tax (£20), National Insurance contributions (£12) and reductions in tax credits (£41). Working parents in receipt of housing benefit or local council tax support can face even higher effective marginal tax rates than this, with some parents seeing effective tax rates in excess of 90 per cent.[20] Overall, half of people claiming tax credits face marginal effective tax rates in excess of 73 per cent, and a fifth face marginal effective tax rates in excess of 82 per cent.[21] The impact of such high effective tax rates can be seen in the fact that four out of 10 families in working poverty who experience an increase of earnings of 10 per cent or more do not escape poverty.[22]

Furthermore, this is not just a temporary issue. **Many parents who get stuck in low-paid work find it almost impossible to escape.** Research carried out for the Commission[23] suggests that of those in low paid work in 2001 – defined as having an hourly wage less than two-thirds of the median – only one in seven had reliably escaped low pay a decade later in 2011.[24]

Looking only at those who were predominately in work, one in four had reliably escaped low pay, with most of the remainder (64 per cent) cycling in and out of low pay (although only 12 per cent of those predominately in work were stuck in low pay throughout the period). Characteristics associated with getting stuck in low pay included being a single parent, working part-time or working in the hospitality industry or a sales occupation. However, recent trends in pay progression are more encouraging – our research suggests that the proportion of adults getting stuck in low pay has fallen significantly since the 1990s (see Figure 5.6).[25]

19 Bradshaw, J. and Main, G., *How Many Working Poor Parents Might Be Able to Work More?*, op. cit.
20 See for example, Policy in Practice, *93% Tax?! Effective Marginal Tax Rates Explained*, October 2015: http://policyinpractice.co.uk/93-tax-effective-tax-rates-explained/
21 Resolution Foundation, *Credit Where It's Due*, March 2015
22 Department for Work and Pensions, *Child Poverty Transitions*, June 2015
23 Social Mobility and Child Poverty Commission, *Escape Plan*, 2014
24 Defined as being in work and not being in low pay in each of the last three years of the decade
25 Social Mobility and Child Poverty Commission, *Escape Plan*, 2014

Figure 5.6: Proportion of low-paid workers escaping low pay over the course of a decade

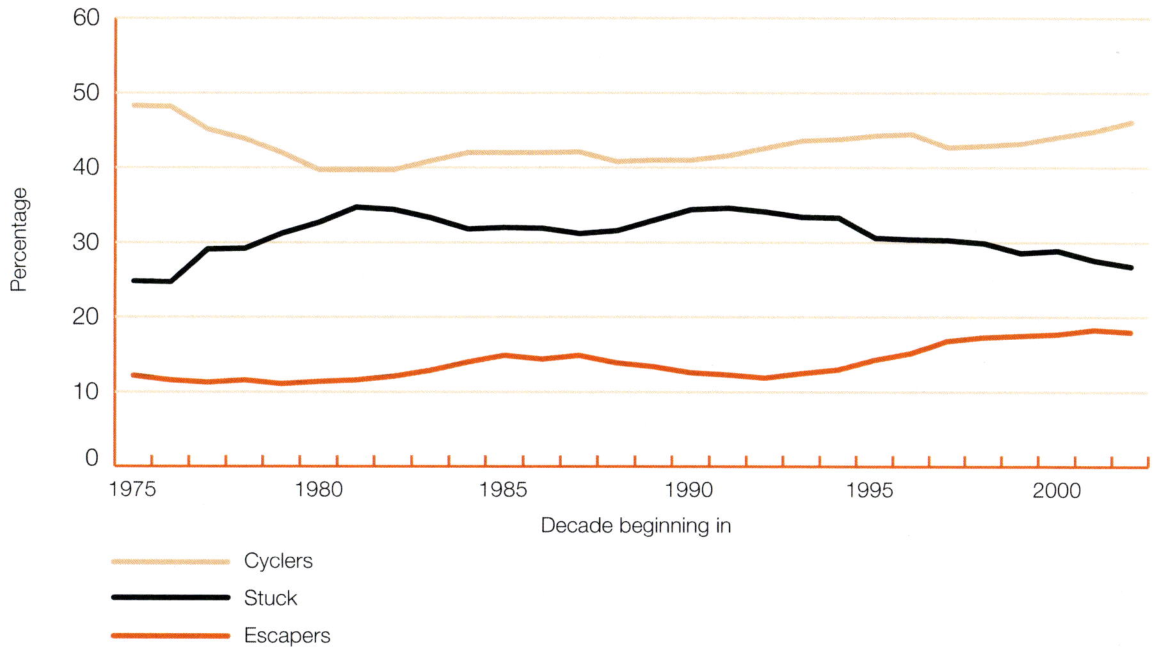

Source: Social Mobility and Child Poverty Commission, *Escape Plan*, 2014

5.3 How are these problems being addressed?

The UK Government has criticised efforts by previous administrations to tackle in-work poverty via expansion of financial support for low-paid working parents through the welfare system. The Prime Minister has described the system as a "merry go round… dealing with the symptoms of the problem: topping up low pay rather than extending the drivers of opportunity – helping to create well paid jobs in the first place",[26] while the Chancellor has said that "it cannot be right that we go on asking taxpayers to subsidise, through the tax credit system, the businesses who pay the lowest wages. Subsidised low pay contributes to our productivity problem",[27] and the Secretary of State for Work and Pensions has described tax credits as "a subsidy for employers which enabled the payment of lower wages".[28]

The UK Government's revised approach for tackling working poverty is based instead around three key elements:

- Stepping up efforts to encourage and support employers to increase pay and productivity, especially of the lowest earners;
- Allowing working families to keep more of what they earn by increasing the income tax personal allowance and increasing childcare support;
- Implementing welfare reforms aimed at encouraging parents to take greater responsibility for increasing their income and standard of living through entering employment, increasing their hours of work and reducing their living costs. It is also hoped that these reforms will encourage employers to increase pay.

Increasing pay and productivity

The UK Government's flagship policy for tackling working poverty is the introduction of a premium in the National Minimum Wage for adults aged 25 or over (excluding apprentices)

26 David Cameron, *Speech on Opportunity*, 22 June 2015: https://www.gov.uk/government/speeches/pm-speech-on-opportunity
27 http://www.publications.parliament.uk/pa/cm201516/cmhansrd/cm150708/debtext/150708-0001.htm, column 337
28 House of Commons, Hansard Debate, 9 July 2015, Col. 486, 2015

through a new National Living Wage. As mentioned previously, this will be introduced in April 2016 at a rate of £7.20, and is intended to increase to reach 60 per cent of median hourly earnings of adults aged 25 and over by 2020, subject to sustained economic growth. It will directly affect up to 2.8 million people over the age of 25 who otherwise would be earning less than the forecast National Living Wage in 2020 and indirectly affect many more, as its effects ripple upwards through the earning distribution.[29] The Commission warmly welcomes this move.

Allowing working families to keep more of what they earn

The second element of the UK Government's strategy is allowing working families to keep more of what they earn. The key policy here is increasing the income tax personal allowance, which will reach £11,000 in April 2016, with the Government pledging to increase it to £12,500 (or 30 hours at the National Minimum Wage rate for 48 weeks a year, if this is higher) by April 2020. The Institute for Fiscal Studies expects that a basic rate taxpayer earning more than £12,500 will pay £208 less tax in 2020–21 than they would have done if the 2015–16 personal allowance were uprated with inflation.[30]

Another important part of the Government's strategy is reducing the need for households to spend money on childcare. Measures include increasing the maximum support for childcare costs available within Universal Credit from the current 70 per cent of eligible costs to 85 per cent in April 2016, extending the current entitlement to 15 hours per week free childcare for three and four year olds to 30 hours where all adults are in work, and the introduction of tax-free childcare from 2017.

Implementing welfare reform

The final element of the strategy is the UK Government's welfare reform programme. The key policy here is the implementation of Universal Credit, which the Government hopes will have a transformative impact on employment through, for example, improving work incentives for workless families, simplifying benefit taper rates, merging the in-work and out-of-work support systems, and improving the government's capacity to help and support families in in-work poverty to increase their earnings.[31]

In addition, the 2015 Summer Budget announced a number of reductions in welfare entitlements – the vast majority of which will affect children and working-age adults in working households – expected to save £12 billion by 2019–20 and far more than that over the long-term as welfare measures are fully implemented. The most important changes (see Table 5.1) were a series of reductions to tax credit and Universal Credit entitlements (together raising £5.5 billion, or 45 per cent of total savings) and freezing all working age benefits and housing benefit in cash terms for four years (which raises £3.9 billion, or one-third of total savings). While the Government has since decided to slow down the pace at which these savings will be delivered by maintaining the current income thresholds and taper rate in the legacy tax credits system, the ultimate impact on working families by the end of the parliament, when most families are expected to be on Universal Credit, will be similar to what was originally intended.

These cuts to in-work support are of grave concern to the Commission, because they will cause real hardship to many working families and undermine the beneficial impact of other welcome initiatives such as the National Living Wage.

However, the UK Government expects that these reforms will change the behaviour of people in receipt of benefits by, for example, encouraging them to enter employment, work longer hours or reduce their living costs by moving to cheaper accommodation or having smaller families. For example, recent analysis of the early impact of Universal Credit for single, unemployed claimants in the 10 Pathfinder areas found that claimants were 6 per cent more likely to be

29 Office for Budget Responsibility, *Economic and Fiscal Outlook*, July 2015
30 Institute for Fiscal Studies, *Taxes and Benefits: The Parties' Plans*, IFS Briefing Note BN172, April 2015
31 Department for Work and Pensions, *Universal Credit: Welfare that Works*, November 2010; Department for Work and Pensions, *Universal Credit: Impact Assessment*, December 2012

in work nine months after starting their claim compared to similar Job Seekers Allowance claimants as Universal Credit was *"making it more worthwhile and easier for people to accept short-term temporary work"*.[32] The Government also hopes that reductions in in-work support will lead to increases in earnings due to the impact of the resulting decrease in effective pay rates on labour supply – they believe that employers will be forced to increase pay in order to be able to continue to attract staff.

The overall impact of welfare reforms on family incomes is uncertain given the impact that such radical changes could have on parental employment and hours of work. However, it seems certain that many low-income working families with children will see big reductions in their income over the next few years, with lone parents, single-earner couples and large families seeing particularly large falls (see Figure 5.7). While things have altered a bit due to the policy changes made in the 2015 Autumn Statement, the distributional impact of changes to tax and benefits implemented between 2015–16 and 2019–20 remains similar.[33]

Figure 5.7: Impact of the 2015 Summer Budget on household incomes in 2020

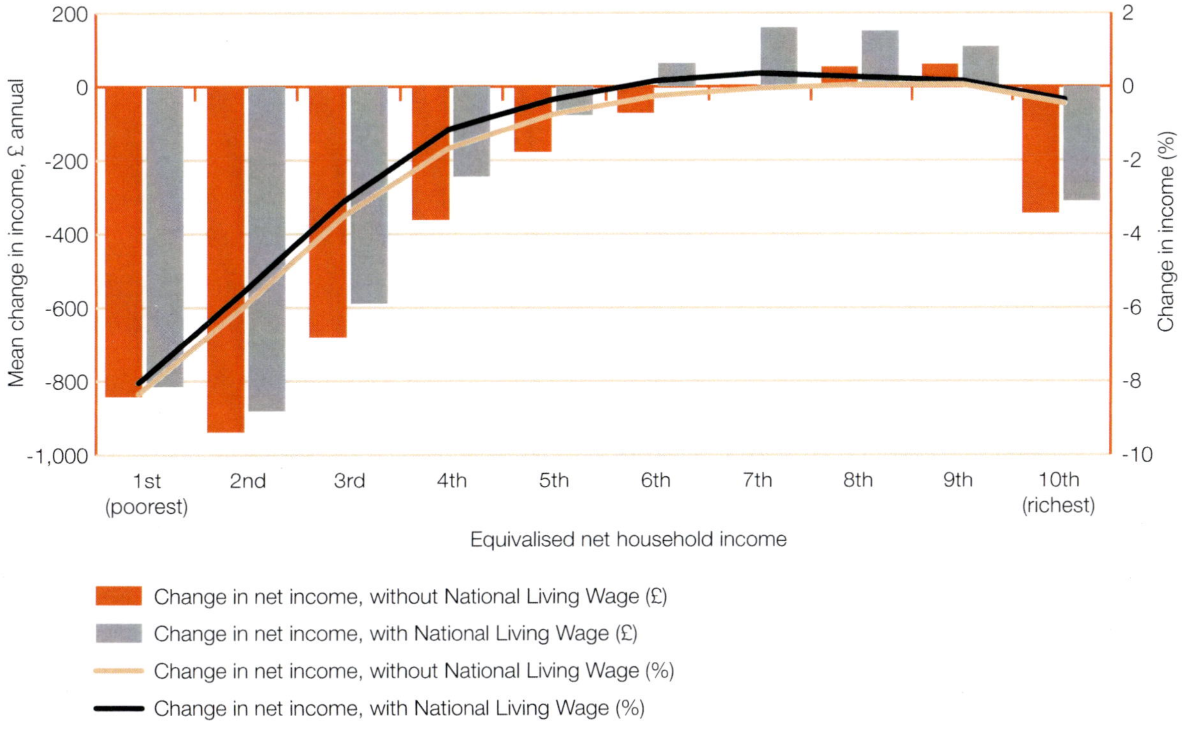

Source: Resolution Foundation, *Higher Ground: Who Gains from the National Living Wage*, 2015

32 Department for Work and Pensions, *Universal Credit – Estimating the Early Labour Market Impacts: Updated Analysis*, December 2015

33 Resolution Foundation, *O, Blessed Revisions: Fiscal Windfall and What To Do With It*, 2015

Table 5.1: Cuts in the welfare budget announced in the 2015 Summer Budget

Measure	Savings in 2019–20 (£ million)	% of total savings	Notes
Uprating: freeze working-age benefits, tax credits and local housing allowances for four years from 2016–17 in cash terms	£3,885	32.2	Frozen in cash terms: equivalent to a 6.4 per cent real terms cut between 2015–16 and 2019–20 based on Office for Budget Responsibility (OBR) Consumer Price Index (CPI) projections
Tax Credits: reduce income thresholds in tax credits and work allowances in Universal Credit from April 2016	£3,310	27.4	The income threshold in tax credits – allowed earnings before benefits begin to be reduced – were planned to be reduced from £6,420 to £3,850. Universal Credit work allowances will be abolished for non-disabled childless claimants, and reduced to £192 per month for those receiving support for housing costs (e.g. a 27 per cent cut in work allowances for single parents from the previous planned level of £263 per month), and £397 per month for those who are not (e.g. a 46 per cent cut in work allowances for single parents from the previous planned level of £734 per month) The 2015 Autumn Statement announced that the Government would not proceed with reductions in income thresholds in tax credits while retaining cuts in work allowances in Universal Credit. This will reduce total savings from this measure to £2,745 million in 2019–20
Housing benefit: reduce social sector rents by 1% each year for four years from 2016–17	£1,320	10.9	This will *increase* the disposable income of social tenants who pay part of their rent themselves – social rents are expected to decrease by 10 per cent in real terms between 2015–16 and 2019–20 (based on OBR CPI projections) – so will improve living standards of many families currently in social housing
Tax credits: limit child element to two children for new births in tax credits and new claims in Universal Credit	£1,055	8.7	This will not affect existing claimants with a continuous claim unless they have additional children
Tax credits: remove family element in tax credits and Universal Credit, and the family premium in housing benefit, for new claims	£555	4.6	This will mean a cut of up to £545 per year for families with children in receipt of tax credits or Universal Credit
Employment and Support Allowance: align Work-Related Activity Group rate with Jobseeker's Allowance for new claims	£445	3.7	From April 2017, the benefit rate paid to new claimants of Employment and Support Allowance (ESA) placed in the Work Related Activity Group (WRAG) will be reduced to align with the Jobseeker's Allowance rate. Similar changes will be made in Universal Credit

Measure	Savings in 2019–20 (£ million)	% of total savings	Notes
Benefit cap: Reduce to £20,000 (£23,000 in London)	£405	3.4	The benefit cap will be cut from £26,000 to £20,000 for: a. Childless couples where no one works >30 hours per week; b. Couples with children where either no one works >16 hours per week, or combined working hours are <24 hours per week; c. single parents working fewer than 16 hours per week. Lower caps will apply for single adults with no children working fewer than 30 hours per week
Tax credits: increase tax credits taper rate to 48%	£345	2.9	The tax credit taper was planned to increase from 41 per cent to 48 per cent of gross income from April 2016 (Universal Credit rates would have been unaffected) The 2015 Autumn Statement announced that the Government would not proceed with this measure
Housing benefit: support for mortgage interest – change from welfare payment to a loan	£255	2.1	Will allow the state to recoup the costs of support for low-income owner-occupiers
Housing benefit: pay to stay – higher income social housing tenants to pay market rents	£245	2.0	Social tenants with incomes of £30,000 per year (£40,000 in London) will pay a market rent or near-market rent, with additional income from council tenants accruing to the Exchequer
Tax credits: reduce income rise disregard in tax credits	£180	1.5	Reducing income disregard from £5,000 to £2,500
Housing benefit: end automatic entitlement for out-of-work 18–21-year-olds	£35	0.3	There will be some exemptions made in circumstances where the Government considers it to be reasonable to support a young person in living independently
Tax credits: Universal Credit parent conditionality from when youngest child turns three	£35	0.3	Introducing a new expectation that lone parents and main carers in couples will work at least part-time when their children are aged three years old (currently five years old)
Total savings by 2019–20	**£12,070**	**100%**	

The Commission was especially concerned about the plans announced in the 2015 Summer Budget to reduce the income thresholds in tax credits and work allowances in Universal Credit, and to increase the taper rate in tax credits from 41 per cent to 48 per cent. These changes would have resulted in millions of families in low-paid work who are 'doing the right thing' and working as much as society expects them to, seeing their annual income fall by thousands of pounds on 1 April 2016.They also would have made it more difficult for these families to work longer hours or find a more highly paid job in order to make good the difference: the effective marginal tax rate of parents who pay income tax and receive tax credits was planned to increase from at least 73 per cent in the current system to at least 80 per cent.

These changes were counter to the Government's objective to create "a country that backs those who work hard and do the right thing"[34], would have worsened working poverty and would have set back the Government's ambitions to improve social mobility. The Government deserves much praise for thinking again and deciding against implementing these cuts in April 2016. The delay will give families more time to adjust to the changes to the benefit system, allow the introduction of the National Living Wage to have a bigger impact on gross earnings of the low paid than otherwise and, on current plans, mean that no existing claimants lose out provided they have a continuous tax credit claim over the next few years unless they experience a significant change in circumstances.

However, cuts in Universal Credit work allowances are still going ahead. It will be very difficult for many affected families to increase their hours of work and hourly pay to avoid big cuts to their incomes compared to the current system. For example, a lone parent working full-time at the minimum wage who receives no support with their housing costs will see a reduction of £2,600 per year – £50 per week – in their income from this measure in isolation.[35] The combined effect of income tax, National Insurance and the Universal Credit taper will mean that Universal Credit claimants who pay income tax will only keep 24 per cent of any increase in their earnings: this means that the parent in this example will have to increase their earnings by some £210 per week – or 72 per cent of expected gross full-time earnings at the minimum wage in 2020[36] – to make up the income losses they will face as a result of the reduction in their work allowance. The £39 per week increase they will see in their earnings as a result of the introduction of the Living Wage[37] will help a little, but is not on the scale required to make up the losses.

A second potential issue is the rules around transitional support for those transferring from the tax credit system to the Universal Credit system and the extent of changes in circumstances that trigger the ending of such support. Given that many families will now be due substantially lower awards under Universal Credit than under the tax credits system, there will be greater incentives for claimants to avoid a change in circumstances that triggers the ending of transitional support. The Government needs to take care that the system is well-designed to avoid this.

34 Prime Minister's Office, *PM Sets Out His Vision for the Country in a One Nation Queen's Speech*, 27 May 2015

35 Their Universal Credit entitlement will be reduced by 65 per cent of their net income between the old (£734/month) and new (£397/month) work allowances

36 Based on Office for Budget Responsibility forecasts, the National Minimum Wage will be an expected £8.25 per hour in 2020 – 35 hours work at this hourly rate gives a weekly gross income of £289

37 The Office for Budget Responsibility forecast that the National Living Wage in 2020 will be £9.35 per hour - £1.10 per hour higher than the expected National Minimum Wage rate

5.4 How can more progress be made?

The UK Government's strategy will have a positive impact on some of the key drivers of working poverty. The focus on tackling low pay and increasing parental employment is particularly welcome. However, there are several implementation risks, and some of the changes that the Government has announced will have a negative impact. This section looks at the opportunities and risks around tackling each of the three working poverty problems identified earlier in the chapter:

- Tackling low pay;
- Increasing parental employment and hours of work;
- Making it easier to escape working poverty.

Tackling low pay

We welcome the introduction of the National Living Wage as an important first step in tackling in-work poverty. We believe that it could make a real difference:

- It will provide a significant boost to the earnings of parents in low-paid work. Based on OBR forecasts, someone aged over 25 working 35 hours a week at the statutory minimum would earn £39 per week, or £2,000 per year more in 2020 before adjusting for inflation as a result;[38]
- It will lead to a significant decrease in the extent of low pay. The Resolution Foundation forecast that the proportion of employees paid less than two-thirds of the median hourly wage will decrease from 21 per cent in 2014 to 19 per cent in 2020, bringing the prevalence of low pay down to levels last seen in 1985;[39]
- Those who remain in low pay will also benefit significantly. The low pay gap – the total increase in pay necessary to bring every employee up to two-thirds of median earnings – will almost half, from £7.9 billion in 2014 to £4.4 billion in 2020;[40]
- It could save small but significant sums of public money (around £800 million per year) if the Government was prepared to take action to avoid the unintended consequences of the National Living Wage on increasing the state pension and working-age benefits.[41]

The Government will need to address a number of issues to ensure that the National Living Wage's potential in tackling in-work poverty can be maximised.

First, there is a risk that the introduction of the National Living Wage could have an unintended consequence in reducing employment growth. The big increase in the wage floor that it represents – equivalent to an 11 per cent year-on-year change on the National Minimum Wage rate that applied in April 2015 – means that the UK will have one of the highest statutory minimum wages in the world. Employers might respond in a number of ways:

- Reducing employment and hours of work. The OBR has forecast that employment will decrease by 60,000, with total weekly hours worked decreasing by 4 million, although it notes that impacts are highly uncertain;
- Cutting back on non-pay conditions of employment, such as holiday pay, staff discount cards and childcare support;

38 Office for Budget Responsibility, *Economic and Fiscal Outlook*, July 2015. The Office for Budget Responsibility forecasts that the National Living Wage will be £9.35 an hour, and the National Minimum Wage will be £8.25 an hour, by 2020
39 Resolution Foundation, *Low Pay Britain* 2015, 2015
40 Resolution Foundation, *Low Pay Britain* 2015, 2015
41 Office for Budget Responsibility, *Economic and Fiscal Outlook*, July 2015. This is the total direct impact on income tax receipts, National Insurance contributions, VAT receipts, corporation tax receipts, out-of-work benefits and in-work benefits, and excludes the knock-on effects on uprating of the state pension and other benefits

- Increasing the use of zero hour and short-hour contracts to give more flexibility to adjust labour costs with demand;
- Substituting young employees or self-employed contractors not entitled to the National Living Wage for older employees who are;
- Investing in capital equipment such as self-checkouts to replace employees;
- Increasing the prices charged for goods and services, or accepting lower profits;
- Redesigning jobs and production processes to try and increase the productivity of low-paid employees.

Second, the National Living Wage will have a far bigger impact in some areas of the country, some industries and some occupations than others. Government will need to work with employers to mitigate undesirable side-effects that this could have on employment in parts of the economy that are particularly vulnerable. The recommendations we made last year about the need to give the Low Pay Commission a more proactive remit around tackling low pay are even more relevant now, given the introduction of the National Living Wage:

- While London will be hardly affected by the introduction of the National Living Wage – fewer than 10 per cent of jobs in London pay less than £7.20 per hour – there are 80 local authority districts in the UK where more than one in five jobs are paid at or below this level;[42]
- By 2020 the National Living Wage will affect six out of 10 workers in the cleaning industry, half of workers in the hospitality and residential care industries, and more than four out of 10 workers in the retail and support services industry;[43]
- The combined impact on the introduction of the National Living Wage with expected above inflation increases in the National Minimum Wage is expected to increase payroll costs for frontline social workers by £3.9 billion in 2020. This is in addition to the severe demographic and financial pressures on social care that the sector will need to deal with over the next few years. There is a risk that these additional pressures lead to increased rationing of social care and knock-on costs for other public services, such as the NHS;[44]
- The government will be effectively setting pay for 15 per cent of private sector employees by 2020 – a huge change in the labour market.[45]

Third, many parents who will see a pay rise as a result of the National Living Wage will not see a big rise in their overall incomes, as increases in income tax payments and National Insurance contributions and reductions in in-work benefits eat away much of the gains. For example, lone parents will only keep on average one-quarter of any increases in their pay resulting from the National Living Wage.[46] Unless high marginal effective tax rates are reduced, the impact of the National Living Wage on living standards will be limited for many families.

Fourth, the National Living Wage is not a true living wage. It is set at a far lower level than the voluntary living wages based on family living costs and household incomes which are promoted by the Living Wage Foundation, and now adopted by more than 2,000 employers covering 68,000 employees.[47] It is crucial that the Government continues to support and encourage employers to go further than the new statutory minimum, especially in those sectors and areas where this will have a limited impact on total labour costs: the voluntary Living Wage is set to increase rapidly over the next few years as the flipside of cuts in in-work support, with the proportion of employees paid below the voluntary Living Wage set

42 Office for National Statistics, *Annual Survey of Hours and Earnings*, 2015
43 Resolution Foundation, *Taking Up the Floor: Exploring the Impact of the National Living Wage on Employers*, 2015
44 Resolution Foundation, *Care to Pay: Meeting the Challenge of Paying the National Living Wage in Social Care*, November 2015
45 Resolution Foundation, *Low Pay Britain* 2015, 2015
46 Resolution Foundation, *Higher Ground: Who Gains from the National Living Wage*, 2015
47 Living Wage Foundation, *Living Wage Rate Increases Announced as Campaigners Call for More Businesses to Go Beyond Legal Minimums*, 30 October 2015

to increase from 22 per cent to 30 per cent between 2014 and 2020.[48] This is especially important in high-cost areas such as London, where the National Living Wage will make little difference to pay and is far below what is necessary to allow working families to sustain a basic standard of living without substantial financial support from the state.

Finally, the direct positive impact of the National Living Wage on the public finances is offset by its unintended impacts on the value of the state pension and working-age benefits. The OBR expects that there will be £1.1 billion of direct savings from higher receipts from income tax, National Insurance and lower in-work benefit payments. After accounting for direct costs arising from higher out-of-work benefit payments and lower corporation tax revenue, the net direct gains are £800 million per year. However, based on current policy, three-quarters of this will be lost through indirect knock-on effects into the state pension (which the Government has guaranteed will rise in line with average earnings growth, and which will be somewhat higher as a result of the National Living Wage) and working-age benefit uprating (inflation is also expected to be higher as a result of the National Living Wage). It is entirely feasible for the Government to claw back these unintended effects of the National Living Wage on the public purse by making compensatory reductions to these other benefits.[49]

Increasing parental employment and hours of work

Successive governments have sought to reduce child poverty by encouraging more women with dependent children, especially lone parents, to take on paid work through a combination of policy measures including:

- Improving work incentives through policies such as the introduction of Working Tax Credit and increases in the income tax personal allowance;
- Significantly increasing work expectations on lone parents, expecting them to look for work when their youngest child is five years old rather than 16 years old – as it was in 2008 before the introduction of Lone Parent Obligations;
- Providing targeted support to help lone parents enter employment;
- Extending the availability of free and subsidised childcare – for example, through the introduction of 15 hours a week free childcare for all three- and four-year-olds and the Childcare Tax Credit;
- Encouraging employers to use flexible working arrangements to help parents combine work and family life.

The Government is taking action intended to drive further increases in the maternal employment rate. For example, the introduction of Universal Credit will introduce the same work expectations for main carers in couples in receipt of tax credits as currently exist for lone parents, expectations on lone parents and second earners are set to increase further by requiring them to enter employment when their youngest child is three years old from April 2017, and the other childcare measures discussed earlier in the chapter will also help support employment.

However, other government policy changes mean that this drive may not lead to a significant shift towards full-time working among lone parents and second earners.[50] For example:

- The introduction of Universal Credit will result in a significant decrease in the incentive for second earners to enter employment and progress in work, as a higher proportion of earnings are clawed back from their benefit payments;
- There is a risk that many parents will choose to reduce their hours of work once the income supplements within Working Tax Credit at 16 and 30 hours in the current system have been removed.

48 Resolution Foundation, *Low Pay Britain* 2015, 2015
49 Office for Budget Responsibility, *Economic and Fiscal Forecast*, July 2015
50 Resolution Foundation, *Credit Where It's Due*, 2015

The net impact of changes to Universal Credit announced in the 2015 Summer Budget on work incentives is largely negative, due to significant reductions in the generosity of work allowances. Analysis by the Resolution Foundation concludes that:

> *The stated aim to boost the incentive to enter work has been significantly reduced… these changes will do very little to improve the incentives for low paid families to find a path into work and then to progress – seen as a key route out of poverty – and for many they will make a difficult situation worse.*[51]

The introduction of in-work conditionality in Universal Credit may mitigate some of these issues, but the system is still under development and policymakers are still far from clear about how it will work in practice. Relying solely on this untested system to prevent parents from acting on the increased financial incentives to reduce their working hours that exist in Universal Credit compared with the current tax credit system – especially families that currently work more hours than the proposed hours requirements, or where parents earn more than the National Minimum Wage – is risky. Further action is required to ensure that work incentives within Universal Credit and the development of the in-work conditionality system support the overall goal of tackling working poverty.

Making it easier to escape working poverty

As we have stated in previous reports, the introduction of Universal Credit provides a big opportunity to help people to progress in work, and to help ensure that entry-level employment is a springboard to higher earnings in the future, rather than a dead end with no prospects for development and progression. Action will be required by employers and government to ensure that entry-level employment can become a more reliable start of a journey to escaping in-work poverty than it currently is.

In the current tax credit system, those stuck in low-paid or low-hours employment are given little support and encouragement to progress. The move to Universal Credit could be transformative in encouraging more people in low-paid work to aspire to progress and linking them up with practical support to help them do so. However, as highlighted above, there is still limited understanding of what will be effective in helping people to progress in work, as the Government continues to test different approaches during 2015 and 2016 ahead of determining its core in-work approach.[52]

One important barrier to progression is that for some parents the relatively low financial returns from moving one step up the career ladder may not outweigh the downsides of career progression, such as a changing work–life balance, disruption to social relationships at work and the risk that promotion just doesn't work out. Our research into this issue[53] found that in many businesses, a promotion only brought a pay rise of 30–50p per hour (or £10–£20 per week). After taking account of the fact that many in receipt of tax credits would only see around a quarter of these gains due to increases in tax and a reduction in in-work benefits, it is clear that not seeking promotion may be a rational decision for many in low-paid work.

This issue is likely to become more pressing over the next few years. The introduction of the National Minimum Wage was associated with significant compression at the lower end of the pay distribution with, for example, the proportion of employees paid within 50p of the statutory minimum doubling from 5 per cent to 10 per cent in the decade 2001–11.[54] Further pay compression is expected as a result of the introduction of the National Living Wage, and there is a risk that this will result in pay escalators grinding to a halt.

Leaving financial incentives aside, factors affecting progression opportunities identified in our research included:

51 Resolution Foundation, *A Budget for Workers? The Impact of the Summer Budget on Work Incentives in Universal Credit*, 2015
52 Department for Work and Pensions, *Universal Credit at Work – Spring 2015*, 2015
53 Social Mobility and Child Poverty Commission, *Escape Plan*, November 2014
54 Resolution Foundation, *Low Pay Britain* 2014

- The organisational culture of employers, including whether policies to encourage and support pay progression are in place and implemented – for example, developing career ladders, supporting those in lower-paid roles to progress and ensuring that promotion opportunities are seen to be fairly allocated;
- The line manager role in encouraging employees to progress and helping them to do so through prioritising development of their staff;
- Internal limits to progression – there are likely to be fewer opportunities for progression than there are able staff at the level below looking to move on, with a risk that encouraging staff to aspire to move up the ladder ends up discouraging many who find their aspirations frustrated;
- A perception that securing promotion requires going 'above and beyond the call of duty' – for example, through a willingness to work unpaid overtime, forgo holiday entitlements, not take time off sick or for family emergencies, and attending work at short notice, freezing out those with caring responsibilities. The increasing use of more flexible forms of employment such as short hours and zero hours contracts may exacerbate this issue;
- Worries among employees about the risks of promotion – for example, around capability to progress, work–life balance, not enjoying a new role and disruption to their social relationships at work.

5.5 Conclusion and Recommendations

If the Government's strategy to improve social mobility and reduce child poverty by making the UK into a higher pay, lower tax, lower welfare society is to have any chance of success, three conditions will need to be satisfied:

- Employers will need to take more responsibility for their employees' living standards by helping them develop their skills, become more productive and progress up the pay scale and combine work and family life;
- The Government will need to set a clear goal for the UK to become a Living Wage country by 2025, and develop a comprehensive pay, progression and productivity strategy to achieve that goal, building on the strong foundations that will be laid by the introduction of the National Living Wage and the implementation of Universal Credit;
- The Government will need to revitalise work incentives in tax credits and Universal Credit so it can more effectively meet its aspiration to make work pay, encourage people to progress in work, and ensure that everyone who 'does the right thing' can enjoy decent living standards.

Recommendation 1: Employers should take more responsibility for their employees' living standards with change led by a vanguard group of 'One Nation Employers' who can act as a beacon for others.

There is a long tradition in the UK and elsewhere of visionary business leaders recognising the importance of ensuring that their workers are able to enjoy a decent standard of living because it makes good business sense as well as making good social sense. An increasing number of large businesses in traditionally low-paying sectors have signed up to the Living Wage set by the Living Wage Foundation, and many other employers make developing their staff and helping them get on in life a core business priority. More and more employers are realising that these kinds of activities are a win-win with a range of benefits – not just for workers, but for businesses in terms of greater staff loyalty, retention, productivity and service quality.

The Government has said that it wants to build on this. It expects employers to take a lot more responsibility for supporting their employees' living standards and helping them get on in life by, for example, filling the gap in working households' budgets that will be left by cuts in in-work support through the benefit system, and increasing their investment in apprenticeships and adult skills.

Realising this profound shift in responsibility from the state to the private sector will require all UK employers to develop strategies to improve the living standards of their lowest-paid employees. Government should catalyse change here by introducing a vanguard group of 'One Nation Employers' who act as a beacon for others. The commitments made by a One Nation Employer[55] should include:

- **Pay and security** – become accredited Living Wage employers with the Living Wage Foundation, and minimise the use of zero hour and short-hour contracts, only using them at the margins to manage fluctuating resource demand rather than as standard employment contracts for most staff;
- **Line management** – increase managers' focus on developing the staff who work for them, including providing practical training for managers on how to be effective in helping their staff develop and by rewarding them on the basis of how they retain and develop their staff, as well as business outcomes such as profit and sales;
- **Communication** – ensure that all workers are able to access information on job and development opportunities, even if they work remotely or have no access to intranet resources, recognise the value of low-paid roles in internal communications, and use human resources data to develop more effective communication with low-paid workers;
- **Skills and progression** – develop and communicate clear progression pathways out of low-paid roles, make development opportunities accessible to all staff, and consider how to develop incremental progression steps to reward staff for higher productivity and incentivise development;
- **Job design** – seek out opportunities to redesign low-paid roles, in order to drive productivity improvements by, for example, giving more autonomy, discretion and ability to innovate to employees in low-paid roles, and looking for ways to improve the scope for workers in service sectors to add value by improving the customer experience;[56]
- **Supporting employees with living costs** – increase the focus of benefits-in-kind on support for low-paid workers, such as staff discounts and loans for one-off costs such as deposits for rented accommodation and season tickets.

55 Built on work carried out on behalf of the Social Mobility and Child Poverty Commission in Business in the Community, *Beyond Pay: An Inquiry into Improving Low-Income Employment*, 2015

56 See for example, Confederation of British Industry (CBI), *A Better Off Britain: Improving Lives by Making Growth Work for Everyone*, 2014; ACAS, *Building Productivity in the UK*, 2015; UK Commission for Employment and Skills, *Growth Through People*, 2014; and Ton, Z., *The Good Jobs Strategy*, 2014 for case studies and research on how changes in job design can boost productivity

The Scotland Business Pledge

The Scottish Government launched the Scotland Business Pledge in May 2015.[57] By making the Pledge, businesses demonstrate their commitment to the goals of boosting productivity, competitiveness, employment, fair work, workforce engagement and development and to delivering them through their actions and future plans.

The Pledge involves nine individual strands of business improvement activity which many companies across Scotland have already adopted:

1. **Paying the Living Wage** – ideally via formal accreditation, but at the very least paying the Living Wage for all employees aged 18 and over;
2. **Not using exploitative zero hours contracts** – committing to appropriate use of zero hour contracts linked to seasonal work, resilience or highly variable workloads, and providing similar employment rights to other staff;
3. **Supporting progressive workforce engagement** – committing to putting in place effective best practice management systems, e.g. a people plan, skills strategy, employee engagement systems and so on;
4. **Investing in youth** – committing to support young people into employment, e.g. partnerships with schools, careers advice, apprenticeships, attaining Investors in Young People status;
5. **Making progress on diversity and gender balance** – committing to developing a better balance in the firm, e.g. by signing up to Partnership for Change to work towards gender balance on boards by 2020;
6. **Committing to an innovation programme** – committing to implement an innovation strategy;
7. **Pursuing international business opportunities** – demonstrating the actions being taken to generate new international business or expand to new markets;
8. **Playing an active role in the community** – demonstrating how the business provides benefits to the local community, e.g. supporting community activities, volunteering, contributing to charity and so on;
9. **Committing to prompt payment** – committing to pay suppliers within 60 days, and working towards a norm of 30 days.

Signatories must be paying the Living Wage and meeting at least two of the other principles immediately and make a commitment to achieving all nine over time. Businesses making a Pledge are allowed to display the Scottish Business Pledge logo on their website and elsewhere.

The website for the initiative sets out the details about each component of the pledge in a user-friendly way, including a summary of its business benefits, why it is included in the pledge, why it is good for Scotland, and how to access help in order to be able to meet that component of the pledge.

It is still too early to gauge the impact that the Scotland Business Pledge has had on business practices in Scotland, but so far 151 businesses have signed up.

Further details are available from https://scottishbusinesspledge.scot

57 Nicola Sturgeon, *Launch of the Scottish Business Pledge*, speech at Tynecastle Stadium, Edinburgh, 26 May 2015

Recommendation 2: The Government should set a clear objective for the UK to become a Living Wage country by 2025 at the latest, and work with business to develop a comprehensive pay, progression and productivity plan that aligns Government programmes behind that goal.

The Commission's report last year recommended that the Government set itself an objective for the UK to become a living wage country by 2025 at the latest. The introduction of the National Living Wage – and the commitments that the Government has made to increase its value to 60 per cent of median hourly earnings by April 2020 – is a very welcome first step towards this goal.

The ultimate goal should be for the UK to make the transition from a low-pay, low-productivity economy to a high-pay, high-productivity economy where everyone earns enough to secure a decent standard of living and those in low-paid roles are able to develop their skills, become more productive and progress over the course of their working lives.

The next stage of this journey is for the Government to commit to Britain becoming a Living Wage country by:

- **Reducing the proportion of people who earn less than two-thirds of median hourly pay to 10 per cent of employees.** This would halve the proportion projected to be in low pay against this measure in 2020 and put the UK on a par with the best performing countries in Europe;
- **Reducing the proportion of people who earn less than the living wages set by the Living Wage Foundation to 15 per cent.** This would halve the proportion of those projected to be in low pay against this measure in 2020, and return it to pre-recession levels;
- **Reducing the proportion of people who get stuck in low pay for more than a decade to 10 per cent.** This would halve the proportion of the population who get stuck in low pay compared to the period 2002–12.

The Government should set intermediate milestones towards achieving these ambitious goals by 2025. Critically, the introduction of the National Living Wage – and further increases in its value – will need to be built on productivity improvements if it is to be sustainable, and avoid the risk of the unintended consequences for those whom the policy is intended to help. The Government cannot afford to cross its fingers and hope that these potential adverse impacts will not happen in practice. It will need to address them.

Key planks of a strategy to make the UK a living wage country by 2025

A shared low pay and earnings progression strategy between the Department for Business, Innovation and Skills, Department for Work and Pensions and the Treasury, to maximise the effectiveness of their programmes (e.g. investment in adult skills training and careers advice support) in achieving the goals of tackling low pay and helping low-income parents to progress in work.

A revitalised role for the Low Pay Commission, giving it a broader, forward-looking remit to tackle low pay, including to make recommendations about what would be required to increase productivity to allow the 2020 target for the National Living Wage to be achieved, and to look beyond the statutory wage floors to cover the issue of low pay more broadly.

A detailed implementation plan for the National Living Wage, including carrying out analysis to ensure that its possible labour market consequences are understood much better than they are at the moment to inform mitigation strategies, looking at the scope for using targeted cuts in business taxation and regulation to support those areas, industries and business which are most affected and considering how faster progress can be made in those sectors that are least vulnerable to increases in pay at the bottom of the earnings distribution.

Lining up existing policies behind the strategic goal of creating a living wage country, including the financial incentives for work programme providers, deployment of the adult skill budget, public sector procurement, support with childcare costs and ensuring that the new in-work support regime in Universal Credit looks beyond those on the National Minimum Wage or working few hours.

Introducing more stringent transparency requirements, such as making the publication of pay ratios and the proportion of workers paid below the living wages set by the Living Wage Foundation a requirement for listed companies and public sector employers.

Developing stronger partnerships with business to improve productivity at the bottom of the labour market, and improve living standards, including encouraging employers to become One Nation Employers (see above) and to rebuild careers ladders and upgrade skills, learning from programmes such as Boston Skillworks in the USA and the UK Commission for Employment and Skills' Futures Programme.

Creating a virtuous circle, by recycling the £800 million direct savings from higher tax receipts and lower welfare spending arising from the introduction of the National Living Wage into anti-poverty policies.

Recommendation 3: Revitalising employment incentives in Universal Credit.

We strongly support the aims of Universal Credit, and believe that it could have a transformational impact on work incentives through the simplification and responsiveness to fluctuations in income that it will bring; through smoothing the high marginal deduction rates that some claimants face; and through allowing more support and encouragement to be given to help those in working poverty increase their earnings.

However, the impact of fiscal pressures on the shape of work incentives in the programme and on the extent of in-work support risk the original aspirations set out by the architects of Universal Credit back in 2009 not being delivered. Worse still, there is a risk that incentives to progress in work for many families could end up being worse than they were in the pre-2010 system. This would be a missed opportunity.

The immediate priority must be taking action to ensure that the introduction of Universal Credit does not make families with children who 'do the right thing' (in terms of working as much as society expects them to) worse off than they would be under the current system. That means reversing the cuts to Universal Credit work allowances enacted through the Universal Credit (Work Allowance) Amendment Regulations 2015 before they are implemented in April 2016.

The medium-term objective should be to make improvements to Universal Credit to improve work incentives by introducing a work allowance for second earners in couple households, adjusting work allowances in step with changes in direct taxation and integrating free school meals and council tax support in the system to avoid creating new cliff edges.

The longer-term objective should be to return Universal Credit to its original aspirations once the national debt starts to fall. Work allowances should be returned to the level originally planned in 2012[58] and uprated in step with increases in earnings since then in order to improve work incentives. The taper rate in Universal Credit should be reduced from 65 per cent to 55 per cent – as originally envisaged by the designers of Universal Credit[59] – to provide better incentives for low-paid workers to progress in work.

58 Department for Work and Pensions, *Universal Credit: Welfare That Works*, November 2010
59 Centre for Social Justice, *Dynamic Benefits: Towards Welfare That Works*, September 2009

Chapter 6: Reducing persistent poverty

- **Over one million children live in persistent poverty. This is caused by a complex range of interrelated factors.**
- **Families in persistent poverty are often struggling with the combined effects of having relatively few skills; a disability or ill health; and high living costs.**
- **The Government's emphasis on getting these families into work is right, but to succeed it will need to focus harder on tackling the multi-causal nature of persistent poverty.**
- **The Government should set a goal of ensuring that by 2020 the UK is one of the top five Organisation for Economic Co-operation and Development (OECD) countries for having the fewest children living in workless households. This would involve reducing the number of children in workless households by half a million and would require a significant reduction both in the number of workless couples and in the number of lone parents who do not work.**
- **This new national effort should be led by a refocused and rebranded Troubled Families initiative tasked with offering personalised help to get persistently poor families into secure employment, and operating closely with the new Work and Health programme and Jobcentre Plus advisors.**
- **To encourage people to invest more of their time and resources into acquiring new skills, long-term unemployed adults should be given personal learning accounts.**

6.1 Introduction

Most people in poverty eventually find a way to improve their situation, often within a couple of years of the events that set them back.[1] But some people get stuck for much longer.[2] Persistent poverty has severe long-term consequences for those it affects and reducing it should be a top priority in any country. But despite many initiatives on the part of Government and others to address the problem, there is currently no cohesive drive to do so. It is time to put that right.

Lacking any financial cushion, families in persistent poverty are more likely than those in temporary poverty to fall behind on their household bills and to run out of money by the end

1 ONS, *Persistent Poverty in the UK and EU, 2008-2013*, 2015
2 Persistent poverty is defined in the UK as having less than 60 per cent of current median income for at least three of the previous four years

of the week.[3] Furthermore, living in persistent poverty has a long-term effect, particularly on children. Not only does growing up in a persistently poor family make for a miserable childhood, but it is likely to damage a child's health, lower their educational performance and reduce social mobility.[4]

Misconceptions about why people end up in this situation are rife. When asked, the public tend to cite parental alcohol/drug addiction and family breakdown as some of the main causes of child poverty.[5] But the reality is that households in persistent poverty share many characteristics with families who experience poverty only temporarily. These include being low skilled, having more than three children or experiencing a long-term disability and illness. What sets them apart, however, is that they are more likely to be suffering from the concentrated effects of a number of these factors at the same time.

The UK Government has made clear that it is committed to tackling the causes of poverty, but it has yet to publish a detailed anti-poverty strategy. This is disappointing, particularly at a time when substantial welfare cuts are being made. The Commission believes that action is needed now. It is time to review our approach to persistent poverty and to adopt new strategies, with a special focus on reducing the number of children living in workless households. Although good progress has been made, Britain still lags behind many other OECD members on this measure. We can and must do better.

6.2 Does today's reality meet the One Nation vision?

Ideally, in a One Nation country poverty would be a thing of the past. At a minimum, child poverty would be a transient experience and would not inflict lasting damage into adulthood. We are far from being that country.

Approximately 2.3 million children live in poverty in the UK.[6] Although there are no official estimates for persistent child poverty since 2008,[7] the long-term trend has been for between 50 and 70 per cent of children in poverty to experience it persistently rather than temporarily.[8] If we assume that the rate of persistent child poverty is still in line with this pattern, this would imply that between 1.1 million and 1.6 million children are living in persistently poor households, a number which even at the lower end is far too high.

Younger children are more likely to experience persistent poverty. The Millennium Cohort Study (MCS), which monitors the experiences of a group of children born in 2000-01, found that, in 2012–13, while fewer than half (47 per cent) of the MCS children had never been touched by income poverty, around one in six (17 per cent) children had been poor in at least four of the five MCS surveys that have taken place so far (Figure 6.1).[9]

3 Department for Work And Pensions, *The Circumstances of Persistently Poor Families with Children: Evidence from the Families and Children Study (FACS)*, 2008

4 JRF, *Does Money Affect Children's Outcomes?: A Systemic Review*, 2013

5 National Centre for Social Research, *Child Poverty in Britain*, 2013

6 Department for Work and Pensions, *Households Below Average Income: An Analysis of the Income Distribution 1994/95 – An Analysis,* Tables 4a and 4b, 2015. To enable international comparisons relative poverty is defined in this chapter as below 60 per cent of contemporary median income, before housing costs. However, relative income poverty among children after housing costs stood at 28 per cent or 3.7 million children in 2013/14

7 This was the last year for which the British Household Panel Study (BHPS) (on which the DWP relied for its estimate) was in operation. Since then the BHPS sample has since been amalgamated into the much larger *Understanding Society* study which started in 2009. With sufficient time having now elapsed to gather the four years of data required, persistent poverty estimates covering the period 2010–2013 should be published next year

8 HMG, *Consultation on Setting the 2020 Persistent Child Poverty Target*, 2014

9 Centre for Longitudinal Studies. *MCS Age 11 Initial Findings*, 2013

Figure 6.1: Poverty across the five surveys of the MCS

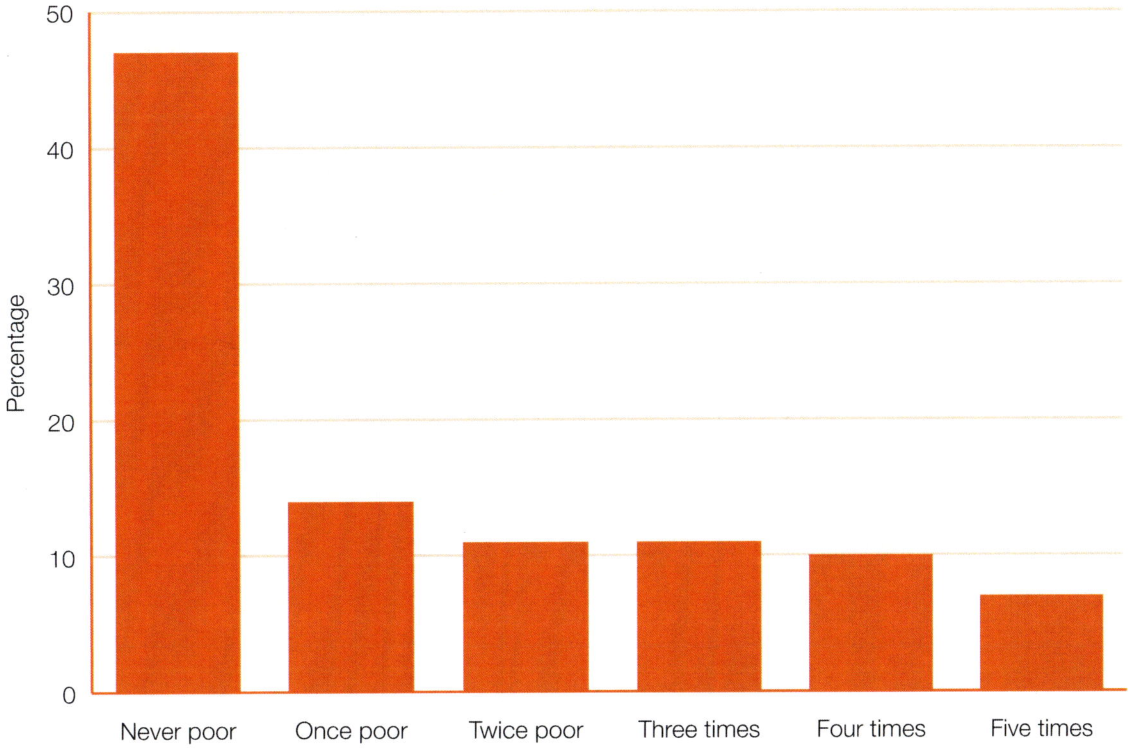

Source: Centre for Longitudinal Studies. *MCS Age 11 Initial Findings*, 2013

Britain's performance on persistent child poverty is similar to that of most of its European neighbours. Set against the EU's richest member states (and Iceland), we stood roughly in the middle of the league table in 2012 (the last year for which there was data), with a rate of persistent child poverty that was slightly lower than the average.[10] However, our performance was significantly below that achieved by countries such as Denmark, proof that low levels of persistent child poverty are entirely possible in advanced economies.

10 The EU 15 are: Austria, Belgium, Denmark, Finland, France, Germany, Greece, Ireland, Italy, Luxembourg, the Netherlands, Portugal, Spain, Sweden and the United Kingdom. The league table excludes Sweden and Ireland, neither of which submitted data for 2012; Eurostat, *Persistent at-risk-of-poverty rates*, online database, 2012, http://knoema.com/ilc_li21/persistent-at-risk-of-poverty-rate-by-sex-and-age-source-silc

Figure 6.2: Persistent poverty rate in 2012

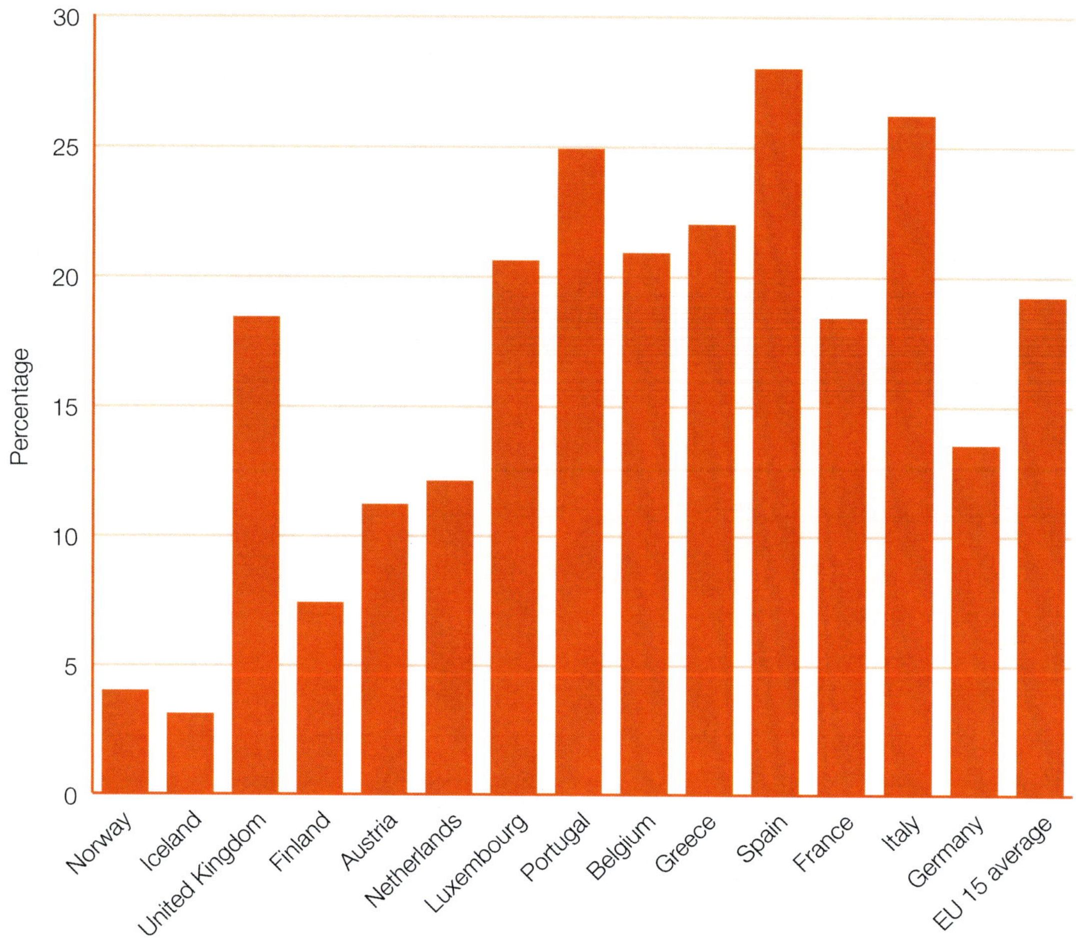

Source: SILC

As well as being too high persistent poverty in the UK is unevenly spread. The MCS Study cited above found greater shares of children in persistent poverty in Wales and Northern Ireland than England and Scotland (21 per cent and 19 per cent, compared to 16 per cent and 13 per cent), a reflection of long-standing regional disparities in wealth and economic opportunities.[11] In the following sections we explore in more detail the causes of persistent poverty and why a more focused strategic response to it is necessary.

Problem 1 – Persistent poverty is typically the product of multiple factors with different households facing different challenges.

At its most basic level, persistent income poverty arises from a long-term imbalance between the incomes of families and the costs of meeting their basic needs. But the precise routes by which different families arrive at this situation span a huge number of individual choices and circumstances. Many people demonstrating some of the main observable risk factors will not fall into persistent poverty, for instance because of support from their wider family. This poses a serious challenge to policymakers when trying to arrive at interventions which are most likely to benefit the largest numbers of people.

The Department for Work and Pensions (DWP) recently tried to fill this gap with a major evidence review of the causes of child poverty, focusing particularly on the factors that make it harder for families to escape. Thirteen family and child characteristics were measured against three criteria: the degree of certainty that a characteristic affects child poverty; the strength of that effect; and the number of people affected.

11 Centre for Longitudinal Studies, *MCS Age 11 Initial Findings*, 2013

The top five factors to emerge from this exercise are listed in Table 6.1. At the head of the list was worklessness and low earnings, underpinned by analysis showing that working even temporarily leads to a substantial reduction in the odds of experiencing persistent poverty. Specifically, a poor two-parent family where one parent is temporarily employed is around five times less likely to experience persistent poverty than a poor family where both parents are persistently out of work.[12] The MCS Age 11 survey also suggests worklessness is a major factor, with half of the children it surveyed in persistent poverty living in workless households.[13]

Table 6.1: The impact of various factors driving child poverty[14]

	% of children in persistent poverty	Probability of leaving poverty	Probability of re-entering poverty
Long-term worklessness and low earnings	38%	If household head is employed +40% If a second adult is employed +60%	If household head is employed -50% If a second adult is employed -50%
Low parental qualifications	20%	If household head has A levels or above +20%	If household head has A levels or above -25%
Larger families (three or more dependent children)	25%	If an additional child joins the household -20% The presence of a child aged 1–5 in the household -30%	If an additional child joins the household +35%
Lone parenthood	23%	If there is an extra adult in the household +25%	Data unavailable
Parental disability/ ill health	22%	Data unavailable	Data unavailable

Source: Low Income Dynamics 1991-2008; Household Below Average Incomes 2011/12

Because some of the studies that influenced the exercise were several years old the Commission asked the Office for National Statistics (ONS) to apply the five risk factors to more recent data on persistent child poverty to check that they were still exerting a large effect. This new analysis confirmed that the associations identified by the evidence review remained strong (Table 6.2), but it also brought out an important point – if anything significant differentiates families in persistent poverty from ones in temporary poverty it is that the former are more likely to suffer from several of the factors at the same time. For example, in 2013 just

12 Barnes, M., Conolly, A., and Tomaszewski, W., *The Circumstances of Persistently Poor Families with Children: Evidence from the Families and Children Study (FACS)*, DWP: London, 2008

13 Centre for Longitudinal Studies, *MCS Age 11 Initial Findings*, 2013

14 This is a simplified version of a table 4 originally published in DWP, *An Evidence Review of the Drivers of Child Poverty for Families in Poverty Now and for Poor Children Growing up to be Poor Adults*, 2014

4 per cent of children in households with one risk factor were in persistent poverty compared with 35 per cent of children in families experiencing four or more risk factors (Table 6.3).

Table 6.2: Dependent children living in persistent poverty or not by family characteristics, 2013

		One adult families	Large families	Low parental qualifications	Long-term illness or disability	Long-term workless families
Persistent poverty	N	395,000	265,000	234,000	222,000	190,000
	%	49	33	29	28	24
Not in persistent poverty	N	1,681,000	2,700,000	1,104,000	1,429,000	895,000
	%	16	25	10	13	8

Source: EU-SILC, General Lifestyle Survey

Table 6.3: Persistent poverty rate for dependent children experiencing different numbers of entrenchment characteristics, 2013

	Number of characteristics experienced				All with dependent children
	0	1	2-3	4-5	
Persistent poverty rate (%)	3	4	20	35	7

Source: EU-SILC, General Lifestyle Survey

This layering effect is best understood looking at specific family types. For instance, the ONS analysis for the Commission suggests that more than one-third of children in persistent poverty now live in families with three or more dependent children, and nearly one-third live with a parent who has a long-term illness or disability (Table 6.2). On one level this is unsurprising – the estimated cost for a household led by a parent couple to achieve a minimally acceptable standard of living (as defined by the general public for each additional child) in 2015 rises by at least one-third if they have more than two children.[15] A similar issue occurs with many families with disabled adults. Analysis by the disability charity Scope suggests that on average, disabled people spend £550 a month on costs directly associated with their disability, while one in 10 spends over £1,000 per month on additional costs arising from their disability.[16]

But in addition to generating additional costs these factors can also affect earning capacity. Large families in persistent poverty are more likely to have children of pre-school age and the DWP's own research indicates that many parents are willing to forego higher incomes from paid work in order to spend time caring for their children when young.[17] This is particularly true for lone parents; of those who have three or more children just 38 per cent are in work.[18] This contrasts with the situation for couple households. Finding it far easier to share the

15 Hirsch, D., *The Cost of a Child in 2015*, CPAG: London, 2015
16 Brawn, E., *Priced Out: Ending the Financial Penalty of Disability by 2020*, 2014
17 DWP, *Making Decisions about Work in Low-income Couple Households: A Report to the Child Poverty Unit*, 2014
18 ONS, *Family Size in 2012*, 2013

responsibilities for caring and undertaking paid work, 87 per cent of couples with three or more children have one adult in work.[19]

Families with disabled adults may find it harder to meet their additional costs due to problems with finding suitable high-quality employment – the rate for people with disabilities continues to be significantly less than for people without a disability or limiting health condition (Table 6.4). When work is found it is also more likely to be low paid – the proportion of employees with a work-limiting disability in low pay is around 10 per cent higher than for other employees.[20]

Table 6.4: Comparative employment status, Equality Act core disabled/not classified as Equality Act core disabled, 2015

	Economically active	In Employment	Unemployed	Economically inactive
Classified as Equality Act core disabled and/or work limiting disabled only	53.9	47.9	11.2	46.1
Not classified as Equality Act core disabled and/or work limiting disabled	83.4	79.4	4.8	16.6

Source: Labour Force Survey, April–June 2015

Other risk factors affecting smaller groups of people can also be significant, for instance ethnicity. The MCS Age 11 survey data showed that 56 per cent of the children interviewed of Pakistani and Bangladeshi origin were in persistent poverty (the rates for other ethnic minority groups, such as children of mixed ethnicity were much lower). Both groups are more likely to have large families than other ethnicities and although most are couple households,[21] thus increasing the scope to share caring responsibilities and work at the same time, they also suffer from some of the highest unemployment levels (17 per cent are unemployed versus 7 per cent of white British people).[22]

Problem 2 –The causes and consequences of persistent child poverty are not being addressed in a strategic way.

Although enshrined as a target in the Child Poverty Act 2010, reducing the number of children living in persistent poverty has not received sustained attention from policymakers or civil society. In part this may be explained by the lack of regular official data in recent years.[23]

Since the causes of persistent poverty and temporary poverty are largely the same, it is tempting to assume that activity designed to tackle the latter will also bring down the former. *The Child Poverty Strategy 2014 to 2017*, for example, contains no specific section outlining how persistent child poverty should be addressed. It focuses on tackling worklessness to reduce levels of child poverty. There is some justification for this. The United Kingdom has made progress over the last 20 years in reducing the number of children living in workless households (down from 19.8 per cent of all children to 11.8 per cent), but it remains behind much of the OECD on this measure (see Figure 6.3).[24]

19 ONS, *Family Size in 2012*, 2013
20 Heslop, P., *Disabled People and Their Relationship with Poverty*, PSE: UK, 2013
21 Connolly, H., and Raha, C., 'Households and families', in Dobbs, J., Green, H., and Zealey, L., (eds), *Focus on Ethnicity and Religion*, Palgrave Macmillan, 2006
22 DWP, *Labour Market Status by Ethnic Group: data to September 2013*, 2014
23 This was the last year for which the British Household Panel Study (BHPS) (on which the DWP relied for its estimate) was in operation. Since then the BHPS sample has since been amalgamated into the much larger *Understanding Society* study which started in 2009. With sufficient time having now elapsed to gather the four years of data required, persistent poverty estimates covering the period 2010–2013 should be published next year
24 Office for National Statistics, *Working and Workless Households*, 2015

Figure 6.3: Children by household employment status in the OECD, 2013

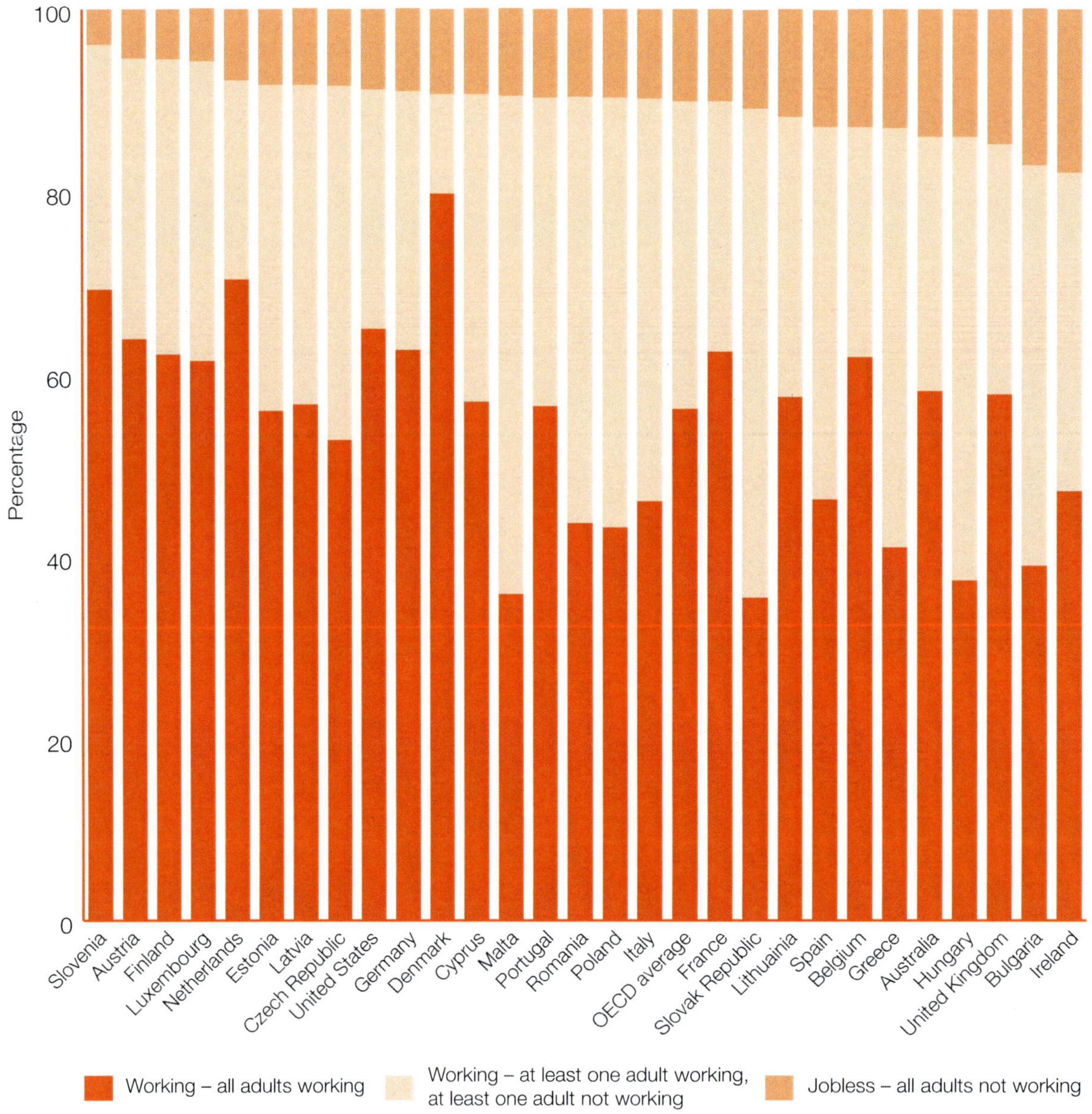

Source: OECD

Note: Data was not submitted to the OECD from Canada, Chile, Iceland, Israel, Japan, Korea, Mexico, New Zealand, Norway, Sweden, Switerzerland, Turkey and Croatia

However, tackling persistent poverty through a focus on worklessness will only be effective if it is based on a clear understanding of the barriers that individually and in combination prevent people from seeking and finding paid work. As it currently stands the Child Poverty Strategy contains no clear measures for assessing progress against long-term worklessness and lacks a detailed plan for how underlying labour market disadvantages, whether related (for example) to ethnicity, disability or a lack of skills among adults, are to be addressed.

The further issue is that conflating the two types of poverty potentially obscures how the experience of persistent poverty can itself push workless parents further from the labour market. A 'discouraged worker effect' has been long observed to be a product of protracted periods of worklessness.[25] The compound effects of that pessimism, coping with multiple issues and having to juggle very tight finances can make the prospect of paid work seem ever more remote.[26]

25 Jahoda, M., *Employment and Unemployment: A Social-psychological Analysis*, 1982
26 Shildrick, T., *et al.*, *Poverty and Insecurity: Life in Low Pay, no Pay Britain*, 2012

This phenomenon helps explain reports from Work Programme advisors that as many as half of their clients have no serious intention of seeking work.[27] This is in stark contrast to other studies which have reported that the vast majority of long-term unemployed people would like to find a job.[28] It is difficult to know what the truth of the matter is here, with both sets of evidence relying on subjective viewpoints for their results. But interviews done by Tracy Shildrick and colleagues with families who have long-term histories of worklessness indicate that it is perfectly possible for a person to clearly understand the advantages of being employed, but at the same time believe their situation – relative to others in the labour market – to be so poor as to render intensive efforts at job search pointless.[29]

Problem 3: Low skills are an increasingly sure route to persistent poverty.

A leading British researcher in this field, Steven Jenkins, has found that if the head of a household in persistent poverty has A levels, they are 20 per cent more likely to exit poverty and, having left poverty, around 25 per cent less likely to re-enter it (all other factors being equal).

The low skills problem can manifest itself in a number of ways. For instance, Pakistani and Bangladeshi families who are in persistent poverty typically have more problems in reading and speaking English than those who are better off.[30] Indeed, separating this from other factors (education level, family type and ethnicity), having English as a first language has been found by one study to reduce the risk of being in persistent poverty by 5 per cent.[31]

The impact of low skills is also seen in the case of lone parent households, who make up a large proportion of the families in persistent poverty (30 per cent in the MCS Age 11 survey;[32] 49 per cent in the ONS data). While there has been a welcome increase in one-parent employment (63 per cent in 2014 compared to 43 per cent in 1996), the positive consequences have been limited by the fact that single mothers (who represent 91 per cent of lone parents) are twice as likely to be in low-paid work (such as cleaning or catering) as mothers in couples.[33]

In part this is because lone parents gravitate towards industries with flexible working patterns.[34] It also may be the case that increased welfare conditionality is pushing some qualified lone parents into jobs which under-utilise their skills.[35] However, a crucial factor is the low skills many lone parents have to begin with. A third (32 per cent) of single parents only have GCSE or equivalent level qualifications, compared to less than a quarter of couple parents and less than a fifth (17 per cent) of people without dependent children. Just 11 per cent of single parents have a degree-level qualification or higher, compared with 23 per cent of couple parents and 20 per cent of people with no dependent children.[36]

Some of this appears to be rooted in the age at which people first have children. With the economy generating fewer manual and lower-skilled jobs on which it is possible to support a family through earnings alone, the vast majority of young people now postpone parenthood in order to pursue qualifications (Table 6.5).

---

27 Dunn, A., 'Activation worker's perception of their long term unemployed clients' attitudes towards employment', *Journal of Social Policy*, Volume 42 / Issue 04, 2013
28 Dean, H., and Taylor-Gooby, P., *Dependency Culture: The Explosion of a Myth*, 1992
29 Shildrick, T., *et al.*, *Poverty and Insecurity: Life in Low Pay, no Pay Britain*, 2012
30 Fisher, P., and Nandi A., *Poverty Across Ethnic Groups Through Recession and Austerity*, 2015
31 Ibid.
32 Insert Centre for Longitudinal Studies, *MCS Age 11 Initial Findings*, 2013
33 ONS, *Families in the Labour Market 2014*, 2014
34 Coleman, N., and Riley, T., *Lone Parent Obligations: Following Lone Parents' Journeys from Benefits to Work*, 2012
35 Dewar, L., *Is the Work Programme Working for Single Parents? An Analysis of the Experience of Single Parents on the Work Programme*, 2014
36 ONS, *Social Trends 39*, Chapter 3, 2009

Table 6.5: Live births by age group of mother and father, 2012 (England and Wales)

	Percentage of live births by age group						
	Under 20	20–24	25–29	30–34	35–39	40–44	45 and over
Mothers	4.6	18.2	27.7	29.6	15.7	3.8	0.3
Fathers	1.7	11.2	21.9	29.4	21.0	10.0	4.8

Source: Office for National Statistics, analysis undertaken by Policy Exchange[37]

Among mothers who had their first child before 20, only 2.1 per cent will go on to have degree-level qualifications or the equivalent, while nearly a quarter have no qualifications whatsoever. Over time this disadvantage sticks and plays out in a range of negative ways, with mothers who had their children young being much more likely to be unemployed or to be working part time (Table 6.6).

Table 6.6: Employment rates of UK single mothers by the estimated age that they had their first child, 2008–12

	Estimated age lone mother had first child					
	16–19	20–23	24–29	30–34	35+	All
Full time	8.90%	15.30%	27.40%	36.20%	30.90%	23.70%
Part time	21.70%	31.80%	34.90%	36.80%	34.50%	32.40%
Unemployed	17.10%	13.20%	8.90%	7.70%	7.40%	10.80%
Inactive	52.30%	39.70%	28.80%	19.30%	27.30%	33.10%

Source: Labour Force Survey, analysis undertaken by Policy Exchange

6.3 How are these problems being addressed?

A number of important factors have – to varying degrees and in different combinations – the power to place obstacles in the path of parents seeking and finding work. These are: a lack of skills; poor health and disability; damaged morale stemming from long-term poverty and worklessness; and heavy caring responsibilities. The Government's approach to unravelling these knots of disadvantage is made up of several parts: a range of measures focused on motivating and supporting people (especially the long-term workless) to take up work; help to access basic skills training; and measures to tackle structural disadvantages in the labour market.[38]

Tackling long-term worklessness

The Government has significantly increased the level of contact between out-of-work benefit claimants and employment advisors to provide more support to those looking for work. Indeed, the UK has built a reputation as a leading moderniser in this area.[39] While certain groups are exempt from the requirement to either prepare for or find work, progressively

37 Tinsley, M., *Parenting Alone: Work and Welfare in Single Parent Households*, Policy Exchange, 2014

38 Because the expanding childcare offer is discussed at length in Chapters 1 and 5 of this report we do not discuss it in this section

39 OECD, *Connecting People with Jobs: Activation Policies in the United Kingdom*, 2014

more individuals are becoming obliged to do so. Until relatively recently lone parents were not required to look for work until their youngest child was 16. The 2001 introduction of mandatory Work Focused Interviews changed this so that lone parents and the main carer of a child in a couple responsible for a child older than one year but younger than five became required to attend periodic interviews with Jobcentre advisors to discuss their plans for getting ready to seek work. The implementation of Lone Parent Obligations in 2008 led to further change with lone parents whose youngest children were above a certain age threshold and who were deemed able to work treated similarly to other Jobseeker's Allowance claimants in that they were required to be available for and actively trying to find paid work.

This changed in 2014 when people with children aged three or four became subject to a requirement to attend courses, volunteer, or undertake other work-related activities. It will soon change again under provisions in the Welfare Reform and Work Bill. Subject to final agreement from Parliament, all parents will be expected to be available for and actively seek work from the time their youngest child turns three in order to claim Universal Credit.[40]

To make employment more attractive the value of many out-of-work benefits relative to real-world costs has also been reduced. The 2015 Summer Budget announced that all working-age benefits, including child benefit, will be frozen for at least four years. The Budget also announced that from 2016, the maximum that out-of-work families can receive on benefits will be decreased from £26,000 to £23,000 a year in London, and £20,000 outside London.[41] For families already on the cap, their net income will reduce by £3,000 a year (£58 a week) in London, and £6,000 a year (£115 a week) outside London. Other families with benefits between the old and new limits will see their incomes reduced by smaller amounts.[42]

If claimants are on benefits for long stretches of time (between six and 12 months) and have not found work they can be referred to the Work Programme by their Jobcentre advisors. This aims to offer more intensive job search support. Services are delivered through providers (or 'primes') from the private, public and voluntary/community sectors. Many of the providers manage networks of sub-contractors who deliver some or all of the employment support services on their behalf. Contracts between primes and the DWP are structured on a payments-by-results basis. Since its inception in 2011, more than 1.7 million people have been referred to the programme, making it the largest such programme in UK history.[43]

Providers are allowed to set the rules for their schemes based on local economic and employment conditions. Consequently, the rules for qualifying to take part in the Work Programme vary from area to area. Jobseeker's Allowance claimants aged between 18 to 24 are expected to take part; as are people aged over 25 who have been out of work for 12 months or more, as well as Employment and Support Allowance claimants, who are expected to be fit for work within 12 months. People on Income Support or Incapacity Benefit can volunteer to take part but are not obliged to. If after two years, people on the programme fail to secure work, responsibility for them returns to Jobcentre Plus. At this point, the claimant is placed on a more intensive regimen of job search, mandatory work-training placements and more frequent meetings with their advisor (under the Help to Work banner).

Between 2015 and 2017, the majority of Work Programme contracts will end. The Government's commissioning strategy, published last year, gave strong clues as to its intentions: a continuing role for the prime contractor model for large-scale national programmes alongside smaller-scale contracts when commissioning specialist services, particularly for people furthest from the labour market. Government has also signalled its intention to allow Jobcentre Plus greater freedom to work in partnership with Local Enterprise Partnerships and local authorities, including pooling resources where appropriate.[44]

40 HM Government, *Welfare Reform and Work Bill*, 2015
41 HM Treasury, *Summer Budget 2015*, 2015
42 Hirsch, D., *The Cost of a Child in 2015*, 2015
43 DWP, *Quarterly Work Programme National Statistics to Dec 2014*, 2015
44 DWP, *Commissioning Strategy*, 2014

For people with disabilities listed in the Equalities Act 2010, more specialised support is available through Work Choice, a specialist employment programme delivered by a prime provider in 28 areas. As with the Work Programme, prime providers sub-contract with a range of other specialist or niche providers to support disabled people deemed both eligible and suitable by Disability Employment advisors. Advisors work with claimants to set goals, help them secure training and work with employers to discuss relevant adjustments, drawing from statutory funding to pay for workplace adjustments where necessary. The majority of the support Work Choice provides takes place in mainstream employment, but some provision is delivered through supported businesses – workplaces historically set up specifically to offer employment to people with disabilities.[45]

Alongside this the Government offers help to employers to make reasonable adaptations in the workplace as well as challenging employers to think about the prejudices that they may hold in employing people with health conditions and disabilities through the Access to Work programme.[46] It has also recently been placing a welcome emphasis on prevention. In the wake of the Black Review of Sickness and Absence, the Government has committed to a number of reforms which aim to keep the 300,000 people who have a job, but who fall ill each year, from drifting too far away from the labour market.[47] The Fit for Work programme, for example, is currently being rolled out across England and Wales, advising GPs, employers and employees to help them develop a progressive back-to-work plan at an early stage of sickness absence.[48] The Government has also over the last two years spent £500,000 in its its 'Disability Confident initiative', an awareness campaign which aims to help businesses become more confident about recruiting people with disabilities.

Finally, the Government is introducing a number of changes to benefit rules to increase work incentives for sickness and disability claimants, including an announcement that support for those allocated to the Employment and Support Allowance (ESA) work-related activity group (claimants who are not currently fit for work but who are predicted to be within the year) would be reduced to the same level as that received by iJobseeker's Allowance claimants.

The Government also recognises that some households may need to work through a number of complex problems prior to finding work and it seeks to respond to this via the Troubled Families programme. In recent months, it has signalled a desire to reorient this programme to focus more squarely on worklessness. In April 2015 the number of employment advisors embedded within existing Troubled Families teams in councils doubled to more than 300. Their role is to work alongside family key workers who provide intensive support to whole families, and provide specialist employment advice and support. Practical support takes the form of CV writing, job interview skills and alerting families to training opportunities and job vacancies in the area. The placements are funded with an additional £10 million provided jointly by the DWP and the Department for Communities and Local Government.

The evolution of the Troubled Families programme has been gradual but steady. Applying to England only, the programme's original focus was on households placing high demands on public resources and causing harm to their communities through anti-social behaviour. A single family worker was assigned to each family to offer intensive support around a range of issues including problems in the home, with health, and with accessing jobs. In late 2014, the programme moved into its second phase, with the intention that councils start working with a larger group of 400,000 families.[49] Eligibility for the scheme was widened, with families who meet the following criteria now being eligible: having a child or children already subject to a Child Protection Plan, or suspected to be in need of one; having members at risk of worklessness at a young age; having a history of domestic violence or abuse; having children or adults who suffer from a range of health problems.

45 Purvis, A., Foster, S., Lane, P., Aston, J., and Davies, M., *Evaluation of the Work Choice Specialist Disability Employment Programme – Findings from the 2011 Early Implementation and 2012 Steady State Waves of the research*, CESI (for the DWP), 2013

46 Ibid.

47 DWP, *Health at Work: An Independent Review of Sickness Absence*, 2011

48 See http://fitforwork.org/about/ for further information

49 DCLG, *Understanding Troubled Families*, 2014

Training and support with skills

The training routes available to unemployed people to redress important skills gaps depend on their age, existing skills and the length of their benefit claim. For adults who have been on benefits for a long time, Jobcentre Plus no longer funds or commissions pre-employment training directly. Instead, advisors refer people on to courses being delivered by colleges and training providers using Skills Funding Agency money. Indeed, unemployed adults with English/English for speakers of other languages (ESOL) and maths needs are now a major source of referrals to the courses in these subjects available through further education and community learning providers. Most are referred at the Pre-Work Programme stage of their benefit claim by their Jobcentre Plus advisor.[50]

For younger people aged 16 to 24 (and for young people with Learning Difficulty Assessments up to academic age 25) who want to work, but who need extra help to gain an apprenticeship or job, traineeships are available. These last a maximum of six months and the core content is a high-quality work placement, work preparation training, and English and maths. Providers and employers are granted flexibility to bring the elements together in the best way to engage and support individual trainees. If adults are in training programmes of more than 16 hours a week, they normally lose their entitlement to benefits but in March 2014, the DWP relaxed the 16-hour rule to allow claimants to take part in traineeship programmes for up to 30 hours a week, without affecting their Jobseeker's Allowance entitlement.

The centrepiece of the Government's skills strategy is the apprenticeship programme, where it has set a target for three million apprenticeships to be entered into in England between 2015 and 2020. This programme is not targeted on the unemployed and those who are furthest from the labour market are unlikely to be able to take it up. Survey data suggests the majority of apprentices were either already working (many for the firm concerned) or applied via a college or learning provider.[51] There are no formal referral routes between apprenticeship programmes and the unemployment service but vacancies can be advertised through the online Universal Job Match system managed by Jobcentre Plus and claimants who meet the basic requirements are encouraged to apply for opportunities by advisors.

6.4 How can more progress be made?

The Commission welcomes the priority that the Government gives to reducing worklessness and supports its decision to increase the contact between people who have been out of work for long periods and the employment support service. With the value of out-of-work benefits falling relative to real-world costs, it would be unconscionable to leave people who are (or could become) capable of securing work alone for long stretches while they and their families make do on ever-shrinking incomes. However, the Commission has serious doubts about whether the system as currently set up can deliver a fall in the number of long-term workless households that is sufficiently large to lead to a sizeable reduction in the number of children in persistent poverty. Our concerns are threefold.

First, labour market disadvantages are an important factor in the worklessness of many persistently poor households but the Government's actions do not match the scale of the problems. Second, the employment support system is currently too impersonal and mechanistic, leading to inappropriate referrals and ineffective interventions. Third, the work currently being done to boost people's skills is generally insufficient to help them plot a realistic route out of poverty.

50 NIACE, *The Work Programme: What is the Role of Skills?*, 2012
51 BIS, *Evaluation of Apprenticeships: Learners*, 2012

Tackling structural labour market disadvantages – more activity is needed to match the scale of the challenges

The Government's commitment in its 2015 election manifesto to halving the disability employment gap was laudable but as of yet there has been little detail of how this will be achieved in practice. This is a glaring omission, especially when the data and wider trends point to the headwinds against this target getting stronger. Analysis of the Labour Force Survey by the disability charity Scope shows that hundreds of thousands more disabled people are leaving work than moving into it each year, in direct opposition to the wider employment trends for the non-disabled.[52]

This is a large challenge and the Government's current activity in this area (a modest awareness-raising campaign and some employer-focused work around prevention) will not be sufficient in magnitude to turn the tide. Specialist employment support and clear targets for making more of Britain's workplaces more inclusive should be the priority. This would include a greater push to encourage flexible working – 40 per cent of all employed disabled people say that modified hours have made the difference to them staying in work; 36 per cent of those out of work say that modified hours could have helped them retain their job.[53]

In the case of ethnic minorities, the current situation is very mixed. Overall, the picture continues to show continuing ethnic minority disadvantage compared to the white British majority group. There is, however, a considerable difference in unemployment rates between ethnic groups. For example, Indian and Chinese workers report relatively high earnings and employment rates whereas people from Pakistani and Bangladeshi backgrounds have less good outcomes. The majority of black and mixed ethnicity groups appear in the middle. Some local authorities are also performing less well than others in terms of unemployment. For example, Birmingham features among the top five local authorities for unemployment for several ethnic groups (for example, Indian, Pakistani, Chinese and African). Concentrated pockets of unemployment are particularly notable for people with an African background in London and parts of the North of England, and in the North West for people with a Pakistani background.[54]

The Government's work on tackling the ethnic minority employment gap is led by the Ethnic Minority Employment Task Force. Policy is driven under three headings: building employability; connecting people to work; and promoting equal opportunities in the workplace. Among its main interventions are: work to improve diversity and equality in public procurement; the launch of an online toolkit for employers to examine any intrinsic bias; and the development of a portal aimed at helping local authorities to access information on ethnic minority employment data for their area.

The latter initiative is a reflection of the growing awareness that a more vigorous approach at the national level needs to be complemented by area-based policies to tackle labour market inequalities locally. Elements of a successful strategy would include:

- Employment support services undertaking targeted outreach at inactive, unemployed or under-employed adults and from ethnic minority groups;
- Jobcentre and Work Programme recruiting staff who reflect the local population;[55]
- Local Enterprise Partnerships supporting and encouraging businesses to create more diverse workforces;[56]
- The public sector taking a lead in recruiting people from ethnic minority groups, particularly those who face systematic disadvantage.[57]

52 Scope, *A Million Futures: Halving the Disability Employment gap*, 2014
53 DWP, *Fulfilling Potential: Building Understanding*, 2013
54 Catney, G., and Sabater, A., *Ethnic Minority Disadvantage in the Labour Market*, 2015
55 NAO, *Increasing Employment for Ethnic Minorities: A Summary of the Research Findings*, 2008
56 Catney, G., and Sabater, A., *Ethnic Minority Disadvantage in the Labour Market,* 2015
57 Ibid.

These types of actions are more likely to occur if there is also clear national leadership. The Prime Minister's commitment in the run-up to the General Election for there to be 660,000 more black minority ethnic (BME) people in employment by 2020 sounded impressive, but actually merely reflects the changing makeup of the working age population (as more BME people enter the labour market) over the next five years and will require no action by the Government for the target to be achieved.[58] Creating more stretching employment targets for ethnic minority groups which systematically appear most disadvantaged should be a policy priority.

Tackling long-term worklessness – a need for greater personalisation

The job requirements for Jobcentre Plus staff are constantly evolving. As Universal Credit is rolled out, the vision is for staff to be freed from simple administration to focus on the employment outcomes that matter most. This is a welcome recognition of the need for change. Time and again studies have identified the design features which are key to welfare-to-work programmes being successful.

First, the timing of interventions is crucial: the longer someone is out of the labour market, the more distanced they become, underlining the importance of early intervention.[59] However, this needs to be balanced with evidence that shows it is important to wait until someone's condition or circumstances are stable before intensive engagement is undertaken. Second, supporting some people back into work can take time and ideally requires continuity of provision.[60]

The current system only partially embodies these principles. Time would be saved if people's circumstances were considered in the round from the outset of their welfare-to-work journey. At present access to various programmes of support is determined by benefit type, a crude mechanism which often focuses on only one set of constraints a family may be experiencing (such as disability) and potentially excludes others which need to be addressed. Work Programme providers have noted repeatedly that a person's benefit-type does not necessarily provide an accurate proxy for the level of support they require.[61] Instead, capability to work and referrals to specialist support should be determined by the whole of a household's circumstances, not just by one aspect such as ill health or length of time outside work.

A version of such reform was recently proposed by the DWP select committee which suggested claimants could be categorised in one of three ways:

- **Relatively work-ready claimants** with a good record of employment in the last four years;
- **Intermediate support group:** claimants with some characteristics restricting their employability, such as lack of qualifications or skills, and a poor record of employment in the last four years;
- **Intensive support group:** claimants with complex or multiple barriers to working, including significant physical or mental ill health; drug or alcohol dependency; housing problems or homelessness; and no record of employment in the last four years.[62]

Adoption of this approach would be a step forward, but it still fails to take account of the wider set of circumstances within a family – alongside their individual characteristics – that can hold people back from working. Instead the Government should adopt the Australian model. There, a wide range of information – including household circumstances, previous benefit, unemployment and employment history, skills and qualifications, language skills, proximity to centres of

58 Khan, O., *Employment Targets for Ethnic Minorities will not Reduce Racial Inequalities*, University of Manchester blog: June 19, 2015
59 OECD, *Activating Job Seekers: How Australia does it*, 2012
60 Mueller, M., and Patton, M., 'Working with poor families: Lessons learned from practice', In Guttman, D., and Sussman, M., (eds.), *Exemplary Social Intervention Programs for Members and their Families* (pp65-90), 1995
61 House of Commons, *Welfare to Work*, 2015
62 House of Commons, *Welfare to Work*, 2015

employment, transport arrangements, ethnicity, country of origin, any specific workplace needs, history of complex needs and criminal record – are considered in a holistic way.

Modelling work undertaken for the DWP by Simon Matty suggests that segmentation tools which incorporate the full circumstances surrounding a claimant (as reported by the claimant through surveys) are better at predicting their likelihood of becoming long-term unemployed than models which only rely on administrative data (such as the length or nature of a claim, for instance those due to long-term illness).[63] This would enable resources to be targeted to where they are most likely to be needed.

The integration of the main working-age benefits into Universal Credit and the current rethink of the work capability assessment (WCA) offer Government a perfect opportunity to consider a change of this kind. A real-world assessment and segmentation process could be integrated into the claimant commitment process with advisors trained in identifying the key issues faced by specific households and determining what support is most likely to enable them to find work. Claimants would then be referred to suitable programmes.

This leaves the question of the nature of support. After a poor start, the Work Programme is now performing at similar levels to the New Deal programmes it replaced and the DWP is forecasting further improvements over the rest of its contractual life. However, the programme is much more effective with some groups than others. For example, outcomes for those aged between 18 and 24 are better than for older claimants (Figure 6.4).

Figure 6.4: Job outcomes as a proportion of referrals by participant characteristics (June 2011–June 2015)

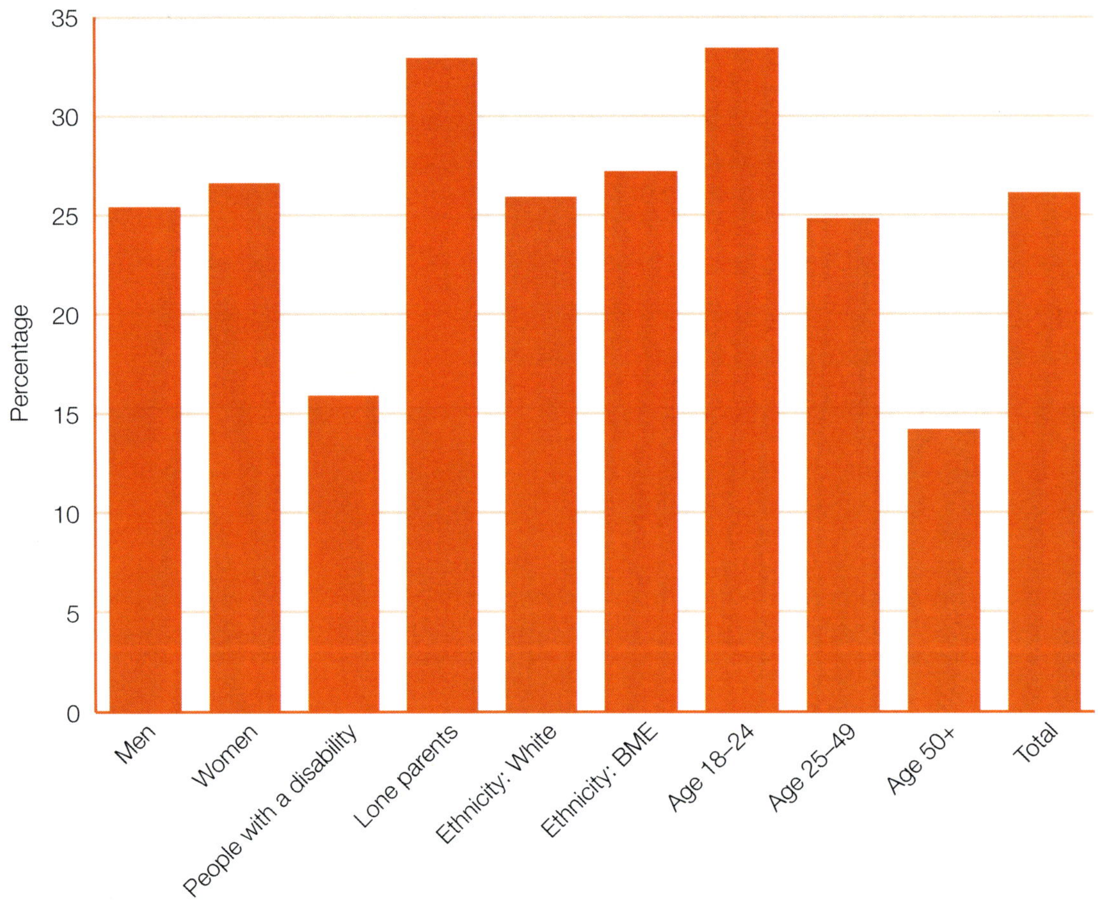

Source: DWP: Information, Governance and Security Directorate; Inclusion calculations

63 Matty, S., *Predicting Likelihood of Long-term Unemployment: The Development of a UK Jobseekers' Classification Instrument*, 2013

The Work Programme also continues to disappoint in relation to people claiming Employment and Support Allowance (ESA). Of the 284,000 people on ESA or incapacity benefit who had moved on to the Work Programme between June 2011 and August 2014, just 7 per cent (18,800) secured a sustained job.[64] The results are an inevitable function of the type of support available through the Work Programme, where a 'work first' approach (job search support to get people quickly into work) dominates. Most participants received help with CVs, job search and interview techniques, which may be of particular value to younger claimants. There is less emphasis on human-capital based approaches (for example, training or health improvement programmes).

This critique is borne out by surveys of participants which report that providers strive to create friendly, mutually respectful relationships between participants and staff, but refer few participants to training provision or to support designed to address specific barriers to employment (for example, health conditions, accommodation problems or caring responsibilities).[65] For example, just 29.4 per cent of people who had a health condition that made work difficult were offered support related to their condition.[66]

After two years on the programme, the roughly 70 per cent of people who don't get a job face the prospect of intense oversight from Jobcentre Plus through the Help to Work progamme.[67] Claimants are expected to be on a training scheme, mandatory work-activity placement or intensive work preparation within days of finishing and can lose their benefits if they fail to comply. They also have to attend the Jobcentre far more frequently than other jobseekers, with weekly signing-on being routine and some people required to do so daily.

For people with disabilities, more tailored support is available through Work Choice. Although subject to some teething troubles, the programme has achieved better employment outcomes than the Work Programme to date, and qualitative evaluations generally provide positive reports of this intervention.[68] Looking at a six-month cohort of Work Choice programme starts between 1 July 2014 and 31 December 2014, there were 7,490 starts to Work Choice in this period. Of these, 4,290 (57.3 per cent) had obtained a job outcome by 30 June 2015.

The stark difference in performance vindicates the Government's decision – announced in the Autumn Statement – to ensure a strong future for specialist employment support by replacing the Work Programme with a new Work and Health Programme once the contracts come to an end. The fact that funding for the Access to Work Scheme is to be increased in real terms and the Fit for Work service expanded suggests that the Government is preparing for a big additional push on this front, something we entirely support, particularly if alongside it substantial efforts are made to make Britain's workplaces more inclusive.

But this leaves open the question of what the journey back to work for long-term unemployed people who are technically fit to work now should look like. Assuming jobs are available locally, the evidence suggests success is most likely to be achieved when an individual is ready and willing to seek work[69] and trusts the motives and skills of those helping them. Based on claimant surveys this trust in part depends on those in the system being willing to listen to the claimant and modify their approach around the claimants' specific needs rather than being governed purely by contractual or institutional imperatives.[70]

64 Davies, B., *In Safe Hands? Rethinking Employment Pathways for ESA Claimants with Mental Health Problems*, 2014
65 Meager, N., Newton, B., and Sainsbury, R., *Work Programme Evaluation: The Participant Experience Report,* 2014
66 Meager, N., Newton, B., Foley, B., Sainsbury, R., Corden, A., Irving, A., Lane, P., and Weston, K., *Work Programme Evalution: Interim Meta Report*, 2013
67 Quarterly Work Programme National Statistics to December 2014
68 Purvis, A., et al, *Evaluation of the Work Choice Specialist Disability Employment Programme*, 2013
69 Dunn, A., 'Activation worker's perception of their long term unemployed clients' attitudes towards employment', *Journal of Social Policy*, Volume 42 / Issue 04, 2013
70 DWP, *Work Programme Evaluation: The Participant Experience Report,* 2014

Given the Government's ongoing commitment to the Jobcentre model,[71] the most efficient way to achieve this would be by instituting more active and continuous partnerships between harder-to-help claimants and Jobcentre advisors assigned to them for the long term. For this reason we support the decision to shorten the amount of time people need to wait before receiving more intensive support from the Help to Work programme. But the choice should not be a binary one between Jobcentre delivered services and more specialist support. Instead claimants and their advisors – having undertaken a more rounded assessment of the kind described above – should be enabled to plot more personalised journeys back to work, drawing on mainstream Jobcentre services, suitable elements of the specialist provision that will be available through the Work and Health programme, as well as any other locally commissioned specialist services.

Underpinning this would be a denser network of referral pathways and protocols that allowed for the maximum possible flexibility (although subject to the current conditionality rules). This would allow claimants and their coaches to more quickly modify their approach as the situation evolves. This should include a more systematic harnessing of the skills being developed within the Troubled Families programme. Feedback from Troubled Families providers indicate that family workers are skilled at building mutually respectful but challenging relationships through home visits.[72] Of the available workforce they are best placed to successfully engage people who are despondent about their prospects due to years of living with a range of serious problems which, combined, have kept them out of the labour market.[73]

Tackling low skills and qualifications

For the new approach outlined above to have real purchase there also needs to be a step change in our approach to skills. Research published in 2012 by the DWP revealed that 31.2 per cent of long-term Jobseeker's Allowance claimants had either no qualifications or unclassifiable qualifications.[74]

The current welfare-to-work model is based on the assumption that participants should find a job first through which they will then gain new skills that increase their chances of staying in work. Unfortunately, for the majority of people with substantial skill deficits, the current 'work first' approach falls down because there are not enough jobs for which employers are willing to recruit people without a basic level of English, maths, ICT and employability skills.[75] Other research suggests that people in low-paid work are the least likely group to receive training support from their employers, limiting their scope for progression once in work (assuming they are able to secure a job on the basis of having basic skills).[76]

The Coalition Government sought to partly address this problem by introducing skills conditionality. This entails Jobcentre Plus referring claimants to a skills training provider, Further Education College or Next Step advisor with potential benefit sanctions for non-participation. Because of the length of time it takes to develop English, maths or ESOL skills, learning providers tend to offer intensive provision for unemployed adults. Although many people find employment on completion of a Level 1 course, others may encounter problems finding sustained employment on that basis (the success rate is currently running at 46 per cent for Level 1 graduates securing sustained job outcomes).[77]

At least some participants would benefit from progressing from English, maths and ESOL at Level 1 to short course Level 1 or Level 2 vocational skills provision. This is backed up by

71 House of Commons, *The Government's Response to the DWP Select Committee Report: The Role of Jobcentre Plus in the Reformed Welfare System* (HC 479), 2014

72 London Councils, *Troubled Families Programme: Lessons for Future Public Service Reform*, 2014

73 Shildrick, T., MacDonald, R., Furlong, A., Roden, J., and Crow, R., *Are Cultures of Worklessness Passed Down the Generations?*, 2012

74 DWP, *Mental Health in Context: The National Study of Work-Search and Wellbeing*, Research Report 810, 2012

75 NIACE, *The Work Programme: What is the Role of Skills?*, 2012

76 UKCES, *Engaging Low-skilled Employees in Workplace Learning*, 2012

77 Gray, R., and Lockhart-Smith, A., *Personal and Social Development Provision: Content, Format and Impact*, 2015

new research suggesting that those in possession of Level 2 qualifications are much less likely to be out of work.[78] Interviews with long-term workless people also reveal that they are keenly aware that much of the skills training they are provided with is of a low level and at best equips them for routine, poorly paid work.[79] The offer of higher-level training and what it represents in terms of a genuine route for progression could increase engagement levels.

But, at present, steady progression from basic skills training to higher qualifications is a goal rather than a reality. A key barrier is that learning providers may find that the costs of supporting participants to achieve higher level skills are not fully covered by the funding they can draw down, or that they have used up their Skills Funding Agency budgets in their delivery of learning to other learners.[80] In this case, the learning provider may have to ask the Work Programme provider to contribute to the costs of the skills provision. No reliable data is available on the number of referrals Work Programme providers make to training providers, but participant surveys suggest they are relatively few.

Support for the long-term workless has also been affected by the fact that the non-apprenticeship adult skills budget has been reduced by almost a quarter (24 per cent) in 2015/16 as the Skills Funding Agency tries to balance its own reduced funding with the need to deliver stretching apprenticeship targets. Casualties of this approach include funding for mandatory ESOL programmes that were introduced for Jobseeker's Allowance claimants with poor spoken English as a condition for their continuing to receive benefits.[81]

The in-year cuts are part of a wider trend that has seen the further education budget reduced by one-third over the last parliament. As a result participation has dropped by almost 11 per cent (more than 350,000 fewer adults) in education and training.[82] The decision made during the Spending Review to freeze spending in cash terms (depending on inflation; a real-terms cut) on 16- to 19-year-old education in school sixth forms, sixth form colleges and further education colleges, as well as the budget for adult skills participation, will mean that community learning providers will need to look for further efficiencies.

It is vital that changes to provision do not disadvantage people who need extra help to become more employable, especially since many will not be eligible to join the apprenticeships programme if their skills fall short of requirements. The decision to initiate a series of locally led Area Reviews – announced in the Autumn Statement – provides a chance to think systematically about how to use skills funding to deliver a further reduction in the numbers of long-term unemployed.

We would argue that the priority must be to create more robust progression ladders so that people without qualifications can achieve basic skills and then higher level skills. Part of this will be about ensuring that funding for Level 1 and Level 2 course provision can be protected. But realistically, to deliver a noticeable upswing in the numbers of adult learners both employers and individual claimants (once in work) will have to be persuaded to contribute more of their own resources. With no prospect of any additional public funding, the respective responsibilities of the state, employers and individuals in relation to building human capital need to be set out much more clearly.

---

78 Bibby, D., Buscha, F., Cerqua, A., Thomson, D., Urwin, P., *Estimation of the Labour Market Returns to Qualifications Gained in English Further Education*, 2014

79 Shildrick, T., MacDonald, R., Furlong, A., Roden, J., Crow, R., *Are Cultures of Worklessness Passed Down Through the Generations?*, 2012

80 NIACE, *The Work Programme: What is the Role of Skills?*, 2012

81 Skills Funding Agency, *Changes to Funding Allocations for 2015 to 2016*, 2015

82 Skills Funding Agency, *Further Education and Skills: Learner Participation: Outcomes and Level of Highest Qualification Held*, 2015

6.5 Conclusions and Recommendations

The UK has rightly been praised for its jobs success, with the number of children in workless households falling from 16.2 per cent in 2010 to 11.8 per cent in 2015 and the parental employment rate at record highs.[83] But as levels of worklessness fall, the question of how best to help those who are still unemployed becomes more pressing. The recommissioning of the Work Programme creates an obvious window to look at the system in total and to consider adjustments to engage and help more of those who are at some distance from finding a job and who are in persistent poverty. The full roll-out of Universal Credit also provides a major opportunity in this regard, freeing up Jobcentre staff from paperwork to focus on the key tasks of assessing need, commissioning specialist services and building strong relationships with their clients. The prize is a more agile welfare-to-work system that fosters the agency of its highest-need clients and expands their sense of what might be possible.

Recommendation 1: The Government should set a goal to make the UK, by 2020, one of the top five countries in the OECD for having the fewest number of children in workless households.

The top five countries in the OECD all have fewer than 7.8 per cent of children living in workless households[84] – this compares with 11.8 per cent in the UK.[85] The target is a realistic but challenging one. It is in line with the current performance of the two best-performing English regions – the South East and the East of England. And it requires the rate of increase in the proportion of children living in working households seen over the last five years – 1 per cent per year – to be maintained for the rest of the decade.[86]

Achieving it would involve a reduction of almost 500,000 in the number of children who live in workless households – or about a third. This goal could be reached if the UK employment rate for families with dependent children were brought into line with those in Sweden and Denmark – 75 per cent of lone parents (currently 64 per cent) and 97 per cent of couples with children (currently 95 per cent) are in work in these countries.[87]

In addition to the labour activation policies already being undertaken, achieving this target would require a concerted push to tackle some of the biggest structural disadvantages currently at play in the labour market. This would involve movement on a range of fronts, with employers, local authorities and education providers playing major roles. The advent of City Deals provides an obvious template through which regions can begin to set ambitious targets for themselves and then start to align local skills strategies, their work supporting businesses and partnerships with Jobcentre Plus to maximum effect.

Recommendation 2: The Government should reform the welfare-to-work system to put personalisation at its heart.

A system that better understands the people it serves will also be a more effective system. The Government should carry out a feasibility review of how the roll-out of Universal Credit could be exploited to create the basis of a richer client record and risk-management tool, and it should commit to a timetable for its delivery. Because Universal Credit is designed around households rather than individuals it should be possible to use the HMRC data it contains, supplemented by other information such as that generated by WCA assessments and case files from Troubled Families workers to identify the individuals and families at greatest risk of

83 ONS, *Working and Workless Households*, 2015
84 OECD, *Familes Database: Table LMF1.1*, 2015
85 Office for National Statistics, *Working and Workless Households*, 2015
86 Office for National Statistics, *Working and Workless Households*, 2015
87 OECD, *Families Database: Tables LMF1.3 and LMF2.2*, 2015

persistent poverty due to worklessness. This would enable Jobcentre teams to plan which people they need to provide more support to, both in terms of time as well as money.

Having identified individuals at the greatest risk, the system should then aim to ensure they can rely on at least one fixed point during what could be a long welfare-to-work journey. This is the relationship between them and their Jobcentre work coach/advisor. Even when referred to the Work Programme and Work Choice regular contact should be maintained.

The Government should also ensure that advisors and their clients are given greater freedom to tailor the approach as time passes; the number of clients left marooned on programmes which have exhausted its suite of interventions should be a tiny minority. Contract flexibilities are needed so clients and their advisors can opt to enter and exit programmes at the right time for the former, rather than only at the time agreed between the DWP and the prime provider.

Recommendation 3: The Troubled Families programme should be renamed and formally brought into the welfare-to-work system.

People with long histories of worklessness, low skills or disabilities (with many of these issues experienced simultaneously) are more likely to benefit from intensive, personalised support from the start of their welfare-to-work journey as well as investment, where necessary, in their human capital. The skills developed by Troubled Families staff over the past five years should be harnessed more systematically.

Based in the public sector, Troubled Families can more easily cross organisational boundaries, aligning local health and social care services with the needs of their client. Caseworkers also have a good track record of developing trusting relationships with their clients and a deep understanding of their overall circumstances.

In line with a broader remit the programme's name should be changed to one with less stigmatising connotations and more in keeping with the substance of its work, for example, the Fresh Start or Families into Work programme. The number of people it aims to help (400,000) should stay the same but the eligibility criteria should be restricted to groups most at risk of worklessness and persistent poverty and entry into the programme jointly agreed between Troubled Families teams working in councils and Jobcentre staff.

Recommendation 4: Introduce personal skills budgets to help people make the leap from basic English and maths to higher-level skills.

The Government should encourage and empower those furthest from the job market by giving them a personal skills budget. One possible model is that proposed by the National Institute for Adult Education. Their 'Help to Train ISA' mirrors the Government's 'Help to Buy ISA' and involves a basic starting element from the DWP or Department for Education which can be topped up by contributions from employers and the individuals (assuming claimants find work). Such an account could also be supplemented by routing funds from other public services, such as mental health or housing since these agencies also have a stake in securing a better outcome for the individual concerned.

The objective should help to develop a system and culture of greater shared investment in learning – from learners, employers and the state. It would of course be important to take the lessons of the Individual Learning Account experiment but there are strong ideas for safeguarding against the mistakes that led to fraud in that instance. Unique Learner Numbers, personal learning records and the register of training organisations could all help to ensure the money was spent properly.

Since basic English and maths continue to be funded by the Skills Funding Agency, the focus should be on using the accounts to help more people on low incomes who have graduated from such training to move on to achieve Level 2 and 3 qualifications. People aged over 25 who have been on a benefit and have completed a Level 1 course or below and not progressed further should be the priority. They are rarely eligible for course fee concessions after that age and are most likely to need pooled funding from agencies and/or an employer in order to progress.

Chapter 7: Social mobility and child poverty in Scotland

- **Child poverty in Scotland is lower than in the rest of the UK, but 140,000 children are still growing up in poor families.**
- **While Scotland has fewer workers paid less than the Living Wage than the rest of the UK and more mothers in couples work, almost one in five employees are low paid.**
- **There is still a long way to go to achieve the vision of eradicating child poverty in Scotland, and the Scottish government will need to put in place a new institutional framework to replace the Child Poverty Act 2010.**
- **Scotland has similar social mobility problems to the rest of the UK, with children from poorer backgrounds doing worse than their peers throughout the educational system.**
- **There has been a welcome increased focus on social mobility, but this has not yet been translated into improved outcomes for less well-off children.**

7.1 Introduction

The Scottish Government has made social justice a core priority. It has an active programme to deliver inclusive growth and tackle child poverty, and is making progress towards its goals. Its approach is similar in some respects to the approaches taken elsewhere in the UK, but has a number of important differences. For example, in contrast to England, Scotland proposes to retain a long-term commitment to meeting the child poverty targets currently set out in the Child Poverty Act 2010, and while social mobility has been a major policy issue in England for at least five years, only recently has it become one in Scotland.

The challenges facing Scotland are not dissimilar to those facing the rest of the UK. Independent forecasters are expecting child poverty in Scotland to rise over the next few years – as in the UK as a whole – not least because of the impacts of welfare reform on the incomes of low-income families. For example, in November 2014 the Institute for Fiscal Studies published projections for child poverty in Scotland which suggested that the proportion of children in relative poverty would increase by 7 per cent and the proportion of children in absolute poverty would increase by 20 per cent, between 2013–14 and 2020–21.[1]

1 Institute for Fiscal Studies, *Child and Working-age Poverty in Northern Ireland over the Next Decade: An Update*, IFS Briefing Note BN154, November 2014. This projected that between 2013–14 and 2020–21 the proportion of children in relative poverty before housing costs would increase from a forecast 20.0 per cent to 23.4 per cent, and the proportion in absolute poverty before housing costs would increase from a forecast 22.6 per cent to 27.1 per cent

These challenges have grown since last year, with the announcement of a further £12 billion of discretionary cuts in the UK welfare budget targeted on children and working-age adults by the incoming UK Government that are not factored into these projections.

In some ways, Scotland is better placed to respond to these challenges than other parts of the UK. The proportion of children in poverty in Scotland against the headline measures is the lowest of all the constituent countries of the UK and decreased between 2012–13 and 2013–14. There are relatively few children in workless households: the parental employment rate is relatively high. Housing costs are low compared to the rest of the UK, meaning that child poverty after housing costs is lower than in any other country or region of the UK.

The most important development around social mobility in Scotland over the last 12 months is the increasing focus among policymakers on tackling the large and unacceptable educational attainment gap between rich and poor that exists in Scotland. This is a very welcome development. The key challenge is delivering on changes that can make a real difference. Scottish society – including central government, local government, schools, further education (FE) colleges, universities, parents and employers – will need to come together to make the vision of a fair Scotland a reality.

7.2 Current position

The most recent annual report on the child poverty strategy in Scotland noted that 2013–14 saw significant falls in child poverty against the relative and absolute poverty measures in the Child Poverty Act 2010, although poverty after housing costs was flat and material deprivation increased.

The Scottish Government's self-assessment of progress in tackling the drivers of poverty was that out of the 37 indicators in its measurement framework, performance was improving against four indicators, worsening against two indicators and being maintained against 30 indicators (time series data could not be reported against the remaining indicator).[2]

The rest of this section explores trends in child poverty and social mobility in more detail, comparing the progress being made in Scotland to elsewhere in the UK, and looking in more detail at the progress being made in improving social mobility beyond the headline indicators in the measurement framework.

Child poverty

On the whole, trends in child poverty are encouraging although there is still a long way to go to hit the targets set out in the Child Poverty Act 2010. Against the headline targets, child poverty is lower in Scotland than in the UK as a whole, and has been falling over time. In 2013–14:

- Relative child poverty before housing costs was 14 per cent, compared to 17 per cent in the UK as a whole and 21 per cent five years earlier in 2008–09;[3]
- Absolute child poverty before housing costs was 15 per cent, compared to 19 per cent in the UK as a whole and 20 per cent five years earlier in 2008–09;
- Material deprivation before housing costs was 13 per cent, the same as in the UK as a whole. This has been rising over the last two years from 9 per cent in 2011–12;
- Relative and absolute poverty before housing costs were both at half the levels seen in 1999–2000 – a significant achievement.

2 Scottish Government, *Annual Report for the Child Poverty Strategy for Scotland*, October 2015

3 All data on child poverty in this chapter is taken from Scottish Government, *Poverty and Income Inequality in Scotland: 2013–14*, 2015 unless otherwise stated

After taking account of housing costs, Scotland has the lowest child poverty rate of any part of the UK. For example, in the three years ending 2013–14, 24 per cent of children in Scotland were in absolute poverty after housing costs, compared to 31 per cent in England and 25 per cent in the best performing English region (the South East).[4]

However, despite this good performance relative to the rest of the UK, progress against the absolute child poverty after housing costs measure stalled in the mid-2000s and the rate has been increasing since 2010–11. As a result, child poverty against this measure was the same in 2013–14 as it was almost a decade earlier in 2004–05.

The trends in one of the key drivers of child poverty – employment – are also encouraging:

- The proportion of children in Scotland who live in workless households has decreased rapidly in recent years and is slightly lower than the UK average – only 10.9 per cent of children in Scotland live in workless households compared to 15.8 per cent in 2012 and 11.8 per cent in the UK as a whole;[5]
- More than six out of 10 (62.5 per cent) children in Scotland live in households where all adults are in work, making Scotland the region with the most 'fully working' households in the UK – for example, only 54.6 per cent of children in England live in households where all adults are in work;[6]
- Scotland has the second highest parental employment rate of any region of the UK: 83.2 per cent of people with dependent children are in work. This is driven by very high employment of mothers in couples; 79.6 per cent of whom are in work compared to 71.9 per cent in England. However, lone parents in Scotland have a relatively low employment rate – only 62.2 per cent are in work (compared to, for example, 69.8 per cent in the East of England and 69.2 per cent in Wales).[7]

Working poverty is becoming relatively more important in Scotland, although this is mainly due to success in tackling workless poverty rather than any significant increase in the prevalence of working poverty:

- 56 per cent of children in poverty in Scotland have at least one parent who is in work compared to, for example, 43 per cent in 2009–10;
- However, the proportion of all children who are in working poor households has been slowly trending downwards over time – in 2013–14, approximately 7 to 8 per cent of children were in working poor households, compared to 9 to 10 per cent in 2007–08, and 12 to 13 per cent in 1998–99; although there has been relatively little change over time after taking housing costs into account;[8]
- A key driver of working poverty is low pay – according to the Office for National Statistics, 441,000 jobs in Scotland pay less than the Living Wage or 19 per cent of jobs. This means that Scotland has the joint lowest prevalence of low pay in the UK, along with London and the South East of England. However, there is a lot of variation between different local areas: the proportion of jobs paying less than the Living Wage ranges from 13.6 per cent in Edinburgh to 33.0 per cent in Angus;[9]
- Another key driver of working poverty is work intensity – children in households where parents do not work many hours or in couple households where only one parent works

4 Department for Work and Pensions, *Households Below Average Income 2013/14*, 2015
5 Office for National Statistics, *Working and Workless Households*, 2015
6 Ibid.
7 Office for National Statistics, *Employment Rates Broken Down by Region and Year, April to June, 1996 to 2015*, Ad Hoc Labour Market Release 004861, 10 November 2015
8 These estimates have been calculated by establishing a lower and upper bound for the level of working poverty in each year from published data on the level of child poverty and the proportion of children in poverty who live in working households, which are both rounded to the nearest percentage point
9 Office for National Statistics, *How Many Jobs Are Paid Less than the Living Wage in Your Area*, 12 October 2015

are far more likely than other children to be in poverty. While the Commission is not aware of any evidence that looks at Scotland specifically, evidence for the UK as a whole, cited earlier in this report, suggests that 37 per cent of children in working poor households live with parents who would be considered to have some 'work capacity' under Universal Credit rules.[10]

Social mobility

While there is a shortage of good-quality published data on social mobility in Scotland, what does exist suggests that Scotland – in common with the rest of the UK – has a serious social mobility problem. Those from less well-off backgrounds fall behind their peers in the early years, and wide educational attainment gaps persist through compulsory school, post-16 education and higher education (HE) and drive worse outcomes during adult life.

Early years

The Scottish Government does not collect or publish any national data that can be used to assess trends year-to-year in cognitive development over the early years of life and development gaps between children from different social backgrounds.

However, there is evidence from the Growing Up in Scotland survey – based on two representative samples of 5,000 children born in 2004–05 and 6,000 children born in 2010–11 – that there are significant gaps by social background in cognitive and social development. For example:

- By the age of five, children from the highest-income quintile are on average around 13 months ahead of their peers in the lowest-income quintile in their knowledge of vocabulary, and 10 months ahead in their problem-solving ability;[11]
- Children from the lowest-income quintile are significantly more likely to exhibit a range of behavioural difficulties on entry to primary school, compared to their peers from the highest-income quintile – they are more than twice as likely to display conduct problems (43 per cent versus 19 per cent), peer problems (24 per cent versus 12 per cent), emotional symptoms (16 per cent versus 6 per cent) and hyperactivity (30 per cent versus 12 per cent).

While international comparisons are difficult to make, evidence from the Millennium Cohort Study[12] suggests that the gap in cognitive development between children from less well-off backgrounds and others is bigger in Scotland than in England, concluding that: "In Scotland it is the poorest children that perform less well than their low-income counterparts in England; high income children in Scotland continue to out-perform high-income children in England throughout the first seven years."

---

10 Bradshaw, J. and Main, G., *How Many Working Parents Might be Able to Work More?*, 19 March 2014 http://spruyork.blogspot.co.uk/2014/03/how-many-working-poor-parents-might-be.html

11 Scottish Government, *Tackling Inequalities in the Early Years: Key Messages from the Growing Up in Scotland Study*, 2015

12 Taylor, C., Rees, G. and Davies, R., *Devolution and Geographies of Education: The Use of the Millennium Cohort Study for 'Home International' Comparisons across the UK*, 2013

School age

The availability of data on the attainment of school-age children is somewhat better than for the early years, with some survey data published on attainment in primary and early secondary school and national data published on school leavers, which both include some information about attainment gaps. However, there is still a severe lack of systematic data published compared to some other parts of the UK, especially England, although this is being resolved through the introduction of national testing by the new National Improvement Framework.

A specific problem with data on the school attainment gap in Scotland is that all the published statistics define disadvantage based on 'living in a deprived area', rather than on individual characteristics. Given that more than half – 54 per cent – of children in low-income families in Scotland (defined using the HM Revenue & Customs (HMRC) Children in Low Income Families measure) live outside of the most deprived 20 per cent Scottish Index of Multiple Deprivation (SIMD) areas, this means that official statistics – and policy interventions aiming to improve the attainment of children from disadvantaged backgrounds – risk ignoring the low attainment of many children from poorer families due to them not living in the most deprived areas.[13]

The *Scottish Survey of Literacy and Numeracy*[14] measures the performance of 10,000 children in Scottish schools against literacy and numeracy on an alternating yearly basis, with performance reported for children in P4 (at age 8–9), P7 (at age 11–12) and S2 (at age 13–14). Children from the most deprived third of areas do a lot worse than their peers across the age range.[15] Focusing on attainment in the second year of secondary school:

- In **numeracy**, children in disadvantaged areas are twice as likely as those in advantaged areas to fail to meet expected levels – 52 per cent do not achieve expected levels (versus 24 per cent), only 25 per cent (versus 52 per cent) perform well, and only 3 per cent (versus 13 per cent) perform very well;
- In **reading**, children in disadvantaged areas are three times as likely as those in advantaged areas to be assessed as not performing well – 5 per cent do not achieve expected levels (versus 1 per cent), 68 per cent (versus 90 per cent) perform well, and 29 per cent (versus 53 per cent) perform very well;
- In **writing**, children in disadvantaged areas were twice as likely to fail to meet expected levels – 19 per cent do not achieve expected levels (versus 9 per cent), 12 per cent (versus 25 per cent) perform well, and only 1 per cent (versus 4 per cent) perform very well;
- In **listening and talking** there was not as much difference between children in disadvantaged areas and those in advantaged areas – a similar proportion of children fail to meet expected levels (18 per cent versus 16 per cent), although there are bigger differences in terms of performing very well (19 per cent versus 28 per cent).

The most recent published data on performance in Standard and Higher level qualifications by disadvantage has three important limitations:

- It merges all school leavers together so performance cannot be differentiated by age;
- It does not attempt to assess attainment at 'expected levels' (e.g. five or more awards at Scottish Credit and Qualifications Framework (SCQF) Level 4/5 or above at the end of S4), and only reports data for achieving 'one or more pass' at each of the SCQF levels;
- It looks at the highest level of qualification achieved and so, for example, records a single D grade at Higher level as a better qualification than any number of Standard Grades.

13 HMRC, *Children in Low Income Families: Local Measure*, 2011 was used to estimate how many children in poverty lived in each of the 6,501 Scottish data zones (2001 boundaries). Scottish Government, *Scottish Index of Multiple Deprivation 2012*, 2012 was used to calculate what proportion of children in poverty lived in data zones in the bottom SIMD quintile

14 All data in this paragraph is taken from Scottish Government, *The Scottish Survey of Literacy and Numeracy*, 2015

15 The data defines 'disadvantaged areas' as the most deprived third of areas and 'advantaged areas' to be the least deprived third of areas

With those caveats, the data suggests that there are very big disadvantage gaps in the attainment of school leavers. In 2013–14, compared to children in the least deprived 10 per cent of areas, children in the poorest 10 per cent of areas were:

- Seven times more likely to leave school without achieving one or more Standard Grades at Credit level – SCQF level 5 – or better (30.3 per cent versus 4.3 per cent);[16]
- Less than half as likely to achieve at least one pass at Higher level (36.8 per cent versus 82.7 per cent);
- Less than one-fifth as likely to achieve at least one pass at Advanced Higher level (6.9 per cent versus 37.6 per cent).

Data from 2012–13 suggests that those from the most deprived 10 per cent of areas are less than half as likely to achieve five or more Standard Grades at Credit level or better than those in the least deprived 10 per cent of areas: 38 per cent versus 85 per cent (data against this measure is no longer published so more recent data is not available).[17]

However, there is evidence of some improvement over the last couple of years. For example, the proportion of children in the most disadvantaged 10 per cent of areas achieving at least one Higher pass increased from 30.0 per cent in 2011–12 to 36.8 per cent in 2013–14; and the proportion failing to achieve at least one Credit grade at Standard level decreased from 37.6 per cent in 2011–12 to 30.3 per cent in 2013–14.

Unpublished data[18] on attainment of school leavers who are registered for free school meals also shows big disadvantage gaps. Compared to their peers, school leavers registered for free school meals are:

- Less than half as likely to leave school with five or more Standard Grades at Credit level or better (32.5 per cent versus 67.8 per cent);
- Half as likely to leave school with numeracy skills at SCQF Level 5 or above (31.1 per cent versus 63.7 per cent);
- Little over half as likely to leave school with literacy skills at SCQF Level 5 or above (41.8 per cent versus 74.4 per cent).
- Only around a quarter as likely to leave school with an Advanced Higher qualification (5.4 per cent versus 20.6 per cent).

There are also large gaps in the attainment of school leavers registered for free school meals between different local areas in Scotland (see Figure 7.1):[19]

- Five out of six young people registered for free school meals in Aberdeen City left school without numeracy at SCQF Level 5, and the same proportion left without five Standard Grades at SCQF Level 5. Only 35 out of 276 school leavers registered for free school meals in Aberdeen and Aberdeenshire in 2013–14 – barely one in eight – left school with a single qualification at Higher level or above, including at most four students registered for free school meals who left school with an Advanced Higher qualification;
- By contrast, more than half of young people registered for free school meals in East Dunbartonshire left school with numeracy at SCQF Level 5 or better, and a similar proportion left with one or more Higher qualification.

16 All data on school leaver attainment and destinations is taken from Scottish Government, *Attainment and School Leaver Destinations: Supplementary Data*, June 2015 unless otherwise stated

17 Education (Scotland) Bill, SPICe Briefing 15/9, 23 April 2015. Data is only published up to 2012/13. Note that holding any Higher qualification is defined as better than five or more passes at Standard Grade, so some of these children will not have achieved at this level

18 The Scottish Government kindly made available unpublished analysis on the attainment of school leavers in 2013/14 by whether they were registered for free school meals by local authority area

19 Ibid.

International comparisons of outcomes for school-age children in Scotland suggest that the attainment gap is similar to in the rest of the UK. For example, the Programme for International Student Assessment (PISA) study concludes that while there are "deep levels of inequality in Scotland, particularly between pupils from different socio-economic groups", the evidence "suggests that there is little to differentiate Scotland in terms of socio-economic inequality from the rest of the UK".[20]

Figure 7.1: Educational attainment of school leavers registered for free school meals: proportion achieving five or more Standard Grades at SCQF Level 5 or better

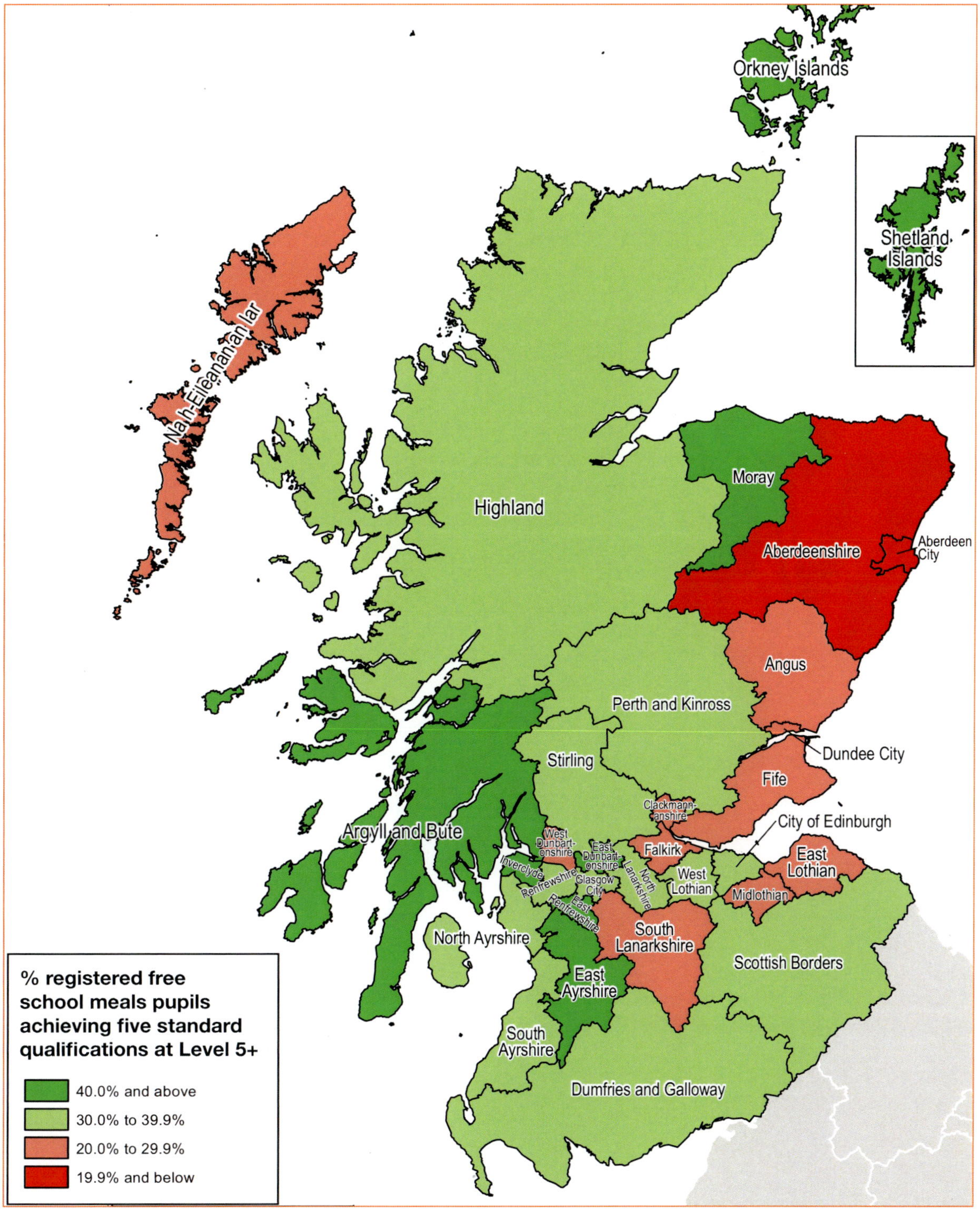

Source: Unpublished analysis on the attainment of school leavers in 2013/14 by whether they were registered for free school meals by local authority area, provided by the Scottish Government

20 Machin, S., McNally, S. and Wyness, G., *Education in a Devolved Scotland: A Quantitative Analysis*, LSE Centre for Economic Performance Special Paper 30, May 2013

Destinations after leaving school and higher education

While the proportion of young people aged 16 to 19 in Scotland who are not in employment, education or training is the lowest since records began (at 8.4 per cent in 2014, compared to 11.3 per cent in 2013), there are big gaps by social background. For example:

- Almost one in six school leavers from the most deprived 10 per cent of areas are unemployed nine months after leaving school – meaning that they are more than six times as likely to be unemployed than those in the least deprived 10 per cent of areas (15.9 per cent versus 2.5 per cent);
- Little over one in five school leavers from the most deprived 10 per cent of areas enter HE within nine months of leaving school – meaning that they are a little over one-third as likely to do so (21.0 per cent versus 62.6 per cent);
- Almost one-third of school leavers from the most deprived 10 per cent of areas enter FE within nine months of leaving school – meaning that they are more than twice as likely to do so than those in the least deprived 10 per cent of areas (32.6 per cent versus 13.7 per cent);
- Looking at destinations of school leavers registered for free school meals (2012–13 data), barely one in eight (12.8 per cent) had entered HE nine months after leaving school (compared to 39.8 per cent of other school leavers), and more than one in five (21.7 per cent) were unemployed (compared to 9.6 per cent of other school leavers).[21]

There is a significant disadvantage gap in HE participation in Scotland. Overall, HE participation rates in Scotland are high: more than half (55.0 per cent) enter HE by the age of 30, and almost half (45.8 per cent) do so by the age of 20.[22] However, little more than a quarter (27.6 per cent) of young people from the most disadvantaged areas enter HE by the age of 20, compared to almost two-thirds (65.1 per cent) of those from the most advantaged areas.[23]

There are also big disadvantage gaps in the type of HE in which students participate. Those from disadvantaged areas are far more likely than other Scottish entrants to enrol in sub-degree courses at FE colleges rather than study towards degree-level courses in universities, especially at the most academically selective institutions:

- More than half of young HE entrants from the most disadvantaged areas study at FE colleges, making them more than two-and-a-half times more likely to do so than young HE entrants from the most advantaged areas (58 per cent versus 23 per cent);
- Little more than one-third of young HE entrants from the most disadvantaged areas study towards a degree, making them only half as likely to do so as young HE entrants from the most advantaged areas (35 per cent versus 70 per cent).[24]

This is important given that sub-degree qualifications have significantly lower lifetime benefits than degrees. For example, evidence from England suggests that the average net lifetime benefit of an undergraduate degree in present value terms is £121,000 for men and £82,000 for women compared to, for example, the lifetime benefits of a Higher National Diploma (HND) of £21,000 for men and £70,000 for women.[25]

Therefore, young people from the most deprived areas are doubly disadvantaged compared to their peers. They are less than half as likely to enter HE in the first place and, if they

21 Scottish Government, *Attainment and Leaver Destinations: Supplementary Data 2012/13*, 2014
22 Scottish Funding Council, *Higher Education Students and Qualifiers at Scottish Institutions, 2013–14*, 2015
23 Ad hoc analysis carried out for the Commission by the Scottish Funding Council. In the rest of this section, 'most disadvantaged' refers to entrants from the most deprived 20 per cent of SIMD areas and 'least disadvantaged' refers to those from the least deprived 20 per cent of SIMD areas
24 Ibid.
25 Department for Business, Innovation and Skills, *The Returns to Higher Education Qualifications*, BIS Research Paper 45, June 2011

do, they are twice as likely to study towards sub-degree-level qualifications which have significantly lower returns in the labour market.

The net effect is that those from the most advantaged areas are more than four-and-a-half times as likely to participate in degree-level higher education by the age of 20 as their peers in the most disadvantaged areas:

- Fewer than one in 10 young people from the most disadvantaged areas begin to study towards a degree by the age of 20 (9.8 per cent);
- Almost half of young people from the most advantaged areas begin to study towards a degree by the age of 20 (45.7 per cent).[26]

Comparing Scotland higher education participation to the rest of the UK

Young people in Scotland – including those from the most disadvantaged areas – are significantly more likely to participate in higher education than people in the rest of the UK. For example, as Table 7.1 shows, far fewer young people in Scotland live in areas with low rates of participation in higher education than elsewhere in the UK.

Table 7.1: Proportion of young people who live in low (bottom 20 per cent) and high (top 20 per cent) participation areas, 2005–09

Country	Proportion of young people living in low participation areas	Proportion of young people living in high participation areas
Scotland	9.9	28.1
Northern Ireland	14.6	27.3
England	20.8	19.1
Wales	25.2	15.3

Source: Higher Education Funding Council for England (HEFCE), POLAR3 data, 2012: http://www.hefce.ac.uk/analysis/yp/POLAR/POLAR3,data/

Note: This is based on the combined participation rate of those aged 18 between 2005 and 2009 participating in higher education between 2005–06 and 2010–11. Low participation areas are the bottom 20 per cent UK-wide and all have young participation rates of below 21 per cent. High participation areas are in the top 20 per cent UK-wide and all have young participation rates of above 47 per cent.

However, participation in higher education in Scotland is less likely to involve attending university than elsewhere in the UK, especially for those from the most disadvantaged backgrounds. For example, data published by UCAS shows that entry rates via an application through the UCAS system are significantly lower in Scotland than elsewhere (Table 7.2).

26 Ad hoc analysis carried out for the Commission by the Scottish Funding Council providing updated data on Table M of Scottish Funding Council, *Participation Rates for Entrants to Scottish Higher Education in 2012–13*, October 2014 by SIMD quintile

Table 7.2: UCAS entry rate at age 18 for young people living in low participation areas (bottom 20 per cent) and high participation areas (top 20 per cent), 2014

Country	UCAS entry rate at age 18 – low participation areas (%)	UCAS entry rate at age 18 – high participation areas (%)
Scotland	9.5	33.6
Northern Ireland	17.4	44.9
England	18.2	45.9
Wales	16.7	42.8

Source: UCAS, *End of Cycle Report 2014*, 2015

The difference between the two measures is driven largely by two key factors. First, as noted above, the average level of deprivation of low participation areas is higher than elsewhere in the UK so it is not a like-for-like comparison. Second, the Scottish HE system differs significantly to that in the rest of the UK. The UCAS participation rate excludes around one-third of young undergraduate entrants in Scotland – those studying towards HE qualifications in FE colleges. These excluded entrants are disproportionately from disadvantaged areas: as highlighted above, 58 per cent of young Scottish entrants from disadvantaged areas study at courses in FE colleges.

So which is the best comparison to use in assessing which country is doing best on social mobility in terms of HE access? Ideally we would be able to look at participation rates of disadvantaged students (rather than those from low participation areas) by level of study: whether students from disadvantaged backgrounds in each country are studying towards first degree qualifications or sub-degree qualifications such as foundation degrees, HNDs and Higher National Certificates (HNCs). Unfortunately, published data on this does not exist, although it seems certain that disadvantaged students in Scotland are less likely than disadvantaged students elsewhere in the UK to be doing degree-level courses.[27]

We would also need to be able to compare the post-HE outcomes of those from disadvantaged backgrounds across the UK in order to shed light on which model of HE was most effective at supporting social mobility.

In terms of fair access to the most selective universities, the four ancient universities – St Andrews, Edinburgh, Glasgow and Aberdeen – are as socially unrepresentative as the 20 English Russell Group universities:

- Entrants to higher education from the most disadvantaged areas are less than half as likely as the rest of the population to enter the four ancient universities, with only 8.1 per cent entering these institutions compared to 17.0 per cent of other entrants;
- Looking at young, full-time first degree entrants to ancient universities,[28] only 76.0 per cent are from state schools, and only 13.1 per cent are from working-class backgrounds[29] (compared to 75.5 per cent from state schools, and 14.2 per cent from working-class backgrounds in the 20 English Russell Group universities);
- Based on the benchmarks set by the Higher Education Statistics Agency – which estimate what admissions would be from widening participation groups if they admitted a representative sample of those 'with the grades' across the UK – there are 415 'missing'

27 For example, analysis by HEFCE concluded that 82 per cent of young HE entrants from the 20 per cent most disadvantaged areas in the UK as a whole were studying towards first degree courses. This compares to only 35 per cent of young entrants from disadvantaged areas in Scotland, based on Scottish Funding Council statistics

28 Further analysis of Higher Education Statistics Agency, *Widening Participation of Underrepresented Groups*, 2015 provided to the Commission by the Higher Education Statistics Agency

29 Defined as being in National Statistics Socio-Economic Classification (NS-SEC) groups 5–7 – 'routine and manual' occupations

students from state schools (meaning a 6 per cent increase in state students would be necessary to meet the Agency benchmarks); and 260 'missing' students from less advantaged socio-economic backgrounds[30] (meaning a 16 per cent increase in less advantaged students would be necessary to hit the benchmarks) – again, similar to the 20 English Russell Group universities.[31]

Finally, on access to higher education, evidence highlighted in the Commission on Widening Access interim report shows that Scottish students are far more likely than their peers to live in the family home while studying: more than half of Scottish students live at home compared to less than one-third of other UK students, with those from disadvantaged backgrounds most likely to live at home. The research suggests that this is due to Scottish students being more debt-averse than young people elsewhere in the UK; with many young people seeing loans to support their living costs as a 'last resort', in part due to misconceptions about student debt and how it is repaid.[32]

This evidence led the Commission on Widening Access to conclude that it is "concerned that young people in Scotland may well be making less than optimal decisions about their future because they do not have access to accurate and detailed advice and guidance on student finance". They also drew attention to worries about the impact that the student finance system may be having on retention rates, degree class and students' ability to make the most of their higher education experience.[33]

Adulthood

There is less information about differences by social background in outcomes during adulthood. Looking at overall labour market outcomes and adult skills,[34] Scotland is similar to the rest of the UK:

- The working age adult employment rate in the year to June 2015 was 72.9 per cent – the same as in the UK as a whole – and the unemployment rate was slightly higher than the UK as a whole;
- The proportion of people in work who were in managerial, professional and associate professional occupations (Standard Occupational Classification 1, 2 and 3) was 41.6 per cent in Scotland, compared to 43.9 per cent in the UK as a whole;
- Average hourly earnings in Scotland in April 2014 were £11.72 per hour compared to £11.61 per hour in the UK as a whole;
- The proportion of 16–64-year-olds not qualified to the equivalent of GCSE or higher (National Vocational Qualification (NVQ) level 2 and above) was 25.2 per cent in Scotland, compared to 26.9 per cent in the UK as a whole.

Looking at access to top jobs in Scotland, our recent *Elitist Scotland* research[35] shows that:

- Almost one-quarter (23 per cent) of people at the top of Scottish society who were educated in Scotland attended private schools for their secondary education. This includes 45 per cent of senior judges, 32 per cent of top media professionals and 28 per cent of UK-educated business leaders. While a lower proportion of those in top professions in Scotland were educated privately than in Great Britain as a whole,[36] there is still significant

30 Defined as being in National Statistics Socio-Economic Classification (NS-SEC) groups 4–7 – this includes all from 'routine and manual backgrounds' and those whose parents are self-employed

31 Commission analysis using the methodology described in the Commission's, *Higher Education: The Fair Access Challenge*, June 2013

32 Minty S., *Young People's Attitudes towards Tuition Fees and Debt in Scotland and England*, paper for British Educational Research Association conference, 16 September 2015

33 Commission on Widening Access, *Interim Report*, November 2015

34 Data taken from Office for National Statistics Annual Population Survey and the Annual Survey of Hours and Earnings via https://www.nomisweb.co.uk/

35 Social Mobility and Child Poverty Commission, *Elitist Scotland*, 2015

36 Social Mobility and Child Poverty Commission, *Elitist Britain*, 2014

over-representation, given that less than 6 per cent of secondary pupils in Scotland are educated privately;

- 43 per cent of people at the top of Scottish society studied for a first degree at one of the four ancient universities in Scotland. This includes 66 per cent of senior judges, 50 per cent of top media professionals and 46 per cent of Scottish MPs. This limits the social diversity of the top of Scottish professions: for example, the data presented above shows that only 13 per cent of full-time, first degree entrants to these universities are from working-class backgrounds (National Statistics Socio-Economic Classification 5–7).

Looking at housing market outcomes:

- In common with the rest of the UK, the proportion of households headed by a young adult (16 to 34-year-olds) who own their own home has fallen significantly over the last 15 years, from 53 per cent in 1999 to 30 per cent in 2014. Over the same period, the proportion renting privately has more than trebled, from 13 per cent in 1999 to 41 per cent in 2014;[37]
- While this decline in owner-occupation among young adults has not translated into a big increase in the numbers of families with children living in the private rented sector to the same degree as in England, there are still 83,000 families with children in Scotland living in private rented housing (13.5 per cent). This may have a negative impact on some of these children, as private rented housing tends to be less stable and more expensive than other tenures. There is wide local variation in the proportion of children who live in the private rented sector – for example, in Edinburgh, more than 20 per cent of families with children live in the private rented sector, including 33 per cent of children in single parent families.[38]

7.3 Key policies

There were no major changes in the Scottish Government's strategic approach towards tackling child poverty since our report last year, with 2015 the second year covered by the *Child Poverty Strategy for Scotland 2014–2017* published in 2014.[39]

The strategy established three main goals for the Scottish Government in tackling child poverty and developed a set of 12 intermediate outcomes that will help these goals to be achieved – with progress being measured using 37 indicators in the strategy's measurement framework:

- Pockets – maximising household resources:
    - Maximised financial entitlements of families on low income;
    - Reduced household spend of families on low income;
    - Families on low income are managing finances appropriately and accessing all financial entitlements;
    - Parents are in good-quality, sustained employment in line with skills and ambitions.
- Prospects – improved life chances of children in poverty:
    - Children from low-income households have improved levels of physical and mental health;
    - Children from low-income households experience social inclusion and display social competence;

37 Scottish Government, *Scotland's People Annual Report: Results from 2014 Scottish Household Survey*, 2015

38 Scottish Government, *Scotland's Census 2011, Table DC4104SC – Tenure by Occupancy Rating (Rooms) by Household Composition*, 2011

39 Scottish Government, *Child Poverty Strategy for Scotland 2014–2017*, 2014

    - Children from low-income households have improving relative levels of educational attainment, achieving their full potential;
    - Children from low-income backgrounds are in good-quality, sustained employment in line with their skills and ambitions.

- Places – children from low-income households live in well-designed, sustainable places:
    - Children from low-income households live in high-quality sustainable housing;
    - Children from low-income households grow up in places that are socially sustainable;
    - Children from low-income households grow up in places that are physically sustainable;
    - Children from low-income households grow up in places that are economically sustainable.

Key policy initiatives identified by the Scottish Government[40] that aim to help support their efforts to meet the statutory child poverty targets include:

- Mitigation of the impact of welfare reform. The Scottish Government will be spending £104 million on this in 2015–16, including the Welfare Fund (£38 million), support for those subject to removal of the spare room subsidy (£35 million) and the council tax reduction scheme (£23 million) among other things;
- Promoting inclusive growth and fair work. The Scottish Economic Strategy, published in March 2015, focuses on tackling inequality as one of two key strategic objectives in Scotland's new economic framework (alongside improving competitiveness). A central part of this is the Fair Work agenda: job security, fair reward and opportunities for personal and workplace development. Initiatives as part of this include the Fair Work Convention (a cross-society advisory body involving employer and employee representatives, who are tasked with developing a fair employment and workplace framework for Scotland by March 2016), the Scottish Business Pledge (see page 141) and the Scottish Government becoming an accredited Living Wage organisation.

A major development since our report last year is the significantly increased focus of the Scottish Government on improving social mobility and the acknowledgement that, in common with the rest of the UK, gaps in life chances between rich and poor in Scotland are unacceptably high. As the First Minister, Nicola Sturgeon, has said:

> *The attainment gap doesn't simply hold back young people who deserve a fair chance to fulfil their potential – it impoverishes all of us as a society. That's why closing the gap is a defining challenge for the government I lead and for our society as a whole... we must never, ever become content to shrug our shoulders and accept that [factors beyond the school gates] make under-attainment in our schools inevitable for some young people.*[41]

The Scottish Government has introduced a number of policy initiatives aiming to make a reality of this commitment to improve social mobility in Scotland, including:

- Plans to increase entitlements to free, high-quality early learning and childcare provision to 30 hours per week during term-time for all three- and four-year-olds and disadvantaged two-year-olds, by 2020;
- Placing a new statutory duty on local authorities and Scottish Government ministers to take action to narrow the socio-economic educational attainment gap and publish reports on progress through the Education (Scotland) Bill 2015;

40 Scottish Government response to the Commission's Call for Evidence 2015
41 Nicola Sturgeon, *A World Leader in Education*, speech at Wester Hailes Education Centre, Edinburgh, 18 August 2015

- Developing a new National Improvement Framework for Scottish Education with a key goal of closing the attainment gap, which will introduce national standardised assessment of literacy and numeracy in P1, P4, P7 and S3 – to be implemented nationally from 2017, allowing the performance of the school system for the most disadvantaged children to be tracked and reported on annually;
- Providing £100 million funding for the Scottish Attainment Challenge over four years, targeted at primary schools in deprived areas of Scotland and aiming to improve children's literacy, numeracy, health and well-being;
- Expanding entitlement to the Education Maintenance Allowance, increasing income thresholds by 20 per cent (to £24,421 for those in families with only one child and £26,884 for those with two or more children), extending eligibility to cover part-time study – meaning that 57,000 young people in Scotland (63 per cent more than in 2013–14) will be eligible for support of £30 per week to stay in education post-16 from January 2016;
- Setting a long-term ambition to equalise the chances of university access between children in the most and least deprived areas in Scotland, and establishing the independent Commission on Widening Access to look at the evidence on widening participation, identify best practice and propose new targets, due to report in Spring 2016.

7.4 Reflections

Child poverty strategy

The most recent Scotland child poverty strategy[42] provides a comprehensive and coherent framework informing the Scottish Government's approach. The 'logic model' approach used in the strategy's outcomes framework ensures that there is a clear understanding of the intermediate outcomes being sought by the strategy as the building blocks for achieving the ultimate goal of eradicating child poverty in Scotland. This can inform the development and detailed design of policies that are able to make a real difference as well as identify gaps in the strategic approach. The new measurement framework is also a very positive development and gives far better information on the progress being made towards achieving the Scottish Government's ambitions than was previously available. Other parts of the UK can learn a lot from the strategic approach taken in Scotland.

Looking ahead, there are a number of ways in which the Scottish approach to tackling poverty could be enhanced to help drive progress over the next few years:

- Increase clarity about what good progress in each of the intermediate outcomes looks like. There is little sense in the strategy of the scale of progress that will be required in each of the intermediate outcomes for the ultimate goal of eradicating child poverty in Scotland to be achieved. Being more specific about what the ambitions of the Government are for improvement in the intermediate outcomes over the next few years will help to focus efforts;
- Increase the focus on taking advantage of the opportunities from welfare reform, as well as on mitigating its risks. While undoubtedly cuts in benefits will create significant challenges for attempts to reduce child poverty, there are also potential opportunities from welfare reform more broadly. For example, the introduction of Universal Credit will mean more scope for a targeted approach to tackling working poverty, through providing in-work support geared towards helping parents increase their pay and work more hours;

42 Scottish Government, *Child Poverty Strategy for Scotland: Our Approach 2014–2017*, 2014

- Increase the focus on helping more parents enter work and increase their hours of work. There is limited emphasis placed on tackling worklessness, helping more parents into work and helping parents to work more hours within the current strategy. Eradicating poverty will require further progress on all of these things. Forty-four per cent of children in poverty in Scotland live in workless households and – if Scotland is similar to the UK as a whole – encouraging more primary caregivers in couple families with school-age children to enter employment, and to increase their hours of work when their children reach their teens, will be key to future success in tackling working poverty;
- Reviewing the indicators used to measure progress towards achieving intermediate outcomes. There is scope to improve some of the indicators used in the strategy's measurement framework, to help them better measure progress towards the intermediate outcomes. For example, the overall parental employment rate is only a partial measure of success in achieving employment outcomes that are sufficient to tackle poverty (intermediate outcome 4). Work intensity – whether all parents in a household are in work and how many hours are worked – is also important. To give a second example, the lack of any indicator of attainment in Standard or Higher exams, or one looking at HE access, is an important omission in trying to measure the extent to which children in low-income households are achieving their potential (intermediate outcome 7);
- Do more to support and encourage local authorities and other public bodies to do their bit to tackle poverty in their local areas. There is much variation between different local areas in how they attempt to tackle poverty in their areas. For example, the strategic approach taken by Renfrewshire – through establishing a Tackling Poverty Commission[43] whose recommendations informed the recent Renfrewshire Tackling Poverty Strategy[44] – is one from which other local areas in Scotland could learn. In addition, the Scottish Government could learn from the approaches taken in England (the Child Poverty Act 2010 gave local authorities in England a range of duties around tackling poverty) and Wales (through the duties given to public authorities through the Children and Families (Wales) Measure 2010).

An important task for the next Scottish Government will be developing a new institutional framework for tackling poverty in Scotland, replacing the current statutory framework in the Child Poverty Act 2010 once the changes that the UK Government is making to it are enacted. At a minimum, we suggest that the new Scottish framework should include:

- A statutory basis in Scottish law embedding the new institutional framework for tackling poverty and improving social mobility in Scotland;
- A duty on Scottish ministers to produce a child poverty strategy which, at the very least, mirrors the current duties set out in UK law;
- New duties on local government and other public bodies that require them to contribute to the cross-national effort to eradicate child poverty in Scotland;
- New accountability arrangements that, for example, formally set out the role that will be played by the Independent Adviser on Poverty or successor arrangements;
- A new measurement framework that is able to track progress towards the ultimate goal of eradicating child poverty and towards achieving the broader intermediate outcomes.

43 Renfrewshire council, *Tackling Poverty in Renfrewshire: Report of Renfrewshire's Tackling Poverty Commission*, 2015
44 Renfrewshire council, *Tackling Poverty 2015–2017*, 2015

Social mobility

We strongly welcome the increased emphasis on tackling the unacceptable gaps that exist in Scotland between the life chances of children from rich and poor backgrounds, and the recent policy developments geared towards tackling them. The key challenge for the Scottish Government is turning rhetoric into reality and delivering – in collaboration with other institutions in Scottish society – on policies that can make a real difference.

One barrier to developing an effective strategy to improve social mobility is the lack of high-quality public data on the issue. This frustrates analysis of the problems and understanding of what the issues are, how best to tackle them and the effectiveness of different policy interventions at improving social mobility. If Scotland is serious about social mobility, it needs to develop easily accessible and comparable data that sets out how well poorer children are doing relative to others at each stage of their education. Scotland can learn a lot from the English approach to collecting and publishing comprehensive data on social mobility outcomes. Some areas to address include:

- Developing a new national school-readiness measure that is able to track year-to-year trends over the whole of Scotland in gaps in early years development and the success (or otherwise) of policy interventions that are intended to close the gap;
- Developing a new national primary attainment measure to track year-to-year trends in the attainment gaps at the end of primary school;
- Developing a clearer measure of attainment by age 16 (the end of S4) based on gaps in achieving at 'expected levels' in the new National 5 exams e.g. five passes at National 5 including English and maths;
- Developing clearer measures of attainment by age 18 (the end of S6) based on gaps in achieving different thresholds of performance at Higher level and at Advanced Higher level e.g. three or more Higher qualifications, three or more Higher qualifications at CCC or above, and so on;
- Developing new individual-level metrics of disadvantage in addition to growing up in a deprived area, acknowledging that more than half of the poorest children in Scotland do not live in the most deprived areas;
- Improving data transparency by ensuring that data on disadvantage gaps is easy to access, published at local authority level, published in sufficient detail to allow a sophisticated understanding of the issues driving them to be built up, and taking an open data approach to help academics and others uncover interesting patterns. The approach taken by the Department for Education in England may provide a good model;
- Policymakers and educational professionals should utilise the emerging evidence base being developed by the Education Endowment Foundation to inform the development of policy in the early years and in school.

A further priority for action is higher education. The debate on access to HE in Scotland is focused largely on access to any HE rather than on differences by social background in the type or quality of HE accessed. There are a number of issues which the Commission for Widening Access will need to focus on as it develops its recommendations:

- The suggestion made in the interim report of the Commission for Widening Access that "current outreach activity may be having a limited impact on overall participation" is a major cause for concern, as is the conclusion that the lack of evidence on the effectiveness of access activity in Scotland makes it "very difficult to make informed judgements on how best to invest and ensure appropriate return on the significant sums of public and institutional resources that are being spent on access programmes".[45] We also agree with the conclusion that there needs to be a lot more co-ordination of access activity in Scotland to ensure that it is coherent and maximise its impact. Resolving these gaps must be a key priority.

- As highlighted above, young people from deprived areas are heavily concentrated in FE colleges studying towards sub-degree qualifications which have lower returns and are not as good at facilitating access into the top jobs in Scotland, while their peers from the wealthiest areas are far more likely to be studying at the elite universities in Scotland towards degrees that prepare them for entry to elite professions. This is a real issue for social mobility in Scotland, and it is essential that there is more emphasis on getting young people from deprived backgrounds into full-time, first degree-level qualifications in university that hold out the prospect of being able to compete for top jobs. Key to this will be tackling the attainment, aspiration, HE access and student funding barriers that prevent this. The final report of the Commission must propose targets around participation of young people from disadvantaged backgrounds in first degree programmes at universities and at the highly selective ancient universities, in addition to the targets that will be proposed for participation in higher education overall.
- Further attention needs to be given to the student support system in Scotland, especially for disadvantaged students. Despite there being no tuition fees in Scotland, the poorest students can still graduate with debts of up to £23,000 for a four-year first degree programme if they take advantage of the full means-tested loans available to them. Scottish graduates face higher loan repayment costs in the early part of their careers (9 per cent of gross income above £17,355, compared to 9 per cent of gross income above £21,000 in England), meaning for example that a Scottish graduate earning £29,000 would repay £1,050 in the first year of their career (or 4.7 per cent of their post-tax earnings) compared to the £720 (or 3.2 per cent of their post-tax earnings) paid by a similar English graduate. While debt levels facing the poorest university students in Scotland are still only about 60 per cent of the level that their peers in England accrue for a typical first degree programme,[46] many of the lowest earning Scottish graduates will also end up paying more for their degrees than their peers in England, as the impact of the more generous repayment terms for low-earning graduates in England exceeds the impact of the higher debt and interest charges that English students face.[47] The evidence cited earlier in this chapter suggests that student debt and associated worries about it among students is having a real impact on the decision-making and higher education choices being made by poorer students in Scotland.

Finally, more focus should be given to working with others to reduce child poverty and improve social mobility. Scotland has some good practice here that the rest of the UK could learn from: around working with employers to improve low-paid employment through the Scottish Business Pledge, launched earlier this year; and through efforts to promote the Living Wage in Scotland. This approach could be usefully replicated in a social mobility context for graduate employers, with the goal of improving access to elite professions, helping employers to do their bit in narrowing the school attainment gap and helping poorer children to aim high and achieve their potential. The UK Government's Social Mobility Business Compact is worth looking at as a model for how employers can be helped to get involved.

45 Commission on Widening Access, *Interim Report*, November 2015

46 See Lucy Hunter Blackburn, *Submission to Commission on Widening Access*, 2015 https://adventuresinevidence.files.wordpress.com/2014/06/annex-to-access-commission-evidence.docx for a fuller discussion of levels of student debt accrued in Scotland relative to other parts of the UK

47 See for example Scottish Parliament, *SPICe Briefing 13/78: Student Loans and Repayments*, November 2013 which suggests that the lowest earning 20 per cent of graduates would face lower lifetime repayments in the English system with a loan of £36,000, than in the Scottish system with a loan of £16,000

7.5 Conclusions and Recommendations

Scotland is relatively well placed to tackle child poverty, with outcomes that compare well with other parts of the UK. Out of the 12 devolved nations and English regions, Scotland has the lowest rate of child poverty after housing costs, the second highest parental employment rate, the fourth lowest proportion of children in workless households, and the third lowest prevalence of low-paid jobs.

However, there is no room for complacency. There is still a very long way to go to eradicate child poverty in Scotland. Continued fiscal consolidation over the next few years will pose a number of challenges and social mobility outcomes appear to be as bad in Scotland as they are in England.

The big priorities over the next few months should be to develop a new institutional framework in Scotland to replace the Child Poverty Act 2010, ensuring that the increased focus on social mobility is translated into improved outcomes, and ensuring that the new powers available to the Scottish Government once the Scotland Bill 2015–16 becomes law are used effectively to drive progress on social mobility and child poverty.

We make four main recommendations for action that the Scottish Government could take to help drive further progress over the next few years:

- Develop a new child poverty and life chances framework for Scotland to build on and replace the provisions currently contained in the Child Poverty Act 2010;
- Collect and publish better data on social mobility and increase data transparency;
- Ensure that the Commission on Widening Access focuses on improving the effectiveness of investment in widening participation, access to degree programmes in university as well as higher education more generally, and the impact of the student support system and student debt levels on the choices made by Scottish students;
- Work with Scottish employers to improve social mobility, through building on the Scottish Business Pledge to develop a Scottish Social Mobility Business Compact aimed at graduate employers.

Chapter 8: Social mobility and child poverty in Wales

- **Child poverty in Wales is higher than in other UK countries and is expected to increase in the next few years.**
- **Trends in employment are moving in the right direction, but Wales has higher rates of low pay than other UK countries, keeping many children in poor working families.**
- **Educational attainment in Wales at all levels, especially for the poorest children, remains unacceptably low despite recent improvements and is significantly below other parts of the UK in terms of Programme for International Student Assessment (PISA) assessments.**
- **The Welsh Government has a welcome focus on tackling disadvantage with a large number of programmes and policies, but a more targeted, evidence-based approach is needed.**
- **More focus is needed to help people move up the social ladder, to accompany commendable efforts to help people at the bottom.**
- **The top priorities for action are to get more good teachers into disadvantaged schools, and to work more closely with employers to improve pay and career prospects.**

8.1 Introduction

The Welsh Government has made tackling child poverty a priority: it has an active programme to reduce disparities in income and educational attainment. Its approach is similar in some respects to the approaches taken elsewhere in the UK, but there are some differences. For example, in contrast to England, Wales has renewed its long-term ambition to meet the child poverty targets currently set out in the Child Poverty Act 2010. It has given less priority to the issue of social mobility.

Child poverty in Wales, as in the rest of the UK, remains stubbornly high, and independent forecasters expect it to increase in the next few years, mainly due to the impact of welfare reform on low-income families. For example, the Institute for Fiscal Studies has published projections suggesting that the proportion of children in relative poverty in England and Wales would increase by 5 per cent, and the proportion of children in absolute poverty would increase by 6 per cent, between 2013–14 and 2020–21.[1] Since the IFS completed this work, the UK Government has announced a further £12 billion of cuts to the welfare budget which will primarily have an impact on children and the working-age population; these more recent changes are not factored into these projections.

The Welsh Government has sought to improve the life chances of the country's children by commissioning several reviews of the country's education system. If the recommendations from these reviews are accepted, this will lead to radical changes to the curriculum and assessment arrangements, from Foundation Phase to Key Stage 4. These changes are overdue, and the Commission commends the Welsh Government for recognising that urgent action is needed.

8.2 Current position

The challenges facing Wales in making progress towards a more socially mobile society with lower rates of child poverty are more severe than in the rest of the UK. In particular, Wales continues to face tough challenges in relation to child poverty:

- Absolute child poverty after housing costs rose to 34 per cent in the three-year period ending 2013/14, from 29 per cent in the three-year period ending 2008/09 (approximately 200,000 children).[2] This compares to 31 per cent in England and 24 per cent in Scotland for the same period. The only part of the UK that has a higher rate of absolute child poverty than Wales is London (41 per cent);[3]
- Absolute child poverty before housing costs is slightly lower at 25 per cent for the three-year period ending in 2013/14. Children in Wales for the three-year period ending 2013/14 were more likely to be in absolute poverty before housing costs than children elsewhere in Great Britain – in England 19 per cent of children lived in absolute poverty, and in Scotland 17 per cent;[4]
- Relative child poverty after housing costs decreased slightly to 31 per cent in the three-year period ending 2013/14, from 32 per cent in the three-year period ending 2008/09. However, the rate in Wales is higher than that of England (28 per cent) and Scotland (21 per cent);[5]
- Relative child poverty before housing costs fell from 26 per cent for the three-year period ending in 2008/09 to 22 per cent for the three-year period ending in 2013/14. The figure for Wales is higher than England at 17 per cent, and Scotland at 16 per cent;[6]
- Children living in Wales were more likely to live in persistent poverty (21 per cent) than England (16 per cent) and Scotland (13 per cent).[7]

Trends in one of the key drivers of poverty in Wales – employment – are moving in the right direction, but there is still some way to go.

Over the last five years there has been a 4.3 percentage point decrease in the number of children living in workless households, although the number remains high (15.1 per cent in 2014). The figure is slightly higher than England (12.7 per cent) and 4.2 percentage points

1 Institute for Fiscal Studies (IFS), *Child and Working-age Poverty in Northern Ireland over the Next Decade: An Update*, IFS Briefing Note BN154, November 2014. This projected that the proportion of children in relative poverty before housing costs in England and Wales would increase from a forecast 19.6 per cent in 2013–14 to 20.6 per cent in 2020–21, and the proportion of children in absolute poverty before housing costs would increase from a forecast 22.8 per cent in 2013–14 to 24.1 per cent in 2020–21
2 Due to small sample size, a three-year average is used
3 Department for Work and Pensions, *Households Below Average Income, 2013/14*, 2015
4 Ibid.
5 Ibid.
6 Ibid.
7 Institute of Education, University of London, *Child Poverty and Deprivation, Initial Findings from the Millennium Cohort Study*, 2014

higher than in Scotland (10.9 per cent).[8] Beneath the national figure, there are wide variations in worklessness by local authority. For example, one in five (22.2 per cent) children in Newport lived in workless households in 2014, compared to less than one in 10 in Powys (7.5 per cent).

It is also striking that in the past year, employment figures for the majority of female age groups in Wales has dropped, particularly for younger females. The biggest drop was seen for 18–24-year-old women, which saw a 4.2 percentage point drop between June 2014 and June 2015 (57.3 per cent to 53.1 per cent): this is compared to a 1.4 percentage point increase for the same age group and time period for men (54.9 per cent to 56.4 per cent). This contrasts strongly with the situation in Scotland, where 63.9 per cent of women aged 18–24 are in work. Overall, unemployment rates for those aged 16 and over in Wales are higher than elsewhere in Great Britain at 6.7 per cent, compared to 5.9 per cent in Scotland and 5.6 per cent in England.[9]

Like the rest of Great Britain, Wales also faces a significant problem of in-work poverty. In the three-year period ending 2013/14, 23 per cent of children living in working families were in poverty. This compares with 13 per cent in Scotland for the same period, and 21 per cent in England.[10] One factor keeping many working families in poverty is low hourly pay, with around 270,000 Welsh workers (25 per cent of the labour force) being paid below two-thirds of the UK median hourly wage.[11]

Employability

The Welsh Government sees improving skills as crucial to reduce worklessness and in-work poverty, and it is encouraging to see some improvement in this area. The proportion of working-age adults (16–64-year-olds) with no qualifications (no GCSEs) decreased from 15 per cent in 2009 to 10 per cent in 2014 (33 per cent), although this masks the wide variations between local authorities. For example, nearly 15 per cent of 16–64-year-olds in Merthyr Tydfil had no qualifications (no GCSEs), compared to just under 7 per cent in Cardiff. In England nearly 9 per cent of working-age adults have no qualifications, compared to 10 per cent in Scotland.[12]

The proportion of working-age adults who are qualified to at least Level 2 has increased since 2009 by 10 per cent.[13] Nonetheless, this still means that nearly one-fifth (18.8 per cent) of working adults don't have the qualifications necessary for finding employment and progressing in work. There are wide variations between local authorities, with nearly one-third of 16–64-year-olds in Merthyr Tydfil not having at least Level 2 qualifications, compared to nearly one in seven in Ceredigion. This compares to 18.4 per cent in England, and 16.4 per cent in Scotland who are not qualified to at least Level 2.[14]

Education and training

The gap between the achievement of children eligible for free school meals and their peers starts young and widens throughout education. At the Foundation Stage the attainment gap has reduced slightly over the past three years, but it remained large at 16.3 percentage points in 2014.[15] [16] The attainment gap at Key Stage 2 is wide at 17.7 percentage points, with 28.1 per cent

8 Office for National Statistics, *Working and Workless Households*, 2015
9 Office for National Statistics, *Regional Labour Market Statistics*, October 2015
10 Joseph Rowntree Foundation and New Policy Institute analyses of Department for Work and Pensions, *Households Below Average Income, 2013/14*, 2015
11 Joseph Rowntree Foundation, *Monitoring Poverty and Social Exclusion in Wales 2015*, 2015; and Office for National Statistics, *Annual Survey of Hours and Earning, 2014*, 2015
12 Office for National Statistics, *Annual Population Survey*, 2014
13 Ibid.
14 Ibid.
15 The Foundation Phase Indicator (FPI) represents the percentage of pupils achieving the expected outcome or above in "Language, literacy and communication skills" (in English, LCE; or Welsh, LCW), 'Personal and social development, well-being and cultural diversity' (PSD) and 'Mathematical development' (MDT) in combination
16 Ibid.

of free school meals children not achieving at least Level 4 compared to 10.4 per cent for non-free school meals pupils.[17] Nearly two-fifths (38.7 per cent) of free school meals pupils are not achieving the expected level for English, maths and science at Level 5 for Key Stage 3, compared to around one-sixth (14.4 per cent) of their peers.[18]

The attainment gap at Key Stage 4 is wide at 33.8 percentage points, with just over one-quarter of free school meals children achieving Level 2 in English and/or Welsh and maths compared to 61.6 per cent of their peers.[19] [20] What this means is that nearly three-fifths (72.2 per cent) of children eligible for free school meals in Wales in 2014 did not obtain the level deemed necessary to undertake good-quality further education (FE) and employment.

Furthermore, four-fifths of children eligible for free school meals in Blaenau Gwent (79.1 per cent) did not achieve Level 2 at Key Stage 4, although the top performing local authority wasn't far behind, with three-quarters of free school meals children not achieving Level 2 at Key Stage 4.[21] In addition, in no local authority did free school meals children achieve higher than the national average for all pupils of 56.2 per cent. Direct comparison is not possible due to key differences in the education systems such as the curriculum, but the attainment gap in English and maths between free school meals students and their peers in England was 26.4 percentage points in 2014.[22]

Looking more generally at educational achievement, Wales performs significantly worse than the rest of the UK in the Programme for International Student Assessment (PISA), with the lowest score and ranking in maths, reading and science of any of the four UK nations. In addition in all three domains, Wales's score is lower than both the UK average and Organisation for Economic Co-operation and Development (OECD) averages (see Table 6.1). The scale of progress required by Wales to be a top 20 PISA nation, and therefore ensure that its children can compete academically with others, is dramatic. Wales would need to increase its score by between 24 and 33 points and increase its ranking by between 16 and 23 places across the three domains.[23]

Table 8.1: PISA 2012 scores and rankings for maths, reading and science

	Mathematics		Reading		Science	
	Mean score	Ranking	Mean score	Ranking	Mean score	Ranking
Wales	468	43	480	41	491	36
England	495	26	500	24	516	18
Scotland	498	25	506	21	513	22
Northern Ireland	487	32	498	25	507	24
UK	494	–	499	–	514	–
OECD	494	–	496	–	501	–

Source: Welsh Government, Programme for International Student Assessment (PISA) 2012/2013

Poor performance in school can lead to disengagement in education and training later in life, with young adults ending up not in education, employment or training (NEET). In Wales since 2009 the proportion of 16–18-year-olds who are NEET has reduced by 1.5 percentage points

17 Ibid.
18 Ibid.
19 Data for 2014/15 for Key Stage 4 has not been used, as new data is not yet available for other key stages or by local authority. To note: In 2015, the gap between pupils eligible for free school meals and their peers still remains wide at 32.4 percentage points, despite moderate increases in performance for both cohorts of students
20 Welsh Government, *Academic Achievement and Entitlement to Free School Meals*, 2014
21 Ibid.
22 Department for Education, *GCSE and Equivalent Attainment by Pupil Characteristics in England, 2013/14*, 2015
23 Welsh Government, *Programme for International Student Assessment (PISA) 2012*, 2013 and National Foundation for Educational Research, *Achievement of 15-Year-Olds in Wales: PISA 2012 National Report*, 2013

(approximately 2,600); yet, more than one in 10 (10.9 per cent) 16–18-year-olds were NEETs in 2014. In England the proportion of 16–18-year-olds who were NEET in 2014 was slightly lower at 7.3 per cent.[24] The proportion of 19–24-year-olds who are NEET has reduced by one percentage point (approximately 400) since 2009, and was more than one in five (20.7 per cent) in 2014.[25]

In addition a greater proportion of young people in Wales live in areas with a low participation in HE: 25.2 per cent compared to 9.9 per cent in Scotland and 20.8 per cent in England.

Improving attainment and training will not improve child poverty and life chances in Wales unless there are suitable employment opportunities within the region. In 2014 nearly one-third (30 per cent) of graduates domiciled in Wales took up employment in England, compared to just over one-tenth (12 per cent) of Scottish graduates. Just 2 per cent of graduates domiciled in England left to take up employment elsewhere.[26]

The Welsh Government has 11 indicators in its Child Poverty Strategy, which it uses to assess its performance on reducing child poverty in Wales. For the eight which have data available, six improved, one worsened and one stayed the same.[27]

8.3 Key policies

The Welsh Government published a revised Child Poverty Strategy in 2015 and reaffirmed its ambition to eradicate child poverty by 2020. The strategy set two new strategic objectives:

- Using all available levers to create a strong economy and a labour market which supports the tackling poverty agenda;
- Doing more to support families through debt and financial advice, and tackling the issue of poor households paying more for goods and services.

It also reiterated the three strategic objectives set out in its 2011 strategy:

- Reducing the number of children in workless households;
- Increasing the skills of parents and young people in low-income households;
- Reducing the inequalities that exist in the education, health and economic outcomes of children and families living in poverty.

The Welsh Government's Tackling Poverty Action Plan is the main mechanism for taking forward and delivering these objectives, and it is revised on an annual basis. It covers a range of different areas.

Early years

In 2013 the Welsh Government published *Building a Brighter Future: The Early Years and Childcare Plan*:[28] a 10-year plan that aims to improve collaboration among early years workers, and bring greater coherence across different policies and programmes impacting on and influencing the early years. It has extended its Flying Start programme, increasing the number of families covered by 18,000. The programme focuses on the most deprived areas and helps families with children aged under four to meet important milestones by providing childcare, a health visiting service, support for parenting and language development and other services.

24 Office for National Statistics, *Young People Not in Education, Employment or Training*, 2015
25 Welsh Government, *Participation of Young People in Education and the Labour Market and Annual Population Survey*, 2015
26 https://www.hesa.ac.uk/stats-dlhe
27 More information regarding the detail of these indicators and data can be found at the Welsh Government website: http://gov.wales/topics/people-and-communities/people/children-and-young-people/child-poverty/?lang=en
28 Welsh Government, *Building a Brighter Future: The Early Years and Childcare Plan*, 2013

The Welsh Government continues to develop its Families First programme which aims to improve outcomes for children, young people and families. Between 2013 and 2014 more than 200 projects were accessed by individuals on almost 200,000 occasions. The Welsh Government extended the Pupil Deprivation Grant to the early years, providing a grant of £300 per eligible child for the next two years for schools and other settings, helping to support learning for three- and four-year-olds in poverty. The Welsh Government is also supporting local authorities in Wales through its Out of School Childcare Grant, which totals £2.3 million this financial year. This grant currently supports local authorities in addressing gaps in childcare, by providing wraparound childcare and play during out-of-school hours and holiday periods.

Education attainment

In 2014 the Welsh Government published *Rewriting the Future: Raising Ambition and Attainment in Welsh Schools*[29] – a programme designed to provide guidance to families on how children can do better in schools, and to provide schools with toolkits to help with engaging families. Implementation is underway and the outcomes are being monitored. Furthermore, new guidance for practitioners on how best to spend the Pupil Deprivation Grant has been published,[30] and assurance has been given to schools about levels of funding for the next two school years. More than £20 million has been allocated for Schools Challenge Cymru, which is targeted at 40 schools facing particular challenges. New guidance was also developed and published in June 2015 – *Families and Community Engagement*[31] – which aims to provide practical support for schools to help them strengthen their approach to family and community engagement.

Young people not in employment, education or training

The Welsh Government published its Youth Engagement and Progression Framework in 2013,[32] which aims to reduce the number of young people who are not in employment, education or training (NEET), and further supports young people into employment through programmes such as Jobs Growth Wales. Jobs Growth Wales aims to give equal opportunities to all young people in Wales with the talent and the skills to do well at work, and aims to create 16,000 jobs over the next four years. The Welsh Government apprenticeship programmes aim to offer more than 50,000 apprenticeships to individuals aged 26 and over, and provide valuable experience and skills to improve their life chances and job prospects. In addition, traineeships are offered to non-employed 16–18-year-olds not otherwise engaged in post-16 education or employment. The programme seeks to improve skill levels through delivery of entry-level qualifications up to National Vocational Qualification (NVQ) Level 1 in a chosen occupational area.

Job opportunities

The Lift Programme launched in 2014 is the vehicle for delivering the commitment in the Welsh Government's Tackling Poverty Action Plan to provide 5,000 training and employment opportunities for people living in workless households by the end of 2017. The programme focuses on people who have been out of work for more than six months and face employment barriers, such as young single parents, adults with few or no formal qualifications, people with poor employment records and disabled people. The programme has provided more than 2,500 training and employment opportunities, including more than 500 people supported in employment, and is now fully operational in nine areas across Wales.

29 Welsh Government, *Rewriting the Future: Raising Ambition and Attainment in Welsh Schools*, 2014

30 Welsh Government, *Pupil Deprivation Grant: Essential Guidance*, 2015

31 Welsh Government, *FaCE the Challenge Together: Family and Community Engagement Toolkit for Schools in Wales – Main Guidance*, 2015

32 Welsh Government, *Implementation Plan: Youth Engagement and Progression Framework*, 2013

8.4 Reflections

Child poverty strategy

The Commission commends the Welsh Government for its commitment to tackling child poverty and for the wide range of policies that it has adopted in this area. Given the scale of the problem, it is vital that the Welsh Government takes a highly disciplined approach, devises realistic plans and moves resources between programmes, depending on their impact and changes in the underlying situation. The Commission is concerned that there are too many overlapping programmes and that resources are spread too thinly. We would encourage the Welsh Government to strengthen its anti-poverty activities by taking a more evidence-based approach and, where evidence is not available, take steps to rectify this.

The Commission welcomes the broader approach to tackling child poverty that was set out in the revised strategy published earlier this year. The Welsh Government is right to prioritise the issue of in-work poverty and to highlight the fact that poorer households often face higher costs than those with higher incomes (the poverty premium). In addition, the strategy is better aligned with the Tackling Poverty Action Plan than the previous edition. However, further work is needed to ensure the two documents work harmoniously together. For example, there needs to be consistency between the two documents in the indicators used to measure success.

Welfare reform

The Institute for Fiscal Studies estimates that changes to the tax and welfare system implemented by the 2010–2015 UK Government will reduce household incomes in Wales by an average of £10.75 a week, or £718 million a year across Wales as a whole, once Universal Credit and Personal Independence Payments are rolled out.[33] However, in light of the further changes to welfare, this figure is likely to rise significantly. The Welsh Government has rightly taken action to mitigate the impact of these changes: for example, it is providing advice so that individuals can understand the impact of welfare cuts and what help is available.

The Commission recognises the financial constraints that the Welsh Government faces, but thinks more could be done to support the families hardest hit by the reduction in benefits. Research commissioned by the Welsh Government highlights the characteristics and areas that will be most affected by cuts; but, the Welsh Government needs to ensure that services and support will be available to all families, including those not located in the most deprived areas. Current methods, such as defining the reach of programmes by the most deprived Lower Super Output Areas (as defined by the Welsh Index of Multiple Deprivation), means that there are many children and families living on low incomes who do not receive services.[34] For example, more than 65,000 children (all ages) whose families received out-of-work benefits or Child Tax Credits (estimated to be more than 130,000 in total) were estimated not to be in areas where the Communities First programme was based.[35] Even children located in the top 40 per cent most deprived areas of Wales are not guaranteed access to services: more than 25,000 children in families who receive out-of-work benefits or Child Tax Credits live in the top 40 per cent most deprived areas within Wales, and were not in areas benefiting from Communities First.[36]

A large number of families in Wales will be affected by housing benefit changes that reduce support for social tenants if they are considered to be under-occupying their property: 20.4 per cent of

33 Institute for Fiscal Studies, *The Distributional Effects of the UK Government's Tax and Welfare Reforms, Wales: An Update*, 2014
34 http://www.ocsi.co.uk/news/wp-content/uploads/OCSI-GettingMeasureRuralDeprivationWales.pdf
35 Communities First has been used within this example as information exists on the location of where the programme is based. Other programmes such as Flying Start are also delivered using a similar model of defining reach by most deprived Lower Super Output Areas, using the Welsh Index of Multiple Deprivation
36 This analysis was produced by the Commission Secretariat using the Welsh Index of Multiple Deprivation, location of Communities First clusters and HM Revenue & Customs (HMRC) data for personal tax credit: children in low-income families local measure to provide estimates. We recognise that this method is not robust and has its limitations

social tenants in Wales will be affected, compared to 19 per cent in Scotland and 15.3 per cent in England.[37] Despite the Welsh Government taking action to boost the number of one and two-bedroom houses, there are still a large number of families who will find it hard to downsize and so will face a reduced income. An increasing number of families have been falling into arrears with their social housing rent (rent arrears increased by 23.3 per cent between April and October 2013). The Commission believes that this is an area where there is scope for more analysis and action.[38]

Welsh councils have expressed concerns with regard to the lack of information and analysis on issues such as overcrowding, tenant debt and the impact on children's education of sharing bedrooms and having to constantly move home. The Welsh Government has a key role to play here: it needs to support local authorities to understand best practice methods, in order to collect and interpret data to ensure that policy to support children in poverty and their families is effective.[39]

Employment

Helping people into work is central to the Welsh Government's strategy to tackle poverty, but the division of policies and programmes between devolved administrations and the UK Government makes the interaction and co-ordination of policies complicated. For example, skills policy is devolved to the Welsh Government, but employment policies – notably, the work programmes, provision of out-of-work benefits and the operation of Jobcentre Plus – remain the responsibilities of the UK Government. As services for employment and skills are increasingly brought together, this will create complex service models.

The Commission recognises that the Welsh Government is developing a more needs-assessed approach to help individuals return to work. However, unless consideration is given to how devolved and UK-wide polices are co-ordinated and delivered more cohesively, this approach will not have the desired impact. The Commission recommends that the Welsh Government should work alongside local authorities to create a clear programme of how it will deliver its objectives to improve employment within Wales using current policies and programmes. This should consider how national and local programmes can be aligned without duplication of effort or conflicting targets and outputs.

The Commission welcomes the fact that the Lift Programme is targeted at those furthest from employment, but notes that access to the programme, as with others, is a postcode lottery – and often does not lead to a job. As at 30 September 2015, the programme had provided more than 2,400 training and employment opportunities, but only 440 individuals were supported into employment.[40] The Welsh Government needs to find ways to increase this success rate, since employment should be the ultimate aim of the programme.

The Welsh Government is committed to tackling in-work poverty, but more could be done to encourage employers themselves to tackle this issue. In 2014, one in four employee jobs in Wales were paid less than the Living Wage (£7.65 per hour).[41] Although the Welsh Government has encouraged Welsh companies to become Living Wage employers, there will be little impact unless there are clear benefits for employers. The Commission recommends that the Welsh Government should work more closely with employers on this issue, and create incentives for them to sign up. For example, the Scottish Government has encouraged firms to sign up to a voluntary accreditation scheme to promote the Living Wage in Scotland. In addition, the Welsh Government could look at other ideas, such as lower business rates for an employer's first year as a Living Wage employer.

37 Auditor General for Wales, *Managing the Impact of Welfare Reform Changes on Social Housing Tenants in Wales*, 2015
38 Ibid.
39 Ibid.
40 Figures provided by the Welsh Government
41 TUC, *In Parts of Britain Half of Jobs Pay Less than the Living Wage*, 2015

Early years

The Commission welcomes the Welsh Government's use of international evidence in designing programmes such as Flying Start and the Foundation Phase, but notes that effectiveness depends on creating a consistent approach across the whole system. The Welsh Government has recognised this challenge and is implementing an Early Years Outcome Framework, which aims to provide a joined-up approach to services from conception to age seven. This framework should be very useful in measuring the impact of policy initiatives.

However, it is surprising that this framework does not have any indicators or published data (live or being developed) to assess child health (beyond low birthweight) and development before the age of two. This is despite these very early years being recognised as paramount in the positive development of the child. The Commission recognises the difficulty in accurately assessing children at such a young age; however, it is imperative that mechanisms are developed to ensure that policy and programmes are working. A joint questionnaire between health and education practitioners – such as the Ages and Stages Questionnaire,[42] filled in by parents and used to inform health and development discussions with professionals – could be one such method of measuring development.

The Commission notes that as part of this framework, the Welsh Government is taking steps to improve the inspection process across early year settings. A clearly articulated and implemented framework would allow for diversity in settings, while offering parity of standards of provision to all children. Currently, short-term provision which operates for two hours or less is not required to register and is not inspected. The framework should be used to standardise expectations for all provision, which would reduce the burden of inspection while avoiding duplication of inspection and enable a risk-led approach to the frequency and type of inspection conducted. For the framework and inspections to make a positive difference, it is imperative that early years professionals receive consistent messages and are offered similar levels of support – otherwise there will be confusion and mistrust from parents and professionals. The Commission recommends that the framework develops guidance based on clear evidence of what works, which will support early years professionals in ensuring that provision is of the highest quality and meets the standards required for inspection.

The Welsh Government has recognised that flexible, affordable childcare of high quality will allow parents to take up or increase hours of work, and will support the healthy development of children. The Welsh Government's Early Years and Childcare Plan highlights how it will improve childcare in Wales: for example, through reviewing the duty on local authorities to conduct Childcare Sufficiency Assessments, and a review of childcare and early education registration, regulation and inspection.

Wales currently has no uniform qualification requirement for the early years workforce, yet there is consistent evidence of the positive impact for children – especially those from disadvantaged backgrounds – of high-quality, qualified teachers.[43] As of 2013/14, only eight non-maintained nursery settings received an excellent rating from Estyn for teacher quality.[44] The Commission recommends that the Welsh Government provide guidance to providers on how to improve teacher quality, and encourages allocation of the best teachers to those in greatest need: for example, through use of the Pupil Deprivation Grant.

Flying Start continues to be one of the Welsh Government's top priorities, and is one of its main policies to improve the lives of deprived children within the early years through programmes such as parenting advice and childcare provision. The Commission is pleased to see that

42 The Ages and Stages Questionnaire is a parent filled-in questionnaire that is altered depending on the age of the child, and helps determine if the child is meeting health and education milestones. It can support professionals in early diagnosis of barriers to learning and health, and provide support and/or treatment

43 Sylva, K., Melhuish, E., Sammons, P., Saraj-Blatchford, I. and Taggart, B., *The Effective Provision of Pre-school Education (EPPE) Project: Findings from Pre-school to the End of Key Stage 1, 2004; Institute for Public Policy Research, Early Developments: Bridging the Gap between Evidence and Policy in Early-Years Education*, 2013

44 Estyn, *Inspection Outcomes Data, 2010–2015, provided by Estyn 2015*

the expansion target of the programme, which was originally set at 36,000 families, has been achieved. The expansion is an important achievement against the backdrop of budget cuts in real terms experienced by the Welsh Government. However, it is disappointing that since 2012/13 there has been little improvement in the proportion of children in receipt of the programme that reach or exceed their milestones, with the figure remaining at around 55 per cent.[45]

Despite the early years being recognised as a key area for focus, too many children are being failed before they even reach school. A report by Save the Children, *Ready to Read*, found that Wales's poorest children start primary school already struggling with language skills, and that one in four children growing up in poverty leaves primary school unable to read.[46] Analysis from the Millennium Cohort Study indicates that poorer children in Wales are twice as likely as their more advantaged peers to score below average in vocabulary at age five. In addition, children living in poverty who had poor language skills at the age of five are more likely to be still behind at age 11.[47] Children who read well by age 11 do better at school, get better exam results and do better at work.[48]

The Welsh Government has a range of policies to tackle the issue of literacy, including the Literacy and Numeracy Framework and annual reading tests, but these policies do not seem to be having sufficient impact. The Commission recommends that in schools with the biggest literacy gaps, staff and parents should have access to a language expert for the early years, with the expectation that this is rolled out to all staff and parents by 2020.

A key area yet to be sufficiently addressed in Wales (or indeed in the rest of the UK) is the quality of the home learning environment and parenting. Effective parenting has a bigger influence on a child's life than wealth, class or education. What parents do is more important than who they are.[49] Children's language development at the age of two is very strongly associated with performance across all subject areas at primary school.[50] A rich, good-quality home learning environment is the foundation for children's success in schools.

Public policy can promote parenting in two main ways: it can reduce the risk factors associated with poor parenting and insecure attachment; and it can intervene early on to address parenting and attachment issues. The Welsh Government's main policy to improve parenting and the home learning environment is Flying Start. The programme provides parents within Flying Start centres with the opportunity to learn skills to positively develop their children, and to provide a positive home learning environment. However, even once the programme is fully rolled out in 2016, only one in four children in Wales will benefit from it.[51]

Ideally, a universal approach to improving parenting is needed, as this reduces the stigma attached to parenting programmes. At a time of austerity this approach is not realistic, so the Commission advises the Welsh Government to focus its efforts on those in greatest need. The Early Years Outcomes Framework should explicitly address the issue of parenting and ensure that there is a holistic, co-ordinated approach to parenting programmes.[52] The Framework also should indicate how the Welsh Government will identify the families who will benefit the most from additional parenting support, and what support they will receive.

45 Welsh Government, *An Annual Report and Termly Updates which Present a Statistical Summary of the Service (Flying Start)*, 2015
46 Save the Children, *Ready to Read*, 2015
47 Centre for Longitudinal analysis, *Millennium Cohort Study*, 2014
48 http://www.wiserd.ac.uk/news/latest-news/wales-poorest-children-already-falling-behind-language-time-they-start-school/#sthash.hKcZYzDd.dpbs
49 Department for Education, *The Impact of Parental Involvement on Children's Education and EPPE, Finding from Pre-school to End of Key Stage 1*, 2008
50 Department for Education, *Investigating the Role of Language in Children's Early Education Outcomes*, 2011
51 Provided by the Welsh Government
52 Eurochild, *Compendium of Inspiring Practices, Early Intervention and Prevention: 'Family and Parenting Support'*, 2012

Education

Increasing the performance of Welsh schools is crucial to improving social mobility and reducing poverty in the long term. Performance against a number of the education indicators in Wales, such as attendance, showed some improvement between 2013 and 2014. Nonetheless, significant challenges remain. Inequality in Welsh schools starts young and continues throughout education, with many children, especially those eligible for free school meals, not meeting the required level across key stages of education.

Despite attainment in Wales increasing year-on-year for all key stages, the proportion of children eligible for free school meals not achieving the required standard at each stage remains unacceptably high. For example:

- Nearly three in 10 pupils (27.6 per cent) eligible for free school meals do not achieve at least the expected outcome at the end of the Foundation Phase, hence they start school without the basics needed to flourish;[53]
- By Key Stage 2 the proportion of pupils eligible for free school meals who do not achieve the expected grade increases to 28.1 per cent, and increases further at Key Stage 3 to nearly two in five (38.7 per cent);[54]
- The proportion of pupils eligible for free school meals who do not achieve Level 2 at Key Stage 4 is very high at nearly three in four pupils (72.2 per cent). This hides wide variation in the performance at Key Stage 4 (see Figure 8.1). For example, Monmouthshire, which achieved the best attainment rate of all local authorities in Wales at 66.2 per cent for all children, is the worst-performing local authority in terms of the gap between children eligible for free school meals and their peers – three in four (75 per cent) children eligible for free school meals do not achieve Level 2 at Key Stage 4.[55]

53 Welsh Government, *Academic Achievement and Entitlement to Free School Meals*, 2014
54 Ibid.
55 Ibid.

Figure 8.1: Attainment gap at GCSE

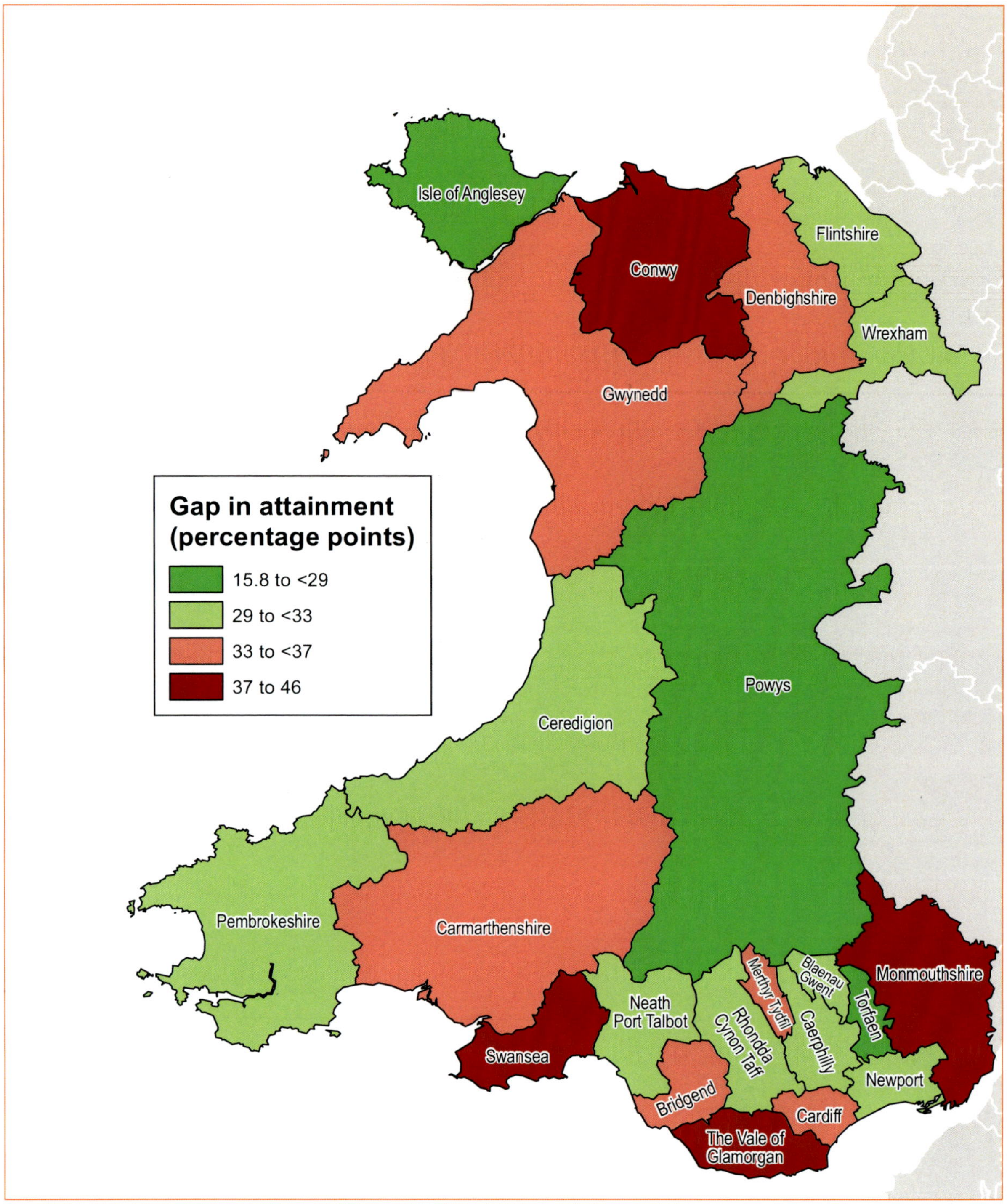

Source: Produced by Department for Education on request using data received from Estyn, *Inspection Outcomes Data*, 2010–15

The Commission recognises that the Welsh Government has a programme to improve educational attainment – including incorporating recommendations from the Donaldson Review[56] – but we remain concerned at the number of children being failed today. In addition to longer-term reform, we would encourage the Welsh Government to take immediate targeted action to improve the performance of the worst schools. We do not think the current light touch approach of 'challenging schools' and providing 'some support' to rectify the situation is a sufficient response to the urgency of the situation.[57]

56 Welsh Government, *Successful Futures: Independent Review of Curriculum and Assessment in Wales by Professor G. Donaldson*, 2015

57 Welsh Government, *Building Resilient Communities – Taking Forward the Tackling Poverty Action Plan Annual Report 2015*, 2015

The Welsh Government and Estyn have recognised the importance of numeracy, and increased efforts to resolve the gap in attainment through the Literacy and Numeracy Framework. Pupils who fail to achieve the basics at primary school are unlikely to meet educational milestones, can become disengaged from school and require expensive late intervention as well as not achieving their potential.

A key barrier to attainment within schools is teacher quality.[58] High-quality teachers have been shown to be a key mechanism to ensure that children from all backgrounds reach their academic potential. But, the practical skills of newly-trained teachers in Wales have been criticised for being below par.[59] In addition, Estyn inspections between 2010 and 2014 highlighted that no secondary school achieved the highest rating (excellent) for teaching quality, and only 3 per cent of primaries did so. It is difficult to see how the inequalities experienced by pupils will be significantly reduced unless teacher quality is seriously addressed, and the pupils who are most disadvantaged have access to excellent teachers.

A report on initial teacher training in Wales by Professor John Furlong – *Teaching Tomorrow's Teachers* – concluded that it was not as strong as it should be, and was falling short of international best practice.[60] The Welsh Government has set up a task-and-finish group to review the recommendations in the Furlong Report. It plans to introduce a four-year education degree rather than the current three, with two years spent learning within schools. It also plans to make entry requirements more difficult. The Commission supports the aim of improving teacher quality, but unless more talented people can be encouraged into the teaching profession within Wales – including individuals from a wider range of backgrounds – it is difficult to see how real change will be achieved.

The Commission would urge the Welsh Government to focus on how to improve the quality of existing teachers as an immediate priority. The Commission recommends that as part of Estyn inspections, schools should have to provide an action plan that identifies the training needs of each of their staff and indicates how this training gap will be addressed. This action plan should highlight how the school is working with others to provide training at lower costs and to share best practice.

The Commission welcomes the fact that the Welsh Government has recognised the importance of parental engagement in improving a child's educational attainment.[61] However, a detailed plan in this area is needed to explain exactly what schools are expected to do, and how the Government will help them engage with hard-to-reach families.

To tackle the issue of poor educational performance in Wales, the Welsh Government has continuously amended policy or introduced new policy and programmes. This has created a confused policy landscape and some simplification would be beneficial. For example, Challenge Cymru aims to tap into the expertise of high-performing leaders in schools in a similar way to two other challenge programmes: the Central South Wales Challenge and the Lead and Emerging Practitioner Schools.

Not in education, employment or training

The number of young people in Wales who are NEET remains stubbornly high,[62] although there has been a marginal fall in the proportion of young people who are NEET. The decrease for 16–18-year-olds between 2010 and 2014 was 0.7 of a percentage point, and for 19–24-year-olds for the same period was 2.2 percentage points.

58 Estyn, *The Annual Report of Her Majesty's Chief Inspector of Education and Training in Wales 2013–2014*, 2015
59 Ibid.
60 Furlong, J., *Teaching Tomorrow's Teachers: Options for the Future of Initial Teacher Education in Wales, 2015*
61 Welsh Government, *Building a Brighter Future: The Early Years and Childcare Plan*, 2013
62 http://www.audit.wales/system/files/publications/NEETs_Report_National_version_2014_English.pdf

The Commission welcomes the fact that the Welsh Government's Youth Engagement and Progression Framework is based on sound evidence and serious engagement with councils. However, some councils have expressed concern about their capacity to implement the framework because of financial pressures.[63] The Commission recommends that the Welsh Government should regularly assess performance against the framework and work with councils to ensure that issues are resolved.

The Commission was pleased to see that the Welsh Government engaged with councils and other stakeholders in the development of its framework. However, young people themselves should have been engaged in the development of the framework, especially those furthest away from employment, education or training.

The new framework should bring clear benefits including improved planning, co-ordination and provision of services – but the Commission agrees with two concerns that Audit Wales has raised in relation to it. First, the framework (and targets) does not differentiate sufficiently between young people who have been NEET for a long time, and those who have just become NEET. There is a danger that the current targets for reducing young people who are NEET could be met by focusing on those that need less support. Second, the framework focuses mainly on young people up to the age of 18, with the assumption that policy and lessons can be applied to those older than 18. It is neither clear that this assumption is valid, nor how the Welsh Government plans to test it. Furthermore, until the Welsh Government and councils make a thorough assessment of the resource required to reduce the number of young people who are NEET, it is difficult to assess whether the targets are realistic.[64]

8.5 Conclusions and Recommendations

The Commission welcomes the Welsh Government's continued ambition to eradicate child poverty, but notes that independent forecasters suggest that due to welfare changes and other factors, the number of children in poverty in Wales may increase by nearly one-third by 2020.[65] The Commission would encourage the Welsh Government to devise a realistic and transparent plan that makes clear what it thinks is achievable in Wales by 2020, and exactly how Welsh Government programmes and policies will contribute to this outcome.

While there is much to praise in the Welsh Government's commitment, the Commission believes that there is scope to take a more disciplined, evidence-driven approach. The Welsh Government is sensitive to the multi-dimensional nature of child poverty, but the Commission is concerned that resources are spread too thinly and that the speed of change means that policies are not given time to mature.

The Welsh Government is inclusive in its approach to reducing child poverty, but more should be done to engage employers in child poverty and social mobility issues. Employers have a key role to play in relation to both the skills and the low pay agenda; they are also central in making recruitment open and fair to everyone. Tackling barriers to employment that are linked to social background can improve the competitive advantage of businesses by giving them access to a wider talent pool.[66] The Commission recommends that the Welsh Government takes an active role to promote fair access to jobs within Wales. For example, it could recruit a set of companies to become champions for this agenda across Wales.

The Commission sets out below three recommendations which it believes would contribute significantly to the goal of reducing child poverty and improving social mobility in Wales.

63 http://www.audit.wales/system/files/publications/NEETs_Report_National_version_2014_English.pdf
64 Ibid.
65 http://www.assembly.wales/laid%20documents/cr-ld10252/cr-ld10252-e.pdf
66 https://www.gov.uk/government/uploads/system/uploads/attachment_data/file/246696/Business_Social_Mobility_Manifesto.pdf

Recommendation 1: Take a more rigorous, evidence-based approach to poverty reduction.

If the Welsh Government is to achieve the greatest impact from its policies and programmes, it needs to undertake a review to ensure that:

- There is clarity about what problem the policies are trying to address, what they will achieve, and how they will achieve it;
- Duplication is avoided and, in particular, that policies and programmes do not cover the same grounds as successful programmes led by non-government bodies;
- There is an overall holistic approach that links policies together to contribute to shared overall objectives;
- Policies are cost-effective and appropriately targeted to maximise impact.

In addition, the Welsh Government should pilot new policies and programmes to assess impact and value for money before they are implemented across the country.

Recommendation 2: Improve the quality of the workforce in schools.

Ensuring that children have access to high-quality teachers in all subjects is fundamental to improving their life chances and preventing poverty from being handed down from generation to generation. The first step to achieving this is to make teaching in Wales more attractive to good-quality teachers, and to encourage students to want to become teachers in Wales. There also needs to be better mechanisms to encourage new students to undertake teacher training in Wales and newly-qualified teachers to work in Wales. Improving careers advice within Wales and communication with universities in other regions of the UK could be one way to entice potential teachers to Wales. Improving teacher training in Wales would also help, as would better identification, provision and assessment of teachers' continuous development. Training costs could be lowered by school governors across schools working more closely together to identify training needs and jointly organising training.

Recommendation 3: Involve business in its drive to reduce child poverty and increase social mobility.

The Welsh Government should increase its efforts to work with companies (including significant employers in Wales who do most of their business outside Wales itself) to create a Business Compact that would promote fairer access to high-quality employment. Engagement with employers can help to focus attention on better training, improved career ladders and greater adoption of the Living Wage. Businesses could be encouraged to:

- Engage strategically with young people and schools;
- Adhere to best practice on internships and apprenticeships;
- Reform the selection process to eliminate unconscious bias;
- Open up well-structured, non-graduate routes to high-quality careers;
- Monitor and evaluate performance on improving access;
- Sign up to the Living Wage.

Annex: Key social mobility and child poverty indicators in England, Scotland and Wales

Area	Outcome	Indicator	England	Scotland	Wales
Child poverty	**Relative poverty**	% children in households with less than 60% median income (before housing costs), three years ending in 2013/14	17	16	22
		% children in households with less than 60% median income (after housing costs), three years ending in 2013/14	28	21	31
	Absolute poverty	% children in households with less than 60% 2010/11 median income (before housing costs), three years ending in 2013/14	19	17	25
		% children in households with less than 60% 2010/11 median income (after housing costs), three years ending in 2013–14	31	24	34
Education	**Age 16 attainment**	% children registered for free school meals achieving exam standard at 16, 2013/14	33.7	32.5	27.8
	Adults with no qualifications	% of working-age adults without any qualifications, 2014	8.6	9.4	10
	Adults with no qualifications at Level 2 or above	% of working-age adults without any Level 2 qualifications (equivalent to 5 or more GCSEs A*–C or Standard Grades at SCQF Level 5), 2014	26.8	25.2	27.5
Living wage	**Employee jobs paid the Living Wage**	% of employee jobs paid less than the living wage, 2014	22.6	19.3	24.9
Youth unemployment	**Young people unemployed**	% of 18–24-year-olds who are unemployed, 2014	13.9	13.6	17.8
Higher education participation	**Young people living in areas with lowest entry to higher education (POLAR 3, Quintile 1)**	% of young people living in areas with lowest level of entry to higher education, 2005–09	20.8	9.9	25.2

Notes:

- Attainment at 16 cannot be directly compared between England, Scotland and Wales due to differences in curricula and exams. These results give an indication of the proportion of disadvantaged pupils who obtain key qualifications that measure similar levels of skills. We have used '5 A*-Cs including English and maths' as this threshold in England and Wales and '5 or more Standard Grades at SCQF Level 5 or any qualifications at Higher or Advanced Higher level' for Scotland.
- Within Scotland, school attainment data is only available for all school leavers, so will include some young people who only achieved this qualification level after the age of 16.

References:

Child poverty: Department for Work and Pensions, *Households Below Average Income 2013/14*, 2015

Education: Age 16 attainment – Department for Education, *GCSE and Equivalent Attainment by Pupil Characteristics in England, 2013/14*, SFR 06/2015, Welsh Government, *Academic Achievement and Entitlement to Free School Meals*, 2014 and data for Scotland provided by the Scottish Government 2014; Adults qualifications – Office for National Statistics, *Annual Population Survey*, 2014

Living Wage: Office for National Statistics, *Annual Survey of Hours and Earnings*, 2015

Youth unemployment: Office for National Statistics, *Regional Labour Market Statistics*, October 2015

Higher education participation: Higher Education Funding Council for England, *Young, UK-domiciled Entrants Registered at Publicly-funded UK Higher Education Institutions (HEIs) plus University of Buckingham, 2005–2009*, 2015